SAM KYDD

The Unpublished Memoirs
Volume One 1945-1952

"Be a Good Boy, Sam."

Edited
by
Jonathan Kydd

Sam Kydd
The Unpublished Memoirs
Volume One 1945-1952
"Be a Good Boy, Sam."
Copyright: Jonathan Kydd 2021
ISBN: 978-1-905912-79-7

Email: jk@jonathankydd.com
Twitter: @Jonathankydd @SamKyddActor
Cover design: Ant Easton, Joe Greco and Jonathan Kydd
Websites: www.jonathankydd.com www.samkydd.com

CONTENTS

ACKNOWLEDGMENTS

Thanks to Jonathan Coy, Andrew Roberts, and Joe Greco for their support and enthusiasm. "You can hear Sam speaking in every sentence."

SAM KYDD The Unpublished Memoirs Volume One is dedicated to Oscar Rabin, Peter Waring, Harry Dubens, Steve Smith, Harry Secombe, Mary Merrall, Jimmy Hanley, Dirk Bogarde, Gary Marsh, Peter Bull, Jack Warner, Jack Lambert, Adelaide Hall, Kenneth More, John Baxter, Basil Dearden, Alberto Cavalcanti, Herbert Wilcox, Andy Worker, Duggie Allen, Major de Lane Lea, Cymbeline Brooks, Freddie Foster, Bill Gollidge, Johnny Gaskin, Cliff Winterbottom, Frank Coburn, Rodney Bashford, Dickie Davis, "Knocker" Noakes, Thelma Graves, Margaret Harper Nelson, Freddie Schiller, all the backroom staff at Ealing Films, the un-known actor on the Piccadilly Line. And of course the wonderful "Pinkie" Kydd.

'He made more films than the M.G.M. Lion.'
Michael Parkinson.

FOREWORD
by
Derek Fowlds

SAM KYDD. Hero, Legend and great friend. I first saw Sam on the big screen in my local Cinema. He seemed to be in every British film made in the forties and fifties. I also used to see him at Stamford Bridge watching his beloved football team Chelsea. I used to say to my friends that's the great Sam Kydd, they were all fans. In 1966 I was thrilled to bits when Sam agreed to play my Dad in the BBC TV Series *Take a Pair of Private Eyes*. It was such a success that the film rights were sold and we only did one series but Sam and I became close friends. I spent many happy hours in his company, with his lovely wife Pinkie. We shared so much fun and laughter. Treasured memories. Sam's first book 'For you the War is Over' was a great read, now this new book that has been found in the loft by Sam's son Jonathan will be a treat for us all to share. Dear Sam, greatly missed but never forgotten. Thank you for being my friend.

PREFACE
by
Jonathan Kydd

An autobiography, or any writing about his acting career he'd attempted, was never published. As Derek Fowlds says in his foreword, my father's record of his time as a prisoner of war between 1939 and 1945, "For You the War is Over" was indeed a good read and was in fact highly successful, selling 40,000 in paperback. But his memoirs, although submitted to several publishers, were never taken up.

I discovered an abandoned manuscript in a battered suitcase in the loft in the family home in Barnes, in London, in 2015, thirty three years after his death in 1982. It was very flimsy paper. The typing had been done with a huge number of 'Tippex' corrections and a worn-out ribbon in places, so some sections were barely legible. I scanned every page into a PDF and attempted to make it into a Word document. This failed miserably. The task for the software was too much and it couldn't interpret the faded and stressed text and reduced it to gobble-de-gook. So I decided to type it out. This turned out to be a very good decision indeed. I found his story fascinating, very little of which he had ever told me. Certainly I'd seen very few of the films, other than the perennial *I'm Alright Jack* or *Angels One Five* or *Reach For the Sky*, which were regularly on TV. The manuscript I discovered, was an in-depth record of his prolific career, from its early struggles around the time of *The Captive Heart, They Made Me a Fugitive* and *Treasure Island,* to intermittent success with films like *Appointment in London* and *They Who Dare,* then a work-crammed period when he was a household name, doing films, dubbing and telly series, including *Pickwick Papers, Shadow Squad, Arthur's Treasured*

Volumes, Treasure of Monte Christo, The Charlie Drake Show, Mess Mates, Island of Terror, Dixon of Dock Green, Fred the Burglar, The Fossett Saga, Crane and *Orlando*; to a final decade of celebrity (which was merely notes in the manuscript), where he was on *This is Your Life, Sykes, Dad's Army, Till Death Us Do Part, Call My Bluff, Play School, Harry Worth, Terry and June,* countless plays and guest-starring roles in series; and then sketchily describing two years into the 80s when he continued acting - he was a regular on *Coronation Street* - with failing health, suffering from his highly debilitating emphysema, until his death in 1982.

This typing out of the manuscript, as well as being an emotional rollercoaster, has fortuitously allowed me to verify a lot of my father's facts, as some names were incorrectly spelt, some films and series he starred in and incidents I personally remember, left out altogether, and in some instances, he got the chronology completely wrong. And sometimes even managed to get what he did in the films wrong! In fact occasionally his involvement in the film on screen, bore little resemblance to what he wrote. At the same time, this analysis encouraged me to cross reference all his diaries, financial records, and letters - and various other bizarre attempts at chronicling his career, written on the back of scripts, envelopes, pieces of cardboard used to stiffen the packaging of shirts in those cellophane bags from the dry cleaner's, or in some instances, betting slips - which I also discovered in boxes in the loft; so consequently, I've added information and stories from these sources which I found amusing, or I felt improved the narrative, or told a more dramatic truth about an incident he'd glossed over. I've also divided his prodigious story into four volumes.

For reasons of copyright, the film dialogue in the book my father quotes, is not the actual dialogue in any of the films he was in, but an approximation.

ONE
Home from Germany, back to Germany, via Ealing

I couldn't believe it!

The sequence of events leading up to the signing of "The Contract" was in itself worthy of a film. It all happened so suddenly that my shattered belief in fairy godmothers and genies and lucky shamrock had reassembled itself and glued itself back together again. My faith in them had undergone a bit of a hammering when I was taken prisoner of war at Calais in May 1940 ("For you ze War is Over Tommies" said the German officer in charge of the Nazi soldiers who captured us on the beach, and indeed it was) and incarcerated in camps in Poland and Germany for the next five years. During that time I made umpteen wishes, rubbed innumerable imaginary rabbits' feet and burnished many a fictitious lamp, but all to no avail. It had been too cold for genies in Poland. And rabbits were all in their holes. The Universe had dealt me a dodgy hand. And I was a rubbish card player anyway. But at least I'd survived the war, with albeit five years of my life having disappeared into limbo; and a new set of teeth from where a German guard had smashed the others out with his rifle butt. But on the positive side, (Yes there is one!) I was alive. My new gleaming dentures had got rid of the gap in my front teeth, and I had a mass of writing and performing under my belt - panto, review, cabaret, theatre (countless productions including *Blithe Spirit, Cuckoo in the Nest, Rookery Nook, Turkey Time, Plunder, Thark, Journey's End, Pygmalion, While Parents Sleep, Babes in the Wood, Dick Whittington,* and many many evenings of song and comedy) even though it had been to a "captive" audience in the prison camp.

On my return to Liverpool from Poland via Russia and the Black Sea in 1945 (I had escaped just as the Germans were escorting the rest of the Camp on a route march back towards the failing Third Reich. I hid in a chicken coop, and then a nunnery) I was transported to a Dispersal camp where I was examined minutely from head to toe by the medical officer, given a couple of injections, ("What will the injections do, sir?" I asked him. "Make me funnier?" A withering look was his stern reply) some extra coupons for food and clothing, and six weeks leave to adjust myself, or I should say re-adjust myself. Not completely re-adjusted, I, along with countless other mal-adjusted (blimey all this adjusting) ex-Prisoners of War, was then ordered to report to the rehabilitation centre just outside Barnsley in Yorkshire. It was no fault of the civilian population that we were not successfully re-habilitated or subjected to much adjustment, "re" or otherwise. We were treated extremely well in Barnsley and on many occasions, handsomely - I have never been offered so many free drinks - but the plain truth was, that the ex-Prisoners of War did not want to be re-habilitated or re-adjusted. They only wanted to be re-leased! Lectures on how to fire a Bren gun ("Is it a different Bren Gun from the one we already know how to fire, Sarge?") and the "New drills," ("I liked the old drills. Could we possibly have a lie down instead, Sarge?") were a complete failure. We were all anti everything military. Not openly, but quietly, desperately and slyly. Mind you, after five years of kicking against the pricks of German discipline and confinement, it was not to be wondered at. Anybody in authority was suspect. In reality, all we wanted was demobilisation. Or in the last resort, desertion! Whilst on parade one morning, several names were read out from a special Royal invitation to attend a Garden Party at Buckingham Palace. Part of the re-adjustment I suppose. I'm not sure what you had to have done to qualify. I certainly wasn't on the list! Those so favoured, were cosseted and cocooned till the day of the "do" and went off in high spirits. At roll call the following Monday, it was apparent that ten of them hadn't returned from the event. ("Perhaps they were overwhelmed meeting His Majesty and needed a few weeks off Sarge?") Some of them were gathered up by the military police, but quite a few never again showed up for their re-habilitation, and self adjusted elsewhere!

Following a succession of dizzy days, drunken nights and lots of intense thumb twiddling - and attempted consumption of all the food we'd been denied in prison camp: eggs, chicken, tea, coffee, bacon, tomatoes, egg and bacon, bacon and tomatoes, egg bacon and tomatoes, and above all, with all of the above, white bread, with as much butter as rationing or the black market would allow - I demanded an appointment with the army psychiatrist. A fellow ex-P.O.W. had done precisely that with great success, and was now demobilised, so he advised me what and what not to say. I had also thought up a list of things to throw in myself that might influence the interview. I'm quoting from it here, written on the back of a re-usable envelope:

1: Weight loss. (He couldn't argue with that. I was all skin and bone).
2: Constant urinating during the night. (Mind you if I'd been to the pub this was always the case).
3: Quick temper. (True also)
4: Nervousness of trains. Was worried they'd crash. (Invented. Possibly too far fetched?)
5: Smoking much too much (Mind you I was making up for the scarcity of cigarettes in prison camp)
6: Headaches (This was true. But aggravated by going to the pub).
7: Skin rash (True as well. Patches of what I believe was eczema. Which was a stress related rash? I could show him a patch on my leg if he wanted.)

The psychiatrist was a sympathetic officer who had a soft spot for old King's Royal Riflemen like myself, knowing what we'd been through. He greeted me kindly.

"I can tell things are difficult for you Private Kydd".

"Yes they are sir. Thank you!" I replied, adopting a lugubrious demeanour, as my mate had suggested. My mate had developed a useful twitch for his interview, but I had that in reserve. As it happened I didn't need it.

"And obviously when you look in the mirror in the mornings, you sometimes don't recognise yourself?" he queried. Ah, what a question. I liked him immensely. I knew what to say to that.

"Yessir. Exactly sir. That's right sir! "Who am I?" I regularly ask myself. And sometimes, "Where am I?"

I put on a suitably confused expression. He studied me for a moment. I was screwing my face up looking as if I hadn't recognised myself at all in the mirror that particular morning. And had probably seen someone else in fact. And then he said, "Don't worry Kydd. I'll see what can be done for you!"

"Thank you sir." I replied emotionally, with a beautifully rehearsed slight "choke" in my voice, looking as if that wasn't my name and what was I doing in his office. And within a week I was on my way to York to pick up my demob suit! I was discharged on psycho-neurotic grounds and although in reality I did feel "strange" ("prickly" some people called it) and was obviously traumatised by my war-time experiences on several levels, something that would come back to haunt me in the future, I outwardly pretended that there was nothing the matter with me. As I journeyed to York I said to myself

"At last! I'm free! Freeeee! Ahahahahaha."

Yes this was somewhat over the top, but it was warranted, as now I could throw aside my soldier's uniform, the battledress which had dominated my life for the last six years, never, I believed, to see it, or its like, again. Little did I know that I'd be constantly putting on outfits exactly like it in my consequent career! This one had served me well in various parts of the world: France, Germany, Poland and Russia, over land and sea, and now finally in England. And I was replacing it with one of Montague Burton's finest demobilisation efforts - a "pepper-and-salt" affair with shirt and tie to match, topped by a dark brown brim-down trilby. I looked like a New York hoodlum. Mind you, so did we all! I emerged from the clothing emporium at York with the world at my Freeman, Hardy and Willis feet, (size 7 and a half) feeling slightly self-conscious. After six years in khaki who wouldn't? I walked past a shop window and caught sight of my reflection and didn't recognise myself!

I had only been home at my mother's house in Bedford Park London W.4. where I'd been deservedly lolling about for about a week, when I saw a news item in the local paper. It stated that Ealing Studios were going to make a film entitled *Lovers Meeting*, the storyline of which was about a Czech officer who assumes the identity of a dead British officer in Prison Camp, and that the Film Company were hoping to get permission to shoot some of the scenes in a real Prisoner of War camp near Hamburg. The Director's name was Basil Dearden and I wrote to him the same evening. I told him that I was an ex P.O.W., that I had acted a lot in Prison Camp and I'd had experience of being a Master of Ceremonies before the war with the Oscar Rabin Band - I'd told jokes, tap danced, sung and done impressions - and if I could be of assistance in any way, such as advising them on the accuracy of a scene, how the clothes should be worn, or the attitude of the Germans etc., I would be only too willing to oblige! In short, rather cleverly I thought, ("Well done, Sam!" I said to myself, recognising myself in the mirror), I offered my services both as an actor and technical adviser. Bizarrely and somewhat welcomingly, as if they'd been waiting eagerly for my letter, their reply came early the day after - I mean I know I only live up the road in Turnham Green, but this was impressive. Today a post-card could take a week!

The quick reply said, "Would you please call at Ealing Studios, if possible on Saturday morning, for an interview with Basil Dearden, the Director, and Michael Relph and Mr. A. de Cavalcanti, the co-Producers of the film…"

It was then of course that a gremlin appeared on my shoulder - a nasty little imp with a sneer on its face - casting doubt as to whether I should go back to Germany after vowing that I would never set foot in that country again, as my experiences there had not been pleasant ones. And I hadn't even got the job yet! Ah, but this was different!

The boot was on the other foot this time, a British Army boot and not a Jackboot. I would be one of the conquerors, not a prisoner, and with my acquired knowledge of German and their humourless behaviour, I could swagger around and lord it over them! Ha ha yes!

"Get me a drink fraulien. Now!" I would say "and make it schnappy!"

Not that I would really, but it would help my mental argument for returning there. Perhaps most of their arrogance would've disappeared by now. Can you lose a war and still be arrogant? It would be weird but interesting, to go back in the new circumstances and conditions.

I mean it could become a sort of working holiday, couldn't it? After all, I had no other plans. I'd no idea at all about how a Film company conducted their business and I was certainly curious. One problem I definitely had though, was that I was extremely thin. I overheard my Uncle speaking to my mother in his camp Northern Irish accent.

"He's very very thin isn't he? Almost emaciated!"

Well I mean either you are or you aren't? I was unsure of myself and neurotic. Not only that, but I was psychoneurotic! It said so on my Soldier's Discharge Book. My AB64. I had "ceased to fulfil Army requirements". That's what it said. Starkly. This might of course be good for the film though. What was I getting worried about? I either had to say Yay or Nay. To confirm my hesitancy, I tossed a coin to decide. Heads I go, tails I don't. It came down tails. I decided to go anyway. And this was before they'd even asked me. In order to bolster my ego and share my news, I phoned up ex-rifleman Steve Smith (the one who had advised me about the psychiatrist routine and had been in the camp with me) and told him what I was up to. He was very impressed, saying, "You lucky sod! Bloody hell, I wish I was on it."

"Well why not?" said I. "Why not come with me to the Studio and perhaps they'll engage us both?"

What was I thinking? As I put the phone down I suddenly

realised that they might choose him instead of me. He was a very good looking fella who could charm the skin off a snake!

The Saturday came and we rendez-voused at Ealing Broadway station and strolled off to the Studios. We met the top brass, Messrs. Dearden, (later to direct *League of Gentlemen, Khartoum* and *Assassination Bureau*) Michael Relph (he had a twenty year partnership with Basil Dearden. Was an academy award nominee for his art direction for *Saraband for Dead Lovers* in 1949) and Alberto Cavalcanti, (he had produced propaganda films during the war, like *Went the Day Well?* and *Dead of Night*. And directed *Nicholas Nickelby* in 1947, for which I had a screen test. But I'm getting ahead of myself!) none of whom seemed at all put out by my bringing Steve along. In fact they made more fuss of him than they did of me! Well, as I said, he was a handsome clean-cut chap, with corn-coloured hair and the deepest blue eyes. Despite coming from Ruislip, he looked Swedish! I naturally imagined him as a very successful actor with the new name of Knut Knudsen.

Cavalcanti, who spoke with a South American accent - he was from Brazil - took a liking to Steve immediately, explaining what the film was all about and mostly addressing him. My heart sank. They asked us to leave for a few minutes while they discussed us. I was in a state in the waiting room. Steve was his cool self.

"Whatever happens, happens, Sammy," he said in his usual annoyingly calm way. He was a sweet bloke though! And we'd been through a lot. (We'd escaped from the "big march" together for a start when all the prisoners were herded together to return to Germany. Hitler had had plans to use the P.O.W.s as hostages, not that we knew that. It was the opposite of what happened when we were captured where we were marched from France to Poland.). We were summoned back in. To our delight and relief, "Cav" (for that is what he liked to be called) said they would be very pleased if we would both join them on the film as technical advisers.....and even better....actors! He added that in time, salaries would be discussed and we would be getting contracts, but in the meantime he invited us to have a drink! We repaired to the local pub just across the Green ("The Grove" if my memory serves me right. A lovely pub that as my career went on and I worked at the studios more often, I found myself frequenting) and agreement was made in whisky!

About three hours later, I left Steve at Ealing Broadway hugely the worse for hospitality, and shakily made my way home to Turnham Green which was only three stations away on the District Line. I woke up at Hammersmith Broadway having missed Turnham Green completely, got out, crossed over the bridge and caught the next train going to Turnham Green. But fell asleep again and found myself at Richmond! I had one more go and finding myself at Hammersmith again, I took a taxi home!

After a week of waiting and watching the post (which a pigeon with only one wing and blind in one eye could've delivered in 10 minutes) a letter finally arrived. My hand shook as I opened the long envelope with the Ealing Studios Insignia - the well-known motif of ears of corn - on the front. It was "The Contract". My fate, although I didn't know it, was sealed. My life as an actor had begun. If that imp on my shoulder had had its way, I wouldn't be writing this book. Or if I was writing a book, it would be about working in a department store, possibly in the bedding department, or as a car salesman, and I wouldn't be writing it!

My mother took it calmly as if acting were some schoolboy crush that I had to get out of my system and said in her lilting Belfast accent, "Oh well. As long as you promise to apply for proper jobs when you're back. You can treat this as a holiday. Though why you'd want to go back somewhere you'd just spent five years hating is beyond me."

I ignored her and after the first hurried perusal of "The Contract" (just to confirm that it was there) I went through it again - slowly. There it was, in black-and-white. My imagination ran wild! I was going to be a film star with my name in lights! Yes! I could see it all in red neon - SAM KYDD. I pondered on it. Might be an idea to change the name. RAYMOND VANDERVELL had a good ring to it. But perhaps not. How about spelling my name backwards? MAS DDYK - Sounds Dutch or Tibetan. No, stick to Sam. After all there were Sam Goldwyn and Sam Weller. They hadn't done too badly. Or how about KNUT KNUDSEN? Nar I didn't look Swedish enough. Steve could have it. I finished fantasising and read the contract again. It said:

EALING STUDIOS LTD.,
Ealing Green,
London W.5.
(and underneath)

Terms of Artiste's Engagement
Film: Lovers Meeting
Name: Sam Kydd
Agent: No agent
Part: Lance Corporal
(I'd only ever been a private! Promoted already and not even begun the film yet).
Starting Date on or about July 30, 1945.
Remuneration on location £17.10s. 0d per week.

Let's repeat that. No let's shout it.
SEVENTEEN-POUNDS-TEN-SHILLINGS-PER-WEEK.
In comparison with the soldier's pay of two shillings a day. This was Film Star's pay! The Contract went on:

"From the day that the Artiste (me) leaves London for the location until the date of his return to London. Should there be an interval between the Artiste's return to London from the location and his first camera day in the studio, the Artiste (still me) shall be paid £9 (nine pounds) per week during such interval."
(NINE POUNDS for being <u>out</u> of work. Better than the Unemployment Bureau!)

Payments to: The Artiste (That Man again)
I agree and confirm etc., etc., and undertake to execute the Standard
Agreement if called upon to do so.
Signed (very quickly) by Samuel Kydd and (not so quickly) by
Margaret Bonnar, Casting Director (wife of the actor Leo Genn as I
later found out).
Michael Relph, Production Manager.
R. Baker, Company Executive.

As I said before, I couldn't believe it! Three months ago I was
virtually still a prisoner in Russia and making my way back on a boat
via Odessa (that was torpedoed!) and now......!!!?

Within two or three days of receiving "The Contract", we were
asked to attend a meeting at the Studios where our wardrobe was to
be checked (meaning the clothes we would be wearing in the film,
which as prisoners wouldn't be much) and we were to be briefed as
to our final destination. It was a bit like an Army Movement Order -
the same chaos prevailed! This was because there were ten of us in
the same category. TEN! And they called us all at the same time! I
had foolishly imagined that Steve and I would be the only technical
advisors. But indeed why shouldn't they have ten? Why not fifteen?
Or even twenty? Anyway, that was the first prick of deflation. Never
mind, I said to myself, recognising myself in the mirror once more, I
would have to make sure that my technical advice was superior to
theirs and in addition, act my socks off to make the grade. So there!

We were a sort of "small parts" band. Actually, "general
dogsbodies" would be a better description. The five pretty ones were
designated or cast as "Officers" in the film and the-not-so-pretty
(which included me, and let's be honest I was looking rough. A bag
of bones and wan; perfect casting) were the "Other Ranks". This
meant I never worked with Steve. We were in separate huts in the
film. In a way this "Other Ranks" decision was to set the seal on my
later roles in all the Service pictures in which I took part. I was always
the cockney "other ranker" and never the officer, though my Irish

father had been an officer in the First World War. I had learned my cockney too well in the prison camp! Though I could switch to an Irish or "posh" English accent at will, which I did in several films and series; in fact I dipped in and out of an Irish accent at home! My "real" accent was a sort of "unaccented" South London. "Well spoken" I suppose is what you'd call it. I'd got that at Dunstable Grammar where I'd been sent after coming over to England from Belfast. Weird to say, but I certainly wasn't a cockney, despite most of my parts being that way. But I had that ability to change my voice according to who I was speaking to. Not deliberately, but sympathetically really! I believe it's called "acting". Though I don't want to give the impression that I wasn't genuine, as I was.

The War Office had arranged for the Unit to shoot the Prisoner of War scenes in a recently vacated P.O.W. camp known as a "Marlag". Here's a translation: Marlag is a corruption of "Marine" (sea) and "Lager". "Lager" is German for camp. - Marinelager became Marlag; it was an ex-camp sailors' camp! There's a lot of it about in Germany. The Jerries have always had this obsession with joining words together. The Americans do it, too. They say "Motionpicturewise" meaning it's something to do with films - sorry, movies. Officers' Camps in Germany became "Offlags" and the Soldiers' or Soldaten Camps became "Stalags" and not as I would've thought "Solags"! "Stalag" I believe was derived from the word "Stammlager" which means Head Camp. This was in fact short for "Kriegsgefangenen-Mannschafts-Stammlager. Blimey! The name of the camp where we were to shoot was Westertimke and our base was to be in a small town called Stade, not far from Hamburg. Well it's actually about 45 miles away, but I suppose it's near enough. There were four hotels. One five-star effort for the stars, four-star for the Director, Producers and various important technical bods, three-star for the riggers, electricians, carpenters, etc., and finally one-star for the small-parts-come-technical-advisers-come-dogsbodies, which included a few chaps from the Production Office side, who although part of the team did not mix socially with the higher-ups! The only

Englishwoman to accompany us was a six-foot, bespectacled rather shy girl named Phyllis Crocker. She was the Continuity or Script girl, and on closer acquaintance I discovered her to be a doll with a great sense of humour. She had to be with <u>that</u> job! She had to make notes as to what the actor had done in the previous shot and work out whether he or she had said the lines differently. And tell the Director that they'd be having another take if there was an error! And tell the actor what mistake they'd made! So if an actor had a new cigarette alight in his left hand and smoked it on the word "Yes!" in the mid shot, then in the close up had a half way down smoked cigarette and used his right hand and smoked it on the word "No!" they'd have to reshoot as the "Continuity" didn't work. Essential deep concentrated work. You had to be brilliant. They only had a pad and a pencil! All done in shorthand! When working in the studio the only other women we saw around were actress Melissa Stribling, wife and one-time secretary of the director, Basil Dearden, and casting director Muriel Cole who was attached to the Production Office under the command of Captain "Slim" Hand, who always seemed to be enquiring about whether the required amount of lavatory paper had been ordered! And believe me this was hugely important!

We were measured for new uniforms - measured? (Wardrobe man holds up battle dress. "This looks as if it will fit you.") - then documented ("Name? "Knut Knudsen!") and given the honorary rank of officers, for travelling purposes. (Oooh. From Private to an Officer in three months!) We were told we would be moving off very shortly. Later that week we travelled rather lazily, by boat, from Ramsgate to Ostend and thence by slow train to Stade, where we meandered to our hotel. Pinned to the noticeboard in the foyer was a written statement signed by the Production Manager. It read:

"The war not having been long over, it is considered a great privilege to be in Germany at all. I must specially ask you to be on your best behaviour at all times.... The Military Governor's orders are held to be sacrosanct and all rules and regulations such as curfew to be strictly observed.... Absolutely no fraternising or intercourse with the ex-enemy."

We didn't think anyone would be paying any attention to that!

The proprietor of our hotel had not yet returned from the "front" and if it was anywhere near the Russians, you could count on another two or three years before he showed up - if ever! However, his comely frau and two strictly (at first) non-fraternising daughters had been persuaded, at the request of the Burgermeister, to open their doors and carry on. They often complained of the looting and bad behaviour of our "Schotlander" troops ("They are awful. They dance, they steal, they drink. They lift their skirts! They wear nozzing underneath!") on their victorious way through, but Steve and I were not impressed, telling them that they really would have had something to beef about had the Russians come through instead! We slept at the hotel but didn't eat there, as we had breakfast and late dinner at the Stade Town Hall and a packed lunch and various tea breaks on the location itself. Not having had regular meals in prison camp, food had become very important to me.

On our first day in Stade we were introduced to the star-studded cast. It was a cast that would be the backbone of the burgeoning British film industry. I would work with many of them time and time again. Heading the list was the hero of the film, Michael Redgrave. (Star of the great British War Film *The Dam Busters*). Following close behind and not necessarily in billing order were Basil Radford, (Star of the Hitchcock Movie *The Lady Vanishes* and frequently paired with Naunton Wayne). Derek Bond, (like me a P.O.W. He played *Nicholas Nickelby*.) The marvellously funny Jimmy Hanley (in the *Huggetts* films and on T.V. in the long running *Jim's Inn*. I was to have a lovely scene with him in *It's Hard to be Good* and more in *Radio Cab Murder*), Mervyn Johns, (prolific film and T.V. actor. A wonderful Bob Cratchet to Alastair Sim's *Scrooge*) Jack Warner, (*Dixon of Dock Green* himself. I was to be in at least 15 different episodes of Dixon, as different criminals. He was to become a good friend.) Gordon

Jackson, (we were to be together in *Death goes to School* and *Price of Silence*. Was later one of the stars of *The Great Escape*) Freddie Schiller (a German actor. We were in *Albert R.N.* and *Reach for the Sky*) and Ernest Richter (also German). The latter two were to play German Officers at the Camp, and Karel Stepanek, a Czech, was cast as a sinister Gestapo official. He made a career out of playing Germans and was in *Heroes of Telemark*, *Operation Crossbow* and *Sink the Bismarck* doing just that. At first we ex-prisoners were in awe of the stars, but we soon got to know most of them and found that they, like ourselves were only mortal! Some of them were initially a little aloof, but even they eventually thawed and deigned to talk to the small-part-come-technical-advisers-dogsbodies. As I said, some of them were to become big pals! At that time the film was called *Lovers Meeting* but was subsequently changed to *The Captive Heart*. After the introductions we were told loudly by the Assistant Director (he shouted a lot) to look at the Call Sheet which would be put up on the notice board in our hotel, which basically informed us when and where we were needed. Our first day's shooting would be "on the morrow", he enunciated theatrically. The notice listed everyone who was required to be on location at Westertimke P.O.W. Camp at 8.00 a.m. We would be picked up by an Army lorry (Bedford truck) and private cars would be provided for the Stars, Director and Producers. Breakfast was at 6 till 6:45 a.m., and we were to leave for the location at 7 a.m. Getting up early reminded me of being a P.O.W. again, but apart from that, I was looking forward with great anticipation and interest to the first day's shooting. Each of us had our own ideas as to what was to happen. As it turned out, it wasn't what we'd imagined. After our arrival at the camp location, which was in effect as you'd expect, a proper camp that had been used to house prisoners only a few months previously, people were hustling and bustling about, setting things up and moving stuff hither and thither and yelling instructions at each other. That made sense. What made it fraught was the constant shrieking of the First Assistant Director (who was the right-hand factotum of the Director), the echoing shriek of the "I CAN DO IT EVEN LOUDER" of the Second Assistant Director and the "I'M LOUDER THAN BOTH OF YOU PUT TOGETHERRRRRR", of the Third Assistant Director. At this time they were just behaving normally, or so I was assured. But the next time they had…aaargh!…the Loudhailers! Then, it became sheer Bedlam. This, coupled with the shouts of the officers and N.C.O.'s who were in charge of the actual soldiers (I had no idea there were any of those. They were from the British Army of the Rhine and were the 51st Highland Division and the 50th A.A. Brigade) who were to be used as "background action" (which made sense in the shots of the camp) all added to the frenetic scene. Confusion and mayhem were the words of the day, but finally, after about two hours - 10.00 a.m. approximately - we were all set up and ready to "go". But then the Lighting Cameraman put his rather necessary oar in. He got his light meter out and decided that the light for filming this particular scene wasn't good enough. The cloud cover was in and out. It was neither one thing or the other. We'd shoot a scene in sunlight and then attempt to shoot it again and the sun had gone in. We all became obsessed with clouds. So we sat around gazing at the sky ("Ooh that bit of cirrus is on its way. We'll never shoot this one in time" and " 'ere. That cloud looks like a dog!") and waited for his assent. One of the first things I discovered, and I'm sure you know this but in all honesty I was Mr. Naive and didn't, was that feature films, unless they're "LIVE", and I don't think I've come across any of those, are shot entirely out of sequence - the middle or the end can be filmed before the beginning. And it's what happens. I mean you may be reading this and thinking, well of course we know that, it's obvious! But I didn't! It's all a question of economics, you see. Get rid of the most expensive sets, scenes and artistes first, is apparently a universal maxim! And this one was no exception. In this case they were concentrating on Mr. Karel Stepanek and the two German officers (Messrs. Schiller and Richter) plus the hundreds of British troops pretending to be Prisoners of War. (And some of them pretending to be German) They cost! Eventually we began with the scene where Karel (playing the sinister man from the Gestapo) was addressing the prisoners, warning them of the dire penalties they would suffer if caught contravening the regulations, etc.. He also spots Michael Redgrave and goes over to talk to him as he has been told he speaks fluent German. And he recognises him from somewhere. Which makes all the British troops suspicious! About page 8 of the script. It was shot from five or six different angles and the same scene was done many times - rehearsed, rehearsed, re-rehearsed and shot! Frequently something wouldn't be right, although to our untutored eyes it seemed to be absolutely fine. "Cut", Basil the Director would say quietly (meaning stop the action. You know this. But it was new to me!) "We've cut!" would blast the First. Echoed emphatically by the Second as if his arm was on fire and then bellowed by the Third as if his trousers had blown off and embedded themselves in a wall. And then after some sotto voce talk in which we were not included, we would start again.

"Quiet everyone. We're going again."

"QUIET ON SET WE'RE GOING AGAIN."

"WE'RE GOOIIINNNGGG AGGGAAINNN QUUIIEET!"

This was utterly knackering, although it may not appear so to the layman, who is probably cocking a snook at my inability not to be weary. But honestly I was exhausted! I suppose it's the mental fatigue of preparing yourself for a scene and doing it over and over. And all I was doing in these scenes was standing. And reacting when the camera tracked across me. And of course offering advice as to whether the scene would have been genuinely like this. All this was shot on the Parade Ground where we, the "Gefangeners" (German for captives. You see I did know a bit of German!) were all lined up. These were huge scenes that required large panoramic views of the whole parade ground and all the men in the camp. Shot by another different camera crew from a crane by what was known as the "second unit". All very impressive. Then Basil Dearden decided to do some reaction shots of the prisoners listening to Karel's speech. He shot sullen reactions, sulky reactions, derisive reactions and one or two dead-pan reactions. Steve had one of those. I did one which was my slightly frightened one. It never made the film. Finally the First bellowed, "Lunch everybody! Back on the set at 2:30 sharp, ready to go."

"2.30! READY TO GO!" echoed the Second and finally belted out like a madman by the Third.

"IT'S LUNCHTIME. BACK AT TWOOOO THIRRRTY RRRRRREEEEAAADDDYYY TO GOOOOOO".

Several teeth fell out, that one was so loud. I wanted to stick his loudhailer up his…….. shirt. Lunchboxes had been distributed earlier. They contained beef sandwiches, custard cakes, an apple and an orange. Tea and coffee were provided, but alas no cheese, port and cigars. How cheapskate! Lunch over, we did all of Karel's other scenes in the same "set-up" as it was called (he addressed us on several different occasions) and we then carried on with the same scene, which necessitated some dialogue at the gates of the camp. Unfortunately the Royal Air Force seemed very interested in our activities, constantly hovering overhead and buzzing about so much, that the Head Sound man was rapidly getting apoplexy. It was completely masking the dialogue. Whenever they came over he'd jump up, whip off his earphones and exaggeratedly shake his fist at them like a sort of Elmer Fudd in a Bugs Bunny cartoon. No doubt the R.A.F. thought he was being extremely friendly and reported later in the Mess, "Jolly charming lot of film chaps over at Westertimke. Always waving at us. We did some wizard zooms at them this afternoon, just to let them know we understood!"

In our Bedford truck, on our way back to the hotel, we were shouted at by the Third to attend a short production meeting to discuss something very important. The meeting was to be held in the foyer just before supper. We were not enlightened as to why it was so important for us all to be there, so there was great chatter about what was up. Some thought that was it. They'd hired too many of us and we were being "let go". One adviser/dogsbody called Roger, (who I think had been in the Navy) was quite distraught despite having no clue about what was going on.

"One of you bastards has rocked the boat and it's turned over so far we're looking at its bottom" he said tearfully.

We found him a bit irritating. Nevertheless, at the appropriate time, we dutifully gathered to wait for the P.M. (Production Manager), who finally arrived, accompanied by the First, Second and Third assistants and Cavilcanti himself, the Executive Producer, and the session duly started. First of all, there was a lot of Cav waffle, where we were thanked for our splendid co-operation during the first day's shooting etc. etc. and told how pleased they were with the amount of screen time achieved etc., etc.. We were not to take too much notice of the minor disturbances which were all part and parcel of the filmmaking, etc., etc.

"But…".

We knew there'd be a "But". And here it was:

"But…" said Cavilcanti ominously, and pausing for effect. The sweat dribbled down our noses.

"But"….

Roger gave an audible sob.

"But…'zere eez one zing to be sorted out."

"What? What is that?" Roger enquired whinily, promoting himself as some sort of overeager spokesman. "Is there something we haven't done and should have done? What are we, in our ignorance, guilty of? We'll do whatever you want, Sir! Anything!"

Personally I thought he was overdoing it and slightly fawning, but it was too late to stop him now.

"Vell" Cav said, fixing him with a beady eye but referring to all of us, "eet was not you exactly, but you are in the best position to correct this zeeng."

We must have looked bewildered. I certainly was. Roger was terrified. He thought he was specifically being blamed. Mind you by now if anything had gone wrong we'd have blamed him anyway. Cav continued, "Eet is" he said…… "zer troops who are working for us as crowd workers on background location in the film…. zey" he went on "are inclined to be un-co-operative and go away 'ven they are needed; not all of zem, but many."

Roger emitted an embarrassing sigh which actually sounded as if he was breaking wind. Perhaps he was as well and the sigh masked it! It was true, the 500 or 600 serving troops who had been detailed as extras or crowd workers (or in some cases prisoners in some of the long shots) had started out with enthusiasm, good humour and willingness to co-operate. It was a laugh, a break from humdrum routine, something to write home about.("Hello Mum I'm in a film with that Jack Warner who has that catchphrase "Mind my bike!")

Pretty soon however, the soldiers found out that they were not going to be paid individually, as they had been led to believe, but that a "donation" for their services would be paid into the Regimental Funds. This, then, was the main reason for the disappearing act. One by one they melted away like the Nazi government – either to hide in the huts, to play cards, or to stay in the lavatories just to chat or smoke and generally waste time! It was not easy to see what we could do exactly. We had no authority or power over them other than appealing to their better nature. It was difficult to ask them to be "extras", supporting artistes, when the crux of the matter was that they weren't getting any dosh! Secretly we all had great sympathy for them, but we said that we would help the Production all we could, and "do our best to round up the malingerers". In honesty we didn't make much effort. The soldiers weren't really interested. I tried, "Oh hello there! Would you like to come and be in the shot? There might be a moment where we see your face in the film and you'd be quite popular with the girls back home!"

But without much success. Consequently there aren't as many of them in the film as the Producers wanted. Not that you'd notice. The film makers made do!

After a quick wash and brush-up and a Pilsener or two, we strode through Stade to the Town Hall where dinner for the whole Film Unit was to be served. It was quite impressive. The tables and chairs were laid out in horseshoe fashion as if for a United Nations conference. In the background was a stage with curtains on either side, no doubt having been used for Nazi meetings as well as local dramatic society shows! The pretty waitresses were mostly German fraulins but there were one or two Hungarian Displaced Persons among them, refugees who had found themselves in Germany. They were all lined up on our arrival as if being presented to Royalty, curtseying and bizarrely bowing as we nodded and went by. One voluptuous German "Madchen" (it's German for "girl"), with her hair styled as if she were wearing earphones, winked at Steve and myself as we moved along. I winked back and said to Steve "Ooh she's gorgeous."

He, acting like a dose of bromide, gave a debonair twist to the corner of his mouth and replied very poshly, "I say old boy! Don't forget the non-fraternising order!"

"Bollocks to that" was my witty response.

The following day's shooting didn't include many background artistes. It was mainly for the Principals, so our soldier friends were not missed when they did "go away"! There were some good card games in the toilets we dipped in and out of. I won one pound two shillings and sixpence with a Royal Flush! Ho ho! As I'd been assigned the role of Lance Corporal as per The Contract (in fact in the repatriation scene when I'm leaving the camp I'm referred to as "Grant"), it meant that I was frequently in scenes where Mervyn Johns, Jack Warner and Jimmy Hanley were involved. I and several others were their "gang" or background dressing of actors. In any "walking-around-the-Camp" shots, or sitting in the hut or canteen area, of which there were many - mostly shot later on in the studio - our gang was always included. I was also in a lot of camp action: singing in the choir, passing red cross parcels, banging in nails to put up photos, raking the vegetable patch etc.. When the light was bad – too dull or dark or insufficient to shoot the normal scenes – the Unit always fell back on what was known as the "Escape Sequence". The lighting necessary for the "Escape Sequence" was provided by several arc lamps, called "Brutes", and the power came from Ealing Studio's own generator or "Jenny". Because the escape, to be made by Jimmy Hanley, took place in the depths of winter and we were filming in August, a carpet of snow was required to cover everything in sight. The snow, incredibly, was provided by the Army Fire Brigade! Massive fire extinguishers would exude their glutinous evil smelling foam ("Foamite", it was called. Hard carbon dioxide) all over the landscape, covering not only the roofs and barbed wire, but also one or two slow-moving extras! As far as the eye could see there was snow - fire extinguisher snow! Through the camera lens the effect was magical. Just like that White Christmas we used to know and were always dreaming of. This operation, of course, took some time to complete and in many instances, by the time it was finished, the light had improved so much that the Escape Sequence was abandoned and we returned to the original one. Unfortunately, unless the foam was almost immediately cleared by water hosing, the chemicals involved created the smell of "rotten cabbages" which permeated the air for a long time afterwards – more so when the sun came out. Consequently, whenever the standby Escape Sequence was mooted and subsequently called for (and it must have been set up about five or six times) there were cries of, "Phworr. Bloody hell, not again! Who's got the clothes' pegs?" and of course much worse than that; the 'f' word being much bandied about! "Farkin 'ell! 'Oo's let one off?"

The fake snow was used a lot and worked perfectly. Especially in the scene where Jimmy Hanley, Basil Radford and Michael Redgrave break into the administration building and change the name "Matthews" to "Mitchell", so Michael Redgrave, who was under investigation by the Gestapo, can be repatriated and avoid being sent to a concentration camp. They have to go through the "snow" to get through the barbed wire to the hut and Jimmy has to wrestle with a guard dog. It looked very realistic to me.

After a week or two, I got some fabulous news. I must have been making an impression, as Basil Dearden and Cavilcanti took me aside and told me that I had been chosen to play the part of the "soldier" in the "Pond Scene". Funnily enough I didn't decline the offer! It was quite a moving "cameo" with about a page and a half of dialogue between two actors. The "soldier" is sailing a model yacht on the camp pond and is seen talking to the padre. Briefly, he is doubting whether he will ever get back to his beloved Woolacombe Bay again. The padre, of course, tries to reassure him, but the soldier, disappointed with life and frustrated with his long years as a prisoner of war, thinks that he will never again see his loved ones and at times doubts his own sanity.

"I'm never getting out of here am I? I'm going to die here. We're all going to die here......There are times padre when I think I'm going round the bend".

The padre was to be played by Jack Lambert who in addition to being a dependable and well-known Scots actor, had also held the rank of Lieutenant Colonel in the war. He had had a reputation for being strict but fair and I thought was well cast as the sympathetic and understanding man of the cloth. I was delighted when told of my new role and my psychoneurotic barometer went up several points!

I applied myself assiduously to learning my lines. Wherever I went, I played the scene over to myself. I became the Soldier. I became the Padre. And once or twice I was the small model yacht – "swoosh" I cried as I sailed past! I went over my lines in the bath, in the bed, in the lavatory. Many of my fellow workers, unaware of the situation, thought I <u>really</u> had gone round the bend!

"He's a goner: they said "First signs. He's talking to himself....."

"He's lost his marbles......"

"Pity, could've made something of his life – what's left of it, that is".

I smiled pityingly at their sallies. This was my big chance, my first steps to stardom. I wasn't going to muff it, least of all by not knowing my lines. But fate plays strange tricks. Before I actually performed the scene, one or two things occurred which dampened my earlier euphoria:

Firstly, the original date for shooting my scene was put back two weeks on the call-sheet and then designated as a "Standby Scene" (Similar to the Escape Sequence) for about ten days! Thus it was written on the call-sheet every day, but we didn't actually get around to doing it, so that when the scene was finally set up, my joyful anticipation had somewhat evaporated.

Secondly, and more importantly, I had a huge quarrel with the Director, Basil Dearden. On the day of the row, I had been dashing around like an over-zealous tour guide; chasing people up, technically advising on several scenes and acting as back-ground action in others. I had had a very heavy day! From my seat in the latrines I was idly reading the genuine P.O.W. notice which stated "Don't drop anything here that the enemy could pick up and use against you" when I faintly heard Basil calling out, "Where's Kydd?... Get Kydd! He should be here. Where is he?"

The Assistant Director echoed his master's voice through the loudhailer:

"KYDD! KYDD TO THE SET. KYDD TO THE SET! ... KYDD!!!!"

The Second had a go:

"KYYYYDDDDD TO THE SET. KYYYYYDDDDD TO THE SETTTT."

And then of course the ludicrous madness of the Third:

"KYYYYDDDDDDDDDDDDDDDDDDDD TOOOOOOOOO THHHHHHEEEEEE SETTTTTTTTTT."

Resentment welled up in me. I thought to myself,

"Let them wait. I've been working my backside off - besides, there are nine other technical advisers around. Let them earn their money for a change."

Just as I reached the end of my musings, the Third Assistant Director came into the latrine area looking for me.

"Ah there you are. You're needed."

"I'm not in the shot, am I?" I asked.

"Well, I'm not sure..... All I know is that he's going mad and I've been sent to find you."

I took my time in my best former P.O.W. deliberate and defiant manner and moved yawningly ultra slowly to where the camera was set up. Basil Dearden saw me and cried out, "Oh Kydd. Here a minute!"

I moved even slower, like a time-wasting footballer, even limping slightly as if I'd been fouled, whilst like an impatient referee about to book me, he walked towards me beckoning.

"Now, Kydd. You know you're not supposed to leave the set without telling the Assistant Director where you're going!"

"Am I in this scene?…" I began to ask.

"No Kydd, (hurriedly, as if not wanting to hear what I had to say) you are not! I know you like to be in front of the camera in every shot, but on this occasion you're not. This shot concerns the officers."

That stung. It was true, but it still stung.

"What I want, Kydd, and what you are here for is technical advice about…"

On reflection perhaps I should have been flattered that out of all the advisers available he wanted me there, but I didn't think of that at the time. I was furious I was being treated like a child, and I did something appalling. I clicked my heels and raised my arm in an exaggerated Hitler salute.

"Heil Hitler" I barked.

He retreated as though I was going to hit him. And I didn't leave it there.

"Get stuffed" I said, and walked off.

Some of those around us looked aghast! A Hitler salute to Basil Dearden? And "Heil Hitler?" And "Get stuffed?" But there was no going back – I had dug a large hole, dived in with a large spade, was digging furiously and had scuppered the yacht scene with the Padre! And possibly my involvement in the film! (Having said that, they couldn't have sacked me because of the continuity. I was in it too often and couldn't disappear….. Could I?) Basil studiously avoided me for the rest of the day and I reciprocated by giving him a "fish-eyed" look in return. Motion-picture-wise, I became the ex-P.O.W. most unlikely to succeed and Basil's unfavourite adviser.

Naturally the "ordure" hit the fan and the following morning, I was asked to attend a short meeting to be held in the Company office. It was rather like a Military Court Tribunal, being attended by the Executive Producer (Cavilcanti), the Production Manager, the First Assistant Director and finally, Basil himself. They faced me as I came in, but I couldn't do the "cap-off" routine because I wasn't wearing one. Cavilcanti acted as a kind of prosecuting counsel and gave us all a resume of my behaviour the previous day, finally asking me to apologise to "Baseel". He went on to say that the location was very important to us, an integral part of the picture and that because the war had only recently ended, we were very lucky and privileged to be in Germany so soon after, and that I should not "muck the boat". (Yes I didn't quite understand that either, but got the gist).

"Many people, Zahm, would geeve zere right leg to be 'ere" he said, looking at me sorrowfully with his South American llama-like eyes. As I had no defending counsel I spoke up for myself.

"You must realise" I said "that I was a P.O.W. for five years and you might not appreciate it, and we may not show it, but it's pretty traumatic for some of us being here in Germany."

I must admit I wasn't traumatised at all but it was a good beginning. And added, "I mean I'm really a pretty easy-going sort of fellow until I feel I'm being exploited."

This was true.

I then went on to say that in view of my long imprisonment, I was sometimes guilty of losing my temper. I continued in this vein, adding that I objected very much to being called by my surname as if I was some menial or should-be-grateful shoe-licking dog! Also I felt that I was doing my best and working hard for the Company and I certainly did not intend to 'muck zee boat." I apologised to 'Bazeel" for my boorish behaviour and at the same time pointed out that some consideration of <u>my</u> position (What position?) would not come amiss. Cavalcanti got up from his seat and came over to me. He put his arm around my shoulder saying, "Be a good boy, Zahm. Let's all be friends and make good peecture. Yes?"

As far as I was concerned the incident was forgotten. But Basil smarted. For quite a while after he always referred to me as Mister Kydd, heavily emphasising the Mister!

"Mister Kydd, is this washing hanging up correctly?"

"What do you think, Mister Kydd" or "Would you see if Mister Kydd is available?" Or even "Mister Kydd to set!" bawled by the Third who joined in the sarcasm!

"MMMMMMMMMMIIIIIIIIISSSTERRRRRRRRRR KYDD......... TO SETTTTTTTTTTTTTTTTTTTTTTTTTTT!"

I felt a bit hurt that Basil should perpetuate the sarcasm and literally bent over backwards to make amends. I thought that I would be deprived of the "Soldier and Padre" scene and would not have been surprised if he had re-cast it. But he didn't. In fact, when we eventually came to shoot it he encouraged me tremendously. But I sensed that underneath he was slightly wary of me and it was only much later on, at a party I was invited to at his house, that I discovered the reason.

As the days went by we got to know the actors more intimately. The ex-P.O.W. technical 10 were invited to the Actors' hotel for drinks and also to the canteen and Sergeant's mess of the soldiers who were working along with us. Jack Warner organised a very successful Concert, aided and abetted by Mervyn Johns and all the others, where we got to see what excellent performers they were! Jack in particular was wonderfully relaxed in front of an audience, compering the evening with great style. Rather cheekily, I have to say, I offered my services, and so did Steve, and he and I found ourselves on stage at the "Zum Kyffhauser, Harburgerstr.", along with Michael Redgrave - who did a bit of Shakespeare, his Chorus from Henry V-Guy Middleton, Basil Radford, Derek Bond et al who sang a few "Bing Crosby" songs, in rather sweet harmony! I told a few jokes and did a few impressions as was my tendency. I had had good practice in the Prison camp! I mean on reflection this was something of a coup for me, on the same bill as these stars!. But I felt so relaxed in everyone's company, and of course had done it professionally before the war, so didn't let myself down at all. I even got a few laughs! Here's one:

"Have you heard the one about the waiter who had a glass eye and he was serving soup and a man passing the table bumped into him and it jolted him so much that his glass eye flew out of its socket and fell into the bowl of soup. The waiter had no idea where the eye had gone as a result of the collision, and thought it had fallen onto the floor and put the bowl down on the table to search for it, obviously without success. The customer at the table, seeing his soup had arrived, swallowed several spoonfuls of the soup and inadvertently gulped down the eye, unaware of what he'd eaten. The following day the customer who'd swallowed the eye had a terrible pain in his guts, and went off to the doctor.

"Ah Mr. Jones. What appears to be the problem?"

"Doctor I've got this awful pain in my stomach. I've had it all day," he said.

So the doc. gave him some medicine which he dutifully took. But to no avail. He went back complaining that the pain had moved to his rectum.

"Take your trousers down" said the doctor. "I'll take a look at you."

The doctor got out his "rectoscope"… yes…rectoscope. It's the thing he uses to peer up your er..recto…and looked into the man's er.. rectobottom. And there was this evil eye staring down at him.

"What's the matter Mr. Jones?" said the doctor. "Don't you trust me?"

And with the theme clearly being ocular, Steve and I did "The Green Eye of the Little Yellow God" together. This was always a handy staple. The essence of the "gag" was that I was standing behind Steve with my arms linked through under Steve's armpits, whilst his were behind his back. My hands were doing all the actions and "demonstrating" the words of the poem. Obviously the audience are aware of the fact that Steve isn't in control of what I might do! We'd done it a lot and had mined a mass of moments that got good reactions! It's the many versed epic poem by J.Milton Hayes:

"There's a one-eyed yellow idol to the north of Khatmandu
(POKE STEVE IN EYE (OW!) THEN POINT UPWARDS AND MOVE STEVE'S HEAD DOWN ROUGHLY)
There's a little marble cross below the town
(DO "LITTLE" WITH FINGERS, TAKE MARBLE OUT OF HIS POCKET AND BOUNCE IT AND DO THE SIGN OF THE CROSS AND MOVE STEVE'S HEAD UP EQUALLY ROUGHLY)
There's a broken-hearted woman…
(TAKE HEART SHAPED PIECE OF PAPER OUT OF STEVE'S POCKET AND TEAR IT UP. MIME FEMALE SHAPE)
…tends the grave of Mad Carew
(MAD "LOOPY" GESTURES),
And the Yellow God forever gazes down……."
(PUSH HEAD UP EVEN MORE ROUGHLY)
Etc….etc….

Obviously as you can see, all my gestures were very specific to the words and were frequently ridiculous and involved doing the opposite of what he was saying or picking his nose or slapping his head, or brushing his teeth, or punching him in the stomach, while taking pre-set items out of his pocket like the marble, the piece of heart shaped paper, a tooth brush, and a tennis ball, and bouncing it - "arrangements had begun to celebrate her birthday with a ball" - whilst he courageously carried on, dramatically and gamely, reciting the poem.

The best part was always the shirt-ripping, followed by the

smashing of an egg on his forehead during the verse which went:

"He returned before the dawn, with his shirt and tunic torn,

(TEAR SHIRT, RIPPING IT AND REVEALING BARE CHEST)

And a gash across his temple dripping red"

(SMASH EGG ON HIS FOREHEAD AND SMEAR IT ALL OVER HIS FACE, CHEST AND DOWN HIS TROUSERS)

The egg of course went everywhere. In fact you'd rub it in! As I said, we went down well. It was a terrific evening.

On the fraulein front I wasted no time in establishing my claim in the "Fraternising Stakes" as it was nicknamed and endeavoured to swiftly make up for my 5 captive years during which my wild oats had been totally un-sowable. In fact, the field was now wide open for collaboration and I used the concert to initiate the first tractor ride! Altogether there must have been about twenty-four of them including the actual kitchen staff who cooked all the food. My plan was to start with the social intercourse chat, leading up to my own personal invasion on "D Day" (or "D" night). For starters, I set my sights on a cuddly well upholstered creature of 19 tender years. She was every man's idea of a blonde buxom barmaid - something to softly lay your hands on, before, during, or after. She originally came from Bromberg in Poland. I knew the area around Bromberg pretty well, having worked there as a prisoner in the sugar-beet factory and this gave me a head start over the others. Her Christian name was Elsa and I started my crusade very gently, making agreeable noises and conversation in German for a couple of days, culminating in overtures with bars of chocolate, cigarettes and soap. It's an interesting statistic which I don't believe has ever been tallied:- how many German girls fell for the troops through the courtesy of Cadburys, Imperial Tobacco and/or Sunlight. On the third night of my wooing, I arranged to meet her in a little thicket just outside the town which I had previously reconnoitred. She said in fact she was very fearful of the thicket - "das dickicht?" she said querulously.

"DAS DICKICHT?" she said again loudly - which made me wonder if it was a well known seduction site, or was booby trapped or was occupied by a hairy ghoul; but a small bar of Milk Tray helped to make up her mind. After a seemingly hesitant, nervous and fumbling start on her part, I realised about five minutes later, that she knew more than she'd been letting on and her whispered "be gentle" soon had me reacting with, "Oi be careful! Don't bite that!"

And before you could say, "We'd better get back before the curfew" it was all over! She put her football shorts (yes, soccer shorts! Hamburg F.C. she said!) which she'd earlier removed for the "Match of the Day", into her handbag and hurriedly smoothing her dress, took my hand and started walking rapidly back to Stade. It was the first of many pleasurable visits to that part of the countryside. And after a couple of weeks, that was that! She said very honestly that she wanted to play the field and began fraternising with an ex P.O.W. who lured her with Woodbines in tins. She didn't actually smoke but could swap them for clothing, like proper knickers, and no doubt a football jersey, and I was forced to look further a-field for fresher fräuleins with whom to fraternise. (Possibly too many 'Fs" there). I f-f-f-found one, the elder of two sisters, who I kissed. But she would go no further. She spoke quite good English, and very firmly told me off for trying to seduce her and I was fortunate the British had won the war, as the Nazis, of which she was one, were far superior.

The film meanwhile, was going from strength to strength. It was up to schedule, we were assured, and the word was passed down that the Highest Authority, in the shape of Michael Balcon, the El Supremo of Ealing Studios, was delighted with what had been shot so far. The "rushes" – the bits and pieces of the various scenes filmed each day, later to be put together in the proper sequence by the film editor, 'rushed' to be ready for approval as soon as possible, so they didn't have to expensively re-shoot and re-engage the actors or re-book the location – were looking extremely good. "Full of atmosphere" they said. And we shot the Pond scene! Yes! It took about an hour and a half. The scene was broken up from a wide establishing shot of us doing the scene at the pond, to a two shot, and then repeated from different angles ending in big close-ups. As I said, Jack Lambert played the padre, in his sweet Scots lilt, and it appeared to work well. I was understandably nervous at first but soon overcame it, being helped by "steady as a rock" Jack. He told me not to worry and explained how I could get the utmost from the scene by "underplaying" it – "Has more impact" he said. But obviously Basil Dearden's expertise as director was of great value to me. Both of them congratulated me at the end of it, and Basil's "Well done, Sam" was praise indeed considering all that had gone before! Jack's advice was on reflection, gold-dust. I've got a lot to thank him for. He was marvellous. Thanks Jack.

I had a good rapport with most of the actors but especially so with Jack Warner, Mervyn Johns, Jimmy Hanley, Ralph Michael and Freddie Schiller. Freddie, a German, as I've said, was playing one of the Camp Officers. Apart from laughing at my jokes, I think he had an affinity with me because of my having been a prisoner of war in his country and he having been interned in mine. He would often give impressions of a B.B.C. radio show called "Workers' Playtime".

"Und now" he would say, as if announcing it, "UND NOW.......IT'S......VERKERS' PLAYTIME".

Then he would shout and cheer madly, endeavouring to recreate the frenetic audience reaction, and then tell a terrible joke with a pun in it.

"Did you hear about zer pessimist who hated German sausage? He alvays feared the Wurst!"

And then he'd cackle loudly, bowing and curtseying as if it was the best joke in zer wurld! After which I would applaud vigorously. He was a friendly German, eager and anxious to please – unlike most of them that I'd encountered!

One day when not "on call", Jimmy Hanley obtained a lift to Hamburg in a car detailed to pick up Gordon Jackson, cast as a blind Scottish P.O.W. in the film. The car arrived back with Gordon, but without our James! Apparently the driver had waited as long as he could and had been forced to return without him. Of course the inevitable happened. Due to a change in schedule, Jimmy was required on the set the following day, but hadn't come back. Hastily the shooting was rearranged and when eventually Jimmy did put in an appearance (after about three or four days) he was only mildly rebuked! His excuse was that he had met some members of his old Commando unit and they had quite naturally celebrated. And he thought his scene was next week! Perhaps Cavalcanti reprimanded him with the "Be a good boy" and "Don't muck zer boat" speech, but Jimmy carried on irrepressibly as before - loudly, cheerfully, kindly and funnily. He was a very friendly fellow with whom I was to work joyously on many occasions. I was shocked when he died so young.

On the "amour" front, I had now switched to a Hungarian girl aged about 30 who answered to the name of Julika (Do you like her) and the answer was - in small doses. She originated from Budapest and I never discovered how she became established in Stade working as a waitress. You can't blame her or anyone else for trying to get away from the hostile environments. Perhaps she'd backed the Germans to be the winners and was thus "displaced". She certainly had no qualms about coming to our hotel, although it was forbidden by the German authorities (and frowned upon by our Central Commission) on pain of dismissal from her serving job at the Town Hall. I never got used to her parading around in the nuddy in my hotel bedroom, smoking the inevitable cigarette in an extra-long holder and saying "Vot you got?", thankfully only referring to cigarettes. Unfortunately she was a chain-smoker. She gave herself to get the fags; to continue smoking, she gave herself. In and out of bed, whatever (or whoever) she was doing, she smoked - especially while she was doing it! She oozed tobacco fumes. The ash got into places I don't dare discuss. She was also insatiable and would be looking for a repeat performance almost before the first session was finished! This idyllic, out-of-control and, let's be frank, pressurised sexual existence couldn't last, of course. I hadn't the know-how or the stamina, and besides, I was beginning to look even more emaciated than I had when I first arrived. Jimmy Hanley said to me, "You'll end up looking like stringy Hungarian goulash if you're not careful!"

Due to her "couldn't-care-less" attitude towards authority, her frequent visits to me at the hotel had become an open secret and in addition her bizarre skills (through my own blabbing) had reached other ears. It didn't surprise me, therefore, that immediately after I threw in the towel, she transferred her allegiance to another technical adviser (also an ex- P.O.W.) from the Royal West Kents. Pretty lusty those Kentish men - it's all those hops at an early age! He too was a chain smoker, so if you'll pardon the pun, they shared an existence of one long "fug"!

After a reasonable period of abstinence to help me regain my strength, I looked around for someone not quite so demanding and again the answer turned up in the shape of one of the coterie of serving girls. This time the trysts were not so frequent or enervating. This little piece of porcelain, Lisa Schmidt, came from Dresden and like the product of her birthplace, was rather fragile and delicate, but pleasant in her attitude to me, so that when the time came for all of us to leave Stade, I had grown rather fond of her. I was very touched when she presented me with a bunch of flowers and a card on which she had written "Ich lieber dich" which means I love you (and not "I Love Dick"). The day before I left, she had given me a keepsake - a small curly haired light blue Dresden china angel in the act of praying, which I have to this day.

When I returned to my home in Bedford Park, W.4., after the film location, I was not needed at the Studio for a fortnight for the interior shots - all the "inside the hut" action was of course shot on theatrical sets created by designers and stocked by props men and built by carpenters - and it gave me time to consider my situation and reflect on my first taste of film-making. It was certainly not as I had imagined, but to be perfectly frank, I don't really know what I had expected. I had believed it consisted entirely of a camera man pointing his camera at whatever was going on and er...that was that!

I'd never really thought about the intricacies of logistics, editing, casting, lighting, keeping up to schedule, props, technical staff, wardrobe, admin, sets, set builders, designers, caterers etc.. I mean how naive had I been? So it had been a huge learning curve! And a great experience working with leading men like Michael Redgrave, Basil Radford, Mervyn Johns, Jimmy Hanley and Jack Warner. In addition to being top actors, they were decent kindly people, ever ready to help and advise. For me to participate in a successful film like this was a complete U-turn of Fate. If anyone a year earlier whilst I was still a P.O.W. had told me that in 12 months time I would be playing a part in a feature film in Germany, I would have given him a pitying look and a scathing reply! But when Fate points at you, and grabs you by the unmentionables, anything can happen.

So. As you'll have gathered, I'd enjoyed it. It was fulfilling and I thought that at least I'd made my mark (no matter how small) in the "Pond" shoot with Jack Lambert.

"An excellent scene" Basil had said, …and very moving".

Cavalcanti had nodded agreement too. But here's the rub – unfortunately and sadly, it was never to be shown, being cut out of the final version! I was bitterly disappointed and upset, though concealing it and pretending that it didn't really matter. Basil Dearden wrote to me before the Press Show:

"Owing to the picture over–running we reluctantly had to cut your Pond scene, a very moving one, from the film. I thought I'd better let you know before you saw the completed picture…."

Well, at least he did apologise! My best (so far) work had been left on the cutting room floor! This was to happen off and on for the rest of my career. In some instances my contribution was completely cut out! *Saraband for Dead Lovers, Train of Events, Pool of London, The Key* and *Heavens Above* are several I did that failed to make it and I don't feature! It's part of the job of course. Though in this instance, I was still in *The Captive Heart*. Just not as much as I thought I would be.

I analysed myself as I thought about my disappointment. I of course, deep down, thought that I'd mucked it up, and Basil was pretending the film was too long. Or as I'd been such a normal character in all the scenes with the boys in the huts, perhaps the contrast of playing such a different unhappy one didn't fit? All I did know was that I was a queer mixture. Ambitious, keen, quick–tempered, sensitive and paradoxically, for an actor, shy. But I knew that I had to overcome my inhibitions before I could ever make it. I was determined not to give up easily. Onward. And upward!!!!

Possibly by way of compensation, presumably knowing that the Pond scene was going to be cut, Basil asked me if I could write a Comedy sketch for a Pantomime extract in the film, exactly what I'd done when I'd been a prisoner. I suggested "Babes in the Wood" which we'd performed in the camp. You needed a chorus of six to eight fairies (naturally chosen from the hairiest prisoners. Those with moustaches always a boon) dressed in the requisite wigs, pleated skirts, little pointy bras, a lot of midriff and army boots. They were to come on stage, preceded by the Chief Fairy for whom I wrote the lines:

"I'm a fairy you know, name of Mary. (PAUSE)
I'm light as a delicate kiss
So I can fly on a leaf or a short piece of grass
And dance on a droplet of…rain!"

Then they all burst into song and do their balletic dance routine. The ensemble was to be led by Jack Warner (Chief Fairy), complete with wand in hand. Basil liked the idea and it was incorporated into the film. I didn't get a credit on the screen but they paid me a couple of guineas for it! They cut the dialogue I'd written down to practically nothing and in the end it's just a small insert, despite having shot a lot more - and used a bit of the song; but Mervyn Johns, Ralph Michael and Jack Lambert made good fairies, and Jimmy and Guy Middleton were ridiculous looking "Babes!" The scene worked all the better as

Basil cleverly cut away from the panto to Basil Radford killing himself laughing whilst the German officers looked bewildered at the "British humour".

Rachel Kempson (Michael Redgrave's real life wife and a big Shakespeare Memorial Theatre in Stratford, starlet) was a fabulous actress and played the heroine in the film, Celia Mitchell, who re-falls in love with her husband via his letters to her (they were about to be divorced) when of course the letters are written by Michael Redgrave who has assumed her dead husband's identity. Not that she knows he's dead of course. (I hope this makes sense. Please watch the film as it works much better on screen than I'm explaining it) and it was fascinating to see how the atmosphere and attitude changed when a woman was present. Not a swear word was heard, which was a complete contrast to their effing and blinding behaviour in Germany! Even the First, Second and Third Assistants were muted! Working in the Studio, I noticed the bonhomie was not quite so marked as it had been on location. The rank-and-file were friendly enough, but we were now back in dear old England where one stuck more strictly to lines of demarcation, so the production staff, from the Producer and Director downwards, kept their distance. A case in point was that the canteen was never used by the executives, who had their own restaurant room and although I didn't see any of the small fry actually barred from going in there, none of the Technical-Ten-Dogsbody-Brigade ever ate there, either by invitation or otherwise.

A well-known stage actress named Gladys Henson played Jack Warner's wife - and his wife in *The Blue Lamp* and *Train of Events*, with Ealing - and I was to encounter her both in films and as a fervent cricket fan at Lord's ground during the years that lay ahead.

"I'll just have a little gin and something to steady my nerves" was one of her favourite sayings, always adding "How about you, dear?"

Margaret Harper Nelson, Muriel Cole and Thelma Graves from the Casting Department were frequent visitors to the set and they, too, were to play an important part in my future acting career which I was now determined to pursue. Though of course I didn't know how vital they would be at the time!

One sequence which caused me a great deal of amazement, as once again I had no idea it was done like this, concerned the opening scene of the film when the various characters were seen being marched to the camp having been captured. In order to recreate this - we'd obviously done shots on location too, but they cut from one to the other in the edit - a large truck was moved onto a big escalator-like track which revolved like a treadmill, which had been laid down on the studio floor. At the same time, behind the column of prisoners in the studio, projected onto a screen, was the background which had been filmed on the roads in Germany. The effect from the front, of this "back projection", when the prisoners were walking, was startling. It was so realistic it seemed as if we were filming in Germany again! The special effects - a wind machine (a huge fan in a cage whirring at high revs), props men off-camera throwing cups of dirty water into shot imitating a truck or vehicle crashing through a puddle, and sound effects (fx.) being created "live" to resemble rumbling tanks and lorries - were magical. This was before sounds were regularly dubbed on in post production. The tools to create the sound of tread and trucks were ingenious, involving oil drums and cranks. Despite seeing the 'smoke and mirrors", after a few takes I really felt as if I were on the road to "captivity" again.

Interestingly, once we were in the studio, Basil gave me lines that I'd actually never been originally assigned; so I suppose on reflection, I must have impressed, as I was clearly trusted despite our "differences". I had lines in four separate scenes:

In the hut where I'm "soldier in top bunk", about the Red Cross parcels not arriving and Jack hitting Jimmy ("Blimey! What'll you do at the peace conference!")

In the canteen where we're reading letters from home.

By the stove where Jack burns his model yacht for firewood "Can't we burn anything else?"

And when "repatriation" is about to take place, I leap into the hut, shouting it!

Those scenes, coupled with all the exterior shots of me raking flowerbeds, or nailing photos to walls, or singing in the choir, or lugging parcels, or washing myself, or just being panned past at roll-call, actually meant that I was quite heavily featured in the film. I even have a big grinning close up as I'm leaving the camp to be repatriated. "Grant" shouts the German guard and I'm off, past the camera and out of the gate! And then there's another girning moment when I've arrived back in 'Blighty' from the boat. This was something I never expected when I'd first signed the contract. Having said that, after such a surprisingly big contribution, I didn't get a credit in the end titles. I'd have to get used to this in the next few years. It appeared to be the policy of so many film makers at the time, to only credit a few.

On the completion of shooting (after we'd "wrapped" as they called it), the Company held an end of picture party, which took place on the sound stage of the studio. Trestle tables were set up with food and drink. A dance band churned out a few polite tunes. Everyone connected with the picture (and some who weren't) was there and the evening, having been initially very quiet and respectable - one might even say polite. Snooty even! ("I say, can you pass the canapés?") - eventually developed into an enormous excessive, drinking, dancing and eating competition between the actual technicians and us the dogsbodies, ending up in victory for the actuals, ten - nil. I clearly wasn't up to it, as I woke up in one of the dressing rooms in my underpants and shoes and socks, with no memory of how I got there, no sign of my suit, and I had a vague idea I'd performed the "Green Eye of the Little Yellow God" with Steve again. (I think I got an egg from the canteen). And then apparently (according to Steve who I spoke to the following day) I'd done a ridiculous strip-tease after reciting it, while Steve sang "The Tiger Rag" (well he shouted out "Hold that Tiger" a lot). I luckily found the suit on a chair in the studio (no sign of the shirt though! Ah well! And it was my best!). No one clearly seemed to care I was in my vest, knickers, shoes and socks. All those revellers left draped on the chairs, had passed out! I staggered home to Turnham Green shirtless, just as the milkman was delivering the milk. It was sad that the picture had finished - well, the actual shooting had finished - and all those people, working and worrying, laughing and living, swapping tales and trysts, for a period of just over four months, were now all going their separate ways.

Ealing were confident that they had a winner on their hands and didn't hesitate to say so. I too was very pleased to be associated with it, but I asked myself, "Will it be my first and only film?"

I'd finished it and what was I supposed to do now? I lay about again. My mother got twitchy. Should I not be trying to find work? Less so though when I told her how much money I'd made.

About three weeks later Basil Dearden's secretary telephoned me with an invitation to a small party at Basil's flat in Lancaster Gate. Quite a number of the Unit were there, mostly heads of Departments - but no other actors! No Jack. No Jimmy. No Mervyn. Steve Smith and I appeared to be the only two of the ex-P.O.W.s to be asked, which was surprising. But I suppose made sense. We had been hugely committed to the project and worked very hard, unlike some of the others who coasted through, not really having any desire to make acting their career. That bloke Roger who'd almost had a nervous breakdown at the beginning, believing he was going to be sacked, when he realised what work-load he was expected to provide, faded away like most of them. Naturally he ended up as a Member of Parliament. (Not really). Needless to say Basil's party was lavish, with caviar and champagne and Basil in a very happy mood. He was extremely funny and entertained everyone with lots of amusing stories – a side of him I hadn't seen before or suspected. At the end of it all, as we filed out into the corridor of the flat to make our noisy "Good-nights", Basil swayed at the open door, shaking hands with everyone as they made their exit. I was the last one to go and when I got to the door he leaned heavily on it and said, "Good night, Sammy. Thank you for all your good work on the film".

"No, I have to thank you Basil" I replied. "I enjoyed it. All of it."

But he went on, "I'm sorry that we haven't always seen eye to eye….."

"Oh, that's all over and done with Basil" I interrupted.

"No, it's not" he said. "You've never really liked me, have you Sammy?"

I was taken aback. Apart from the "flare-up" on location and one or two frosty moments when he'd given me his well-known "what-am-I-saddled-with-here" look, I had never conveyed that I didn't like him. Maybe I might have shown by my expression that I wasn't completely in agreement with some cynical remark that he had made - he was good at that - but as for saying that I disliked him - definitely not!

"It's not true, Basil" I said, beginning to feel embarrassed.

"Oh yes it is" he ploughed on. "You've never thought much of me from that day that you heard that I wasn't on active service like yourself."

I didn't know what to say. I had no knowledge of Basil's war service, nor had I expressed any wish to know. I knew that he had directed some shows for E.N.S.A. ("Entertainments National Service Association". Or the cruel version: "Every Night Something Awful") with Basil Dean, but that was all.

"Look Basil" I said, emphasising my words "I don't know where you got this idea about my disliking you. As a matter of fact, I was just thinking how much I owe you for taking the time and trouble with me on the film." (Creep!)

"Oh no" he persisted, swaying a little as he spoke. "You've never liked the idea of me getting out of the war and you having been a prisoner for so long."

"Basil, if I could have got out of it, I would have. I don't know why you're saying all this. I admire you a lot."

There was an embarrassed silence and then he shook my hand and, with his hand still pressed in mine, said, "Never mind, never mind. I'll do what I can for you."

And he nearly fell over. On that unsteady note I left, thinking to myself that I was the one supposed to be neurotic, not Basil! He never referred to the conversation again and I met him many times, both working for him and playing cricket with him and Harry Kratz, his favourite First Assistant Director whose "Howzats" were wonderfully loud as you'd expect, and on many occasions persuaded the batsman into giving themselves out when they weren't. Harry Frampton (the man in charge of make-up) was also a keen cricketer, as was editor Sidney Cole (who eventually produced all 105 episodes of the T.V. series of "Robin Hood") helping to create an enthusiastic team for the Ealing Studios XI. Basil was a useful bowler and took quite a few wickets, although, modestly, he never considered himself to be any good. He was madly keen on football, too, and had a seat not far from me in Chelsea's East Stand at Stamford Bridge. It was a great loss when he was killed in a motor accident, on the way back from Pinewood Studios, some years later. I had a lot to thank him for, as did the British Film Industry.

The Captive Heart opened at the Odeon, Leicester Square and was widely acclaimed by the critics.

"Superbly authentic atmosphere" figured in many reviews and the acting and documentary feel were highly praised. Steve and I had played a good part in making sure the environment was as real as possible!

"Well observed genuine performances" was also said of it.

When I saw it, I naturally re-lived all the circumstances appertaining to my appearances. I thought I looked awful. Skinny as a rake. Ill. Drawn. In fact exactly how a P.O.W. should look! At the time I remember I was worried I'd got tense and gabbled my several lines, but no there was no evidence of that. Though I would have liked to have seen the Pond scene included of course. That rankled for some time. "If only" I kept saying to myself. And to the tree in the garden. And next door's cat. I became slightly obsessed with it. I saw the film about eight times.

(Once I sat through four showings in the cinema on one day.

This was an era where you could get away with sitting in the auditorium for as long as you liked.) I took my mother to the Odeon, Leicester Square, to see my worldwide acting debut and when the film was coming round to my first bit of dialogue, about the Red Cross, delivered from the bunk, I nudged her arm in advance with my elbow. Unfortunately she was cleaning her spectacles at the time and dropped them. My lines boomed out with me failing to find her specs. As I frantically grovelled for them under the seat, incurring the wrath of the people behind and beside me as I inadvertently touched a few legs in the dark, I heard my voice coming from the screen speaking my next immortal supposedly funny line to Jack Warner and Mervyn Johns after he's punched him, about his "being needed at the peace conference!" End of scene. Big laugh! (hopefully). There was silence. Had I gabbled it? Is that why there was no laugh? Some people had laughed when I'd seen it before. My mother sensed that I was fed up.

"Don't worry" she whispered "we'll sit through it again till you come on."

"I am on again Mother. In a few minutes. It's alright. I was just worried I didn't get a laugh."

"Oh good. Have you got more lines?"

"Yes Mother. Several."

"Oh well in that case we only need to see it once!"

"Okay. Thanks," said I, pleased at her enthusiasm but then realising she didn't want to sit through it again which was dispiriting. But by the next time I was on, which as I've said, was soon after, she had fallen asleep and I hadn't the heart to wake her. She slept for the rest of the film. Missing me entirely. She pretended she'd seen me as we went out. She said, "You were very good. Very thin, of course. But very good."

Later she was to see me in many films and television shows, but the first on the big screen was rather special as far as I was concerned. Well at least she'd made the effort. From then on I decided to try and see every film I was ever in, despite being my own worst critic. At the time of course, I wasn't sure if I'd ever make many more.

After the film I was in the wilderness for sometime. I mean I had no idea what to do to be an actor at all. My mother, remembering my success in the bedding department at Whiteleys of Bayswater before the war - despite my having been sacked for suggesting I have a 2/6d a week pay rise - kept asking, "When are you going to settle down and get a proper job with a pension attached?"

Adding subtly, "Shall we go for a stroll around a department store? You like them don't you!"

And unsubtly making a beeline for the bedding department when we got there. This was the burning conundrum. Acting was not proper. If this was the sixteenth century I would be buried in an unmarked grave outside the walls of the city if I was a thespian and poked with a shitty stick. So I searched. In the papers. (possibly the wrong thing to do. But I had no idea). But without any luck. And asked lot of questions. Probably of all the wrong people. And then one day on the P.O.W. grapevine, Steve Smith, (still not "Knut Knudsen") returning the *Captive Heart* favour, told me he'd heard that the Revue *Back Home Again,* which entirely consisted of ex-prisoners of war (mainly flying types from Stalag Luft 111) was going on tour. The show had originally been presented by Jack Hylton at the Stoll Theatre, Kingsway - Jack was a famous band leader turned impresario of the time - under the direction and production of fine friendly funnymen Peter Butterworth and Talbot (Tolly) Rothwell (both subsequently to become very well-known, the former as an actor in, and the latter a writer of, the *Carry Ons*) and consisted of a series of sketches and revue numbers, as performed in a (supposed) prison camp. Tolly, as well as writing practically everything, did an ace impersonation of Groucho Marx, acted in a few skits, and Peter organised, produced everything, and appeared in some of the sketches. The show had had an extended run at the Stoll and was a fair success. The touring version, however, was licked into shape by

Producer/Writer Val Guest (ultimately the great Hammer Horror director and with whom I would work on the *Quatermass Experiment* and *Up the Creek*) and the chorus girls were to be real girls, not like those employed at the Stoll and in the prison Camps - "ersatz" - who were men dressed as women! I sent a letter mentioning my having been a P.O.W. and having done a lot of revue in the camp, asking for a meeting, and was granted one with Mr. Guest, who was a charming man, in his office. As per my letter, I explained I'd had huge experience in a real Prison Camp putting on a mass of shows and acting in them...and writing a few! I was asked to audition! I did a routine I'd done before the war when I was the M.C. for the Oscar Rabin Band: a few gags, and some impersonations, which included:

"My wife's so conscientious, that when she goes to the local baths, when she gets out, she gives the lifeguard a penny".(This was a Syd Walker joke and of course was about a time when the cubicles in the lavatories cost a penny. As in "spending a penny"). And for those who don't get it, it's a "risque" gag about weeing in the swimming pool.

"Do you like Violet in the bath? Who the hell wouldn't!"
A Vic Oliver gag. Said in my best Vic Oliver!

A quick song (Louis Armstrong's "I'll be Glad when you're dead you Rascal You") and a tap dance.

And to my delight I got the job! My mother, as you will appreciate, wasn't very pleased. Especially as she'd just got me an interview to work in the food hall at Barker's of Kensington. She loved going there and was clearly thinking of the possibility of cheap cheddar.

We rehearsed in London and later at Wolverhampton where we were to open, at the Hippodrome. In reality, we were a Variety Bill with the girls being included for good old sex appeal. Unfortunately I didn't seem to appeal to the girls, but these were early days!

Show-wise, I was in a couple of "Black-Out" sketches (silly shenanigans in the dark!

"Ooh sorry constable is that your truncheon?").

A sketch with Tolly called "Dr. Fradler's Dilemma" where I played a butler called Whitewings, with lines like:

"Sir, you appear to have a hedgehog attached to your head sir."
"It's a hat, Whitewings."
"Your hat is moving, sir."
"Argh! If this is a hedgehog, where's my hat?"
"I think you just gave it a saucer of milk sir."

Cue comedy props hedgehog (cleverly made out of cloth) being thrown into the wings with loud "Ouch" from the darkness!

A sketch called "It takes a Tough Guy to Be a Leading Lady" where I did a very over-the-top camp character – I was good at them – called "the Dresser" where all the "ladies" were of course "men".

Another sketch where I acted with Peter Butterworth called "On my Return" written and narrated by Tolly about all the scenarios of returning from the war and meeting up with your girl-friend. My character Johnnie saw his girlfriend arrive with her new boyfriend!

A song called "Dream Boogie" where I think I did quite well crooning sleepily as if in the bath.

And then the Big Finale Song Scene based round "Strolling in the Park". The girls came on from the opposite side of the stage to us and we met in the middle and paired off. Mine was a blonde with a gap in her teeth and a slight moustache. It glistened in the lights! We were suitably garbed in blazers, tight high-waisted cream trousers, gaudy red bow ties, white gloves and straw boaters. At each line of the song we made the appropriate action like stringed puppets. For instance, the third line went….

"I was surprised……" (hands raised coyly in shock Al Jolson "Mammy" fashion, face melodramatically aghast).

Then the stolen heart bit meant you pointed to where your heart should be (Left side, you fool!) and made flying-away bird motions with hands and much fluttering of eyelids.

"I smiled"…. (Teeth or gums revealed by stretching or drawing back of lips across the mouth in grinning grimace as if for toothpaste commercial).

"I raised my hat"…… (frequently that hat was dropped!) And "Something……dar dar dar dude dum dee" (me and my partner did a bit of a complicated twirl here so I looked suitably arch and let those who were just bobbing do the lyrics).

We whistled the next chorus, repeating all the gestures and strutting at the same time. We looked good in a "naive-old-fashioned-hair-smarmed-Gold-Diggers-of-1946" sort of way. When we opened, a long tour was envisaged, promised and supposedly booked. We moved on to Proud Preston and there we were subjected to "cuts" - pruning and re-rehearsing until we achieved what was needed. The show went well that week at Preston and everybody felt happy, thinking we were onto a winner. To celebrate our success I invited one of the girls, Martha ('Rambling Rose of the Wild Wood' was her character in the show) to go with me to Blackpool. I tried to make love to her on the sands, but unfortunately she wasn't having any of that. Well, not at Blackpool…

"Wait till Brighton" she whispered in my candy flossed ear.

We returned to London to enjoy a week out – no wages, of course. No play, no pay! But I was looking forward to our week in Brighton where we were due to "wow!" them at the Hippodrome. We arrived on Friday to make it a long week-end, only to find that the show was a no show! The tour was off, finished, caput. No, wait a minute – they might be able to resurrect something from the ruins.

"Would we take less money?"

We didn't think so, but on second thoughts, well, maybe. (I was getting £15 per week). But it was no good. Jack Hylton had seen the light… but it wasn't turned in our direction. Now we were out of work and in Brighton! Four of us had booked a large flat on the sea

two weeks holiday and to Hell with it all! I
a ("Rambling Rose of the Wild Wood". Yes,
e in with us but she said she didn't believe in
r words) so that was out. I don't know why
: orgies! Nobody mentioned that to me! We
er did find out why the show was cancelled.
Booker, was reputed to have said that it wasn't
what? She had more power than Jack Hylton
well had said. So if she said it was "off", it was
people out of work.

ked about, as one could whimsically put it, to
of my possible acting career. I tramped around
aving obtained a list of names from Mrs. Betty
the Actor's Directory, once again someone who
contact. Good old Knut that never was! She was
ge of the place at that time and having very kindly
of woe, had within minutes produced a list for me.

ed cricket with her addicted husband - to cricket I
mean - who soon became el supremo of their offices in Cranbourn
Street. What a lovely googly he had. We'd all like one like that.

The "Spotlight" Directory amongst other things, supplies
information concerning Directors, Producers, Productions, Agents,
etc., etc., but mainly, even now, it's concerned with actors and
actresses. The Directory includes photographs (supplied by the
artistes) with details of all (or most of) their past work (or their best
work) enumerated next to the photograph. Mind you if you haven't
done much, it's all your best work! It also gives information as to
height, colour of eyes and hair, plus any outstanding abilities such as
glider pilot, winner of standing still competitions, or camel wrestler.
In addition, the names and telephone numbers of the Agent
representing each artiste are included with each photograph. Or not,
if you haven't got one. In which case it says "Care of Spotlight" who
have your details. The end product is a massive book which
resembles a telephone directory – a sort of marketplace - for Theatre,

Telly or Film. Anyone connected with Theatrical Productions in any shape or form, usually possesses a copy of "Spotlight" which is a "must" for every Casting Director in the United Kingdom. B.B.C. Television And Sound are littered with copies of "Spotlight" as are Independent Television – Granada, Harlech, Yorkshire, Southern, Scottish, Border, Ulster And Westward: All the Independent TV companies. I've even seen 20-year-old copies in Doctors' and Dentists' waiting rooms and two thirds of the actors shown had long ago taken their final curtains with no chance of an encore! Of course, this profitable enterprise has to be paid for, and this is where the actors come in. They supply the photographs, they pay for the blocks and they are charged annually for the insertion in "Spotlight". It's not cheap! But it's a good shop window, so they say. Having said that, I've never met anyone who said "I got a smashing job through "Spotlight" the other week".

But I can appreciate an American or European Director leafing through the pages and being interested in someone who takes his fancy. If you know what I mean.

To continue… I was recounting how I had to go around all the Agents and what ensued. Well, I can recount it in one word – nothing! Zilch! De nada. Naff all. Nobody wanted to know. Some were uselessly sympathetic. They said, "When you get a job let me know where you are appearing and I'll come and see you working!"

Others said, "Your teeth need straightening. Get that done and then come and see us again."

They of course knew a good dentist. Or… "You're too thin. Get some meat on your bones and come back when you're fatter."

They knew a good cook. Or the worst one I got… "You need some elocution lessons and a personality. Come back when you've got both."

Ouch! I made many temporary friends and acquaintances – mostly secretaries (now called Personal Assistants) and shorthand typists, who worked at the offices. I had numerous buckshee cups of tea but I never got a job, not even a hint of one; indigestion, wet arm pits and tired feet, but no work. My having to be constantly enthusiastic was exhausting. I perused the columns of the professional newspapers, "The Stage" and "The Performer" without any luck. Mostly there were ads from venues wanting ventriloquists, chorus girls, singers and dancers to audition. There were also some by Variety acts giving details of their act such as…

"Mother Goose. Last year Cleethorpes, this year vacant and available. Own Eggs." Which was exactly what I was – very vacant and very available. And not an egg to my name. The following is an example, in dialogue, of my many encounters with Agents:

ME:(Holding up photo) This is from my latest picture, "The Captive Heart".

AGENT: Which one is you? That one?

ME: No that's Jack Warner.

AGENT: That one?

ME: No that's Jimmy Hanley.

AGENT: Oh is that you? The scrawny one?

ME: Er…yes.

AGENT: What are you up to?

ME: Well I'm here!

AGENT: No. Work wise.

ME: Oh. I'm "resting" at the moment. On my laurels. Ha-Ha-Ha. (No reaction from Agent). Do you think you might be able to get me, er… something…er…suitable?

AGENT: Suitable for what?

ME: Ha-ha-ha (cackling falsely) Well, you know…a small part in a film…. or a play…..or stage manager?…..or …or…(blank look from agent)…I'll let myself out. Thanks. (For what?)

Here's another encounter:

AGENT: What did you say the name was - Sam Kid? No relation to Sam Son? Ha! Ha! Ha! (laughs too long at own feeble joke) Or Billy the Kid? Ha! Ha! Ha! Ha! Ha! Ha! Ha! Ha! Ha! Ha! Ha! Ha! Where's your pistol? Ha ha ha ha ha ha ha ha ha ha ha ha! Well, what do you do? Juggle? Sing? Vent?

ME: Well actually I've just been in….(The telephone rings)

AGENT: Just a second…Long distance call. Can you come back again sometime? This is confidential……And bring the dummy with you next time.

ME: But I'm not a vent act and…….

AGENT: Ah Bill. Of course it's convenient! I'm on my own! I've just shooed out a guy who's a vent act and he didn't bring his dummy! Yeah! Would you believe it? Like an actor coming in without his head! (I am reminded of the door) How's Chicago treating you?"

(I exit with tail firmly between legs).

There were a mass of them. I'd put notes about some of the more accessible ones in my diary:

"Robert Layton Ltd. Frith Street. Small parts his specialty. Snooty secretary."

"Mary Buxton in Jermyn Street. Nice woman but secretary doesn't answer the bell. Don't ring either as she'll not answer the phone to actors. Write only. They'll call you in."

"Bill Watt, also of Jermyn Street, opposite the Plaza. Theatre only. Stern man. Lisp."

"Henry Serek of 69 Piccadilly. Nice man. Sympathetic friendly secretary. Films."

"Kitty Slack of the Company of Four. Seen her once. Got tea and a biscuit! Has a list of actors she uses but try again."

"Frank De Woolfe in Cambridge Circus. Rude, but secretary lovely."

"Harry Blue at 18 Charing Cross Road. Lovely man. With the friendly Margaret Berry as secretary. Tea and biscuits."

"Hyman Zahl of Chandlers Avenue. Secretary is a battleaxe. Assistant is gorgeous. Variety only."

"Dennis Van Thall Independent Producers Guild 117 Regent Street". Producer. Seen him several times. Never had a sniff. Nice man though".

"Mr. Palmer of Tom Arnold Productions (I never did find out his first name) Sympathetic but a bit deaf. Blown up at Arnhem."

"Dorothy Mather of Wardour Street. Secretary is Pearl. Looks like my aunt".

Amongst many others.

One day towards the end of the week I called at an establishment named "Plays And Players - the John Charles Agency" that Ealing Films had helped me seek out. It was run by Miss Fanny Noble, a large, ebullient lady. I had been there before without any joy and was prepared for my usual rebuttal, but this time, after the usual skirmishing, she suddenly said, "You speak German, don't you?"

"Er yes" I replied guardedly. "Why?"

"I may have a job for you" she answered. "There's the part of a German guard going in *Men in Shadow* at the Theatre Royal, Windsor".

This was written by Mary Helen Bell, married to John Mills and mother of Hayley and Juliet. She wrote *Whistle Down the Wind*.

She continued, "It's all about the resistance movement. What height are you?"

I didn't know which way to reply. If I exaggerated my height she wouldn't believe me and if I made it too low I might not get the part. On the other hand, either way I might not get it! Desperately I plunged in, almost sotto voce and half coughing so that she couldn't distinguish what I said.

"I'm roundabout 5 foot…cough". (my actual height is 5 foot 8 1/2, except when I'm depressed).

"When does it start?" I asked, to distract her, so that she wouldn't check my height.

"Four weeks time" she said. "What did you say your height

was?"

"Five foot er…." I coughed again.

"Oh for goodness sake you're deliberately coughing."

"No I'm not."

"Yes you are! How tall are you?"

"Sorry. Five foot ten. And a half."

"You don't look like 5'10 and a half to me. More like 5'6".

"I'm more than that" I said indignantly. "And anyway, they're not so strict about height in the German army. It's not like the Coldstream Guards, you know. Only the S.S. are six footers. And they're elite troops. I know. I was there."

  She was unimpressed.

"Well, they don't want a tiny guard, do they dear, especially if you have a scene with the hero. You'd have to stand on a box. It's a dramatic thriller. The part is not for a cod German in a comedy."

"Oh, I understand" I replied miserably. I could see the part running away from me down the corridor, sticking its tongue out.

"I could put some "lifts" in my Jackboots?" I said desperately.

"Oh yes, you could do that, I suppose" she said, as if beginning to regret having even mentioned the part.

"I may as well tell you, the producer liked your photo" she said. "The only doubt was your height."

She looked me up and down disparagingly, as if tape-measuring me with her eyes.

"Oh, I suppose you'll do. You'll pass in a dark light. All your scenes take place at night time, anyway. You'll have to meet him first. Rehearse two weeks, maybe two and a half. You are free, aren't you?"

"Oh yes, I'm free."(As the wind, as the air. Fancy free. If the truth were known, I'd have done it for free!)

"Right" she replied. "£5 per week for rehearsals and £15 for the week that you do it. Usual terms, 10% commission. Okay? I've got your telephone number and I'll phone to confirm the meeting or otherwise."

Otherwise? That would mean I hadn't got it.

"Otherwise".

What a horrible word. I rang her three times the following day but her secretary said she was out. The next day was a Sunday so I couldn't telephone. I thought about it though! On the Monday morning I rang again, but this time she wasn't due in till after lunch. I phoned at 3 o'clock and at 4 o'clock and again at 5 o'clock and just in case at 5.15 and each time I got, "Oh sorry! You are so unlucky! She's just popped out!"

I was beginning to wonder what were the chances of my getting her when she'd "popped in"!

"But are you sure she didn't say anything about Windsor?" I asked.

"Windsor? The Horse Show?"

"No! The Theatre! Are there jobs going in the Horse Show?"

I was suddenly interested.

"Not that I'm aware of. But no she hasn't mentioned the theatre. Perhaps the job's not happening anymore?"

"Oh I hope not."

"Anyway, keep phoning. You're bound to contact her eventually."

(God what a life!) I foolishly tried every day for a week but without success. I mean let's be honest I was clearly being fobbed off, wasn't I. So I gave up. The job had clearly gone to a taller man, from Dusseldorf, with his own gun!

"Otherwise!"

And then just as I about to pluck up courage to ask the local butcher if he needed someone to sweep up in the shop, she rang! I was ludicrously overjoyed!

"Oh you've phoned! Yes! Yes! Yes!"

"That is Sam Kydd isn't it? You sound as if you're about nine!"

"Yes it is! The line's a bit squeaky. Have I got the part?"

"Not yet. As I said you have to meet John Counsell the Producer first. The appointment is next Tuesday at the theatre. And make sure you put your lifts in and stay on tiptoe!"

"Of course! And I'll make sure I stretch every day till I see him!"

I said this slightly facetiously, but I had been hanging from a tree branch in the garden just in case. Naturally as is typical of these situations, my height wasn't referred to when I met him! He was very friendly and the audition seemed to go well. I did a bit of Henry Higgins from *Pygmalion* and an inappropriate speech from *Blithe Spirit* (Madame Arcati, the medium in fact. "I may go into a slight trance, Mr. Condomine. But if I do…pay no attention", in a high pitched voice which amused John Counsell a lot) and I had to bark a bit in German (which I could do standing on my head having been barked at so much in the last five years) and I did it making myself as tall as possible despite it not being mentioned, just in case. I must have done something right as I got the part! It was all about the Resistance Movement, set in the the loft of an old disused mill, next to a farmhouse and I had to say lines, outside the farmhouse, in German, like, "Jahvol, Herr Kapitan." (Right, Captain)

And "Ha ha ha! Dumbkoff!" (Ha ha ha! Foolish person!)

And "Achtung!" (Oi! Watch it!) as we were looking for the Resisters.

I was "Willi, First German Soldier". The officer in charge of me was played by a friendly slightly pompous actor called Philo Hauser who I have to say I never worked with again. We did all our scenes together in darkness! The only woman in it, playing "Cherie", was a beautifully voiced actress called Violet Gould with a fine, if very loud ("projected darling") French accent, who I happily encountered again in "Pickwick Papers" in 1952 where she played Mrs. Cluppins. She did various *Dixon of Dock Greens* playing delightful old ladies.

My helmet fell off one night because it was too big for my small wizened cranium - I had stuffed it with newspaper in order to make it fit. A lot of the audience laughed as it rolled towards the footlights and in trying to retrieve it I dropped my rifle, tripping over it before I finally gained my composure! Naturally after a comedic success like that, I asked if I could keep the whole routine in, but was dissuaded by the Company Manager after a brief discussion. ("No. Don't be ridiculous. This is a serious drama"). I enjoyed the play. The cast were pretty good, the piece was engaging, and the audience seemed to like it! I'm not sure if Her Majesty saw it - she may not have been in residence that week! Or if she did sneak in, she hid her crown in her handbag. Out of my £15 I had to pay commission of 10% plus my fares every day, by Green Line Bus, for rehearsals and the day we performed the show: in all about £10, so I had made £3 approximately each week, some of which I spent in the pub with the friendly cast. As they say in the Army - "I should never have joined." But really I wasn't counting the cost, it was the work I wanted!

After my enjoyable but financially disastrous stay at Windsor, I was once again on the endless circuit of trailing round for acting work. It really was soul destroying, this constant treadmill of calling on Agents and Managements and being ignored, or given little bits of tantalising information that very rarely led to anything. These days it's more civilised because you usually sign an agreement with one particular Agent - if he thinks you're a good investment! When I felt fed-up or cheesed off after some abortive "chasing about" I used to nip into a News Cinema and often watch the programme round three times! No one would ask you to leave. It cost sixpence for the front rows and one shilling for the rear stalls, and I found it an excellent place to snooze. Until you were rudely shaken in the middle of a snore and told to "Belt up!" However, what happened to me one day was very peculiar and not to say a little scary. One Tuesday, after another fruitless demoralising attempt at getting an acting job, I went to the Tatler News Cinema (as it then was) in the Strand, with the specific intention of having a nap. I found the warmth of the place and the drone of the news items the perfect environment for a major kip. Going to the theatre is another perfect sleep inducing set-up, especially if the show is a bit rubbish! Or even if it's not! Except I feel duty bound not to doze in front of a live performance as it's not fair on the actors to hear snores coming from the auditorium! In this instance, before my visit to the comfort of the seats, I performed a slick manoeuvre. I went to the "Gents", which was situated half-way up the hall, came out after my "gosh-I-needed-that" pee, cleverly turned left instead of right, and under cover of the darkness, sneaked a seat in the Upper Echelon where the rich people and the more "discerning" sat.

I was having a gentle, soothing saunter about the Land of Nod when I was tapped on the arm and woke up instantly saying "Wazamatter", guiltily fearing the usherette was wanting to check my ticket. And of course I would be banished down to the cheaper front row! But my fears were groundless. I had been awakened by a charming woman of about forty who was enquiring if I had a match or the means of ignition for her cigarette. I gave her a light for her cork tipped Craven 'A', using my "Mark five "Zunder" German Lighter" which she immediately recognised, telling me she was Norwegian and had seen similar lighters in Norway during the Occupation! And was I German? "No I'm Irish!" I said. It was all slightly awkward and to be honest I was suddenly starving. It occurred to me I hadn't had any lunch. After a few whispered platitudes, whispered so as not to disturb the four other people in the cinema, "How was she finding London?...Did she come here often?.... Had she ever eaten Fish and Chips? etc." (I was feeling very peckish by then) I got up to depart, nodding farewell to her as I left. What next happened was this - your honour. When I reached the foyer and stopped to buy some chocolate, I found she had somehow preceded me and was in the process of hailing a taxi. She spotted me and called out "Come" and beckoned me to join her with her elegant gloved hand, rasping 'Fortnum & Mason' to the driver - Cross my heart. That's what happened M'Lud - I have to admit that I was more interested in the grub than her! The Fortnum and Mason teas were legendarily scrumptious! I leaped into the taxi, hard on her high heels, and before I could say "I'm a hungry ex-P.O.W. out-of-work-actor", I was given the full Fortnum's treatment: tea, toast, strawberry jam, Dundee Cake, choice biscuits, interesting sandwiches etc.... and a few crumbs of Norwegian chat. My fairy godmother's name was Anna Maier and she was en route from Paris, spending a few days in

London before returning to Norway. She was staying at the Dorchester and she assured me that she was not in the habit of inviting strange men to share a taxi, but she was lonely, and wanted someone to talk to. I discovered that she was married to a German/Norwegian, and had two children, a boy and a girl, and was fascinated with my being a P.O.W.. And she and her husband believed in separate holidays - her story your Worship - and she handed me her card, with her name and address printed on it, saying that if I ever went to Helsingfors I was to get in touch.

"Of course. I'd love to!" I said, slightly over eagerly (the chances of me being in Helsingfors were, how can I put it, slim) hiding the card away in my wallet in so safe a place that I've never seen it again, and attacking a cucumber sandwich. She told me she spoke German and French in addition to English, and had got married when she was only 17.

"Long before the war", she added.

She was a huge Anglophile, she said. I once again have to admit I was really concentrating on the food rather than her information. I nodded, wondering where all this was going to end and hoping I didn't have to pay the bill.

I didn't have long to wait because by the time my fourth cup of Darjeeling was finished and I'd started on the tarts, she had asked, would I go and have dinner with her that very evening at the Dorchester? Dinner? Yes! A steak would be wonderful. I hadn't had one since before the war! But - and this was true - unfortunately I was already heavily committed with some relatives arriving from Ireland and had to decline. I expected that to be the end of it, but she was persistent and suggested that tomorrow we go on a bus journey in and around the Capital's places of interest? And just in case would I care to telephone in the morning to confirm that everything was okay?

"Of course" I replied, noting that she was taking a fiver out of a leather purse. Phew!

That evening I got on the bus to Turnham Green and pondered.

What was this all about? Was I taking advantage of her? Was she taking advantage of me? I thought the former, so decided not to call. Yet the following morning I changed my mind. It was an adventure! I hadn't done anything like this for six years. Come on Sam! Enjoy yourself! So I phoned. And would you believe it, the concierge said Anna had left for Paris following an urgent call.

"Oh well! C'est la vie!" I said. But he added, "She has asked, would you please telephone the hotel in the evening and if unsuccessful, try again the following morning to see if she is back?"

"Oh! O.K. Yes I will! Thanks!" I said, not sure if I would.

In fact I didn't make the evening phone call. I was having second thoughts actually. I mean she wasn't really my type. But the following morning, the thought of a steak (I really can't explain how the thought of a meal like this was so enticing) made me phone.

"Why did you not ring last night?" She said sounding slightly peeved. I made some lame excuse ("er the Irish relatives stayed an extra day. And you know how relatives are!") and enquired about what she was up to. She said she'd like to go on the bus trip and in the evening would I go to dinner with her at the Dorchester as she had suggested before? As she was apparently leaving the following day and appeared anxious for me to accept, and I was rather keen on the idea of the classy feast, I acquiesced. I had been so deprived of these luxuries in prison camp, it was slightly alarming how important this meal was becoming!

After the pleasant bus tour when nothing untoward happened (mind you what could happen on the open top deck of a busy bus?) I shot off home to change into my Dinner Jacket for my dinner date at the Dorch, questioning myself as to what was I really doing? I ridiculously made sure that my lighter was working - changed the cotton wool and put a new flint in the striking mechanism - placed it in my trouser pocket and bought a rose from a seller near Park Lane and in due course presented it to her. On reflection perhaps this was leading her on, but ho-hum. The late-night bite at the Dorchester was extremely pleasant and correct - I had an unusually small but rather excellent medium rare Chateaubriand. Mind you there was still rationing - and she regaled me with stories of the German occupation, whilst I in turn reciprocated with tales from my experiences in the camp. She was most attractive when she smiled, but in repose her face and manner were inclined to be solemn and serious, so I endeavoured to keep her amused. At the coffee and brandy stage of the dinner, when I produced my lighter for the inevitable cigarettes, she suddenly grabbed my hand and drew me towards her and said huskily

"Every time I see someone with a lighter like that at home, I will think of you."

Let's be honest. I mean, come on. What a bizarre theatrical line. It was all very peculiar. In a burst of generosity and to prevent myself from giggling, I offered it to her but she was adamant that she would not take it.

"No no. I mustn't! she said. "It is so…. you!"

This was a Bob Hope film. Wasn't it?

She looked in to my eyes.

"I would like to ask you to my room. But I am afraid."

"Afraid?" I said "Afraid of what? There is nothing to be afraid of… Other than fear itself."

I couldn't believe how corny that was. I think it had originally been used by Franklin D. Roosevelt. I was being sucked into the melodrama. She grabbed my hand tightly and looked at me very sternly and shook her head vigorously as if dislodging a fly from her nose. She scrutinised my face. Her breath smelt of cigarettes. On cue and as if this was a very bad play, the head waiter arrived with a note from reception to say that she was wanted on the telephone. It was an overseas call from Norway! She left the table hurriedly, throwing a frantic glance in my direction, and I waited what seemed like forever for her to return, but was in fact time enough for me to eat seven bread sticks. When she did reappear, she immediately asked me for a cigarette "lit with ... the lighter!"

She proceeded to smoke two Capstans in great agitation and

ordered another brandy, peering over her shoulder nervously. I looked around for a hidden film camera. And then just to cap it all, the head waiter returned to say someone wanted to speak to her urgently in the foyer. A Mr. "Frobisher"? She went as white as a sheet.

"Quick. I haven't much time. Someone will deliver a package to this address next Thursday. I want you to pick it up," she said with mad eyes, scribbling on a piece of paper and stuffing it into my top pocket.

"What?"

My 'what' was one of wanting an explanation. But she repeated in a loud screechy whisper like a cat.

"Someone will deliver a package for me to the address in your top pocket next Thursday. I want you to pick it up."

"Yes! Yes! Allright! Ow!" She'd dug her fingers into my wrist.

"You have my address. Bring me the package!" She flung two five pound notes onto the table and bolted out through an exit. A bloke looking like a Gestapo thug with a crewcut in a leather over coat ran into the restaurant and shouted at me.

"Where is she? Where is she? Where is Nadja?" in a German accent. Nadja? I thought she was Anna!

"She went that a way!" I said in true Wild West fashion pointing in the wrong direction.

"What's your name?" he spat.

"Knut Knudsen!" I shouted.

A waiter walked towards him distracting him for an instant and I chose that moment to run out past him towards the foyer, and straight out of the hotel entrance. I sprinted into the park, where I hid behind a bush. Blimey! In no way was I getting involved in any of that! So I didn't pick up the package. Or go anywhere near the address she gave me which was in Hackney.

What was that all about?

When I didn't patronise the News Cinemas for my regular snooze, (I never met another Anna. Or was it Nadja!) I went either to the Tea Centre in Regent Street or the Nuffield Centre in Adelaide Street, the club for ex-service men and women created by the wonderfully generous Lord Nuffield, where you could get a very cheap cuppa. I must say I preferred the Indian variety of tea served in the Tea centre - the tannin was stronger and the girls were prettier in their beautiful multicoloured saris. If I was merely wanting company, I used to visit well known Producer Firth Shepherd's secretary in her office. (One of their big West End successes in the 30s was *The Gusher!* I'd seen it!") She was a very sweet woman called Edith Savill. She saved my life on many occasions, by always having a kind and comforting word when I was feeling low, which was frequently. When you visited the Firth Shepherd's company offices in the Charing Cross Road, they had a rather pleasant little annexe where they had hung all the posters of their past successes amongst the plant pots! Not every show was a hit of course, but with their label on, it could never be called a complete disaster! Edith liked me and took pity on me. She would say, "Come and see me whenever you need somebody to talk to."

And she would invariably produce a smashing cup of Sergeant Major's Special, (very sweet tea!) a couple of biscuits and a sympathetic ear. She would tell me of the management's plans and would always say, "Ah Sammy. We must look out to see if there's anything in it for you".

It never materialised, mind you, but the fact that I was made welcome was almost enough! She was fantastic though, for keeping me up to speed with what was happening in the theatre world, which was of course of benefit. I owed her a lot. Though my next warning of a possible job came from a very strange source!

Naturally, the longer I was involved in the perpetual tramping around for work, the more agitated my mother became. And the more desperate I looked, despite having lovely people like Edith Savill to cheer me up! It wasn't suiting my fragile disposition. And of course I didn't have any money. Mother got more belligerent this time.

She asked me again to give up the idea of becoming an actor. The world of retail was her preferred route for me as I think we've established. She liked the idea of having a son working in a shiny department store selling shiny modern things that she wouldn't mind having in her not particularly shiny home. The dingy yellow nicotine stains on the cream walls were something you just accepted. But then everyone in the household smoked. Though the brown paint in the sitting room below the dado rail was certainly glossy. Her brother Jimmy, with whom she lived in the house in Fairfax Road, Turnham Green (and brother Jack and younger sister Edie and her husband Alec - it was a big house!) ran the car park outside Selfridges so it was in the blood! Once again I almost gave in. Once again she arranged for an interview for me, this time across the road from Jimmy, at Selfridges, citing my experience in the bedding in Whiteley's before the war in the letter, as she always did. We had an in depth heart to heart:

"Sam."

"Yes?"

"You will go for this interview."

"Yes Mother."

When suddenly something fortuitous happened: I got some work in a very weird and wonderful sort of way. I was travelling to the West End on the Piccadilly Line early one morning (Turnham Green to Hammersmith on the District and change) and because the train was full and all the seats were taken, I was obliged to stand near the doors, squashed against a bowler hatted City type who was scanning the Financial Times, a pretty West Indian girl, and two young suited men.

I was so close to the two fellas that I could not avoid overhearing their conversation about acting and agents. How unbelievably rude of me! I mean how very dare I? I was of course in fact straining my ears to hear what they were saying, but unfortunately every time the train stopped at the station, I was forced to move away from them in order to allow passengers to get out and in. South Kensington was the worst. A mass of people who'd been to the Science Museum got on and I was pushed against the opposite door. Each time the train restarted I had to squirm my way over to my original position, to the disgust of the Financial Times geezer.

"Oh for Goodness Sake!" he blurted.

Ignoring him, I squeezed ever so slowly over so as not to miss a word. And it was all good stuff! Other than a momentary digression in which the spottier of the two discussed an unfortunate rash. They were both actors and were talking about an interview one of them was to have with a certain Mr. Forbes Russell that very morning, at the Lionel Wallace agency in Charing Cross Road! It appeared that Mr. Forbes Russell was presenting a repertory season at Butlin's holiday camp at Skegness and artistes were being interviewed all day today, and this particular actor, Kevin I think his name was, was due for an appointment at 11 o'clock that morning! The train then lurched just before entering Hyde Park station, and my inquisitive listening lugole, and then my face, appeared abruptly over his shoulder. He gave me a withering look as if to say "do you think you could sling your 'ook, fishface?" Slightly embarrassed I pretended I was not interested in his riveting conversation at all and looked up at the adverts. There was a particularly fine one for Pepto-Bismal anti-indigestion liquid that became of great interest, whilst I affected a grimace that gave the impression that I found what he was saying utterly distasteful and I really disliked all actors. Meanwhile though, the job antennae were twitching as I took in and saved every single piece of juicy information he was giving me. So. This was the gist:

"David Forbes Russell. Lionel Wallace agency, Charing Cross Road! 4 plays. Skegness."

Yes. I knew it. I had been to the agency before, looking for work and passing the time of day. I got out at Leicester Square and jogged smartly to my destination. There were two offices: the outer where the hoi- polloi congregated i.e. the actors; and an inner sanctum where interviews and contracts and anything to do with financial matters were dealt with. Sitting on rickety chairs in the outer office, two actors were already there, discussing their chances, pouring scorn on plays and performances they'd seen recently, and discussing breakfast. Typical. The girl at the reception nodded to me pleasantly and assuming I had an appointment, asked me what time I was being seen. I toyed with the idea of lying, but thought it better in this case to tell the truth, so I gushingly said while being sheepish (a difficult skill) that I didn't have an appointment and I had heard about the show through the grapevine, ha ha ha etc.. I paused......She smiled and didn't throw me out. Luckily she was very forthcoming and told me all I wanted to know. The engagement was for the whole season at Butlin's holiday camp, at the newly built Skegness summer theatre. Four plays were on, in 'repertory' - *Blithe Spirit* by Noel Coward, *Night Must Fall* by Emlyn Williams, *While Parents Sleep*, by Antony Kimmins and *George and Margaret* by Gerald Savoury. But, unfortunately, she sadly pointed out, as I didn't have an appointment, there wasn't anything she could do. I put on my "whipped cur" expression, where the eyeballs bulge, the mouth drops at the corners, and the eyebrows almost disappear into the hairline (this is not something to do without practicing as you can do yourself a mischief and tear an eyelash) and spoke in a small pleading pathetic "Is-there-any-hope" voice.

"Do you think there's any possible chance of my being fitted in somewhere? Please?"

She gave me an understanding quizzical smile, as if to say "Poor bastard he's doing his nut" and then scanning the list suddenly said, "Oh! You're in luck! One of the actors has phoned to say he'll be delayed, so if you don't mind waiting….?"

(Mind waiting? I'd wait all day if necessary!) She even gave me permission to nip out and buy a packet of cigarettes ("Oh yes you've got time!") and on the way to the tobacconist I nearly bumped into the actor whose conversation I'd overheard on the train. I turned and looked straight at the wall and smoothed it, as if I was a brick layer assessing some other brick layer's handiwork and giving it nine out of ten! I returned and was soon ushered into see Mr. Forbes Russell and

Miss. Wallace of the Agency. After my (deep breath) introduction and listening to details of my limited professional theatrical experience (it went O.K. actually) they asked me what it was like being a P .O W.. I talked about all the plays I'd done, but then piled on the deprivation and they were most sympathetic. During a lull when some coffee was brought in by the secretary, (from whom I got a grin) I overheard Mr. Russell saying out of the corner of his mouth to Miss. Wallace, "Hmm. Yes. He'd be alright for Jerry in *While Parents Sleep* or Hubert in *Night Must Fall* or Dudley in *George And Margaret*. And Miss. W. replied, also from the corner of her mouth, "Yes but there'd be nothing for him in *Blithe Spirit*".

"Good God, no!" said Mr. F.R..

I felt slightly insulted! I could play in a Coward! I'd played Madame Arcati in prison camp! But beggars couldn't be choosers. By this time they were looking out of the window and the discussion continued. I had to crane my neck and listen whilst not appearing to listen. It was clearly a day for that. They continued their whispering.

"And he could combine stage manager with business manager. He seems pretty sharp."

(Sharp? I was both red hot pepper and cut throat razor! Not an easy thing to be, let me tell you!). They both turned as if to confirm their comments, and two seconds later I was offered the job! Hooray! To be business manager and assistant stage manager and to perform as cast at £10 pounds per week! Accommodation in a holiday camp chalet for £3 per week. Food not included. I accepted with over the top alacrity. The whole enterprise, they told me, was under the banner of Mr. John Watt, a top variety producer from the B.B.C., who was also supplying a musical revue for the evenings. We would play matinees only, from Monday to Saturday, doing three different plays per week. (As a matter of fact, the Saturday performance was cancelled as it coincided with the arrival of the new campers and the departure of the old ones, and nobody wanted to see the plays whilst coming and going). They were clearly being very lovely to me at the Wallace agency, suspecting correctly that my business management experience was nil and that I had never stage-managed anything in my life! They put me at my ease by saying, "Don't worry you'll soon get the hang of it, and anything you're not sure of, just ask."

Luckily one of my character traits was that of being a willing and enthusiastic learner (and always saying "yes" to being able to do something even if I couldn't) and I would apply this trait with the work ethic I had put into the mattresses at Whiteley's. Mother would be pleased! (I hoped! No she wouldn't.) As I mentioned before, the whole theatre season was under the auspices of John Watt who was the B.B.C. Radio Senior Light Entertainment Producer. I learned that at one time he was head of B.B.C. Comedy and this was a new departure for him. Forbes Russell had obtained the contract from John Watt who in turn was answerable to the Butlin organisation. Mr. Watt was represented by his agent, Harry Blue, who concentrated on variety bookings. Consequently all requirements for the repertory company had to go through the Harry Blue office which was very adjacent to the Wallace Agency in the Charing Cross Road. Harry was a nice man and as well as the lovely Margaret Berry who I've mentioned before, had an equally lovely blonde secretary named Bridie who was very understanding towards me and more than helpful. Her role in the Butlin's job was to check on all the money spent on props, set dressing, and "special extras" (things that we hadn't thought of that might just raise their ugly heads), in fact everything needed for the four plays. There was something that didn't cost anything! Ronson lighters were supplied free of charge in exchange for free programme advertising. Receipts were required for all the money paid out and also my written notes for expenses, petty and not so petty! Already I was trying to work out what I could get away with! I had to stop myself. It was the P.O.W. in me! Bridie, as well as providing me with copious cups of tea, was a God-send. I couldn't have done it without her. She spent ages explaining amongst other things "the intricacies of the agency business in relation to the mounting of theatrical enterprises" (a bit of a mouthful) and basic accounting. When she learned that I had been a P.O.W., her attitude visibly softened and she invited me round to the office after hours to "get a grip with more complicated accounting", and to imbibe a touch of the hard stuff! We were getting down to it when the phone rang! Breathless and dishevelled (it's hard work that complicated accounting) Bridie answered the inconvenient call and slightly annoyed, handed the receiver to me saying "it's for yew John", in her distinctive Scottish accent. It was indeed for me - it was the Lionel Wallace agency asking me to go and see them the following day. I rang off and "went through the ins and outs of accounts" once more, pouring myself a generous scotch before each lesson!

I prepared myself for the job with the few savings I had left, knowing I was on a tenner a week minus the chalet pay and grub and 10% to save once I was on it. So my make-up box cost £3. I bought a new suit from G.Wildes for £20, an overcoat from Jennings for £30, a pair of shoes for 60 shillings. And had some photos taken for £5 with the repros (reproductions) at £2.

I had decided to call myself John Kydd in my career as a "thespic artiste" - though I'd been Sam in *The Captive Heart* - and for some time that indeed was my name (though of course I had flirted with Knut Knudsen) until I discovered that there was another actor - John Kidd - with a name clearly one letter of the alphabet very near mine. When I started getting his bills and he started getting my cheques, and there was the possibility he would be getting my auditions, I thought it was time to revert to Sam or Sammy. Sam was my father's name as well as being my real one, so I stuck to that. But at Butlin's theatre I was still John - "Puir wee John" Bridie would breathlessly say, referring to my immediate past, not to my size or state of health - she was a grand "wee girrl" herself and she helped me considerably in my dual role of business and assistant stage manager. As well as "aiding my rehabilitation."

TWO
Skeggy Billy Butlin

Eventually the day had come to move off to Butlin's Theatre in the holiday camp in Ingoldmells, Skegness, Lincolnshire. I was in the company of seven or eight actors and actresses, (as well as being A.S.M.) including the charming Nigel Plunkett Green who later saw the light and became a very successful theatrical agent, and Muriel Martin Harvey, a very sweet scatty lady who had trouble seeing a lot of things, being somewhat short sighted, who was cast to play the lead in *Blithe Spirit* only. She'd been a silent films actress in her youth. There were three other leading ladies - Olga May, Pamela Roberts and Betty Huntley Wright. All very fine actresses. Years later I met one of them working in Derry and Toms department store in Kensington, in the ironmongery Department .

"Better than resting, dear" she said. "And you get a knowledge of tools."

Eventually we were joined by a young ingenue named Cymbeline Brooks to play in *While Parents Sleep* and *George and Margaret.* I got on with Cymbeline very very very well indeed and she was rather wonderful (Gulp); but when she wanted the relationship to be a more serious one, I had to resist her many alluring attributes and blandishments. I really didn't want to settle down so quickly after my war experiences. But I have to admit I almost fell. She was absolutely gorgeous. Absolutely. Sigh. As far as the Company went, we were all happy and friendly - just as well really, as we were inaugurating that barn of a theatre. I mean it really was a monster of an auditorium, the size of a football pitch. When you think about it we were quite privileged to be involved in the very beginning of this project of supplying "Theatre for the campers" and the instigators of the whole thing, in the shape of the celebrated holiday camp entrepreneur Billy Butlin (later a Knight of the realm) and Col. Basil Brown, his A.D.C. (aide-de-camp; the man who helped around the camp!) were extremely anxious that the whole thing should be a swinging success. They welcomed us all with champagne, and Billy made a short speech saying, "I 'ope you all 'ave an 'appy stay at our first season at Butlin's, Skegness, Ingoldmells!"

That kindly portly Colonel alongside him, Basil, also addressed us, twinkling at the girls at the same time.

"If by any chance anything is amiss you can contact me through the company office where my manager will attend to it."

We were to give free shows in the afternoons, but the campers would pay for the evening entertainment in the shape of the musical revue - called *The Stars Look Down*. .....("Their Noses", someone wrote on the poster. Presumably before they'd seen it, because there weren't any Stars in it. Well Jack Haig was in it. But he was yet to be a star).

The camp had not long been vacated by the Naval Authorities who had requisitioned it during the war and great pains had been taken to obliterate any signs of the recent occupation, by using a strong application of Butlin's light blue paint. Nevertheless there were one or two graffiti messages still around. In the Gents especially: "please adjust your dress before leaving" and somebody had written underneath "ooh of course dear!" And on an official notice of "Help the Sailors Society" someone had added "Third cubicle, next Friday, 4:30." One constant piece of graffiti I agreed with, was "turn that sodding Tannoy off!"

Eric Winstone and his Band played every night in the Ballroom and with them for Sunday concerts were the mellifluous Beverly Sisters, just embarking on a famous career. I used to watch them and listen to their harmonies with great interest, admiration and yes I admit it, awe. You just knew they were bound for the top of the tree. They were very assured, confident and professional, as indeed was Eric's band. I especially listened to them, because we had played so much of their music in prison camp - "Oasis", Eric's big hit number, being one of our favourite songs. The holiday camp was enormous and had many amenities for the post-war campers. The Red Coats certainly earned their money, the way they cosseted and shepherded their flock. These young men and women worked together in teams to organise everything and never appeared to have any rest periods. You had to applaud their industry. Meanwhile back at the theatre, my role - I wasn't running the shows. We had another S.M. for that - was that of "re-checker". The lighting, the sets, the props, the house lights, the sound equipment, the tabs and the massive metal Safety Curtain which kept sticking halfway down - or was it halfway up? The answer to this problem, I said to the local Fire Inspector, was not to use it at all. But this was out of the question.

"It's got to be used, Mr. Kydd, to comply with safety and fire regulations, hasn't it! Where will the audience go if there should be a fire?" he asked.

"Well" I said, "They've got six exits they can use and they're not likely to jump onto the stage to get out are they?"

"Ah" he went on, adopting a "you haven't thought it through" look.

"But what about if there's an explosion? They'd be jumping up there in a flash."

I gave him a look. This was ultimately hugely excessive, judging by the number of people we got for an audience. About 200 was the fullest I saw it and it seated 2500. The whole place could've been emptied in minutes. Luckily a curtain engineer came from Lincoln Theatre Royal and after much fiddling and faffing, it descended smoothly, if unbelievably noisily. But we had to make do with the din. At least it now worked. "It was a cog" our saviour said mysteriously. The Fire Chief grinned like a Cheshire Cat.

Came the day of our opening and everyone was on tenterhooks. The Tannoy boomed out at irritating ten minute intervals with plummy information about the show, punched out in madly hammy Pathe News tones:

"Today sees the grand opening of the repertory players first production *"Blithe Spirit"* by Noel Coward, starring Muriel Martin Harvey related to the famous Sir John Martin Harvey. Admission Free! (This was said at four times the volume of the rest of it. And repeated) Yes! You heard me! FREE! Doors open 2 p.m.. Come and see this wonderful West End production. Presented by the Forbes Russell players in repertory. FREEE only to Butlin's campers! FREEEEE!!!!! And in case you missed it, it's FREEEEEEEEE!!!!!!!!!!!

About 100 people turned up and it went down like a lead balloon. If you sat at the back of the stalls you couldn't hear anything. About 35 drifted off at the interval - the sun had started to come out or they felt like an early tea. Those who remained didn't react much (apart from the children who held races in the aisles) and the afternoon passed away quite peacefully. Surprisingly, there wasn't much reaction from the cast either. They seemed to accept it as "just one of those things". Nothing had gone radically wrong. Miss Martin Harvey exited through the French windows when she should've gone out of the door, and the curtains took a ridiculous time to close, like a slow shunting train, leaving the actors having to wait on stage as if playing statues. Miss M-H. only had to be prompted twice, causing her to do the same page of dialogue a second time, but nobody noticed - not even the cast! The campers seemed more inclined to patronise their own entertainment, such as amateur talent night and the knobbly knees contest, which took place in a hall next to the dance floor, but we were content with the thought that these were early days and the revue people had yet to present their extravaganza. As it subsequently turned out, their reception was even colder than ours and before long the revue was abandoned and a new policy of weekly variety instated.

In the meantime I had yet to make my acting debut as a member of the cast. It was in *Night Must Fall* that I made my first entrance - actually I was already on stage with curtains parted, sitting in an armchair downstage left, reading a newspaper and just in case I forgot anything, my whole part as Hubert, was typed out and pasted into the pages.

In other words I cheated - I read it. All of it. Then one day the paper was missing, later to be found in the gents lavatory being used symbolically as loo paper and for that performance, I stammered my responses to the rest of the cast! Much to their amusement. Though one of the cast said, "Let that be a lesson to you!"

He was of course right - always learn your lines no matter how few. Failing that, always have a spare copy of the newspaper you can hide your lines in, and keep it in a secret place known only to yourself! Preferably down your trousers. In the meantime my life was repetitive. I was either seeking a meeting with the account manager in an effort to get some special privilege for the rest of the cast (like real cake on stage in an eating scene); or going to the bank in Skegness to draw out the money to pay the actors; or rehearsing the present play and the next one (*While Parents Sleep*) concurrently. It was therefore "all go"!

After the cool reception for *Blithe Spirit* (and it didn't improve) the management decided to withdraw Coward's masterpiece and concentrate on the three other plays which were to be performed in one week – Tuesday Wednesday and Thursday.

"I don't know how you actors do it. All them lines to learn. How is it you don't get them all mixed up?"

"Don't worry lady. We do!"

Night Must Fall came and went, and then we did *While Parents Sleep* in which I played Jerry, the juvenile lead. This was a part more suitable, so I thought, to my (ahem) comedy playing talent. However this too fell on stoney ground. In fact, I think I would have got more of a reaction had I stood in the middle of Shepherd's Bush Green and read the telephone directory out loud, naked, in a broad cockney accent. Mind you I'd have been arrested as well, but at least it would have been a reaction. So much for my magnetic drawing power. Meanwhile, we toiled on rehearsing *George and Margaret*. I was playing the part of "Paddy", the young son. In prison camp, I had played

"Alice" the mother and "Malcolm" the father (at different times, not in the same show, I'm not that versatile!). And now it was "Dudley" the son – a singular record, I would've thought. Years later, when I met Gerald Savoury, the author of *George and Margaret*, I told him of my, I thought, unique, triple casting. "And?" he said witheringly, "So what. It's been done before!" What a load of rubbish. Even if it had been done before, he needn't have been so crushing. But I'd have thought the chances of anyone playing mother, father, and son in that show were minimal. He was just being an ass.

From a secondhand shop in Skeggy I bought an electric kettle which I plugged into the electric light in my chalet to provide the usual early-morning cup of tea and at any time of day, if I so wished. In addition I made up a complicated Heath Robinson affair of strings and brackets which enabled me to switch the electric light, off or on, without getting out of bed. Sometimes, very early in the morning, just before dawn, I had a dip in the freezing sea. The path behind my chalet led down to some sand dunes, which in turn led to the beach and water. It took about five minutes to get there, plunge in and thrash around for another five, doing a bit of breast stroke (it was always cold, Eskimo cold!) get out A.S.A.P., run along the beach, retrace my steps and be back in the chalet all within 25 minutes, ready for a quick rub down (or up, depending on which way I was facing) and the inevitable cup of tea. It was, quite frankly, a bit too bracing. Yes, an abstemious life, but I wasn't in prison camp and I began to feel and (kidding myself) look, fitter. For a long time though I was saddled with that ultra lean look. Or to put it realistically. I was a scraggy, wizened, b*stard. That was why I did my bathing very early in the morning. And definitely not in the daytime. I had this complex about my body, so I avoided undressing and showing it in front of others. Mind you, it was different in the dark!

My chalet was situated in the section allocated to the staff of the camp and I was right alongside two of the Redcoats. As I mentioned before, they worked very hard organising everything for the campers but as they seemed to enjoy it, you could hardly call it exhausting.

Nothing is, if you enjoy it! Two prominent members of the profession - Des O'Connor and Dave Allen - were both Redcoats at one time, but not at Skegness, so I was given to understand. The staff, which included the Redcoats, decided to put on a one act play called *Hewers of Coal,* a worthy piece by the poet/miner Joe Corrie, and they invited me to play a part, which I happily accepted. I also ended up directing it. The production was mainly about an explosion in a coal mine and all of us playing exploded miners wore coal dust make up! In fact you couldn't tell who was who, as on the first and only night the keenest actors put on too much Leichner black Greasepaint, and what with the lighting being possibly too much on the dim side, as we were in the mine, it made following the plot quite difficult. Though considering none of them laid any claim to being an actor, I thought they acquitted themselves extremely well. On reflection each of us carrying a pick and a tin water bottle was an artistic decision that possibly I could have re-thought. There was a lot of clanking.

The Tannoy loud-speakers, an essential though noisy part of holiday-camp life, large cone-like affairs and called "horns", were to be found at the end of each section of the chalets on long poles, blaring music unceasingly and could be heard all over Lincoln when the wind was in the right direction. If it was not blaring music, it was being used for announcements which seemed to occur every hour on the hour and sometimes on the half or the quarter hour too. In a way it was the forerunner of the ceaseless chattering disk jockey. This was obviously necessary for the smooth running of the camp, but what I and several of my good companions objected to was the early-morning forced heartiness shout of "Wakey Wakey! Rise and Shine!" which drove us all round the twist! Then would follow a list of the day's happenings – droning on and on. One day I could contain my hatred no longer, so in true P.O.W. fashion I found the cable that fed our nearest Tannoy and before you could say "Good morning campers" the verbal diarrhoea was clipped in the bud! For a couple of days we had peace and tranquillity. But then the repair man came round and fixed it. Whatever my own feelings were about the Holiday Camp, I did come to appreciate, after talking to many campers, the satisfaction they got from their holiday. For a family with an economy budget to live on, a Butlin's holiday was ideal. Everyone was catered for – old, young, and very young. Some very old! - in all the activities. Committees were elected for the two weeks or one week's holiday and complaints and suggestions were listened to. The war had not been long over and things were still hard to come by – food was still rationed and clothing coupons were still being issued. For a working man it was really reasonable. For an ex-P.O.W. actor/assistant stage manager/funny-business manager, it wasn't too bad either! The Butlin's Repertory Theatre was an experiment which had a shaky start – we were the innovators – but today it still flourishes and long may it continue.

We pressed on, and everything was going well with the productions, except that on one occasion the old safety curtain problem reared its ugly head again. This time it started to descend on its own during a performance of *While Parents Sleep*. It stopped about 3 feet from the stage floor, refusing to budge either up or down, as it did previously and despite my pressing the two Safety Curtain up/down buttons hundreds of different ways, the show had to be abandoned amidst loud cat calls and laughter ringing in our ears. The slow hand clapping from the up till then, quite responsive audience of 146 people was followed by a chorus of "Why are we waiting!?" (to the tune of "Come all ye Faithful"). Colonel Basil was called for and in rather clipped posh tones he announced from the stage, "Ladies and gentlemen, I'm afraid we are unable to continue."

There were cries of "Why not? We can see their feet. They'll just have to bend over and talk louder."

"Because we can't at the moment raise the safety curtain…" was Basil's measured unruffled response.

"Pull the tassle. Then roll it up."

Huge guffaws emitted from the audience.

Basil soldiered on. "If you would care to return next week at this time…"

"Can't. Too late. Going home!"

"We will be performing the play once again…"

"Why bother mate – it's rubbish!"

Cue more laughs. Basil gave up. Although the whole thing had provided what is known as a rather amusing "divertissement", I got the blame for the curtain sticking – along with the Fire Inspector! We got the engineer from Lincoln Theatre Royal in again.

"It's the cog" he said.

On another occasion I had to understudy an actor whose mother was ill and he was allowed a couple of days off (again during a performance of *While Parents Sleep*) and as well as going on with the book to read his lines (he only had a couple of scenes) I had to sing and play the piano. In order to make my playing realistic (I'm not a good pianist) we rigged up an electric button which was controlled by my foot to give a signal to the real pianist offstage. In other words, when he got my one buzz signal, he played; when he got two buzzes, he stopped. Simple you'd have thought. The difficulty was that the pianist off stage couldn't see me because his piano was situated at the rear end of the stage - the only place it could go - and he relied entirely on my buzzer. I, of course, mimed my piano playing onstage to coincide with his playing offstage. Pretty simple to coordinate you'd have thought. On this particular occasion we had quite a large audience – this was due to the fact it had rained in monsoon fashion since 8 o'clock in the morning and all 700 of them crammed into the stalls - we didn't open the circle - were quite appreciative for once! Then the time came for my piano playing debut. I sat down, pressed the button with my foot pretending to play, the ivories were tinkled by the piano up the way, I mimed (rather expertly I thought) and crooned the song. When I reached the end of the chorus I pressed twice for the pianist to stop, and at that moment, got up coolly from the stool to carry on with the show. Unfortunately the piano playing started again. Quick as a flash I returned to my seat and again simulated my ability with the keyboard, at the same time seriously putting my foot on the button to warn my cohort every four bars, and finally not caring about the timing anymore, I just feverishly stepped on the buzzer button as if stepping on a wasp. But of course unbeknownst to me the buzzer wasn't working! Eventually I had to croon, "Okay I'm finishing now."

And I stood up. But still the music continued. The audience loved it and some wag shouted, "Do a little dance!"

Another requested an encore. When I retorted that it was a pianola he called out, "Put another penny in then!"

The show went down well that afternoon; in fact, as usual after the success of my non piano playing - the getting up early got a huge laugh - and my chat with the audience, I suggested keeping the mishap in. Of course the management did not concur.

"This is the theatre, Kydd, not the music hall!" said the company manager, dourly. Apropos this remark, it was noticeable to me that there was a distinct gap between those who called themselves actors and actresses and others who were Variety artistes. It was very apparent then that they were separated into two classes, the Variety people being relegated to the "working-class" and the acting fraternity elevated to the "middle-class" with a sprinkling of "upper!" Neither faction mixed much with the other, although I patronised both and was apt to think that the comedians or single acts were something to be envied and admired. For me, the concentration and courage to pit yourself on your own against the audience was the most vulnerable thing you could do. Perhaps it was a throwback to my early days before the war, when I had done an impressions and gags act mainly in an amateur way. I'd also entered lots of talent contests with some success. And of course I'd been a professional when I was M.C. for the Oscar Rabin Band. And I'd done a lot of compering in prison camp. However, the division was definitely there and even these days there is still a slight barrier, although we are all "Brothers" in the same union, the V.A.F. (Variety Artists Federation) now having submerged its identity with British Actors Equity. The V.A.F was a worthy institution consisting mainly of comedians, conjurers, acrobats, high wire walkers, trampoline tramplers, ventriloquists, camel wrestlers etc.. But chorus boys and girls, and dancers (including ballet) have always been under the Equity banner. And within the last few years Stage Managers and Assistant Stage Managers have had an Equity card. In the main, Equity do an excellent job. For instance, actors not being renowned for their business acumen, Equity keep an eye on rogue film producers and impresarios and agents who tend to exploit us! I had first applied for an Equity card (a provisional one. I think I needed to do about forty weeks professional work before I got a full one) when I was in prison camp; 1943 in fact! I was in so many shows in the camp, and I'd worked for Oscar before I was captured - I thought I'd try to take advantage of the situation, so even under lock and key I was optimistically considering an acting career. I got a letter back saying I had been approved! It was strange and uplifting having this sane communication with them in the middle of the insanity of war, but they hadn't closed down. There were still masses of shows going on all over the British Isles, and you had to be in the Union to be in them! They rather kindly let me off paying my sub, but as I hadn't been in many professional productions, I was still a provisional member.

After the incident of the non-stop piano, nothing much of note (ho ho!) happened that I recall, except that a new producer arrived – he was the husband of one of the girls in the show. The original producer had to go off to initiate the same sort of set up at Butlin's camp at Filey. It was to be the number 2 Forbes Russell company, so it was obviously paying off for somebody! At a guess I would say Mr. Forbes Russell plus our Billy, the dynamic Mr. Butlin. Little did I know it, but the new man had it in for me!

We got a very good review!

"The plays are put over by a first rate cast, including such talented artists as Ann Jackson, Sidney Trevelyan, Olga May, John Kydd, Cymbeline Brooks and John Seebold, who is in charge of production. Playgoers are assured of a tip-top afternoon's entertainment."

Mind you it was the reviewer from the "Butlin's Holiday Times", so possibly he was a bit biased.

As far as my romantic life was concerned, I was so involved and busy for the first four hectic weeks that I didn't have time to er "consolidate" anything. I had had one or two flirty skirmishes with a sweet married member of the cast who consumed copious cups of tea in my chalet, whilst I quaffed lousy instant coffee in hers. Finally she invited me over one Saturday night for fish and chips, red wine, and so I was led to believe, "afters". Just as we were getting to the end of the countdown and coming up to blast off, we were intruded upon by three other members of the cast, one of whom shared the chalet with her, bearing bottles of beer and numerous packets of crisps. I had to eject from the capsule and we hastily splashed down behind the bed to put our clothes back on. She did ask me to stick around until the end of the festivities but the others were going to "party" till 6 o'clock and as I had my usual early start, the moment was lost! The following week we agreed to have another fish supper and would you believe it, she got food poisoning in the afternoon, and was poorly for three days, and by the time she was well again, her husband had joined the Company and that was that!

When the box office receipts had fallen to a new low, it was decided to bury the revue and introduce the new scheme, which I mentioned earlier, in connection with the Variety performances. A "big star" would top the bill and the rest of the supporting acts would be the usual artistes: jugglers, tumblers, acrobats, musicians, singers, dancers – according to the handouts it was about to become the "Palladium of the East Coast"! I spent most of my free time in the evenings, watching from the side of the stage. Sandy Powell (with a brilliant comedy vent act) Bennett and Williams, Issy Bonn, Naughton and Gold, The Two Leslies, and many others. One of the bill "toppers" at the inauguration was a very successful comedian called Peter Waring. I had heard him several times on the radio in a programme entitled "Music Hall" and he was extremely amusing with terrific laconic timing. His catchphrase, borrowed from the Royal Air Force was "Press on regardless" later to become abbreviated to "Oh well, press on!" Peter would appear at the microphone immaculately dressed in white tie and tails, speaking in a rather cultured voice and smoking the inevitable cigarette. He would chat to the audience, using a smooth, man about town delivery, telling anecdotes, and drawling out the punch lines. For example:

"I was talking to a beautiful half naked dancing girl at the side of the stage and she said, "What......now?""

Or (referring to English girls and Yankee soldiers) …

"You've seen the Americans here and there – mostly there!"

Or…

"She turned out to be a very good girl – unfortunately!"

Or…

"I stayed at the Palace Hotel during the war, and only made one mistake. I met a woman in the Bar and asked her if she was going to have one. And she said "Oh no. It's the cut of my uniform.""

Or….

"I went to a nudist's fancy dress ball and met a rather attractive young lady who went as a road map! By midnight I found myself in Shepherd's Bush".

And…

"I met a lovely girl and we were married by candlelight. But it only lasted a wick."

He assuredly spat 'em out and if they didn't get a laugh he was on to the next one.

I came to realise that his was more of a nightclub act, suave and sophisticated, but he was an enormous success with the ex-servicemen. Today, of course, it would be very mild stuff, but I thought his performance was very amusing and told him so. He spoke to me after the early show at the beginning of the week and invited me to his dressing room for a "dish of tea". He was hooked on tea like most of us and would drink it at any time of the day or night – tea with milk, tea with lemon or even tea with tea. With a few sugars thrown in of course! My P.O.W. stories enthralled him and if ever we were interrupted whilst I was recounting them he'd always come back to the subject, asking me what happened next! He seemed to enjoy my company and we got on really well. After he'd been to see me in one of our matinees, I took him on a tour of the camp, showing all the facilities and activities - he was staying in a hotel in the town - and he finished up in my chalet for a cuppa and a snack. We settled down to demolish the tea, cake and biscuits I had in the cupboard and after two cups of tea each and more water on the boil for a further session, he once again showed his interest in my P.O.W. experiences by asking, "Tell me, how did the Germans really treat you? How did you manage to exist like that, for five years? I would've died. I couldn't have done it. How did you keep your temper when you were goaded by some "sadistic hulk of a Hun" lording it over you?"

I told him the truth. Your self preservation instinct kicked in. You knew the consequences of retaliating would be dire so held your tongue. I recounted the story of having a rifle butt in my face when I did question something. The false teeth that were its legacy were a constant reminder. So you learnt to seethe inwardly and deal with it. But how you were tempted. Peter told me that he himself had served in the Royal Navy as a Paymaster Officer. He had been wounded and bore a permanently twisted wrist to prove it; in fact, he was so self-conscious about this injury that he had his shirts and jackets especially enlarged to cover his "offending disfigurement". He had an eye for the ladies and was in every way a good catch, with his handsome looks, fine manners, great sense of humour and above all, that priceless possession of making people feel important when he talked to them. During the course of our conversation he told me that he had been asked to star in a B.B.C. Radio series starting in the autumn. The Producer was Charles Maxwell (the *Navy Mixture* producer, later to be associated with the very successful *Take it from*

Here) and Peter wondered if I'd be interested in playing a regular featured part in the new autumn series? Would I be interested!?! I could have jumped over the chalet and held up the safety curtain single-handed I was so interested! I took a deep breath and helped myself to two more lumps of sugar, putting one in my tea and the other in my mouth to steady my nerves like an over excited horse.

"I'll get you an interview with the producer, if you like" Peter said. "You'll probably have to audition, though. Would you mind doing that?"

Mind? He could have all the rest of my disability pension (seven shillings and sixpence a week) if it would persuade him.

"Of course I don't mind" I answered, and overdoing the obsequiousness, followed up with, "And thanks a lot for thinking of me."

"Well" he said, "you're wasting your time up here and you deserve something better after the way life has treated you."

I mentally arranged to send him a year's supply of Darjeeling Orange Pekoe to thank him for his kindness. (In fact I sent him several cartons of Lyons Red Label which was the nearest I could afford).

He went on: "It won't be for some time yet but I'll contact you as soon as I fix it up."

What a great guy. I had done nothing other than talk to him and provide him with tea and cake. Strangely enough, he was lonely. Nobody spoke to him much, mainly because they were in awe of him. He had a slightly distant manner and "was very well spoken" and he could on occasions be very curt and sarcastic if things didn't go as they should. For instance, if the microphone was placed in the wrong position or the cigarette holder and the newspaper he used in his act were not in the right place, or if the sound equipment didn't function properly, he would be very quick to blame the staff and the management. But then it was him under the spotlight. These errors could cause him to lose the audience or fluff a set-up and go down badly. Consequently he was given the "touch of the forelock" treatment by some who in private thought he was a bit grand. Before Peter left Butlin's, we exchanged telephone numbers; he told me he lived in a small flat in Devonshire Mews near Portland Place and hoped I would see him there when I returned to London.

After Peter had gone, I carried on as before, but hugging my secret to myself (typically Aquarian) waiting for the day when I would receive the call for my B.B.C. radio audition. This meant so much to me! To work for B.B.C. Radio would be another rung climbed in my fledgling acting career! And what might it lead to? In fact, the call didn't arrive until about five weeks later and when it did come, it didn't work out exactly as I'd envisaged. In the meantime I carried on with my daily round and trivial tasks - business managing, assistant stage managing (which wasn't onerous) and cavorting in a suspicious manner: sometimes known as "actin".

Meanwhile I became stupidly smitten with the daughter of a magician whose act was on the Variety bill:

"All the way from the Orient ! The Magical Chang Ching Chow! (or something like that) Owing to enormous success," (It said) "retained for another week!"

She, with her father (the chief magician) her mother and two sisters, all took part in the act. They were heavily made up to simulate the corny Western idea of Chinese people from the Fu-Manchu era and when I first saw the act, they had me fooled! I thought they really were from the Orient, but subsequently found out that the credit was strictly due to Max Factor and terrific characterisation. During the show the father spoke guttural broken English very slowly, in short sentences:

"Abberaahh…Kadabberaaah!.. Me make… Ladee disappear… Like so!"

And he'd do it! "Chang Chin Chow" in actual fact, was Alan from Bradford and spoke like a true Yorkshireman.

"Ello Sam. Fancy a cuppa?"

His daughter too! Her stage persona was "number two daughter

Rotusfrower!" But she was Janet.

"Eee Sahm" she'd say in her delicious accent. "Whatever are you oop to?"

When it was perfectly obvious what I was up to. She was extremely pretty in a doll like fashion. And slim, petite and maddening.

"Oooh. Me father would kill me if he found me like this!"

It was rapidly killing me too. I walked with a limp after each encounter.

"And you do understand Sammy" she panted, changing position, "that I want to save myself for Mr. Right."

"Yes but Janet, that's my real name! Sam Wright!"

In spite of the frustration, I liked her and I understood. I also appreciated her fear of her father. After all she was only 18. And he was very strict, waving a mental and irrefutable rod of iron over her every movement, wanting to know where she was going, what she was doing and with whom.

"He'd kill you too if anything happened!"

And to be fair he did have a very big sword which he brandished on stage as part of the act, cutting up lengths of rope that then miraculously became all joined up again!

After initially being friendly, he began to regard me suspiciously, as if I were intent on seducing his precious daughter. Which of course I was, but never did! Besides I didn't want to hurt her or upset her. She had an impish charm which was very becoming, and when she was in an embrace, the roguish side of her was all for giving in.

"Oh yes Sammy. Oh yesss."

But the serious side wasn't having any of it!

"No Sammy. Stop! NO!"

Years later I met her when I was working for Granada Television in Manchester. She was very happily married to a Fu-Mancunian. She introduced me to her two beautiful daughters who looked somewhat bewildered when I said, "Abberacadaberrah!...You 'ave two young ladies appear! Like so!"

From the beginnings of my career as an actor I was always extremely nervous – outwardly serene but a mass of nerves inwardly. Despite my mucking about with the psychiatrist, I did have symptoms and was discharged from the army suffering from neurosis. Being a psychoneurotic entitled me as I've said, to the magnificent sum of seven shillings and sixpence per week and to keep pace with the cost of living it was later increased by two shillings and sixpence to ten bob! At a medical tribunal I was asked to attend, I was advised by a British Legion officious official to accept a lump sum to pay me off. (They were always having tribunals to see if your condition had improved so that they could reduce the pension).

"Well" the pompous moustachioed man said, talking all over me, "I've seen lots of neurotics like you and to be very frank, and I know you wouldn't want me to be otherwise, would you…?"

"Er no!" (Or was I supposed to say "yes"?)

"But you seem perfectly normal to me."

"Ah. Well I…".

"How long do you think they will go on paying you?"

"Well I was hoping …"

"If I was you I would get the generous lump sum."

"Oh. I don't think I…"

"It's £50."

"I don't think I want…"

"Good I'll accept for you."

I later realised that he must've been on the side of the medical board. £50 was only two years worth and it wasn't going to go away just like that. I'd probably be affected for the rest of my life.

So I got given £50. But despite initially making light of them, my P.O.W. experiences had left their mark on me and for a long time, as I suspected, the condition persisted, so that I had to steel myself on entering a crowded room, imagining that all eyes were on me. It was some considerable time before I overcame it. And yet, paradoxically enough, I enjoyed people watching me act.

One other notable thing happened before I received a call for my B.B.C. interview – my mother came to Skegness to see me give my "Jerry' in *While Parents Sleep*. She was accompanied by a lady friend (a lodger in fact) Mrs. Hummel. They sat in the third row of the front stalls with a handful of campers and four usherettes. It was a lovely day outside and as usual hardly anyone had turned up. She peered in my direction most of the time, even when others were speaking, as if assessing my prospects in the bedding department and didn't seem to laugh much. Afterwards she said limply that she'd enjoyed it, adding that I was looking much better than the last time she saw me, as if I was an inmate of an institution! After the matinee, I took them both on a tour of the camp which aroused a flicker of interest, and then gave them tea and buttered scones in my chalet, finally seeing them off at the station. Just before my mother got on the train, I told her my news of the upcoming audition at the B.B.C.

"Oh yes?" She paused and looked thoughtful and said, mournfully, sagging like a deflating bellows, "I hope it all works out the way you want it son."

But this wasn't the way *she* wanted it. Her eyes focussed on a distant seagull. And she was clearly thinking of pillows and eiderdowns. And how I was ruining my life. To her, I was stumbling headlong into the filth, degradation and drunkenness of the appalling licentious life of an actor and above all dragging the family name through the mud. I got all of that through her one look at a seabird. The train steamed out leaving me wistful and low.

On the Friday of the following week the telephone rang with a call from Peter Waring.

"Hello Sammy! Could you get to the B.B.C., the Aeolian Hall in Bond Street, at 10.30 on Monday morning for an interview with the producer? Just a formality - the job is as good as fixed. Anyway, good luck see you there."

I made enquiries at the station and found out that to be back in Skegness in time for the afternoon performance I would have to catch the 10.30 a.m. train from London, in which time I was supposed to see Charles Maxwell, the producer! Obviously I would have to telephone him to ask if he could see me earlier. I decided to travel to London late on Saturday evening and rang my mother to let her know that I would be going home the following weekend. Next I had to get in touch with the producer in order to change the interview time. I had great difficulty in getting connected and even then I wasn't able to speak to him personally as he had gone out.

"Don't worry" said his secretary. "I'm sure it will be alright but just in case could you ring later and in the meantime I'll tell him when he comes in."

After that I rang Peter telling him about the tricky situation that had developed and hoped he could arrive earlier at the Aeolian Hall. He couldn't, so that was a disappointment, as I wanted his moral support. However, he did say that I hadn't anything to worry about. Later I telephoned the B.B.C. again and this time the secretary informed me that my appointment had been changed to 9.45. Leaving later on Saturday didn't bother me, but as the interview came closer I became more and more nervous. I was in Bond Street at 8.30 a.m. sharp, pacing up and down, aimlessly looking in shop windows until the appointed time. I had three cups of coffee in a nearby cafe and then had to hurry in case I was late! I needn't have worried – the producer didn't turn up till 10 o'clock. He talked to me briefly, asking me what experience I had had. I told him the truth, embellishing it a little, but admitting that I had never broadcast before. Finally he asked me to read something from the script, which I did – very badly and stammering several times. I was extremely nervous and thought I detected a slight touch of hostility in him.

"Yes...... Well.... Thanks." He said.

Although Peter Waring had been adamant that the interview was "Only a formality" and "the job was as good as fixed", my inferiority complex was working overtime. And I became even more neurotic when I looked at the clock in his office – it read 10.20. I was distracted. I couldn't possibly catch the 10.30 train now, which meant I wouldn't be back in Skegness in time for the show. My only course was to phone and tell them what had happened. I talked for another two minutes with Charles Maxwell. He seemed very concerned about my lack of experience. And then departed. It was a most uninspiring interview and I received the impression that the producer resented my trying to get into a radio show via Peter's recommendation. I sensed that he wasn't going to let me in at all – not in <u>his</u> show, anyway. I felt completely fed up. I took a taxi to the station in the forlorn hope that the train might be delayed, but of course it had gone out on time.

I tried to telephone Butlin's from a phone kiosk in the station, but at first I couldn't get through. Then when I was finally connected I was cut off! I tried again and got the wrong number by which time the person waiting outside the kiosk was banging on the door asking, "How much bloody longer are you going to be?"

T'was ever thus in the face of adversity. Undaunted I ploughed on, sweat gurgling from my furrowed brow. Eventually I got through to the girl who was employed in the box office at the theatre. Unfortunately she forgot to deliver my message till the following day, by which time it was evidence for the prosecution .

"Ee sid 'ee weren't coming till later!"

When I returned to Butlin's, I received a weeks notice of dismissal. I think the producer wanted an an excuse as he was a jealous man and suspected me of trifling with his wife's affections. Which I'd have liked to have done, but because he turned up, I didn't. And to add to my misery as I suspected, I didn't get the job on the radio series either – it seems that Charles Maxwell thought my voice was dull and monotonous. Apart from that he liked me!

So there I was, languishing at Butlin's for a week, working out my notice and not being able to leave until they got a replacement three days later. I was sorry to go. But the producer was adamant – "Broken your contract haven't you, old boy" he said vindictively.

No. He didn't like me. Just when I thought my fortunes were improving, I felt resentful that Fate should treat me so unkindly. On the other hand, I did bring it up upon myself. When I returned to

London, as an outward manifestation of an inner turmoil, I suddenly developed a violent eczema rash on my face which made it extremely difficult to shave, so that in the end I gave up shaving – and washing. I felt and began to look like a P.O.W. who had "let himself go" – there had been a lot of them about in the camp. But I had never joined them. Smearing excrement on the wall was never my idea of a good time. My mother's Irish Doctor, Hennigan, ("Ask Hennigan. He'll know what to do. He cleared up your Uncle's piles in no time" she said helpfully) put me in touch with a skin specialist from South Kensington and that doubled the bill immediately. He diagnosed "Barber's Rash" and prescribed a special penicillin cream, at the same time forbidding me to use any soap other than one with a coal tar base. I hardly dared show my face in public and when I did go out (mainly to see him) I wore my *Brief Encounter* faded trilby well down over my forehead, and dark glasses to hide my bloodshot sea green eyes. A muffler, pulled up over my nose and mouth, yashmak fashion, completed the disguise. I got several funny looks, as you would expect. Some lactic concoction had to be dabbed liberally on my face, three times daily with cotton wool. It was a long and tedious process. But eventually I was given the all clear and I gratefully discarded my disguise. But I was warned by the specialist to be most careful of what I put on my face - even a hot towel. And to this day every time I get a whiff of coal tar soap and see a wad of cotton wool, I think of the huge medical hole in my meagre bank balance.

Eventually the near leprosy feeling cleared up and I was able to look several agents in the eye again and one such was called Gino Arbib, who had an office in Lower Regent Street. He was a large, bear-like, affable Frenchman who specialised, according to his billing, in "foreign types" for films. He had "vide connections" he said, which I think meant he was a consultant as well as being a casting director. Or perhaps it meant he was a casting consultant? I looked it up in a dictionary and it said it was the Latin, videre, to see, as in *"vide"* in books, when directing a reader somewhere else, so was none the wiser. Whatever it was - and I think it was something he'd made up -

I knew he was in a position to cast actors, and apparently he arranged dates for cabaret acts and variety theatres as well. But in my case, I was the perfect "foreign type" for a French film he was casting, so he said. Well I think that was the case. My lack of French was making it an uphill struggle. And his vanity was such he thought he was speaking English. It was a weird combination of the two.

"I 'ave vide connections but pour vous I only take 10% commission, oui?"

I had absolutely no idea what he was talking about but he was taking the usual percentage so I was happy about that!

"Oui!" I said, nodding in case he couldn't understand my French.

"C'est necessary pour moi pour le travail." he continued.

"Oh oui!" I said, still worried about what "vide" meant. Was I supposed to be naked with donkeys? Was it that sort of film? I had taken along to his office some of my stills from *The Captive Heart*. He was most interested in them. He said, "I ham unvolved doing avec un film francais qui vient in Angleterre pour location scenes. Eet call itself *Le Battalion du Ciel* (The Sky Battalion) et I chooze you pour le British soldier "le Premier soldat anglais.""

I gathered with difficulty that my character was to be on guard over one particular plane which was consigned to carry the French "Skywaymen" (parachutists) to their dropping zone in Germany. Things were clearly moving after this initial "rendez-vous", as I then met the director Alexandre Esway, at an interview arranged by Gino. Alexandre was most pleasant, and scrutinised one particular photo of me which he held up against me and said, as if to confirm his incredulity, "Eet ees not possible! No! Incroyable!"

He stood back as if checking that it truly was me standing there before him; his eyes narrowed, his head wobbled, so, panicking slightly, as once again I wasn't sure what was going on, I decided to give him a sickly smile. I think it worked. I still to this day have no idea what was or wasn't "possible" but as it clearly got me the part, whatever it was, I didn't question it! He didn't even ask me to do anything in a soldierly fashion! I could have auditioned as the German guard if he'd liked, after my experience at Windsor!

It was four or five days guaranteed over three weeks at Ringway Airport, Manchester. Headquarters were at the Midland Hotel. There was nothing particularly sensationally different in the way the French unit worked from the English. They were true to filmic fashion in their despairing "Oh mon Dieu" attitude to some things, especially the light going in and out, but at other times they were positively dilatory and unworried if things didn't go right. Pierre Blanchar was the star of the film - he'd played Napoleon at one stage so he told me - along with Raymond Bussieres - both hugely experienced French film actors - and I acted with Pierre; but I was never given the whole of the plot, so I never found out really what was going on. This seemed to be the theme of things with this film. My scenes were handed to me in the shape of four typewritten sheets of paper and I was mainly concerned with guarding the aeroplane. Despite the small amount of screen time I had, the filming took ages! When it came to the acting, I didn't have to extend myself at all! My part consisted of a few reaction shots, "Halt who goes there?" shots, "running round the plane" shots, a few "Who's that?" shots, and that was my lot - of shots! Just in case (of what, I wasn't sure), they kept me there, in the Hotel, I presume, to make sure there weren't any forgotten "what have we forgotten?" shots! Much of the time was wasted, mainly due to misunderstandings and wrongly interpreted messages. Quelle surprise! There weren't any interpreters anywhere! I conversed with the film crew and Pierre in a mixture of schoolboy French and simple English. They were most respectful towards me, especially when I told them of my captivity as a prisoner of war and how I'd mingled with the Vichyites and French P.O.W.s in Berlin. They referred to me as "Monsieur Keed, le Prisonnier". I quite liked that! "Monsieur Keed!" It was a very unstressful shoot. After two weeks they'd finally shot all my bits.

"Ecoutez! (listen) Tout le monde! (everybody) Apres ce shot" I said "je suis fini avec le production *Le Battalion Du Ciel*. I 'ave ad un jolie bon temps," I said, clearly incorrectly but heartfeltly.

"Ah oui Monsieur Keed le Prisonnier. We ave bin tres amusing by you" was the equally incorrect response. The focus puller (le "puller de focus" as I called him) fancied himself as a linguist and said, "What doings you ave approximate, Keed le Prisonnier?"

I gleaned he meant "what was I up to next".

Speaking as a fellow linguist I answered, "Je ees 'aving un meeting avec le exchange de labour at Chiswick."

My response was completely out of his league.

"Quoi Monsieur Keed le Prisonnier?" he said.

I repeated it even less clearly: "J'attends le Dole Office for le dosh pour le non-work."

He looked suitably perplexed but fortunately was called away before I had any more explaining to do! I asked M. Sphuren, the Production Manager, for my train fare to London, prepared for a language "bataille", but he understood "la monnaie pour le voyage to London" so gave it to me sans hesitation; and then I promptly begged a lift in a freight plane heading for Northolt, thus being able to keep the money for not using the train!

During the early period of my homecoming from Germany, as I said earlier, I had gone to the Nuffield Centre, which was an informal Club in Central London, opened for use by all members of the forces. In fact when I'd first returned from Russia and we were on our initial "long leave" of six weeks (they gave us that before we returned to be demobbed or sent elsewhere. It was initially uncertain), I had done a double act there with fellow P.O.W. Frank Coburn. These were different more ignorant times and of course I wouldn't do it nowadays, being more aware of its significance, but it was quite normal then, and we blacked up as a sort of "Alexander and Mose" cross-talk act, (they were famous for the "Chicken Chaser" sketch and were in fact well known 30s comic Billy Bennett - a top comedian in his own right - and Australian Albert Whelen) and it had gone down well.

Here's a taster of the dialogue:

ME: What you bin doin?

FRANK: I'm a pilot.

ME: In the airforce?

FRANK: No sir. A pilot on the farm.

ME: A pilot on a farm?

FRANK: Yes sir. I pile it here and pile it there and sometimes I pile it on the rhubarb.

ME: You know a song?

FRANK: Yes sir. It's entitled "I used to kiss my sweetie on the cheek. Now it's all over."

ME: I know it. I'll join in.

BOTH: Snow is white

Coal is black.

If your pants is loose

Pull in the slack. Etc..

And

FRANK: What you call it when a gal gets married three times? Bigotry?

ME: You surely are an ignoramus. When a gal gets married two times, that's bigotry. Three times that's trigonometry!"

And

ME: What would be the first thing you'd do if you had hydrophobia?

FRANK: I'd ask for a pencil and some paper.

ME: To make your will?

FRANK: No. To make a list of the people I want to bite.

On reflection my desire to perform as often as possible was so necessary for me - and something my mother never ever really grasped - that the first thing I'd done on returning from captivity was to see family, obviously, but also to get in front of an audience. It spelt out normality. And that was what I was craving. Another thing of course that I did to express the "normality" I was seeking, was, along with 100,000 others, to watch Chelsea F.C. play against Moscow Dynamo at Stamford Bridge. It was a huge outpouring of emotion amidst the appalling uncertainty and deprivation we'd all experienced.

The Nuffield centre, which resembled the "Stage Door Canteen" in Piccadilly, was run by a charming gentlewoman called Kathleen Waite and one would never have cast this sweet, demure, well-spoken woman in the part of Manager of an establishment devoted to entertaining the forces. However, appearances can be deceptive and she kept us all in order, always "cocking a deaf 'un" to the crude language which could be heard from time to time. She was assisted, nobly, by Mary Cooke, who eventually superseded her and later worked for the B.B.C. booking department. At the club, one could have a cheap meal, cheap drinks, and spend many hours playing billiards, snooker, or table tennis. And on certain evenings we could enjoy cabaret and dancing. In addition, free theatre tickets for all the West End shows were often available. I used to go there frequently, sometimes to perform as compere to the shows, or to do a turn (I would try out material and new impressions. Or might even guest in a sketch or two) or just to help out with sandwiches and drinks for the artistes. I tried a speedy doctor routine with Johnny Gaskin from the camp:

JOHNNY: Are you taking the medicine regularly?
ME: I tasted it and decided I'd rather have the cough.

JOHNNY: Why are you bouncing up and down like that?
ME: I just took some medicine and forgot to shake the bottle.

ME: Doctor you'll have to help me
JOHNNY: What's the matter?

ME: I'm so absent minded I keep slamming the wife and kissing the door.

And

ME: Doctor as you know my wife's been very ill and you told me I should take her to the seaside.
JOHNNY: Yes. And did you?
ME: Well I wondered why I should if I could create the same sea breezes effect at home
JOHNNY: And how do you do that?
ME: I fan her with a herring.

Not great gags I know, but all done as "rapid fire", so if you didn't get a laugh you were onto the next one!

Performances were held every Tuesday and Friday and served a dual purpose: they entertained the troops and troopesses and at the same time they were seen by agents and bookers for cabaret. B.B.C. bookers were always very much in evidence. After the normal show, usually of two hours duration, hospitality, in the form of drinks and a running buffet, were the order of the day and were always available. Many of the present day stars did a stint at the Nuffield, among them Benny Hill who was a great favourite there, with whom I was to work many times on T.V. in the 50s. Producer Kenneth Carter in fact did several shows with Benny from the Nuffield for the B.B.C.. In addition to Benny there was Frankie Howerd, (always friendly. More of him soon) cheerful Australian Bill Kerr, whose opening line was "I've only got four minutes" and of course he'd go on much longer. He was later in all the Hancocks. Also there was the "Bumper Fun Book" man, Robert Moreton. I liked him immensely. He'd pretend to be an amateur performer reading jokes out of the "book" and would follow the punchline - and laughter - with "Oh get in there Moreton!" He was very funny indeed. He sadly subsequently committed suicide. It would be interesting to see the Nuffield Centre

Visitors Book of that time, if one could find it! One or two representatives of the C. S. E. U. (Combined Services Entertainment Units) came to see the acts, amongst them Colonel Richard Stone (later to become a highly successful theatrical agent) and a Major Brightwell, with whom I had a nodding acquaintance. I was to get to know them even better in the months that lay ahead.

I was constantly advised in this period to have one sole agent, but any effort I'd made - mostly via the Royal Mail - was rebuffed. Apparently, I still didn't have enough experience. I'd enclosed a stamped addressed envelope and when they actually bothered to reply I'd get responses like:

"Thankyou for your recent letter but we're not taking anyone on at the moment."

And...

"As yet we do not feel you are experienced enough."

Or ...

"We have someone exactly like you" (Did I have a twin and not know it?)

And that old chestnut.....

"The position of cleaner has been filled".

So I decided to play the field alone – well it was forced upon me. So whoever got me work, got the commission. When I worked for the Forbes Russell company at Butlin's, the Lionel Wallace Agency took the commission. And when I was employed by the F.F.M. (French Film Makers) - I never got to know the name of the Production Company - Gino Arbib took ten percent "only". He was doing me a favour with his "ten percent only" so he said. So having made £100, less insurance and 10%, on that deal, I wasn't doing too badly. (I'd have to pay tax of course) But the longer I was out of work, the further the money had to be spread over. Well, it follows doesn't it?

As far as the labour exchange, the job centre, is concerned, they're not in a position to offer work to theatrical people - those kind of jobs don't go through them - so it was quietly suggested by the supervisor that it might be a good thing if I took a job other than one connected with the theatre or films. I wondered if he was friendly with my mother?

"How about lift attendant or tally clerk (I didn't even know what that was) or even a night watchman?" he suggested.

Ah no. He didn't know my mother. No mention of department stores. I was just debating whether or not to consider his "teasing" job offer, when there came a phone call from good old Peter Waring asking me if I was interested in a tour of Germany. Germany again? For goodness sake. What are the chances of that? Hadn't I spent five years there as an unwilling P. O. W.? Hadn't I been three months on location there for *The Captive Heart*? Hadn't I asked to be nailed to my seat rather than return there? I was very keen on going anywhere, Cyprus, the States, the Middle East, even the Arctic Circle. But Germany?… Oh alright. I was going to be paid and I was going to do the job I clearly loved. It was no contest. Life began to look up again. Aided by the marvellously generous Peter Waring, who was disappointed it hadn't worked out with Charles Maxwell, but still had faith in me. He suggested that I should go round and see him at his place in Devonshire Mews, not far from Portland Place, which is notable for its famous B.B.C. building with its statues of Prospero and Ariel by Eric Gill and its mass of er.. aerials. So I did. It was a very compact and neat little mews house, presided over by his general factotum, a likeable ex-R.A.F. chap called Bill Montague. Peter had never mentioned him before, so he was a surprise! Bill had met Peter after leaving the Air Force and had been offered the job of generally looking after him and putting up with his peccadilloes! At the beginning everything was sweetness and honey just like a new marriage, but Bill eventually got fed up "working like a bloody manservant" – which was a bit odd as that was what he was! Perhaps at the time Bill's laid back approach to his work warranted a strong admonishment, but not when it was usually delivered in front of an audience. And that's what Peter did! He folded his experiences with Bill into his patter. Having a "man" suited his stage persona.

"My "man" is in the dog-house. He made me a sausage sandwich….. Without the sausage! Bread and butter and….thin air!" Said very lugubriously!

"My manservant is in the wings. ..Bill…. Very short…. Comes up to here on me. (Indicates his waist) I can balance a tray on his head…. Fits perfectly. He's got a very flat head. That can be very convenient if I'm hungry and standing up!… He doesn't like it of course. Especially when I bang him on the head with the tray. But then why would he?"

He got a lot of laughs at Bill's expense! But apart from some long dark looks from Peter and what-the-hell-have-I-got-myself-into expressions from Bill, life went on fairly smoothly. Over a cup of strong tea, Peter put me in the picture. Shortly after finishing his successful Radio series for the B.B.C. - the one I wasn't in - he had been approached by the C.S.E.U. about the possibility of starring in a revue which would tour every part of Germany occupied by our troops, all our performances to take place in German theatres. Peter said the opportunity was there, if I wanted it, to be in the sketches yet to be written. But first I had to see Major Brightwell of the C.S.E.U., to get his approval. Luckily I already knew him via the Nuffield, so that shouldn't have been a problem. So, the next day I went along to C.S.E.U. Headquarters at 60 Eaton Square, expecting to audition, but no! He knew my work! He'd seen me performing at the Nuffield! And also I was highly recommended by old flame Cymmy Brooks who I'd known at Butlin's and who knew him! How lovely of her! (Ah, Cymmy. What might have been with Cymmy! Ah………) Anyway, I was warmly welcomed and offered the job! It was arranged that in addition to acting in the production, because of my experience at Butlin's, I would also be assistant stage manager and business manager. And I was to be paid £10 per week – £3 for the acting work and £7 for the managing jobs! The same money and tasks as Butlin's. They'd been comparing notes! (Well, Cymmy had warned them as to my competence! Ah Cymmy!) Hotels and food would all be arranged by the C.S.E.U., and I was to liaise with them if I had any difficulties. The tour was to kick-off at Hamburg and then go to Celle, Luneburg, Wuppertal, Brunswick, Minden, Berlin and Dusseldorf.

THREE
More Germany Bitte

We rehearsed at the Dinely Studios in Baker Street. As I was only involved in the sketches, I had to wait until the written material arrived. Meanwhile, I managed. The scriptwriter, one Denis Norden (ultimately the hugely successful writer and Radio and T.V. personality) was a long, lean young man, with dark darting eyes. He more or less produced the show, aided and "interfered with" by Peter Waring. It was Denis's first excursion as a producer/director and as Peter was the star, nobody disputed his helping hand.

Members of the cast contributing individual acts were:

Adelaide Hall, the internationally famous vocalist (what a brilliant piece of casting it was to have her. Her famous songs were "River Stay Away From my Door" "Lonesome Road" "Some of these Days You're Gonna Miss me Honey" and "The Dark Town Strutter's Ball").

Harry Robins, a maestro on the xylophone.

Sheila Matthews, ingenue, singer, dancer, and actress.

Pamela Cundell, comedienne of much skill.

Ken Brown, singer, noted for his rendition of "Summertime".

The Ascots, a dancing act consisting of two girls and a boy.

And last but not least, a young, slim, (yes, slim!) shortsighted comedian called Harry Secombe!

There were also dancers and a band of course. And they were all excellent as you'd expect. Especially with the great Adelaide Hall singing! We had only two weeks of rather "patchy" rehearsals - more time seemed to be spent on talking, drinking tea, waiting for scripts, rewriting them, acquiring coats, dresses, moustaches, comedy chickens etc. and other props necessary for routines (part of my job as A.S.M.). I suppose the pressure wasn't on, as each act was indeed doing their "act". Which obviously they knew rather well! Finally, we were told to go along to the medical centre to receive our going-abroad injections. Some of the cast were a little apprehensive, though nobody actually passed out. Naturally I went weak at the knees, felt a bit faint and frothed at the mouth. And this was before I'd even had an injection! But otherwise all was fine.

The title of the show was Peter's catchphrase *Press on Regardless*. I took part in several sketches involving Peter, Harry Secombe, Sheila Matthews and Pamela Cundell. But my favourite was an amusing chat-cum-song number written by Denis Norden, entitled "Three Carroll Levis Discoveries" (Carroll Levis of course hosted the B.B.C. Radio talent show of the 30s and 40s which then transferred to T.V.) in which I played a milkman, Harry was a lavatory attendant, and Pamela Cundell was a charlady. In the sketch, all of us had won talent contests. And each of us did a bit of the "act" that our characters had won with. And then interacted with each other in the sketch. So Pamela sang and did a monologue about charring, "With me big bottle of smelly disinfectant, And a big tub of elbow grease at hand………".

I did my milkman:

"On me rounds…..I love it with the cream on top…… I got a friendly 'orse I call 'im "Milky". He pulls me cart into the 'earts of all the girls!…"

And Harry sang about loos as his character worked in a public lavatory:

"Oh I'm an expert with my brush..in the lavvy…in the lavvy…in the lav-er-tory's where I am… If your bowl 'appens to be dirty. Really dirty. Very filthy I'll ave it sparklin clean in two shakes of a lamb…… "

Whenever we performed this particular sketch, it was a showstopper. This was mainly attributable to Harry's antics. (And his great voice of course). I have never known blowing a raspberry to be so funny. (Cockney rhyming slang. "Raspberry tart - fart". Squelchy noises made with the tongue between the lips. Harry specialises in the Rhonda Valley variety!). His impressions of the noises in his "white tiled establishment" were hilarious. Although the sketch was enormously successful, Peter was constantly making suggestions for improving it and it became evident that he would have liked to have played Harry's part. The fact was that Peter and Harry were two very clever comedians, but completely different – Peter with his quiet sophistication and quick repartee and Harry with his hilarious, boisterous, infectious manner of delivering lines or even non-lines, later to be used with such glorious effect in the *Goon Show*. Added to which, he had this superb Welsh deaf defying "We'll keep a welcome in the Valleys" singing voice. So it was possible that Peter felt his position as star was being usurped. For instance, Harry could extract the maximum amount of amusement out of very ordinary situations. His variety act, which he underrated, was entirely based on the various ways in which men shave themselves, e.g. the very shy shaver who couldn't shave without cutting himself badly and another who shaved in very cold water with a blunt blade. Describing it like this, can't possibly do justice to the performance. Seeing it was an education in how a clever comedian works. The audience loved it. One of my funniest memories of Harry was watching him on the balcony of our hotel in Berlin, wearing a Hitler style moustache and delivering a speech in mutilated German to the assembled people below. Quite a puzzled crowd had gathered, wondering whether the Führer had risen from the bunker!

We arrived in Hamburg to see that parts of the city were absolutely devastated – even the ruins had ruins! As far as the eye could see, it looked as if there had been a succession of major earthquakes, with bricks and wood and filth spewed across the roads. Whole areas of streets and avenues had totally disappeared, but at the same time, curiously, several hotels and shops in and around the station were intact. The station itself, although patched and pitted, had miraculously survived. In prison camp we had always doubted the Jerry war communiqués, which tended to exaggerate their gains and minimise their losses: the laconic Wermacht handouts which stated "There was some slight air activity over Hamburg yesterday" were somewhat understating the truth! Towards the end of the war one of their regular old favourites had been, "In order to shorten our Front, our troops today took part in a strategic withdrawal and retired to previously prepared positions." In other words, they retreated! A large number of the German soldiers who guarded us in the camp were always complaining about the suffering their comrades were enduring at the hands of the Soviets and the miserable conditions that abounded on the eastern front. But from what could be seen, a number of the civilians had obviously suffered just as much, if not more than the soldiers of the Third Reich. The "carpet" bombing had been devastatingly effective. Whole areas - the size of say, Hammersmith, for example - had been completely flattened. Mini Hiroshimas. My feelings were divided. One half of me said "That's your hard luck mate!" And the other half said, "Poor devils."

On Sundays, people congregated at the railway station and the park surrounding the beautiful Lake Alster, where they peddled their goods and personal possessions for coffee, tinned beef and cigarettes. I certainly appreciated their feelings because I had experienced the same pangs of hunger and want in my time in captivity. But I resisted the impulse to barter cigarettes for their precious goods and chattels. It was strange how life had moved full circle. It had taken seven years to happen, but happened, it had.

As business manager of the outfit, I had arranged to draw money from the British Army Pay Corps, for the artistes to buy little extras like drinks and cigarettes or gifts to be purchased at the local N.A.A.F.I. (Navy, Army and Air Force Institutes). This was in the majority of cases, including my own, exactly half the weekly salary agreed upon with the C.S.E.U. in London. Peter, being Peter, had a separate arrangement of course. He told me with great emphasis that the idea of some "minion" handling his money and doling it out to him did not meet with his approval.

"But it's me doing the doling" I said. "I'm the minion!"

"No no not you my dear fellow! Some other minion! Who isn't you. As you're not one!"

Despite what Peter felt, his status was nowhere near that of Colonel Richard Stone. *Press On* was actually directed, lit and polished on tour by the Colonel, who fortunately for us, had taken care of several productions at the same theatres in the recent past. Peter was quite willing to defer to his theatrical knowledge when it came to making it work on the stage. After three days perfecting, and hectic last-minute rehearsing, we opened at the local Hamburg theatre, renamed "The Garrison Theatre" for the benefit of the British troops, which was intact amidst the rubble. Before the war, it had been famous for its Opera, for which it was originally designed, and the stage, which revolved, was of a vast size and not entirely suited to an intimate revue like ours. But this sort of show worked well at the front of the stage, as a "front cloth", so we took up residence there. Unfortunately our presence coincided with the breakdown of the central heating and while snow was falling steadily outside, the barometer did likewise inside, and the artistes flapped and flailed, cursing the frozen pipes. The girls in the cast were particularly affected by the freezing temperature, being slightly less well clad than the men in some of the scenes, but Harry had them all jumping about doing exercises to banish the low temperatures! (Some of the girls got the old "don't jump about too much or the audience's temperature might go through the roof" gag from Peter). And Harry even got the audience doing the exercises as well! He also appeared to have his own personal built in heater. He was never cold. His motto, taking inspiration from "The Windmill", was "we never froze". It must have been his abundant energy, especially on stage, where you could see he was destined for stardom. The audiences loved him.

The troops were of course hungry for entertainment, having

been deprived of it, and showed their appreciation with wild applause, long shouts of "Encore" and a deafening stamping of their feet, which also warmed them up too! After the first week, which was a broken one, as we hadn't turned up till the Tuesday, we arranged to play for another ten days - arranged? The C.S.E.U. decreed it! So appropriately we had a celebration party on the Saturday after the show, with a small running buffet and stacks of booze. Some of the workers from the Hotel joined us, as did most of the theatre staff! Everybody who could perform entertained us with a party piece. I did some new impressions: Flanagan and Allen, (playing both of them in a rendition of Underneath the Arches, accompanied by some of the band who had brought their instruments), and Bob Hope and Bing Crosby singing "Road to Morocco" - Harry sang the Bing part - which went very well indeed. My Claude Dampier, who I'd done before, who was ultra posh, and known as a "silly ass" type, was a bit hit and miss. If you said his catchphrase "It's meeee" and there was no reaction, you knew you were onto a loser. Sometimes he went down wonderfully. Sometimes the silence could be deafening. Tonight he was a success! Phew!

Long after the twitching hour, the party broke up and in the morning, I found myself in a strange bed in a strange room in the hotel. Oddly enough, it was just along the corridor from my own room and not so odd in that it was the bedroom of one of our dancers, the lovely Pat van den Bergh. We had got along splendidly since our first meeting in London and this seemed to confirm it! She had been married to a Dutch sailor, but was now separated from him. Her mother took care of her baby son in a house in Islington. She was inclined to smother me which I pretended I hated, but secretly enjoyed. We liked each other a lot! She was a pretty girl - a nifty dancer and a very good mover. She grew quite fond of me, and I of her, and I've often wondered what course my life would have taken if we'd been hitched "in sickness and in health". And she'd promised to love, honour and Oh Boy! She was very loving. And that is of course all we need. Well, so the Beatles said.

Our next port of call was a town called Celle. It was a tremendous success. All the "turns" went down brilliantly. Especially Adelaide. Let's face it, it was a fabulous bill. Our "Carroll Levis" sketch was once again greeted ecstatically. Peter watched it from the wings and as usual gave us notes, but we continued to do it as we'd rehearsed it!

Next was Luneburg, where General Montgomery had overseen the surrender of the German armies and where Himmler committed suicide. A beautiful medieval town strangely unaffected by the war. As far as we were concerned though, the only thing Luneberg was notable for, was the fact that Harry contracted food poisoning, and we were forced to leave him behind in the Army hospital. His place in the "Carroll Levis" sketch was, naturally, taken by the ludicrously eager Peter, who'd been hankering after it all this time and now had his chance to impress!

"Slow it down and relish the lines" had been his constant advice.

So Peter followed his own direction and slowed it down. And relished. And lo and behold, guess what? It almost ground to a halt. It didn't work, as we already had a rhythm. And he was also unable to assume a cockney accent when he played the part of the lavatory attendant who had found fame.

"What a lovely lavvy, Larry.
A toilet whose tiles are glistening, Gary
My bright white urinals, Lionel
You'll find are so sweetly smellin' Nigel,
Are all the best'll little urinals in the land.....ll
Don't splash! Don't splash! As in wiv me brush I'll dash........
Coz I'm an expert with my brush..in the lavvy...in the lavvy...in the lav-er-tory's where I am..."

And didn't bring to it the "earthiness" which it required. His well spoken "posh" voice didn't work at all! And let's be frank, he was no Harry. His singing voice wasn't up to it. Nor were his raspberries! It was all a bit rubbish. He was very apologetic and highly embarrassed. He hardly got a single laugh. We were very glad when Harry recovered, after a couple of days of our misfiring with Peter, and the show came bubbling back to normal. Peter never gave us a note again.

At Wupertal, on the Friday, Peter had some sort of seizure just after he'd finished his routine. He collapsed dramatically just after the curtain had closed and was in so much pain, holding his stomach, that he was writhing. It was rather worrying. Bill Montague was alerted and rushed up with some tablets. None of us in fact ever found out what was wrong. Peter wasn't willing to divulge anything.

"Oh bit of a bloke's thing, you know. Nothing to worry about! All good now!"

This was all we managed to get out of him. He certainly looked extremely the worse for wear. Bill and myself held him up and carried/walked him to his dressing room. He improved slightly and managed to limp unaided back to the hotel, which was just around the corner. We had a conflab with Richard Stone. Bill suggested he take his boss's place the following night if he hadn't improved; somewhat gleefully I felt! Bill had apparently, like a good understudy, so he said, learnt all his boss's lines just in case. And backstage Bill did a few minutes of Peter's act for Richard (and us all) as a sort of audition. It was uncannily good. Bill winked at me. This would be his revenge, for all those gags about him. Bill could do Peter's act! The following night all was prepared for Bill's impersonation. There'd been rehearsals through the day and some cuts made, when Peter out of the blue and against doctor's orders, returned from his sick bed and barged on, the moment Bill had started. Peter's timing was immaculate. He shoved him off in fact .

"Thankyou so much for warming them up. Whoever you are! I'll take over now!"

Ouch! Bill was ordered to hang about in the wings by Richard Stone, who was in attendance, in case anything untoward happened. But there was never any doubt that Peter wouldn't survive -

especially after he got his first ripple of laughter. Bill had been thwarted. We never got to see him "do" his boss in the show which was a great shame, as the dress rehearsal had been hilarious. Mind you we were appreciating the impression, not the actual performance, so perhaps it's just as well he never went on.

The tour continued, being rapturously received wherever we performed - none more so than Minden. There were so many encores the show was 45 minutes over its usual length! Then followed Berlin, the Western Sector. In order to get there we first had to negotiate the checkpoints where we were repeatedly stopped by the scary poker-faced Soviets. They regarded everyone and everything with suspicion. Our props and costumes were scrutinised minutely. They poked our comedy chicken all over (it featured very briefly in a doctor sketch) as if they were worried it was a sophisticated bomb and would explode any minute, and ultimately placed it in a bucket of water; and our papers were examined minutely as if they were all the work of a master forger. The waiting about was interminable and deliberate. They tried to make it as uncomfortable as possible. Eventually when we did get into the western sector, we were told, very firmly, to avoid going anywhere near the eastern sector. There were some scaremongering stories about people accidentally finding themselves in East Berlin who had never been heard of since! However, on one occasion whilst I was travelling in the Berlin underground, I found myself whizzing towards Dresden, very much off course, and naturally became very apprehensive about regaining entry back into the western sector. But I needn't have worried. I told the official who questioned me that I was an actor ("ich bin schauspieler") and was appearing at the local Opera/Garrison Theatre for the troops. He was most interested and a pre war film fan and helped me on my way having asked me in broken English if I knew any film stars. When I said I knew Gary Cooper, (well he'd been at the same school as me, Dunstable, so it was almost true) he was very impressed! I think in reality everyone was suspected of being involved with the hundreds of blackmarketeers who were rife before the Berlin Wall was built. We were approached by many shady individuals offering to sell us rare goods - nylons, eggs, butter and forged passports - at knockdown prices. We were told not to be tempted. Association with these types could lead to arrest and disappearance into a gulag.

After Berlin, where we had again been an enormous success, we went to Düsseldorf which was our last stop. Here we had to perform on another vast stage, built for opera, as in Hamburg. And like the Hamburg theatre there was a huge turntable, which naturally, we decided to use. Of course it jammed halfway through the performance, and then mysteriously unjammed and then jammed again, possibly deliberately, as much mirth was had by all, as props and actors were stuck facing in the wrong direction and then thrown to the floor with the jolt of the restart. Harry of course was at his best during such situations, pretending to crank the stage with an imaginary starting handle and making noises to give the impression he was winding up a rubber band, and asking the audience if anyone would like to come up and help push the furniture about. Several of course did! He then asked if there were any engineers in the house and when 10 soldiers put up their hands he'd question them and then invite them all to have a look at the machinery.

"We need oil! Anyone got any oil? No?…What?…..You've got a bottle of beer? Well that's rather tasty but I don't think it's going to be much help….Oh and the machinery needs to be cranked! We need a crank to crank it. Anybody got a crank? Then we need someone to do the cranking. You sir you look like a cranker! Could you do some mimed solo cranking for us sir so we can get an idea? …Oh you look like you're starting a very small jeep. Yes. Bit bigger. Mind you, you sir, you look as if you've sprained your wrist…I'm not quite sure what you're doing sir. Is there a small animal involved? etc.."

He disappeared with them under the stage and we heard a lot of shouted under-stage dialogue about what they were up to. Of course with Secombe commentary.

"We're under the stage! We can't see a bloody thing! Someone turn a light on! Help! (CUE MASSIVE INFECTIOUS SECOMBE GIGGLE).

Harry would then regularly maintain the subterfuge that he was trapped under the stage after everyone was back in their seats.

"Help! I'm stuck! Anybody there? Help! ...Heeelp!..It's scary down here! (CUE RASPBERRY) Oops sorry!"

It'd been a great tour with much fun, merriment and camaraderie. Peter, to whom I owed so much for his faith in me, and to whom I was eternally grateful had rescued me from becoming a night watchman, Harry and I have remained friends ever since, and I'd done myself a lot of good with Forbes Russell! On returning to London I made tracks for the paymaster at Eaton Square to hand in my counterfoils, bills and receipts and collect the rest of the weekly stipend. It appeared that the C.S.E.U. had received glowing reports of our tour and I was asked if I would like to go further afield in a similar capacity. The Middle East was mooted, to which I keenly said "yes" and true to custom, I never heard another word. I went home to my mother at Chiswick and after two weeks of home comforts, I felt in need of a different kind of comforting and cosseting so I telephoned my dancer friend Pat and we had tea and toast at her place. Unfortunately that week she had to dash off to Holland to contest the custody of her child and when she came back she went on tour again, so gradually the fire dampened down and finally went out. It was a shame. I was very fond of her.

To keep my name in circulation I had on several occasions phoned Margaret Harper Nelson (Casting) and her assistant Thelma Graves at Ealing. And sometimes I had a chat with Muriel Cole who was always polite and interested in my welfare. They were all great to me, as they had been when I first met them at the Studios, and Margaret when not too busy, would invite me along to see them. We usually talked about what I was doing and what films they were involved in. I got the impression that they felt responsible for me and endeavoured to find work for me, if and when they could. I was one of their ex P.O.W. boys. And of course it helped that the film *The Captive Heart* had been a great success.

Unlike Charles Maxwell, who had found my voice monotonous (ooh, I won't let this go will I), Forbes Russell had had the opportunity to hear my vocal range and began to find me one or two - or three or four or five - post-syncing jobs (which meant that my voice would be re-recorded over scenes already filmed, "post synchronisation"). In some instances, where some voices were supposed to be heard on screen, but the characters were not actually in vision and the soundman hadn't actually recorded them at the time, I did some of those voices too. This is known as A.D.R. or Additional Dialogue Recording. You know that indistinct background noise in a scene, say, a restaurant? It's rarely the sound of the supporting artistes, who are occasionally actually told not to speak at all, but to pretend to speak, just in case they're too loud for the actual dialogue in the scene. That background noise, that "rhubarb", is an actor in a recording studio coming up with improvised dialogue, but it's being turned right down so it's barely heard, so as not to interfere with the lines in the scene. For actual "dubbing", replacing the original dialogue or original actor's voice, if the director didn't like the tone quality of the voice of an actor playing a small part, (and sometimes even big parts!) my voice would be re-recorded over that actor's. The process went like this: a microphone was placed in front of the screen in a recording theatre. The scene that had been filmed was projected onto the screen which I would watch intently, at the same time attempting to match the words to the lip movements of the person on the screen. (It's now done with a "wipe", which is a line advancing across the screen, and three spaced beep noises to help you time it.) The danger in listening to the original dialogue was that if I wasn't careful I found myself taking on the tone or delivery pattern of the voice I was replacing. (They now turn the original dialogue off for this very reason). Sometimes the voice of the actor to be dubbed was not distinct or perhaps too light or not even light enough. Luckily my vocal range meant I could do both high and low. The odd voices I did in these recording studios were rewarded at the then not to be sneezed at sum of £5! This was worked out at half the daily rate for the acting job which at that time was £10. The number of characters who ended up being post synced (or even "post-sunk") in films was enormous. I had no idea so many were! I often visualised the outraged feelings of the actors concerned when hearing my voice emanating from their image. At one time, and some still do, a colony of foreign artistes made a career out of dubbing the voices of outstanding American stars such as James Stuart, Clark Gable, Gary Cooper, Edward G Robinson, Marlon Brando etc. into their own languages. So an actor might be known as the French Clark Gable, for example. The only snag was that once the actor's voice and been identified with that of a particular actor, the actor concerned was unable to use his voice for anyone else. And if the actor died, the foreign dubbing man effectively passed away too and had to find an alternative career! Probably not in a bedding department. I did a mass of post-syncing and dubbing which was always most welcome. Over the following years my post-syncing was a fulfilling part of my career. I'm in lots of films re-voicing small parts that even I've forgotten about. I watched *Carlton Browne of the F.O.* recently on T.V. where I played a radio operator opposite Terry-Thomas and Thorley Walters, and I've also dubbed one of the soldiers in the scene afterwards.

"I recognise that voice!" I thought.

You may think, at this stage of my life, that things weren't going too badly for me. On the surface possibly. But underneath I can assure you that were still many moments of self doubt. In fact at this time, just after Germany, things began to look pretty bleak. The work wasn't consistent you see. It never was. Even when I was working regularly, I still didn't believe I was a success. There's almost a feeling that you'll be found out. Someone will tap you on the shoulder and say, "Oh dear. You're a bit rubbish at this acting lark, aren't you? It's all been a big fluke hasn't it?" And you bow your head and agree. Especially after the appalling uncertainty of the prison camp, where we frequently thought we'd all be taken out and shot.

At this period, after several weeks had gone by and I was still out of work, and my mother was giving me that "soft bedding" look again and I had exhausted the contacts I had made during my short span of employment, the disenchanted feeling with my chosen, overcrowded profession and everything it stood for, could be overwhelming. Perversely even when the work started to become regular, I assumed it would go on improving - getting better every time, rather like er…bacon and egg! But then that is the actor's desire. You hope that the graph of your career goes forever upwards. Whereas frequently it's mountainous peaks and troughs!

On our return from Germany to the U.K., as is nearly always the case, everyone had wandered off, vowing to see each other as soon as possible. But life takes over. And we became ships in the night. Peter and Harry already had some work lined up. Peter so he told me, as well as a large number of "gigs", was doing more episodes of the radio show *Heigh Ho* (which I'd failed to get into) scripted by Frank Muir and starring Peter, Kenneth Horne (ultimately of the brilliant *Round the Horne*) and charming actor Maurice Denham which had been such a huge success when it was first aired. And, naturally, as it was produced by good old Charles Maxwell, there was no chance of a part for me! Harry was much in demand and was soon to be hoisted to stardom via the *Goon Show*. But it was hardly surprising as he was a phenomenal talent.

As to the others, we all exchanged phone numbers, as you do, and vowed to keep in touch. Some I've never seen again - the lovely loose limbed dancers "The Ascots" for example. I wonder whatever happened to them? But others I've bumped into on the street and it's as if we've just got off the boat again! I love that about this business. You can not see someone for years, but you're mates again instantly.

I saw Adelaide Hall immediately on getting back. Her husband, a terrifically friendly Trinidadian called Bertram Hicks who was also her business manager, who eventually ran "The Calypso Club" in Regent Street, invited me to tea in their luxurious house in the

Boltons, Kensington. I had become a great admirer of Adelaide after watching her on tour where she took encore after encore. She had such a pure soaring voice. She was already a big star, but her career went from strength to strength. She worked most famously with Duke Ellington and Fats Waller and had been a regular at the Cotton Club in Harlem in New York. She told me she was the first person ever to use nitrogen smoke on stage! During the war she'd been a famous E.N.S.A. performer. She even taught Queen Elizabeth the Charleston!

About 20 years later I was assisting at a Covent Garden charity concert and saw this glamorous black lady retreating along the corridor. Thinking it was Adelaide who was on the bill, I rushed up to her, calling "Adelaide, Adelaide," flinging my arms wide in melodramatic fashion and shouted "Remember me? It's Sam!" She turned round and said, "In future I shall forget to remember you honey! I'm Elizabeth Welch!"

Unfortunately there was no hole in the ground for me to crawl into. To be fair, there was a resemblance! They were about the same age. And both equally talented! "Stormy Weather" was Elizabeth's great song. And annoyingly I didn't manage to see Adelaide!

When I've been mistaken for someone else I tend not to disappoint and deny I'm who they want me to be. I remember once watching Chelsea at Stamford Bridge and left to get back to the car, parked near the Earl's Court Road. A man ran up to me, panting, and said, "Hello! You certainly walk quickly. I've had to run to catch up with you!"

"Oh really?" I replied. "Yes, well, it is a bit cold to be dawdling".

I wondered if this was all he was going to say and he had just wanted to criticise my swift walking style as there was a pause. But he continued... "I've seen you several times at the football and I was determined to get your autograph. I love everything you're in and always look forward to you being on the telly."

No that was lovely. What a nice man.

"Oh thanks very much!" I said beaming. This was extra nice as

Chelsea had lost 3-0.

"My mother will be so pleased as she's a great fan of yours too."

"Oh good! Lovely! Thanks. It's O.K. I've got a pen." I got out my Osmiroid. He handed me a piece of paper.

"Could you make it out to Dave please Dermot?"

Dermot? What? He thought I was Dermot Kelly with whom I was in the T.V. sitcom *Mess Mates*! (He was also Arthur Haynes' sidekick in his T.V. series.) So I signed it Sam Dermot Kydd. Well I suppose in certain lights, one Irishman looks like another. Then gave him a signed Sam Kydd photo I had in my jacket. I drove off with him looking a bit confused.

On other occasions I've been mistaken for Sidney James:

"Oi Sid I love you in them "Ancocks"."

And Eric Sykes:

"Oh Mr. Sykes, can I have an autograph? It's not for me you understand it's for my sister. I don't like you as much as she does."

And once, bizarrely, Cary Grant. But I think the autograph hunter had had too many beers.

In November I heard from Thelma Graves of Ealing Studios. She told me they were doing a film called *A Convict has Escaped* at Riverside Studios, Hammersmith. It was a "film noir" (beautifully atmospheric black and white shots of the docks etc. and huge close ups of leering faces. I know this is a generalisation, but it looked spooky and evocative and was very "of the moment") and the plot was about the post war black market, smuggling and murder. It was to be directed by Cavalcanti, "Be a good boy Sam", himself! Nora Roberts, the casting director of the film who cast me, reminded me of a severe school teacher. Her particular forte was her superior ability with facts and figures. She was a tough negotiator, especially if you went to see her not through an agent, as I did. If I'd had an agent he would have shielded me from such anxious bargaining. And possibly got me more money. Her favourite line was, "Oh, we can't possibly pay you that dear. The budget won't allow it!"

The one positive I initially gained from meeting her, was that she had heard of me! (Really? Yes!) She possessed a photograph of me from *The Captive Heart* and apparently I had been earmarked by Cavilcanti to play a gang member in this film – who didn't have many lines but was featured a lot. In fact I was in every scene set in the "Valhalla" undertakers, the front for the blackmarket activities of the gang, and in the warehouse where they kept their stock of purloined goods. And the plot had us at both locations for rather a large number of scenes. I have to admit my part did have me hovering in the background a lot, or just being in rather well set-up group shots, with me peering over someone's shoulder or visible just in the gap.

"Sam we can't see you. Shift a bit to your left please," Otto Heller the cameraman would advise me. The stars of *A Convict has Escaped,* shot by the Alliance Group (they owned Twickenham, Southall and Riverside Studios) were Trevor Howard, Sally Gray and Griffiths Jones. About half way through the making of the film they decided to re-title it to *They Made Me a Fugitive* – a subtle, more dramatic, change. My wardrobe for the film consisted of dirty trousers, jacket, a roll neck sweater and an old soiled raincoat. I myself looked like a "fugitive" but that part was played by Trevor Howard; he was the man on the run and an up-and-coming star – he'd already done the brilliantly received *Brief Encounter* - who was later to become one of the best leading character actors in the business. The *Third Man* was soon to be his rocket to stardom. He was a nice bloke – matey, congenial and mad about cricket – his interest in the latter giving him a big plus in my estimation.

Griffith Jones, playing the lead criminal Narsy (short for Narcissus) was very pleasant too – a nervous, shy man who gave me the impression of being highly strung; nevertheless he was easy to get on with. He'd been the Earl of Salisbury in Olivier's *Henry V*, and had been in many stage shows in the 30s. He was on the verge of an excellent career. I'm not surprised. He was really good. His character in this was really narsy. He had an extremeley credible London accent, despite being very well spoken indeed. And he was such a nice chap! Ah! It's called acting!

Sally Gray was wonderfully glamorous. She'd worked before the war in several films with Stanley Lupino, including his *Lambeth Walk* movie of the musical and was just becoming a huge sultry star and offered a contract to go to the States with R.K.O., but got married to a Baron instead and retired! His Lordship's gain was cinema's loss. I thought she was fabulous. I had one gang group scene with her after she's been kidnapped. She was in *Obsession,* a film I was in in 1949.

The gang consisted of Jack McNaughton, (we were to be in *Trent's Last Case* together. And also fellow cricketers when I first played for the Stage Cricket Club), Cyril Smith, (we were both in *The Steel Key*) John Penrose, (in *Kind Hearts and Coronets* as Lionel) Michael Brennan, (our paths crossed a lot, especially on T.V. and a gripping scene in *Tale of Two Cities*) Charles Farrell (subsequently voicing fairytales on *Childrens' Hour* on radio) and myself. The over-seer of these dubious villains in the film was played by that delightful lady and charismatic actress Mary Merrall (she was later Mrs. Nickleby in Cav's *Nicholas Nickleby)* playing the gang's sort of "co-ordinator" in a quirky northern cum posh accent. Sensing my insecurity - it was a top feature this was, with a top cast and director and to be frank, despite my blooding in *Captive Heart,* I was a bit nervous - she took me under her wing, both in and out of the film, and we had several "nips" in her dressing room and at the bar in the Chancellors pub just across the street in Crisp Road. She had a fund of amusing stories which she recounted with her droll sense of fun.

"Be careful if working with Robert Morley" she told me.

(I would do so in several films in the next few years. He was indeed a character).

"He'll upstage you the moment he comes on. He's so competitive. Very funny and lovely amidst it all. I wouldn't let him upstage me. I pinched him on the bottom the moment he tried anything. He'd yelp mid sentence. And by the way Sammy, apropos that very same thing. You're a sensitive chap. Don't let these other actors bully you. Stand up for yourself all the time. Some of them would take the food from out of your mouth as soon as look at you –

wouldn't you dear?"

She would address the last remark to one of her unfavourite actors who happened to be near at the time.

"What's that dear?" he would say not having heard.

"I was just saying how good you can be my dear, and warning my friend Sam to look out when he was playing the scene with you, because you're liable to overlap him. This is for the good of the scene, of course!"

Then we would all laugh, including the maligned actor who was not quite sure what was going on. She did have a point.

I was the junior there. And everyone knew each other. And I didn't know any of them. And some were bit stand-offish.

I had a few lines and I really did feel the pressure to get them said before someone would say theirs. It was all slightly intimidating, as Mary was alluding to. Even my "Hello" to Michael Brennan as he snatches my cigarette, had to be said at pace or Michael was in snatching. As was my, "It's not as much of a risk as leaving it in the Valhalla" talking about the chances of the police possibly finding the contraband whisky in the office or in the warehouse. You try saying that quickly in a cockney accent and being understood.

But my other line was the worst, said in the midst of intense dialogue. I still have nightmares about it to this day. It was difficult enough remembering it, let alone saying it without gabbling, with all the actors around me picking up the cues and "overlapping me".

"Yes. And only have her goin' squealin' to every blasted copper she sees."

This line concerned one of the gang member's girlfriends, who we had crying in front of us, pleading for her life, who we were sure, if we let her go, was going to tell the police we were out to kill her boyfriend, Soapy.

This line was a tongue twister amongst tongue twisters. You say it. And make it clear and audible at high speed.

"Yes. And only have her goin' squealin' to every blasted copper she sees."

Exactly. This line has become a tick. Even now, I can be frying bacon and egg and I'll suddenly find myself saying that line. I'll be tying my shoe laces and it'll pop into my head. I can be daydreaming in the car and ..bam..there it is. It was traumatic.

"Yusnowneeeavergawnsqueelytarevweeblustycawpersharzeez". That's how I said it.

Cav suggested after the first long take.

"Zam I theek you need to be clearer with the squealy line." which was a tactful understatement. So the pressure…gulp… was on. In the second take, as with every take, all my other lines were fine; but the "squealy" line crashed into my cue. The third I got it right, but it was probably unintelligible and anyway there'd been a lighting problem and we went again. The fourth I was slow and spoken over (Mary was right) and although not my fault, the Second did that thing of coming over and showing me the line in the script, which was (and is) a bit embarrassing.

"This is your line."

Of course it was. Who else's was it? And then (oh my Gawd) he said it to me as if I had never seen it before:

"Yes…. An… only… have… her… goin… squealin'… to… every… blasted… copper… she… sees."

"Thanks" I said. While wanting to crawl under a carpet and just lie there. And be stepped on. And then he added, "And the cue is "She can cause us problems". Yes? "She…. can…. cause…. us…. problems?".

This was said as if English was a language I'd only been studying for a fortnight. I wanted to say, "Yes for goodness sake. I know it. I know it. I've just got a bit of a complex about the whole scene."

But of course I didn't. I just nodded. And said, "Thanks" once more.

The fifth take was fine (well I didn't fluff), and is the one that was used; and if you watch the scene, there's a kind of blind concentrated panic in my face as I leap in to say the line, enunciating, but trying to stay calm and making sense. I'm not in fact acting, I'm saving my career. And then I had the line, "An' walk smack into 'em?" talking about Curly, a gang member being picked up by the police. Spat out quickly. It's, "Ang-awk-smik-innerem?"

If you listen to me saying the line, you'll see. It is. Very. Spat. But at least I got that in in time. There was no having the Second speak it to me as if I'd just landed on planet earth from a distant galaxy.

But mostly, my part consisted of just sitting there playing cards or standing observing, and on one occasion, handing Griffith my knuckle duster and then my gun. Interestingly, my role in the piece was that of someone who always stayed behind looking after Aggie, Mary's character. And my status amongst the cast was consequently slightly that of an actor with a lesser part. Anyway that's what my inferiority complex told me. And the fact that despite being in a large amount of the film, I didn't get a credit, didn't help either.

I remember that Mary had a "running gag" where she always requested that any illegal deliveries that arrived in the coffins (that's how they moved the black market goods about) she should get a slice of, to give to her boyfriend. ("Keep about twenty bottles for me. My boyfriend drinks like a fish.")

There was something slightly lascivious about her mentioning this boyfriend with his taste in food, booze and cigarettes as she was a supposedly genteel woman in her sixties. The lines that stuck in my mind were, "Limpy's on the phone....la la la la la la" (she sang a little tune while crossing from the stairs). Narsy... He wants some New Zealand mutton. My boyfriend loves mutton. Keep me some."

And for some unknown reason I have never forgotten them or her. She made such an impression on me. She was delightful and idiosyncratic and supportive and it was early in my career. She said these lines in such an amusing way, expertly getting a laugh from nothing, which I love. Consequently every time I hear the word "mutton", which isn't often these days (well there's not much call for it, is there?) I think of those lines and her.

One day during the shooting we were all together on the set and just about to embark on a scene, when a huge arc lamp, aptly known as a "brute", came hurtling down from the gantry and nearly decapitated Griffith Jones in the process. It was a terrifying moment. Filming was halted for some time while all the lights and lamps and cradles were checked. Griffith, bless him, had a couple of stiff brandies and offered to continue immediately. But I think the enforced intermission, despite his altruistic and professional desire not to halt the filming, did him a load of good. For the rest of the film though, he was perpetually looking up at the gantry. Though I noticed he was less concerned about it whilst embracing the delectable Sally Gray.

The film company generously decided to hold an end of film Ball for the whole unit, so it was arranged that all the actors, the technicians and the studio staff, with their other halves, dancing partners, etc. would be invited to Hammersmith Town Hall, just up the road from the studios at Riverside, for a shindig. It was held on a Friday evening and the bar was doubly stacked up. On getting there I danced a little. It was Joe Loss! A top notch band! And at first, drank a little.

"Yes I don't drink much. It's just a small one!"

And dipped in and out of the overflowing buffet. There were egg and cress sandwiches! And mini sausages! And those prawn wotsits in pastry! And I danced some more and drank even more, and helped myself to the pork pies! And generally swanned around, as you do. I had hoped to invite the continuity girl, Shirley Barnes, who was a terribly efficient and not bad looking young lady, but she had previously been spoken for by the camera operator. I won't say that I didn't have designs on her, but I certainly never attempted anything, and any thoughts that 1 may have had in that direction were soon quashed by the fact that she had brought her sister along to the dance, and my fate, as they say, was sealed. And so was hers, come to that – poor girl! Though we didn't become an item immediately. We dated on and off. Sometimes more off than on! Shirley's sister's nickname was "Pinkie", which stemmed from the fact that as a baby she was pink all over and it's still the case! Well not entirely all over.

Soft cream with a dash of pink really! She was a big shot in table tennis, having played for both Surrey and England and was the winner of many championships. She was ultimately the World 1949 Womens' Doubles Final Runner-Up and Champion of the Netherlands amongst other honours. During the war she'd given exhibitions all over with Peggy Franks. They were billed as the Blond Bombshell and the Black Beauty! Pinkie, being black haired, was the latter. She worked as a copywriter in advertising, one of the first females to do this job in England and I liked her vivacity, her lovely eyes and her firm hand clasp. (All those table tennis bats!). She'd worked at one time as secretary to R.H.Naylor the Astrologist, and regularly attended the London Spiritualist Alliance in South Kensington. She had a flair for palmistry, inherited from her mother, and was intensely interested in it. In fact she was so good at it, people would get annoyed with her insights.

"Who told you about my health / love-life / financial arrangements?"

Was an often angry cry when she'd come up with an intimate detail that she'd spotted in someone's hand that the owner of the hand considered too personal.

She was also partial to ex service men - Army, not Civil Service! She had been pursued for some time by an officer who had subsequently gone abroad and fallen in love with a nurse, so she was now fancy free. After about the thirteenth dance, including several "Gentlemen's Excuse Me's", one "Lambeth Walk", one "Palais Glide' and a couple of "Paul Jones's", we repaired to the bar for the umpteenth scotch. I told her I was an Aquarian: a whisky and water man, and she took my hand and started to read my palm. She smelt like Chanel number five mixed with Teachers whisky! And the Teacher's was just me! She had a great sense of humour which I found hugely attractive.

"It's all there in your palm" she said, gypsy-like, outlining my right hand with her finger as she spoke, and it tickled!

"An eventful life. And a successful one. I see good fortune for you. You have a great deal of energy, your Mound of Venus is well-developed."

(My what?) She squeezed it as she pointed it out. It's that fleshy bit below your thumb. She examined my fingers.

"Your fate line is excellent. You will have a long and happy life, provided you end up with the right partner."

How could she tell all that? I squinted and almost fell off the chair.

"You must take care of your lungs" she said "or you will suffer in later life".

She must have seen the tobacco stains on my fingers. But she was on target – I've had to stop smoking! I asked for her phone number and said I would call to arrange a date. I later learned from her that she took pity on me because:

a) I looked so emaciated and forlorn

b) She was captivated by my large green Irish eyes (she meant bloodshot) and…

c) I had been five years as a P.O.W. (There's a pattern here. My having been a prisoner did create an enormous amount of sympathy.) As the hand reading session went on, I was rapidly beginning to see two of her, and the annex after time, seemed to float and swim around in astrological circles. In short, or should I say in doubles, I was drunk! I withdrew my hand, bade my pretty palmist and everyone else a "Fugitives" farewell and hurried shakily and woozily into the cold night. A car had thoughtfully been provided by the company for drunks such as I, and in no time at all I was whisked to Chiswick (which fortunately is not far from Hammersmith as we know) fell up the stairs at Fairfax Road and was soon dribbling on my pillow.

When *They Made Me a Fugitive* was finished, I almost became one myself. There was no work on the horizon, not even any post syncing from Ealing, although I constantly phoned them to enquire whether they needed me. When I think back, I had a lot of cheek in those days. In a peculiar way though, because they had taken me to their bosom, as it were, I thought I was something special to them, to be cared for and be responsible for – after all they had introduced me to this celluloid society, and ignited the spark and fanned the flames of my burning ambition with *The Captive Heart*. What a load of rubbish. I must've been a bloody nuisance to them. But they never demurred, always finding time for me and making me feel wanted. I was shattered when some years later the Ealing Studios were disbanded, having been bought by the B.B.C.. As far as I knew I was the only ex-prisoner of war of the original technical-advisors-dogsbodies from Ealing who had Thespian aspirations, but I found out later that Paul Hardwick, Donald Tandy and George Carr had soldiered on. Paul got a job with the Old Vic and was in the film *Night to Remember*. Don was working as an actor - he was in *Chance of a Lifetime* in 1950 that I was also in - and George was writing scripts and plays. And Steve Smith? My big P.O.W. pal? "Knut Knudsen" who never was? He'd given up. And had gone to the States. We lost touch. Which I regret. We'd been through the mill together.

As an A.O.O.W. (actor out of work. It's not an official title. I've just made that up) you cling to the possibility of something that's been "mooted", coming off. So I was still half hoping for the reappearance of the attractive Middle East tour. But after a few unproductive phone calls, there was clearly no sign of it taking place, now, or in the foreseeable future. I therefore settled for a two or three weeks holiday (well not a holiday really, just mooching about and a few days in Margate) and then half-heartedly recommenced the dismal round of fruitless wandering to various "favourite" agents - the ones with nice receptionists who would be pleasant and not dismissive.

Once in the midst of this unceasing circle of disappointment, I came to a terrible conclusion. In fact it was the Prophet of Doom, perched on my shoulder, lisping seductively in my ear, who came to the conclusion: Nobody wanted me and that I would never work as an actor again. After a cash seeking appearance at the Labour Exchange, I took a bus to Hammersmith and haphazardly pootling about, thinking dark thoughts, called in at the public library in the

Shepherd's Bush Road, which is opposite the Hammersmith Palais, and after a visit to the Gents (which had been my real reason for going in there) repaired to the reading room for a leisurely look through the newspapers and magazines, to seek an alternative career that did not include sheets or divans. The library reading room was always so crowded you almost had to queue up for your favourite paper or magazine. I gave up my desire to read the Mirror as it was spoken for, and wandered idly through the Melody Maker, published mainly for musicians, and by utter fluke came upon an advertisement for Oscar Rabin's Band (Supplementary Band.).

"Apply Cambridge Circus now" it said.

Ah. Dear old Oscar. He was a great guy. A kind, considerate and generous man. The advert brought back good memories. I had been employed by Oscar in 1938/39 after he'd seen me in a Talent Contest, as a member of his "Hotshots", which included vocalist Gary Cowan (known for "My Prayer"), scat singer Billy Nichols ("Hold Tight! Voodle ee acky sacky!") and the incomparable and much sought after Beryl Davis. I loved her singing "I'm Waiting for Ships that Never Come in" and used to be in complete awe of her talent. She'd sung with Glenn Miller during the war and eventually found even more fame in the U.S.A. singing with Frank Sinatra on *Your Hit Parade* the huge radio show. In 1938 I'd toured, (Bud Flanagan was the top of the bill. He was a nice encouraging man) and in 1939 I had compered and told jokes in front of "Oscar Rabin's Broadcasting Band" - on radio at the Golder's Green Hippodrome and elsewhere - and at the Palais. And also M.C.'d the resident band at *Scarborough Scala Land*, which was a cross between a seaside concert party and a Pin Table arcade: 3 o'clock till 5.30 and 7 o'clock till 9.30 p.m. which meant two sessions daily (except Sunday). Nice work if you can last out! But as it happened we didn't have to. We got peremptorily closed down by the threat of Adolf Hitler and his Hotshots. Whilst in prison camp I had written to Oscar to let him know of my change of address and "circumstances" and to see if he could arrange for any music to be sent out for the camp orchestras —

dance, light, or otherwise. Needless to say, he rose to the occasion and a thick envelope of dots duly arrived! At that time Oscar lived in a pleasant house in Dewhurst Road, which is just up the road from the Palais, with his wife and three sons, Bernard, Ivor, and David. I had okkey-cokeyed and cut a rug many a time at the Palais as a member of the audience, as well as performing there, so it was a sort of home from home. He was like a father figure and advisor to me – he advised and I figured out if it was worth it! Having seen the advertisement, I decided to call in at their office. Two days later I found myself in Cambridge Circus where the agency was situated. I climbed two flights of stairs and announced my identity to the neatly coiffured receptionist.

"Sam 'oo?" she asked.

"Sam Kydd…Kydd with a Y" I replied.

"Oh, I see" she squeaked – but I'm not sure that she did. She disappeared behind a partition and I could hear her spelling it out.

"There's a man called Kiddy. Sam Kiddy. K-I-D-D-Y. He's very thin!"

Almost before she'd finished I was snowed under by Bernard and Ivor and David who welcomed me with open arms. It was like the return of the Prodigal son.

"Sam, Sam, Sam you mensch! When did you get back?"

"Why didn't you come and see us sooner?"

"Bloody hell, Dad will be pleased to see you. He's never stopped talking about you!"

"Oh Sammy. It's so good to see you!"

I sipped tea, ate mounds of biscuits, and bit off more than I could chew with the ginger cake.

"Go on – eat up" said Bernard. "You look like a bag of bones in a glue factory. Have as much ginger cake as you like. We've got another."

Jewish people can be so warm and swamp you with kindness. I love 'em. I sat back and wallowed in their cosseting and questions. They were most interested in my P.O.W. experiences and I gave them a short resume of my life since 1940, addressing myself mostly to Bernard with whom I'd been associated in Scarborough in 1939. David and Ivor were new to me but I obviously wasn't unknown to them – the "old man" must've talked about me a hell of a lot.

"Some geezer from your regiment, the K.R.R.s, told Oscar that he'd seen you blown up at Calais Station. Dad was in two minds whether to tell your mother or not". (Luckily he didn't tell her. She'd received a card saying I was missing in action as it was and this would have pushed her over the edge.)

"And he was so delighted when he had a letter from you asking for some music to be sent out, that he never stopped talking about it!"

I told them of my acting career and how it had temporarily stumbled to a halt, and of my hopes and fears. The telephone rang and David answered, putting on his brisk business manner.

"As long as we get a percentage, it's okay! Okay?"

There was a short silence after he replaced the receiver and then Bernard said

"I've been thinking Sammy. How would you feel about working for us?"

"Oh that sounds interesting" I said, sounding interested.

"In what capacity?" I queried.

"Well, you know we're maybe opening a new ballroom soon not far from town?"

(I didn't know, but I nodded sagely).

"The details haven't been finalised yet, but we will need a new trustworthy manager, like yourself. To look after things." (I'd told them about being an A.S.M. and money man in Germany and Skeggy).

"Well, yes of course. It sounds interesting," I said repeating myself. And added "But I don't know anything about managing a dance hall."

"Oh there's nothing to it" he said, "I'll take you along to Wimbledon Palais (they owned it) and you can see how easy it is."

"It's very kind of you" I replied "but in all honesty I'm really not (careful Sam, don't sound ungrateful) er…sure I'd be any good?"

"Tell me after you've seen the Wimbledon setup."

I thought a moment and then said, "On the understanding that it would only be a stop-gap until something big comes along, (I like that. "Till something big comes along" – how hoity-toity is that! What a swank!) I wouldn't mind having a go. What's the money situation?"

"About a tenner a week. No, just because it's you, maybe 12 quid a week and then we can take our commission, 10%."

"What?!" I spluttered into my slice of ginger cake.

"Well, all right. In your case I'll waive it. You'd be responsible for the takings, publicity, the band salary (They'd be on a percentage) and our public relations representative. Think it over and then come and see us next week – if it's confirmed."

We shook hands on it and I tucked in to more cake before realising I hadn't seen their father.

"Er. Can I see your father?" I asked.

"He's not here! He's at home today. We phoned him. He wants you to come over for dinner in the week. He's so looking forward to seeing you."

I went, and was royally entertained. Thanks so much Oscar.

FOUR
Southend Shenanigans

The Palace Hotel Southend, had been purchased by impresario Prince Littler, and the ballroom, which was originally part of the hotel, was to be turned into a money-making concern, with dancing every night. I went to Wimbledon with Bernard for a shufty of the set-up there and of course was hugely impressed. The band were cooking and the joint was jumping. Before I finally accepted, I took a swift train to Southend to "'ave a butcher's", and find out if there were any snags! Southend was a very popular seaside resort in an era where people all holidayed in Great Britain. Crowds of people went past the hotel, down the slight hill, on their way to the Kursaal, the well-known amusement and fairground complex, which for me, was not exactly virgin territory. I'd been known to stumble down the hill in my teens and early twenties. On the Esplanade between the hill and the Kursaal, there were a multitude of public houses and whelks stalls dotted about the promenade. And on Saturdays and holidays, there was music and dancing in the streets, (the Palace Hotel didn't have the monopoly) of the "knees up mother brown whoops I've had too many argh I've fallen over" variety. The hotel at that time seemed to be from a different era: genteel and very English, their afternoon teas being typical, with their cucumber sandwiches and strawberries and cream. They had had a regular clientele who visited them for years up to the outbreak of war, but during the 1939/40 crisis, it was, I was told, off-limits to all except the troops. While I was there, it was never more than half-full and some customers were residents on special terms, as I was later to be. Coincidentally, someone who I'd met at Butlin's Skegness was permanently installed at the Palace Hotel; he was a fellow artiste named Vincent Tyldesley who as well as acting, organised and produced a vocal act called the Mastersingers. I think there were about eight of them and they were originally part of the John Watt bill at Butlin's theatre. Vincent's mother and father lived permanently at the Palace Hotel and his father the Very Rev. Robert Tyldesley, who had retired from being a Vicar, was extremely kind to me, inviting me in regularly for tea. He was a very jocular man, easy to get along with, who had a fund of amusing anecdotes to tell, which originally appeared in the Church Times about his time as a Reverend. Like his having to reprimand a member of the congregation who regularly wrote the names of horses in the back of the prayer book.

"I know you may not find my sermons of much interest but I'd rather not believe that you were thinking more about the two thirty at Uttoxter, than He who is the chief jockey of us all. But interestingly the verger put a small bet on one of them and won £1. 2s 6d so not all is bad."

And…

"The man who wrote that the graveyard will be closed all next week for stock taking, in chalk on the church wall, was amusing, but possibly not going down too well with Him Upstairs."

His knowledge of ridiculous Church parish notices was marvellous. He reeled them off at will:

"The church ladies have cast off clothing of every sort and they may be seen in the crypt on Friday."

"The Reverend John Root came up with a snappy new slogan for those wishing to donate: "I Upped My Donation - Up Yours.""

"Our new Vicar is to be the Reverend Henry Green. We could not get a better man." Etc. etc..

I suggested he should have been a comedian! He was a brilliant person to discuss philosophical questions about life. My religious beliefs were in turmoil since the war, but having been brought up as a practicing Christian and a choirboy at St. Stephens Church in Lancaster Gate, I was always willing to listen to a man of the cloth and The Very Rev. Robert was a wise one. The amount of death despair and deprivation I had experienced during the war had effectively played havoc with my Faith, but he listened to my reasoning with great sympathy and never lectured me. His help was wonderful. But I was still "Confused" of Chiswick.

The ballroom was built onto the hotel and had been used for Palm Court type concerts, plus monthly "Old Tyme and Ladies Invitation Dances" – none of the modern "Big Apple" jiving stuff left over by the Yanks! I enquired of the hotel manager whether I would be given a special concession for staying at the hotel while I was working there and was told that it could be arranged providing I "played my cards right" whatever that was supposed to mean. I never did find out. I liked the phrase though! So when the following week David Rabin confirmed that the deal was on and I was to get £12 per week, with the amicably veiled warning that I wasn't to try to fiddle any extras, I replied indignantly that nothing was further from my thoughts and that I intended to "play my cards right"!

"What's that supposed to mean?" said the hard man, David.

"Never you mind" replied his new employee, putting on the indignant face used for fooling the Germans.

"But I never thought that you would accuse me… a friend of your father's, an ex P.O.W. who has just returned from five years suffering in the wilderness… of trying to bite the hand that feeds one!"

I said slightly incorrectly. David clapped sarcastically.

"Regardless of what sob story you present me with (ouch!) I have business interests to protect" he said and then, "We know all about your suffering – just watch it!"

Blimey! This side of him wasn't very nice! Before then nothing like that had entered my kleptomaniacal head. But David having sown the seed and been so confrontational, prompted me to look around to see who, or what, I could financially exploit!

After I'd been installed for a week or two at the hotel and had at first made daily and then weekly reports, Bernard and David came down to see me and having scrutinised what I was up to and being satisfied I wasn't "biting the hand that fed one", and was indeed "playing my cards right" pronounced themselves satisfied with "Operation Dance Hall, Southend." Thus another branch of the Rabin Empire had been successfully launched!

I had to engage two part-time cashiers for the ballroom, and someone as a sort of assistant to do jobs for me. I went through an interview process via an agency and spent far too much time chatting to the few that applied, mostly about their war experiences, which I really enjoyed. Some of them had had stressful times like a lot of us. So that was the cashiers sorted. The job of the Assistant was easily filled. A chap named Benjamin Downe, a small mild-mannered man with an infectious giggle who'd been in Tobruk, and was once upon a time a knife thrower in the circus, stood out. Well, only he and a man with a dreadful cough turned up for the interview. The man with the cough was clearly so ill I didn't dare take him on and suggested he go and see a doctor as soon as possible. So Benjamin got it. Benjamin's job amongst others, was to take tickets at the door, issue pass-out vouchers to the people returning from the lavatories, which were next door in the hotel, move beer barrels, (with help of course. The barrels were bigger than him) do filing etc. etc. and just generally help me out. He was known to all and sundry, obviously, being about five foot one, as "Big Ben". On Gala nights, usually Fridays and Saturdays but sometimes Thursdays, (this was a strange tradition as nowhere near as many people came on the Thursday) it was practically impossible to deal with the exodus and return of lavatory users. Even Mick McManus the I.T.V. wrestler would have had trouble grappling with this feverish crowd, girls as well as blokes! As the lavatories were part of the hotel, a favourite ploy perpetrated by those who wished to avoid buying tickets in the normal way, would be to come in through the exit door pretending they had lost their pass-out vouchers which were being issued to them by the aforementioned tiny Benjamin. This also was the favourite gimmick of the Greyhound racetrack gangs who patronised the bars at the hotel. Dealing with them could be quite daunting. More about this later.

One of my chores was to check on all the posters advertising the various popular dance bands who each appeared for just one week. We had some terrific line ups: Oscar's band of course, Eric Robinson, (later to be musical director of the *Eurovision Song Contest*) with the Brew Rockets, Harry Parry, (star of the B.B.C.'s Radio Rhythm Club) Joe Loss (one of the greats of the big band era) and the celebrated Squadronnaires (The Royal Air Force Dance Orchestra), who would be performing in the ballroom.

I also had to check on the content of the poster and design it, (with the help of the printer who knew about these things) fork out for the usual sites the posters would be on, and insert adverts in the local daily and weekly papers. I was asked in a whisper by Bernard (as if someone would be listening!) to look around for some "pirate" sites, such as windows of shops which were unoccupied, or put them up in public conveniences.

"You've got a captive audience there and good footfall" he said bewilderingly as I couldn't see how they'd stick to the tiles. "Put up as many as you can" said Bernard "without having to pay for the space!"

To the uninitiated this is called "fly-posting". It was my task to go cycling around with a bucket of paste and a dollopy paintbrush, plus the all important and informative posters. Large trees were the favourite targets, preferably situated in Mablethorpe and Westcliff on Sea, on the outskirts of Southend. At first I approached the job with enthusiastic anticipation, having admired poster pasters ever since I was a small boy. The way they slapped on the paste and expertly flapped on the halves and quarters of the posters had always fascinated me. However, after two or three days of cycling with a full bucket of paste precariously swinging to and fro on the handlebars (which frequently found itself on my person) and pasting on unreceptive trees – cycling and pasting, pasting and cycling – on the fences, on the walls, even on the pavement when I dropped the poster, it all got a bit unrewarding and in the end I hated the sight of bloody posters. If you add to this the fact that my exquisite handiwork was completely wasted (Benjamin occasionally accompanied me and was very encouraging about my poster pasting skills) because some interloper, probably from the council, systematically followed my trail, tearing them down and desecrating those that he couldn't remove, you can see why it was a job to get fed up with! I was also responsible for the distribution of publicity cards, detailing our weekly activities, to places like the Castle and the Greyhound track or any other area of entertainment where the world and his wife gathered. The establishments were happy to have them displayed or left in piles on bars or at restaurant entrances. In addition I employed two men with sandwich boards who also handed out free admission tickets and tokens for the odd pint of bitter. This worked quite well. And was all my idea! Though I didn't get any credit for it. Once or twice I was sorely tempted to tell Bernard where he could stick my dollopy paintbrush! But my good nature prevailed and I carried on.

The copy on everything was simple:

> "At the Palace Ballroom.
> Oscar Rabin Enterprises present,
> For One Week Only:
> (Insert name of band here)"

Each night after the money had been counted it was entrusted to the hotel safe by Sidney Smith, who after checking and rechecking, gave me a receipt. Sydney had been a manager for Stoll theatres, and was now principally Prince Littler's general manager. (Prince Littler the impresario, owned the ballroom. The Rabins leased it.) He was an agreeable, good-natured man and luckily for me, pretty unflappable. His wife Betty was also very friendly and helpful; what's more, she always laughed at my jokes which was good for my ego and my morale! They had both been associated with show business for a long time (Mrs. Smith was originally a dancer) and to use an Irish expression were "good value". And they both had a fund of rude stories about the profession, which I never tired of hearing!

"Now Ivor Novello. What a nice man. Ivor Davies was his real name. Was Welsh! Sydney encountered him and his boyfriend Bobbie a lot. They occasionally "dragged up" you know. Made good women. Very funny of course. But too much stubble! We had the good fortune of working with Nolly Coward. A potty mouth. Never stopped swearing. Huge use of the 'c' word. But a very funny man. A genius you know. Would burst into song and be brilliant. Once said of an actress "she wouldn't get a laugh if she came on with a haddock dangling from her fanny."

I suggested they write a book.

"Oh no. We couldn't. We'd be giving away their secrets."

"Nobody would believe us. And anyway we'd be done for libel!"

As each band was on a percentage, it was my job every Saturday night to calculate what to pay them from the profits.

I had to neatly type it all out with daily details and then write out and sign the cheque and finally hand it to the manager of the band concerned. At first I approached this part of my work with apprehension but with the help of Sydney and a Ready Reckoner - calculators were in their infancy and as big as a house - my fears were finally put to rest. In the end I became quite efficient and computer-like, much to Sydney's astonishment. When he first helped me he had that slightly "leave–this–to–me–the–man's–an-idiot" look about his visage, but towards the end of our acquaintance it changed to more of a "not–a–bad–pupil–after–all–see–what–you– can–do–if–you–try-I-never-thought-it-would-happen-but-he's-actually-quite-good" look!

I was advised by the Rabins to split up the various evenings into "Speciality" nights – for instance, "Ladies night" on Tuesday, "Holiday night" on Thursday, "Late-night" on Friday and "Anybody's night" on Saturday. I made occasional announcements from the stage in front of the band, such as, "There will be an Adam and Eve Ball at 7:30 p.m. on Friday the 13th. Leaves off at 1 a.m.."

Or…

"Come to the Palace ballroom. Clean and decent dancing every night. Except Sunday."

From June onwards the venture improved with rapid progression and by the time we reached August it was a sell-out!

My being attached to the hotel (if only temporarily) had a number of advantages. After all, it was only two years since war had ceased; rationing and utility goods were still with us and looked as if they would be for some time, so living in the hotel at a reduced rate suited me admirably. Added to which there was a considerable amount of female pulchritude around, all very pleasant and good to look upon. One such, whom I shall call Celia, was a receptionist who was the perfect cheeky cockney sparrow. If she was up for a film you'd cast her as that. About five foot two with brown feathers and a beak. She flirted outrageously with all the men and in so doing obviously got her own way with most things – without any danger to herself! Like myself, most of the girls I fancied lived in the hotel and at the close of the evening dancing activities, I always went to the restaurant where a cold supper had been left out for me. Usually I was joined by Celia, on late reception duty, whose intention was to satisfy the inner woman – to start with. We ate together until our appetites had been assuaged and then we got to know each other a little bit better. We indulged in a snogging session, mostly light-hearted kissing and cuddling (can it ever be heavyhearted? - perhaps when you've got indigestion or stomach ache!) At that time in history the "pill" was unknown and unheard of (though no doubt being tested somewhere - but certainly not at the Palace Hotel), so favours were not so fully and freely given. In other words one had to fight for it and finally I gave up! She unfortunately didn't– at least not to me. One late evening when I was too occupied (counting the money) to meet her, she drank more wine than she should have in the company of another, and thereafter threw all precautions to the wind, to the benefit of the new assistant manager who suddenly found it was "All systems go". Later the local doctor confirmed her worst fears. She had fallen! Once again the ethics of the age frowned upon such "out of wedlock" activity and she and he were swiftly married!

Another one I was rather taken with was Pam Pam, a dark haired curvaceous waitress who lived in a flat flat not far far from the hotel hotel and made made steak steak for late late supper supper to keep up my strength.

There was also a strange mannish Amazonian woman called Stella who regularly came to the Thursday night dances and sometimes would weirdly dance on her own. She was initially tentative, just saying 'hello" and "it's me again" but then one evening had clearly had too much to drink, as she wandered up to me in the bar and said, "Sammy." (she'd found out my name). "I've been observing you."

"Oh yes?" I replied wondering if she'd been sent down by the Rabins as a sort of job-checker. But no.

"I want you to bend me to your will. Force me. Make me give in…."

Luckily Big Ben came over and asked me to help him in the cellar and I was able to flee before my will was tested.

For a short period in August the management tried out "Thé Dansant", tea dances being very popular before the war, (you essentially danced at about four o'clock. Tea time. And had "tea") and at first it looked as though it might succeed. Due to rationing, the 'tea' for each person was a salmon and shrimp paste sandwich cut into four pieces, one piece of Swiss roll, and a stale fairy cake with a cherry on top. Plus one very small cup of tea, with of course extra hot water, milk and barely enough sugar to cover a dancer's toenail! The physical effort involved in organising these afternoon jollities, coupled with the little financial return, finally put paid to the venture and it was withdrawn. The gig band engaged for the tea dancing had helped to put the mockers on it. They virtually had a tea break between each number and actually consumed more sandwiches and fairy cakes than the paying customers. They were worse than out of work actors, renowned for their guzzling ability, (they never know where their next meal's coming from) and that's saying something!

"Must be the sea air" I said to Sydney Smith when he remarked on it. Anyway the axe was introduced and that was that. The evening dancing, however, continued to flourish and David asked me if I was prepared to be resident manager right through the winter. Undecided and not knowing what the future was to bring (can anyone be certain?) I answered yes, providing my salary was increased.

"Oi wait a minute" said David.

"You will have less work to do in the winter with a much smaller residential band, and apart from weekends you'll be able to bolster your income in some other way by working in radio or as a male model on Mondays Tuesdays and Wednesdays."

A male model? I hadn't thought of that! Though I wasn't convinced anybody would want this emaciated frame to be modelling anything! I could certainly do a "before" in a "before and after" sequence in a "You don't want to look like this when you could look like this" advert. I'd be the one who had sand kicked in his face! David made it sound so easy. He was being helpful wasn't he??? As things turned out, he was eerily right and I did get some "still" work as opposed to the film "moving" work. That is, a continuing photographic sequential advertisement campaign! I was phoned by one of the agents who had remembered me for being so thin, and sent off to meet the producers of the campaign at the Ministry of Information.

"Bloody hell!" blurted out one of the young "creatives".

"You're absolutely perfect! You look really ill!"

It was about tuberculosis.

"WHAT TO DO WHEN YOU GET TB?" was the title. It was a series of thirteen posters. I was in eleven of them. The first one was just a caption. I was John Smith.

Number one: "Caught in Time"
This was just information. No pictures of me as yet.

"About 1000 new cases of T.B. are reported in England and

Wales every week. (Nothing about Scotland and Northern Ireland!) There is a good chance of quick recovery if T.B. is detected early enough: that is why early detection is a vital weapon in the fight against T.B."

Number two: In the second poster, it's me. I'm with the boss who tells me I'm doing well, but I'd better take care of my cough which I put down to smoking. The speech bubbles are saying this:

BOSS: (Spectacled and boss like) "I've got good news for you Smith. We're going to put you in charge of the new department when it's ready next month. You must take care of that cough of yours you know.

ME: (Turning away coughing into my hand) Oh it's nothing much. I think it's the tobacco I've been smoking."

Number three: Going home and greeting the wife who is worried about me despite my promotion:

ME: (Expression deliriously happy.) We'll be able to afford a really good holiday this year Mary! I'm being promoted next month.

MARY: That's wonderful John. But I do wish you'd see a doctor about that cough of yours. It really has gone on too long.

MY GREEDY SON "Will I be able to have a new bicycle daddy?

MY DAUGHTER: Silent

Number four: Photograph of me at the doctor's surgery being scrutinised by a doc with a stethoscope. Expression not particularly upset - in fact a smirk is playing about my lips (why did they choose that photo?) but then I suppose I'm still not diagnosed as ill yet.

DOC: I'm afraid there are one or two things that worry me…A persistent cough like yours can be dangerous if neglected. I should like you to go to the chest clinic and have an X-Ray."

ME: I wish I'd taken my wife's advice and seen you earlier.

Number five: At the chest clinic. The awful truth – photo of me downcast, chatting to X-ray technician, looking at the ghastly dark X-rays of my rib cage. I'm looking rather dapper though!

RADIOGRAPHER: It's very unpleasant news for you, Mr. Smith. But luckily, you've had the good sense to come to us before it has gone very far so you've got a good chance of a quick recovery

ME: Who'd have thought that I had T.B.. This will be a blow to my wife. And as for my job….

Number six: In this one I'm in bed in stripy pyjamas (I could be playing for Brentford in that top) gazing forlornly up at a well - dressed woman with a huge handbag in which she possibly has a cat. She is wearing a large pair of highly inappropriate furry gloves and a nifty beret. She is informing my wife (who's in a rather pretty white blouse) that:

"We're going to treat your husband at home until he can get a bed in a sanatorium. The specialist, your family doctor and I will visit him regularly. You'll see he gets plenty of rest and proper food, won't you? And don't let him worry. He's in good hands."

My wife replies, getting out a gun:

"Eat lead nursey. This is a Colt 45 and we're going to dance into the early hours and drink all the whisky we can lay our hands on. Ha ha ha! Bang!"

No of course she didn't say that. She said:

"Yes nurse. And I'll see that the window is kept open, and I'll keep the children out of the room. They're going to the chest clinic for a check-up tomorrow.

Number seven: Going to hospital (We were ferried to an attractive village Hospital in Kent which was devoted to the care and cure of T.B. patients). Photo of me arriving at the gates of hospital, complete with small suitcase containing my pyjamas, toothpaste, teddy bear etc..

Number eight: Still of me being tucked up in bed by nurse, who was not unlike Tommy Cooper in drag.

Number nine: Temperature and blood pressure being taken. Pale and ill. Made up to look very sickly.

Number ten: Gradually, after treatment, recovering my self assurance. Shot of me walking, striding out in my khaki shorts, with the expression on my face as if the light was beginning to dawn that I was cured.

Number eleven: Still of me leaving hospital, waving farewell to Tommy Cooper and shaking hands with Doctor at gate.

Number twelve: Photos of me returning to the bosom of my family, entering while the children are playing, with a
"Hello, it's me. I'm back" look (just in case they didn't recognise me).
Various reaction shots of family – sickly cheesy grins from kids, half-hearted smile from wife, unsolicited picture of dog baring teeth in affection! (Handler twisting dog's tail).
In the last one, number thirteen, they just had a picture of mass radiography, urging everyone to get an x-ray if the x-ray units visited their area.

I was paid £25 pounds less 10% and every surgery and hospital and London County Council establishment I happened to visit during the next five years, had a poster of me on the wall! People would stop me and say they were pleased I was looking so much better and how were my wife and kids? And did my boy get his bicycle? I was tempted to invent a story of dreadful unhappiness for these people who believed I was indeed John Smith:

"Unfortunately we're no longer together. My wife went off with the radiographer."
And
"Yes, my boy got the bicycle, but sold it to a school friend after he'd got into debt, gambling."

But of course didn't. Coincidentally, years later when I was suffering from a chest infection, it was discovered from my X-rays that I had actually had T.B., no doubt incurred during my incarceration as a P.O.W., but fortunately my lungs had healed. The tell-tale scars on the X-ray photos were an eerie and gloomy sight, not to mention a shattering one! But it made sense as I'd been very poorly on several occasions when I'd been in solitary confinement, in the damp dungeons under the castle moat, sent there for bartering chocolate with Polish farm workers.

On a more serious note, the campaign was hugely successful. The mass X-ray programme created by the Ministry of Health which sent mobile screening units all over the country, caused a large number of the population to be tested for tuberculosis. Before these posters and the mass testing, there had been a sort of stigma attached to having it. It had been considered a "poor person's disease". A poor person in fact who had been living a licentious life (a bit like the way my mother considered actors!). But my character John Smith was middle class and a family man, and he'd caught it. And got cured. So it completely destroyed the stereotype. I was rather proud to have been involved.

FIVE
Greyhound Night

At the Palace Hotel, as I've said, Friday evening was always the Southend greyhounds' race meeting night, and on one particular Friday I needed all my powers to avoid serious injury. The lavatories for use of the ballroom patrons were situated at the end of a wide corridor which lead directly from the hotel bar. Access from the ballroom to these loos was through a small door, at the rear of the ballroom, which was permanently manned by my trusted employee and once upon a time, knife thrower, Benjamin, who religiously handed out passes to those who needed them. To re-enter the dance hall, the permits had to be given back to Benjamin. This simple system worked quite well usually, but on this particular occasion – Greyhound Night – my "Honest Big Ben" had been overwhelmed by a gang of 10 louts who forced their way in, pretending that they had lost their passes. The intruders, all from the Greyhound meeting, had been drinking in the bar to celebrate a successful night's betting on the dogs, but were now loathe to pay the entrance fee to the ballroom. B.B. came to me in a panic and related what had happened. They had threatened to manhandle him if he didn't let them through and although he had protested, he had had to acquiesce through sheer weight of their numbers.

"They just pushed, kept on pushing, and passed by me, Mr. Kydd, without as much as a by your leave. I tried to stop them but it was impossible, just impossible."

He was quite tearful.

"Don't worry" said I. "Leave it to me."

(What a poor innocent fool I was, thinking I could appeal to their better nature). Benjamin followed in my wake, keeping in step as if he were my "shadow, walking down the avenue…."

"That's them, over there" he whispered, pointing to a noisy cigar smoking group near the door. I nodded, advanced and addressed one of them.

"Excuse me", I said. "I'm sorry to bother you".… (I must've been mad. The man was twice the width of a wardrobe) …. "But this gentleman here tells me that you forced your way in without a pass and without paying."

The man I addressed was cracking a joke with his cronies who were all Superman size and bursting out of their jazzy broad check suits. He turned and looked down at me from his great height, saying, "Are you talking to me, shitface?"

I soldiered on…. "I understand..(GULP).. I understand that you and your friends came in without showing your passes?"

(I was rapidly beginning to feel that it was all a mistake and I should've forgotten the whole thing.)

"Ow yuss?" he replied. Then to his mates "Did you 'ear that?.. "I understand... I understand…" (Mimicking my voice in a very whiny version) "This prick of a penguin" (I was wearing my dinner jacket and black bowtie) "sez as 'ow we didn't show our passes!"

"You don't say!" said one of his pals. "Well, tell him to eff off, old boy!"

Whereupon Wardrobe Man turned to me and said very loudly and precisely

"My friend tole me to tell you to f*ck off!"

"Now listen" I said, foolishly putting up a restraining hand "that's enough of that language. There are ladies present, you know!"

He towered above me, speaking in a little mincing voice, once more pretending to sound like me. I was tempted to say "that sounds nothing like me", but the moment passed.

"Ooh! There are ladies present, yew knaow!" And then "Well show us the f*cking ladies!"

This elicited big guffaws from his mates, especially when he thrust at me with his not inconsiderable belly so that I fell back a pace.

"Now, please, please" I protested weakly, becoming acutely aware that I was rapidly approaching the point of no return.

"Neeow please, <u>please</u>" he mimicked again and did the quick action replay of the barging belly bit. I cannoned into little Ben who was cowering behind me.

"Look we don't want any trouble" I said in a supplicating voice. Actually, supplicating is wrong. Now I was whining.

"Please. Please."

I again foolishly put up my hand as if to ward him off but I didn't touch him. I wouldn't have dared! He ran into me.

"Jus' a minute" said the deep menacing voice behind me. It certainly wasn't Ben.

"Jus' a f*ckin' minute! I saw that!"

"What? Saw what?" I asked, bewildered, half turning.

"You! 'Avin' a go at my friend, that's what!"

"Me, 'avin'... I mean.... having a go? Me?"

"You're not gonna stand for that are you, 'Arry?"

"I certainly am f*cking not."

Now it was like some mad inescapable nightmare. If only I could wake up and find myself in room 504 with Alice Cassidy, the assistant housekeeper, sorting out the sheets. Or something. Anything. But 'Arry boy was not to be denied.

"But I didn't touch you" I protested meekly.

"Oh no?" said 'Appy 'Arry.

Whereupon he grabbed me by the lapels and shirt and held me up struggling. Kent Walton the commentator on I.T.V. wrestling, would have approved of the hold: the Ballroom Neck-lock.

"When you're in the presence of your betters, cock sparrow" he said. "Just keep your f*cking lip buttoned. Understand?"

From my cramped position on high, I maintained my dignity and tried to nod. By this time a small crowd of my devoted admirers who had collected during the melee was calling out to him to put me down.

"Put him down" they cried, meaning to release me rather than put me out of my misery. Other cries rang out, such as "leave him alone you bully!"–

"Get the manager!"

"He is the manager!"

"Oh bloody hell, poor sod!"

"Get an ambulance!"

This last one was a bit premature but was wonderfully prophetic. Wardrobe Man's twin leered into my face and thrust his teak forehead into mine – in other words he head-butted me. There seemed to be an explosion of starry insects and I had a quick preview of the Southend illuminations. He followed up by sticking his fingers in V for Victory style as hard as he could up both my nostrils and I fell to the floor with blood oozing vividly over my newly laundered white dress shirt. Some of my supporters joined in the fray and soon pockets of fighting were breaking out all over the dance floor. Big Ben seem to be squashed under me, whimpering. A girl screamed, "Stop it. Stop it!"

I don't know if she was referring to the fighting or whether she was ordering me to do my managerial duties. There was the sound of breaking glass and tables being overturned. Then an astute bystander blew a police whistle which he obviously just happened to have on him at the time. Someone shouted, "The Coppers are here." Even though they weren't. And within seconds, as if by magic, order was restored and the Greyhound Gang had vanished. The police did eventually arrive in response to a stranger's phone call, but I was advised by my counsellor in chief, Mr. Sidney Smith, for the good of the hotel and for the good of my health, not to make a complaint. A kindly band member offered to take me to hospital; but once my nose had stopped bleeding, I felt O.K.. The nasty egg on my forehead stayed for several days. For a long time after the incident, I was particularly wary on Greyhound racing night. Well in fact, we let everyone in for free who'd come in via the lavatories. I wasn't going through that again.

Coincidentally, not long afterwards, I played the part of a greyhound track "bookies runner" in the film *The Blue Lamp* at White City Stadium, Shepherd's Bush. This was a course an Ealing Studios production and was directed and produced by the old firm of Basil Dearden and Michael Relph. They'd come good for me again! At the time I don't think I appreciated what a coup it was being in it. It was difficult to get a perspective on small parts, especially when they were proving so hard to come by. But this film was another huge success and on reflection, being associated with it, was very good indeed for the C.V.. I had a line describing the killer, Dirk Bogarde, in a three shot around the board displaying the odds, which was "Thin chap. Black hair." And several be-trilbied close ups while the plot was unraveling for Dirk and the tic-tac men were spreading the news that he'd been spotted amongst the crowd. One of my two lines was cut, along with a "handing-over-money-to-a-punter shot, but you learnt to get used to that. It fitted in perfectly with Southend. Well I made it fit. B.B. and Sidney Smith manned the fort, and it was in the off-season. I was used for two days at £15 a day. Minus eventual tax and National Insurance deductions! Don't forget them! And it was shot with the real punters in the stadium on the race evenings, which gave it terrific authenticity. This was of course the first appearance of Jack Warner's policeman, Sergeant George Dixon. And despite him being murdered in the film, his character was resurrected for T.V. by the B.B.C., creating the iconic Saturday night hero so beloved by the British public for twenty years. I was ultimately very fortunate to appear in at least 12 of the episodes as different villains, usually "with a heart of gold". (To be frank I've forgotten how many) But that's for later. There was no fighting to be done near this dog track, I'm happy to say. I shared a few beers with Bernard Lee in his car (He had huge success in *The Third Man* and of course was "M" in the James Bond films. A marvellous actor. I got on very well with him). I didn't work in a scene with Dirk on this film, (I said hello though!) but was to do so at least six times over the next few years.

Meanwhile back at Southend I was approached - approached?

Sorry wrong word. I was "ordered" - to get hold of a gig band to take over the winter sessions, and as if it had been ordained, I immediately thought of Nigel Plunkett.

Nigel was a former P.O.W. mate of mine who had shared a lot of vicissitudes and one or two good times with me in prison camp. He had been a professional musician before the war and I was determined to give him the job if he was still in the business. Happily, when I finally located him in Wimbledon Park via the phone directory, he was still playing the guitar professionally. Nigel was a delightfully vague sort of chap, so immersed in his guitar playing that he seemed to live in another world. But there was none finer than he. I met him in Charing Cross and after the usual salutations and the "do you remember when", "have you seen him?" and "how did you get back?" reminiscences - like me he'd escaped from the march and I'd had no idea he had - we went along to visit David Rabin and arranged the whole thing. Nigel "fixed" the other musicians, and his Quartet were to share alternative sessions with "The Stardusters", a very well-known group of musicians led by pianist Dennis Wilson who went on to compose so much hummable music for B.B.C. T.V. shows - The "Till Death Us Do Part" and "Marriage Lines" theme tunes were his - that he deserves a third of the licence money!

I compered every evening, told a few gags -

"My girlfriend thinks I'm a surgeon. She keeps saying "Cut that out! Cut that out!"

"My brother's in hospital. It's not looking good. I took him a couple of magazines. He asked me if I could bring him some more. "Of course" I said. "But don't start any serials".

"I was out with my wife the other day. A young lady walked past and smiled at me. I said to my wife "Did you see that? That young lady smiled at me!"
"That's nothing". She said. "The first time I saw you I laughed

out loud!"

And I did my impersonation of Maurice Chevalier singing "Louise" and "You brought a new kind of love to me!" And my gravely voiced Leslie Henson! But all to no avail. Unfortunately after the main holiday month of August and dwindling September, we were very thinly attended for October, and finally we stuttered to a stop, so the ballroom venture from Oscar Rabin's angle for that season, fizzled out!

When all the bills had been cleared up and my fond farewells given out, with promises to return (how many of us ever go back?) I accompanied Nigel to London. We said goodbye over a couple of drinks and I've never seen him since! If you ever come across him - I heard he's moved to Sydney and is playing on the jazz circuit - he has thick curly reddish-grey hair, twinkling eyes seen through steel rimmed glasses, a goatee beard, and a guitar which he'll pick and strum with such cleverness and style, that you'll have to listen in spite of yourself. If by chance he's not around any more (and as I write a number of ex-P.O.W.'s are dropping off like flies on a hot window-pane) then the world is a poorer place to be without his kind.

During the winter months of my sojourn in Southend, I had on four occasions worked on a day here and a day there on Documentary Public Information films for a company called "Basic Films". I'd sent them a letter and had an interview with director Kay Mander with whom something clearly clicked, as she introduced me to J.B. Napier-Bell and he used me too! They had intriguing titles like *How, What, and Why*, *The A.B.C. of Gas* and *Balance: An Introduction to Laboratory Weighing Practice*. The ones I worked on were *24 Square Miles* which was all about the town of Banbury near Oxford, *Type 170* concerning the aircraft industry (I played a gunner in the R.A.F.), *Take Thou* about administering prescriptions and *Souring of Milk* which was all about er ...milk souring! I played a farmer. Because they were documentaries, they were obviously supposed to be concerning and using members of the public, but in transition scenes it was easier to use actors to keep the story going or "push the narrative" as they say. And that's where I came in. They obviously helped me keep my head above water and were good training for being on the ball. You needed to be word perfect of course. The dialogue was frequently quite technical and required a good memory, correct diction, and a lot of concentration to get right. I remember in *Souring of Milk* having a complicated speech about how cheese was made, so was saying the words "lactose", "lactobacillus bacterium" and "casein" whilst being as real as I could be, in a pub. It's quite a tricky skill.

Things were suddenly, post Southend, on the up! I soon discovered that my being in *The Captive Heart, They Made Me a Fugitive* and *The Blue Lamp* seemed to be a passport to gaining access to all sorts of films, as my written requests for interviews now nearly always bore fruit, whereas before I'd been denied access and greeted with silence. Some of the films I found myself in were for kids, some independent low-budget: *Mine Own Executioner* at London Film Studios in Isleworth for writer/director Anthony Kimmins – then *River Patrol - Fight to the Fortune - Just William's Luck - School for Soldiers - Monday Next - Saturday Morning - Penny Doctor* - I got the princely sum of £4 for that one - and *The Last Load* for John Baxter. (I'll be frank, I think some of those titles changed!) Then *How What and Why No. 1* for Kay Mander - both direction and continuity were her excellent specialties - a cine-magazine made for Children's Cinema Clubs. We shot an imaginary scene from a film and I talked about how you approached a role! And then for Norman Lee I was in *The Case of Charles Peace* starring the effective pinched "rodent" performance of squeaky Michael Martin Harvey, brother of Muriel. (I was actually edited out of this one! I'd been in a pub). And *Trapped by the Terror* at Merton for five guineas. This was a Children's Entertainment film directed by Cecil Musk set in Revolutionary France. I was a soldier. But with a rather attractive French hat and interesting musket. These were all small parts with one or two lines in one or two scenes, but it was all great experience. Some actors you worked with could be snooty. Some were friendly. It was always like this.

One of John Baxter's I was in, soon after meeting him, was *Fortune Lane*, in which a boy gives his savings to a friend to see an ill relation. I played a draughtsman designing trains. I earned £12 for the two days I was on it. I got on very well with John and he seemed to take a liking to me; in fact, in the years which lay ahead, he employed me on several occasions, and recommend me to many other directors.

"You come highly recommended by John Baxter" was a regular piece of praise. He'd been an actor himself and had performed in the music hall, which appeared to make him very understanding of the performer's role. He was, on the surface, a bumbling Pickwickian figure, but very sharp underneath it all! He had achieved great success during the war years with *Love on the Dole* by Walter Greenwood and all the "Flanagan and Allen" films and was a major founder of the National Film Finance Corporation. As I mentioned, we had a good relationship from the start. Phone calls being rarely successful, I'd dropped him a line. There was never a great deal of money to be made from his children's films but that was offset by the fun and good humour which emanated from the head-man. Eventually we were on the kind of footing where I could ring him up prior to his next production and ask what the score was – which meant which part was I playing and how many days? In the immediate years ahead, his employing me or giving me news of other films was to be the saving of me when work appeared to have dried up. One of the things about him that appealed to me most was his calmness. When it came to filming a new scene he would say, "Well now. What does it say in the book of words?"

Then he would reach for the script and rehearse the scene gently. If an actor or actress suggested trying something different, John was always amenable. "Yes, of course, let's have a go and see what happens". And if things went wrong, as of course they sometimes did, he would put up his hands and say quietly, "Don't worry, we've got plenty of time, we can always go again".

He was unique as far as I was concerned, being the only director who allowed me time off to do another job. while I was filming something else. In this instance whilst I was doing *Ramsbottom Rides Again.*

He allowed me to go to Pinewood to play a couple of important scenes for director Jack Lee (who directed the marvellous Classic, *The Wooden Horse*) in the excellent *A Town like Alice. Ramsbottom,* which starred Arthur Askey and a host of well-known character actors, including Sidney James (terrific comedy actor from *Hancock* to the *Carry Ons* to T.V. sitcoms) and Thora Hird, (dear Thora, a delightful actress. More about her later) was being made at Beaconsfield and it was fortunate for me that Pinewood was not so far away – about seven or 8 miles. And after he had confirmed it would be okay, he intimated that if I was delayed at Pinewood he would "shoot round me" until I was available. This is the kind of treatment handed out to the big stars, not to unknown shrimps like me! I never heard a word of dissent against John Baxter. He always received respect and affection. I was very fond of him.

Another thing I managed to slide in during Southend was something called a "Sunday Thought". These were directed by the very efficient Norman Waker. (He had to be with the tiny budgets he had, he told me). This was a "wear your own clothes" job. These "sermons" were shown in the cinema, as you'd expect, only on a Sunday because of their religious, moral content. With titles like *For Those in Peril* (like the hymn), *The Malicious Tongue* and *Benefit of the Doubt,* you knew where you were with these little homilies. My first one, that only took me one day and for which I got a fiver - well I suppose it was, in a strange way, for a good cause - was called *Question of Trust.* I played a slippery n'er do well and came to a sticky end in a motocycle accident. My character deserved it! I was horrid to everyone. I must have impressed as Norman got me back in for one called *Jumping to Conclusions* where my character made a decision about someone's character that was completely wrong and consequently gave him a lot of misery. Was I apologetic? Nar! Ooh I was a nasty piece of work! Guess what? Once again I came to a sticky end. This time I was sacked from my job! And then he got me in once more for one called *Ashes from the Altar*. But I was only a helpful tractor driver in this one. A goodie. Tchah! The atmosphere on all these films was as you'd expect, ridiculously and somewhat surreally respectful. There was almost a reverential hush about the proceedings! No one ever swore! Everyone was on their best behaviour! And of course the money you were getting gave the impression that most of your fee had gone to the local church! 4 quid for the day

On my return to London from Southend, I rejoined my mother in her house in Bedford Park where she had been talked into taking in (by me), as lodgers, three ex P.O.W.s with whom I'd been closely associated in prison camp through the many shows we did together. They were: Clifford Winterbottom (a likeable colour sergeant from Dublin, who was in the regular army and later posted to Korea), Johnny Gaskin (a Northern Ireland regular soldier soon to be discharged and to become friend and advisor to Sir Anthony Blunt, the art historian) and Frank Coburn - who I mentioned as the man I did the act with at the Nuffield - although a tough uncompromising soldier who was mentioned in dispatches for his bravery, he specialised in playing dame parts in prison and was known to all and sundry as "Phyllis", later appearing in the chorus of *Piccadilly Hayride,* which starred the great Sid Field (one of my favourite performers ever), at the Prince of Wales Theatre. This then was the "set-up" at home which obviously provided much reminiscing and always a lot of laughs – with no Jerries to bother us! Naturally we created a sketch troupe, and after rehearsals and run throughs in my room, did three nights at the Nuffield with our ten minute act! It went down marvellously. "Phyllis" in all his dragged up glamour, could get laughs just by walking on stage.

"What are you looking at?" being his opening sally in a deep brown voice when he was wolf whistled or cat-called. We all had decent singing voices and our rendition of "Sonny Boy" interjected by Winterbottom (as he was known) in a little boy's voice with a lisp raised the roof!

US: Climb upon my knee, Sonny Boy!

WINTERBOTTOM: Whath my name?

US: Sssh. Though you're only three Sonny Boy…

WINTERBOTTOM: Whath my name?

US: Sssh.

WINTERBOTTOM: Whath my bloody name!

US: Will you shut up!

WINTERBOTTOM: Can I have a thandwich? etc. as the little boy interrupts non-stop.

But everyone had different commitments and it eventually faded away which was such a shame.

I was phoned by an agent with whom I had previously left one of my precious photographs. He said he was at the Henry Fox Agency. He asked me to go and see the director of a film being made at Merton Park Studios, not far from Wimbledon. It was a friendly, pleasant little studio in those days, compact and homely. The film was about the French Revolution and the character concerned was one of Robespierre's renegades named "Le Duc". I read for the part in my rather elegant "Frainch accent". It was for five days work and I got the part, which I played with garlic driven gusto! I never discovered the names of the other revolutionaries. I hadn't met any of the other actors before (or since) – I wish I had, because I could've compared my treatment with theirs: five days at £5 pounds per day less the usual deductions – 10% to the agent plus the National Insurance stamp. But I waited in vain for my money. When I rang the agent there was no reply. The number was "unobtainable". The agent had done a moonlight flit. He had gone, vanished, vamoosed, buggered off, with my cheque and doubtless several others with him. This wasn't the first time this would happen in my career. It's easy to be too trusting unfortunately.

I had managed to save £60 from my Southend Ballroom experience which could stand me in good stead for the time of unemployment that inevitably lay ahead. To be frank, I wasn't actually enamoured of the dance hall scene. I'd liked the compère game, yes, but the management side was too stressful. As you will have gathered, I wanted to perform, that was where my future lay. Obviously if the occasion arose again and I needed the work, I would have considered it. Luckily I never needed to. I thanked the Rabins and they thanked me for a job done well. I'd "played my cards right!" They remained friends and were very encouraging in my career.

My old "pal" Cav rang me to ask me if I'd go and see him at Ealing Studios. I arrived in time for tea. There was cake! Cav greeted me warmly, telling me he was shortly going to direct *Nicholas Nickleby* and he thought I might be right for the part of Smike, and would I mind testing for it? I was thrilled and flattered that he would think of me. I naturally said yes to the test and was all agog and keen for it to happen. It took place in Ealing's smallest studio and was lined up by Gordon Dines the lighting cameraman as if it were the actual scene in the film, except that the lines were spoken by a "stooge", someone standing to deliver the lines from just off camera, in this instance Derek Bond, who'd been cast already as Nicholas. We knew each other from *The Captive Heart* of course. It was the scene where Smike died - highly emotional and supposedly deeply moving - and I was lying on my back emoting. I wasn't satisfied with it and neither was Cav. Derek was non-committal which was fair enough. We did it three more times and that was it! After a week of deliberation which I obviously wasn't a party to - in fact I'd given up hope - Cav phoned and asked me to do another one! He said that the other test was "not correct technically!" I think basically he wasn't sure and wanted me to have another go!

The second session disastrously, was worse than the first.

I wasn't comfortable at all although I knew the scene backwards by now. We did seven takes. Cav was gentle with me just asking me to underplay more and more.

"It's a bit too beeg Zam" he said.

But then asked me to do one take "much bigger". He could see I was struggling. Perhaps I was too nervous. Or the possibilities of my getting the part were weighing too heavily on me. Then Cav told me it was "splendid work" thereby confusing me completely. Sidney Cole the producer who was there was also full of praise! Perhaps I'd been fine and it was all in my head. But the proof of the pudding was in the casting. They chose the excellent Aubrey Woods! And he was good! Different from me obviously. But good! It was Aubrey's first film. He had a terrific career ahead of him. He was also a fine singer and was the Candyman in the film of *Charlie and the Chocolate Factory*. I was of course disappointed but I didn't dwell on it. You can't let these matters fester inside you and cause you to be bitter. I mean the positive thing was that it was excellent to have been thought of in the first place! Wasn't it? Well yes. But in fact, you need to get these jobs. And I knew it. But what can you do about it? Short of dispensing with your rival. And even then there's no guarantee of getting the part. Dear me. Why was I thinking like this??

Unusually Cav arranged for me to see my first test. I was grateful and could see where I'd gone wrong. Smike is dying from tuberculosis and I'd gone for it with the coughing and gasping. About a minute's worth. Then he finally manages to say

"I'm (pause for gasp).... goin' sir...I'm.....goin'..."

It all took so long I felt like saying "I wish he'd hurry up and go."

On the other hand I certainly looked right for the part, still being very thin as I was, and could have played it satisfactorily. But it was not to be. I'm still not sure why he showed it to me. He didn't offer advice and I was too embarrassed to ask. He could have always told me to have died more quickly.

The film itself was not a great success although it had a terrific cast including Cedric Hardwicke, Sally Ann Howes, Bernard Miles, and many Ealing stalwarts like Gladys Henson and Stanley Holloway. As I write Aubrey Woods and Derek Bond live just up the road from me in Barnes within a stones throw of the failed Smike!

SIX
Oo-err. Summoned to the Foreign Office

Then something strange happened. Out of the blue I received an unusual buff envelope and cryptic note within, telling me, nay ordering me, to get in touch with the War Office Intelligence Department. I telephoned the number on the letter and was asked in guarded tones to, "Come along to the War Office on official business."

I was intrigued, and replied that, yes, I could go on the date stated and asked if they could possibly tell me what it was all about?

"No." Came the stern reply. "Not on the telephone."

Blimey! Mysterious or what? My imagination ran riot. I had read stories about secret agents. Was I going to become one? Did I know any and not know it? Had I been one and forgotten? Was I a sleeper, and would suddenly remember I was actually Russian? Samski Kydsov? On the Tuesday in question I turned up at the War Office at the appointed time and stated my business to the security commissionaire. After checking my identity and my appointment, he led the way through various corridors, till we finally arrived at my secret rendezvous. Room 413. Or was it 314? Or even 143? I'm not allowed to tell you to this day! (I've forgotten anyway. I don't think I even knew at the time). I was ushered in and met by a most courteous and very correct Colonel, who bade me sit down and shouted out slightly too loudly,

"A cup of tea for Mr. Kydd, please," to no one in particular.

As if on cue, a man appeared from out of nowhere (probably from the next door room) at my elbow, in army uniform, with a strong cup of army tea. Plus two lumps of sugar and a rather tasty Ginger Snap. After exchanging a few pleasantries about the weather and rationing, and my having swiftly polished off the tea and biscuit, I sat back and waited for the interrogation to begin. The assistant then presented a fairly bulky file which had my complete military history therein! From my Territorial Army involvement, to my calling-up days in the Queen Victoria Rifles, then the K.R.R., to my eventual discharge in 1945. My times in solitary in the prison camp, my shows and writing, my editorship of the "Prisoner's Pie" periodical, my escape from the camp, my journey back to Liverpool via the Black Sea, my being torpedoed, my interview with the doctor etc.. Everything that I had done (officially, that is!) was recorded. It shook me to find that some unseen or all seeing eye had chalked up my life-story, and I said so.

"You'd be surprised what we know about you, old boy." said the colonel, preening himself.

"We have detailed dossiers about most people we're interested in."

Interested in? Shades of Orwell's Big Brother here surely! Who were the informers? The compilers? I foolishly asked the question.

"Oh I'm not allowed to disclose that, old chap!" said the Colonel.

"No?" I queried, querulously.

"No. What I <u>can</u> say, is that you've had a very interesting life so far. (So far?) And we need your help to identify someone."

I was intrigued. Who was it I had to identify? A traitorous fellow P.O.W.? A German or Polish contact? Another Lord Haw-Haw? The Padre who left us in the lurch at Warsaw? (On my escape we'd been 'helped' by a Priest who had hidden us and then informed the local Nazi sympathisers where we were. Luckily we got wind of his treachery. None of us trusted him. And we had moved on to another location.) Some Englander in the British Free Corps who'd joined from our Prison Camp? (The hated B.F.C. was a unit of the Waffen S.S. made up of P.O.W.s recruited by the Nazis. I'd been interviewed by an American Nazi to join them. I had of course declined.) The Colonel put paid to further speculation by producing a file of photographs. Most of them had been "blown up" or enlarged so that they were now 10 x 8s and on each photo the same particular individual was ringed or arrowed. Some were out of focus.

"We want you to identify this man" said the Colonel. "We can't tell you anything about him, by which I mean that we're not allowed to tell you about him; other than the fact that he was in your P.O.W. area in Poland and later after the arrival of the Russians, he was photographed in the centre of Thorn. Or should I say, Torun."

He showed me a photo of a street market in Bromberg with the ringed individual concerned standing near a stall. With the aid of a powerful magnifying glass, I took a closer look at the man. He was nobody I recognised. He could've been Irish – he had an impish, quizzical Celtic face.

"He might be an Irishman" I said.

"What makes you think that?" asked the Colonel.

"He's not unlike Liam Redmond" I replied. (Liam was a terrific Irish actor and sweet man. I was to have some excellent scenes with him on *Final Appointment*. He'd starred for W.B. Yeats in his celebrated *The Death of Cuchallain* at the renowned Abbey Theatre).

"Who?" said the Colonel. Sharply. Menacingly. Making a note of the name.

"An actor called Liam Redmond – he's quite well-known.

I don't mean him being this man. I mean this man looks like him. Or in fact I mean he looks like this man".

(I was digging a hole here. Poor old Liam. I had visions of him being dragged out of his bed at three o'clock in the morning as a consequence of my idiocy.)

"No" said the Colonel. "I don't think it could be him,"

pulling me out. But I wouldn't let it go and got out the spade again.

"I wasn't suggesting that it was him. I was just saying he was not unlike him."

"He wasn't a prisoner with you in the camp, we know that."

"What this bloke? No."

"No. Liam Redmond."

"No it's not Liam Redmond. Just a similarity."

"Yes we know that."

He was rightly irritated. I had been a bit foolish. I decided to put the Liam confusion to bed once and for all.

"Yes I'm saying…that it wasn't Liam Redmond…It isn't…who wasn't in the camp with me…Neither was this man…But he resembles him…Liam does…but it's…isn't…Liam…This man…isn't him."

The Colonel looked to the heavens. A tense silence ensued. In it, I studied the photos in more detail. In some of the photographs our mysterious stranger was dressed like a Polish or German businessman, wearing a black Gestapo like hat, scarf and a long double-breasted leather overcoat, the inevitable briefcase being carried under his arm. In other photographs he was garbed in semi-military uniform with a Russian soldier's headgear, i.e. a padded hat with huge flaps pulled down covering the ears and neck from the Siberian blasts, and tied up under his chin. After I had scrutinised several photographs, the Colonel sensed my negativity and said, "No luck?"

I replied, "No. I don't know him.... And yet…."

"Yes?" He thrust his head forwards. I flinched. "He does remind me vaguely of someone. Have you a more clean-shaven photo somewhere?"

They hadn't. Our victim was not an enthusiastic shaver. He believed in growing it and keeping it – in fact there was more fungus showing than face.

"I don't know how you could identify anyone under that beard!" I said.

The Colonel winced. I shook my head. I didn't know him……… And yet…… "We could go on like this for hours, couldn't we Colonel!" I said.

The Colonel gave me a withering look, saying, "Are you absolutely sure that you can't recognise him, either from Poland or since you've been back home?"

"Here? Here in England?" I was taken aback. Had I met him in England? Had they seen me with him?

"Yes. Please look again."

I looked closely again at the photos, zipping them through my fingers like giant playing cards. I gave up. No. I couldn't identify him. I said as much to the Colonel and then went on:

"What do you want him for? Desertion? Is he English, German, Polish, Russian?"

The Colonel shook his head from side to side to everything.

"I'm sorry. I can't tell you anything. I was hoping that <u>you'd</u> be able to tell <u>me</u>!"

I left with the sinking feeling that someone had been watching me and documenting my life intently for the past few years. I peered over my shoulder. Were they watching me now? Were they adding all my acting experiences into my dossier? And if so, who had I worked with who'd been spying on me?

Of course while returning home - these kinds of things take some time to percolate through the mind - on the tube, I realised where I had seen that face. He was the man who'd asked me "which way did she go?" in the Dorchester that odd evening with the Norwegian woman I'd met in the News Cinema, who wanted me to deliver a package. He was clean shaven of course.

Meanwhile I got back to the daily grind of sending out letters and hanging about Casting Directors' offices. One afternoon I was sitting in the waiting room adjoining Ronnie Curtis's office; Ronnie was the casting director for the Film Producers Guild in St Martin's Lane. (The Film Producers Guild owned and shot documentaries at Merton Park Studios). I was surrounded by 15 or 20 other non-working actors and actresses who had drifted in, all in the hope of getting a job in one of the many documentaries which the Film Producers Guild were engaged upon. (As I've said, these documentaries had actors who spoke lines in them). Something was always going on there! Not much money in it (5 pounds per day was the maximum) but you'd get some work eventually. The procedure was to play the waiting game, sitting on a bench or chair and either hope to be noticed by Ronnie, or just have a chat with other actors to find out what was going on elsewhere. This networking was so essential. Sometimes it did happen that I would get a tip which would send me scurrying off to call at some office about a film or play, only to find that I was too late – it was all cast! Apart from that, the waiting room was a very good place to go if it was raining and perhaps chat up one of the pretty actresses who could always be found there. On one particular occasion I was doing precisely that – she was a very nubile young actress who I had noticed many times before and she was showing me her album of photographs in various poses but none actually from any production. This was because she had not as yet worked on anything, although the photographer had obviously worked on her to good effect! The photos were pretty exotic; in fact, one or two of them were decidedly erotic! This was somewhat unusual, to be shown these in a casting environment - in fact let's be honest, in <u>any</u> environment. Especially to an out of work actor like myself; and no doubt to any in-work actor too! Anyway, we were sitting side-by-side, giggling and chatting. Probably flirting too! And I was commenting on the photographs.

"Oh that's good." I said. "I like that one with the broom very much. That should get you a great deal of work." (And possibly arrested.)

"Do you really think so?" she asked coyly.

"Of course! And I love the way that flimsy er shawl..er...thing... is draped over your chest revealing the beauty of your er... beauty! If I were in charge I'd give you a part right away."

I wasn't kidding.

"Do you think I'll ever make it?"... She queried, anxiously.

"Well...You'll certainly get a great reaction from the producers. Perhaps we could discuss this more over a cup of ....?"

At that precise moment Ronnie Curtis came striding out of his office and stood surveying us like Captain Bligh inspecting his villainous crew in *Mutiny on the Bounty*. In fact he looked like Charles Laughton. Not normally. But just then. Everyone stopped talking and gazed up expectantly, like little puppies fawning at their master. Some even had their tongues hanging out. Ronnie, in love with the moment, did his famous slow panning "look-at-all-the-actors-and-actresses-oh-I-love-the-power" shot.

Everyone sparkled in anticipation. "Oh please can I be chosen!" they almost said.

And having scrutinised the room, he finally stopped at me. I returned his gaze, hoping, but not speaking (I've been caught like that before – Ronnie's eyes were slightly crossed and I was never quite sure whether he was looking at me or not.) To my surprise and directing his remarks vaguely in my direction, Ronnie said, "You were in the army, weren't you?"

The actor next to me, a large pipe smoking Northern chap said, "No. I were in't mines."

But cross eyed Ronnie said abruptly, "No not you. <u>You</u>."

I still wasn't sure. He was forced to point. At me. "<u>You</u>."

"Me?" I answered, surprised.

"Yes you!" said Ronnie again as if I was being an idiot. Who else could he be talking to?

"Oh yes, I was in the army", I blurted out as if pained. And then dramatically. "Five years behind barbed wire."

Blimey I was good. A tear thought about running slowly down my face, but didn't have time, as Ronnie said sympathetically but totally incorrectly, "Yes of course. I remember very well. Burma. Building a railway. Terrible hardship you poor poor man. Come into the office."

Casting all thoughts of social intercourse (or the other) aside, concerning my meeting with the girl and her photo album - I knew where my priorities lay - I bounded after him into the office, almost colliding with him as he turned to offer me a cup of lukewarm tea. But no biscuit. The bastard.

"It's for *Call Up* he said. "A film about the army, for the War Office and it's being directed by Jeffrey Dell. Do you know him?"

"Ah, no," I said. "But I've certainly heard of him." I lied. I had no idea who he was. Luckily Ronnie didn't care.

"Well, you can go and see him this afternoon. It'll be yours if you play your cards right".

(What was it with this phrase?)

"You're perfect casting."

He ushered me out of the door.

"And by the way. He'll keep you out of trouble!"

"Trouble?" What on earth did he mean? "Trouble?" "Cards right?" Did I have a reputation I didn't know about?

"He's in this building. Fourth floor. The money will be the same as usual."

I started to thank him but he cut me short.

"Don't thank me! You haven't got the job yet!"

"Well, er I mean er.. thank you for the opportunity to be seen by the director" said the crawling creepy desperate out-of-work creep, creepily.

But… I got the part! Jeffrey Dell liked me! As I said, it was called *Call Up.* It turned out to be a sort of documentary instructional film, not about the army at all, but for the R.A.F., and I met Geoffrey Keen (an instantly recognisable lovely actor - we were to be in *Treasure Island* and *Passage Home* together in which he was brilliant - later to star in T.V.'s *The Troubleshooters*), when we gathered together at the Royal Air Force depot at Uxbridge, where the majority of the scenes were shot. I was a gunner! I'm not quite sure what relevance my having been "in the army" as Ronnie demanded, had at all!

I gathered later that the film was very well received by the War Office (I wonder whether it appeared in my dossier) and it gave me a great start to a working friendship with Jeffrey Dell (who directed *Carlton Browne of the F.O* in 1959 which I was in) and Julian Wintle (the producer, later to produce *The Avengers* on T.V.). In addition to being a director, and a sympathetic one, Jeffrey was also a writer of some repute, penning both film scripts and books. His book *Nobody Ordered Wolves* was a masterpiece of satire concerning the film industry. Uncharacteristically, in his spare time he managed his own farm, doing quite a number of the chores himself! He had several cows who were his pals, he said.

"Much easier than dealing with temperamental actors".

From 1948 onwards there was no serviceman that I was not to portray – Sailor, Airman, or Soldier. And always the private, the ranker, the rating, the erk. Possibly a lance corporal or even a sergeant. Or a stoker. But never - ever - the officer. In actual fact, the nearest I ever got to becoming an officer was before the war, when I applied for a short service commission. I'd passed the oral examination board and was almost there, when I was advised by the medical officer to have my sinuses operated on. Not having the money handy, I had to forego the opportunity. And the commission slipped away. How different my war - and my acting life - might have been had I got it! Mind you I might never have become one, taking that route. My father was an officer in the 1914-18 war, having been promoted in the field! I think I would've done O.K. if I'd had the opportunity, but I was never cast as such, no doubt due to my thin, sharp ex-P.O.W. features, and I became type-cast early on! Michael Caine changed type in *Zulu* playing an officer with a cut glass accent instead of his usual normal laconic cockney, and look what happened to him! Obviously, my cockney, polished in the prisoner of war camp, was pretty good and definitely more marketable at the time than my native Northern Irish! Though I was also to use my Belfast accent frequently to good effect.

On Christmas Day 1948 my mother and I got up early and went to St. Stephen's Church Bayswater for the 8.00 a.m. Communion service. As I said before, for three or four years I'd warbled there in the choir and had been a very active member of the Boys' Club attached to the church, and when I was taken prisoner, a short account of my parochial exertions had been published in the church magazine. Kildare Terrace, Bayswater (where we lived when we originally came to London from Northern Ireland) adjoins the church and I possessed many happy memories of the place where much of my childhood had been spent. Like all things, it's never the same going back. Many of my contemporaries had left the district. Some had been killed in the war and many had moved far away. The streets were the same, the sounds in the church were the same, and the pews were exactly the same, but the faces were all different; except for the wizened churchwarden. Strangely enough, he hardly looked any older! But oh he was. He was so ancient he only just made it to the altar with the collection. And after a respectful wait, he turned and made his limping, faltering way back to his well-worn seat halfway up the aisle, all eyes upon him, everyone with the same thought: is he going to make it? The original Vicar, the Very Reverend Llewellyn Hughes, had moved onto greater things. It was quite a good promotion – Senior Chaplain to the Armed Forces. He once expelled me from the church for whispering and giggling during his sermon. Oh, the humiliation of it! I had been passed a crude drawing of a nude girl being chased by a chorister, the latter's sole item of clothing being a very short surplice (of course with his rampantness very much to the fore) and I was trying to suppress my laughter and pass it on, when the Rev. Hughes turned round in the pulpit and saw me stifling a laugh. It was during evensong.

"That boy" he thundered in his Welsh theatrical way.

"That boy...."

"Who me sir?"

"Yes you. Go to the vestry at once and wait for me there."

I was conscious that the whole congregation was looking at me. I stumbled embarrassed behind the other choirboys, turned right to go past the altar, genuflected and of course nearly fell over in the process. Catching my floor-sweeping cassock up in my arms, I eventually reached the vestry. He entered fuming at the end of the Service. I got it with both barrels. I was banned for a month and lost all my payments of one shilling a week extra for weddings and funerals, paid for by the bridegroom in the former case. And no doubt from the estate of the deceased in the latter!

The way home from the church was by number 27 bus to Notting Hill Gate and then number 88 to Turnham Green where we alighted at the "Tabard" public house which is only a short step to Bedford Park. On the 88 bus my mother told me in muted, almost regal, tones, that she had said a prayer for me. I nodded my thanks and remained silent while the bus drove down Holland Park Avenue. I appreciated she had thought about me, but found it difficult to communicate. I knew what she was going to say. My silence encouraged her to speak. She gave me a wigging, once again clearly having spent an afternoon in Barker's of Kensington department store where she knew a lady in the canteen, so she told me. It was becoming more and more apparent that my mother had fingers in many major departmental store pies. She started her sermon. From her point of view it was now sometime since I had returned from the War and knowing the vicissitudes of the profession I was following, and the dim view everyone took of it, she was concerned, as she simply put it, about my work status; that I was "more out than in!" She was a very very strong character, a fighter, having brought me up alone in London after the early death of my father, as a consequence of his being gassed in World War One. Overprotective and inclined to be slightly Victorian in attitude, (she had never been slow in giving me a good slippering if she felt I'd gone too far) she was convinced in her heart, that actors were loose livers and not to be encouraged. In fact she'd never said this before, but she said it was not a profession she would ever want a son of hers to be in, with all its appalling distractions and dreadful morals and could I not see how awful the whole thing was? All her friends were in agreement with her, especially Mrs. Hummel, her principal lodger, and quite frankly I was going down the plug 'ole. She finished her somewhat bitter speech informing me that I didn't have a cat's chance in hell of "making it" and when was I going to realise that? I didn't reply immediately. I was insulted. The bus tootled along. I observed clusters of people hurrying home in the cold. A seagull squawked, despite us being nowhere near the sea. A cat played the banjo, cleaning itself. A newspaper blew lazily along the pavement. I decided I would initially repeat what I'd been saying since I'd started acting and see what happened.

"Give me another year and let's see how things go. If I'm a flop I'll think about your advice and I'll look around for something else."

Of course she wouldn't have it. She wouldn't accept that same response. And it was her reply that made me decide that this conversation was over forever.

"You are" she said angrily, "over 30 and still undecided about a worthwhile career. What are you going to make of your life? Isn't it time to think seriously about settling down to a good job – a job with a pension. Before it's too late? Why don't you decide now? This Christmas Day?"

Why I had to "decide" on 25th. December, that very day, as if it had any specific significance, (other than the birth of Jesus of course) to do what she wanted and in fact "give up", was beyond me and now I wasn't going to pay any attention anyway. Her quilted and plumped dreams of sheets and pillow cases would have to be firmly stuffed into life's laundry basket… where they could softly fade away!!!

I paused for a few seconds while the bus was passing Shepherd's Bush Green - I noticed a man being sick into a rubbish bin - and decided to put the whole thing to bed (ho ho) for ever.

I was quite impressive though I say so myself! I said, "Mother."

I let that ring out. Several people on the top deck jumped and turned round. She looked startled. I carried on.

"You know my work is unpredictable. And you'll have to acclimatise yourself to that situation. And I know you mean well and are trying to do your best for me."

Then a bit louder…

"But could you stop presuming I am making a hash of my life which I'm not and let me get on with it! Please!"

People had turned to listen. A man my age smiled. An older

woman in the front tutted. An old bloke with a strawberry mark on his face gave me a thumbs up. The rest of the trip was a silent one. She could of course have thrown me out of the house. But she didn't. In any case, my future wasn't dim. I had recently seen Basil Dearden who promised me a role in his latest production *Saraband for Dead Lovers* starring Stewart Granger. It turned out to be several days in the marketplace where the "Lord of Misrule" carnival was taking place (a worker is chosen to be "King for a day" but it's a sort of mad revelling nightmarish version of being a monarch). You'd have difficulty picking me out! Mainly because I'm not in it! My brush with the gorgeous Joan Greenwood - she of the lovely larynx - amidst the leering masked revellers, didn't make it to the final cut! Luckily Mother never saw it or she might have thought I was making the job up.

In terms of other work, I'd only recently played a police inspector in a B.B.C. Light Programme show called *The Upsetting Business of the Musical Snuffbox*. And I also had another radio job the day after Boxing day, live from Alexander Palace. I'd written a letter with a brief C.V., was called for an interview where I'd had to read for both parts for the same producer - an "evenin' all" voice for the copper and a lot of shouting in battle for the latter one - and was offered both. The second was a drama called *The Malindens*, "The Story of a Family" written by Jonquil Anthony. I played a soldier in once again a very loud scene. And another one (with a different accent) and a somewhat well spoken character called Anthony Viccars. Norman Shelley was interestingly in it. He was ultimately Colonel Danby in *The Archers* but I remember was rumoured as having stood in for Winston Churchill during the war for some of his speeches, when Winston was "otherwise engaged" and was in fact thought to have impersonated him for the "we will fight on the beaches" and "this is their finest hour" House of Commons orations when they were repeated on radio.

I actually asked him about this and he confirmed it, but was still reluctant to talk about it. Another member of the cast told me

Norman had been given grief about it by too many people, so preferred to keep it under his hat. Fascinating. I got both jobs entirely because of *Captive Heart*. The producer said he'd loved the film and remembered me in it! That was nice! Even if I only had a couple of lines in these two radios. The experience was great, if quick, and new to me. I wanted to do more. The creative tension of a live radio performance was very appealing. And the sound image of the battle scene I was in was very realistic. The great radio actress Gladys Young was in *The Malindens*. I didn't have a scene with her but got to shake her hand and hoped some of her talent would rub off.

Since *The Captive Heart*, Basil Dearden had been extremely kind to me. This doesn't mean that I wasn't to feel the lash of his tongue when he was in the directorial seat. I was criticised along with all the others. He did tell me (and no doubt Michael Relph, his permanent producer, would confirm it) that he always looked through the script to see what was suitable for me. And he was true to his word. I had a part in *Frieda* starring David Farrar which was a hugely relevant story at the time about an ex P.O.W. - I think I know why I was cast in this one - who has escaped through the help of a German woman - played by Mai Zetterling - who he brings back to England with him. She is initially shunned and they find love. Mai, who I didn't get to meet or work with, is a lovely funny Swedish actress who had initial success with Ingmarr Bergman and then a big English film and T.V. career, starring soon after this one in the hugely successful *Quartet*. She was married to Norwegian Tutte Lemkov, with whom I was to have many a merry time. He and I were in *Treasure of Monte Cristo* together in 1961 amongst many other films and tellies.

Then I was in *Train of Events* in which poor Jack Warner injured himself whilst playing a train driver and fell out of the cabin. He ended up with a permanent limp that got worse in his later years as Dixon. He didn't do much walking in the later T.V. episodes and was frequently shot standing behind his desk!

The film was interesting because it was four films in one. The idea was a good one. You start with a train crash and then zoom in on four passengers and have stories, or in this case separate films, about them, starting three days earlier. One was called *Prisoner of War*. I was of course in this one, in a scene with Laurence Payne, later to play Sexton Blake, who was being an on-the-run ex German P.O.W.. Alas, the scene was cut. A shame. Coz it was a goodie I thought! But then I would! This run of being edited out was frustrating to say the least, and as always caused a niggle of self-doubt. I wished I could rid myself of that. But that's the business.

Meanwhile, I hadn't phoned immediately, as to be frank I was a little bit scared of the whole situation, but I plucked up the courage to phone the War Office about the man I thought I'd seen at the Dorchester. I used the number I'd originally been given.

I attempted to explain the nature of my business, "Hello is that the War Office?"

"Who's this?"

"I came recently to discuss something with er someone."

"What?"

"You sent me a letter and I turned up and discussed something about someone? With er someone?"

"Who?"

"I'm afraid I don't know. And I don't think I'm supposed to tell you anyway if I did. Sorry."

"What?"

"Yes."

"What do you mean, yes? Who is this?"

"Sam Kydd."

"Who?"

"Sam Kydd. You said you had a dossier on me and asked me about someone. I think I remember where I've seen them now."

"Who?"

"This other someone. Not the Colonel someone."

"Do you have a name of this…someone?"

"Which one? Your someone? Or the someone whose photos I looked at?"

"Is your name spelt K-Y-D-D?"

"Yes."

The phone went dead. I phoned back again on the number I'd been given. A long note of a noise rang out. I phoned the Operator.

"Hello there I've been phoning the following number in Whitehall, WHI. 3456 and I'm getting a heterodyne noise."

"A what?"

"A long sort of beep."

"WHI. 3456?'

"Yes. Is it out of order?"

"I'm afraid it doesn't exist sir."

"But I was just speaking to someone!"

"Immensely unlikely sir. We don't have it listed."

Blimey!

Following almost immediately after *Train of Events* came *Scott of the Antarctic* directed by Charles Frend (again an Ealing Studios film) starring John Mills (I was to sit next to him and Richard Attenborough in the East Stand at Chelsea. He was of course a terrific actor, sprung to stardom by *Great Expectations*) and featuring amongst others, the ubiquitous Kenneth Moore. Charles Frend, almost like his surname, was a very likeable man. Meeting him for the first time, one would see someone tall and distinguished, of very serious mien; after working with him, it proved how deceptive appearances can be – what good value he was! And so good at praising everyone.

"Well done everyone. Terrific! Great take! On we go!"

I'd had a scene saying goodbye to the cheering multitude on the quay as the boat, the Terra Nova, left (and had made up "saying goodbye" dialogue with an imaginary family who I pretended I was shouting and waving and pointing at) but my big moment came when I had to present the ship's cat to Captain Scott as a token of good luck. I was a Royal Navy stoker, Edward MacKenzie (not doing any stoking though). We were all at the end of the gangway with the mock up of the ship behind us. I had the following lines with John as

Scott:

ME: Excuse me Sir. Can you take the cat with you to the Pole, Sir….You wouldn't lose it against the snow!
(THE CAT IS BLACK)
ALL: Hear hear, Sir.

John replies by saying it's not a good idea as the cat is "good luck" and he'd be taking the luck away from the ship were he to take it with him. And the cat makes its own decision and bounds back on board!

So…. picture this. I've been handed the cat. I'm waiting to approach John, as the scene is about to start, holding it. This feline, who was supposed to have been trained as a professional, and would supposedly do everything in one take on "action", (in this instance, just be handed over) became bewildered and confused by all the shouting and noise going on around him, despite it being his supposed tolerance of this that got him the part in the first place. You could tell all was not well as he tensed up and began squirming. On the loud call of "we're going for a take," and its echoed responses, he nipped out of my arms very sharply, scratching while exiting, and disappeared behind me under the enormous set of the ship in the mock ice flow.

"What's the problem?" said Charles.
"We appear to be one light in the scene Charles." said the First.
"Who's that?"
"The cat."
"Ah. Where is he?"
"Under the boat somewhere Charles."
"Ah. Can the handler get it out?"
"He's trying Charles."
"Ah."

For over three hours he defied all blandishments and encouragements to move from his hidey-hole in the fake ice flow.

The amount of cat food that was lain down just out of his reach to attempt to lure him out. I reckon they went through every flavour of Kit-E-Kat known to man. But to no avail. Perhaps he was secretly a vegetarian. Heaven knows what it cost to get that shot; certainly more than they paid me. Charles Frend got increasingly exasperated and when eventually the poor pussycat was recovered, looking frightened and cowed, his handler tried to make out I'd been holding him incorrectly, and it was my fault and I'd scared him! But the First (I liked him!) was having none of that and told him so, and everyone gave the handler the "fish eye" for daring to suggest it was all of my doing. The cat was hired after all, as a film cat, supposedly able to cope with the stresses and strains of having people holding him saying lines. Now that he was once again in my arms, I was ordered this time to hold onto him on pain of death. I think I damaged his leg in doing so. He certainly limped after the scene was over, flinging me a reproachful glance at the same time. Well, it was either him or me. It would have been quicker to have used the mangy Studio cat and doped him for the occasion. Failing that, a stuffed one from the Moggy Museum would've sufficed. Or even a cat puppet of some sort! However well trained, nearly all animals are tricky to deal with in films or T.V. and should be used with the utmost caution. Anyway, after we'd "recovered" him, he "stayed" in my arms until handed over to John, and if you remember was supposed to bolt back towards the ship, escaping from John's grasp. But in fact, the cat had become so useless by this time, that John had to tip him out of his arms towards the direction of the boat ("tipping cat out to make it look as if he's jumped towards the boat" acting) and in fact, did nothing but just be tipped out, like a sack of potatoes (well, one large spud) whereupon he crouched at my feet, clearly petrified, the poor animal. Luckily he wasn't in shot - Charles was shooting the group at waist height - and we walked back towards the ship trying not to step on him, pretending he'd beaten us onboard. Any opportunity for a "cat running up gangway" shot which was supposedly scheduled, was of course completely scuppered.

Scott was a terrific film. I spent eight days on it, so at £12 a day, less National Insurance and 10% to the agent who booked the job, my daily rate was going up (I kidded myself). Of course if I came face-to-face with a budget which couldn't pay that, and I needed to work very badly...... I accepted a lower rate!

Incidentally and coincidentally, the cat scene was filmed on 16th January 1948, the date of the annual "Antarctic Club" dinner. This was a dinner for those who'd spent their winters in the Antarctic on British expeditions and Ealing Studios rather thoughtfully invited anyone from the expeditions to come along and watch the filming, which about 30 of them did, including Admiral Reginald Skelton who'd been on the Majestic with Scott, and Edward McKenzie, my character, who'd been the leading stoker. I was rather pleased to shake his hand. I of course looked or sounded, nothing like him!

SEVEN
I'm Sid King

By this time, January 1948, with an ever improving list of work on my C.V., I was taken on by a sole agent, one Harry Dubens Esquire, although in fact I never had a contract with him. He was like that. Loyal and trustworthy. I had met his son Stanley, who was his assistant, at a party, and was attracted to the set-up because of his good list of actors - Harry at this stage only represented actors who'd been on active service, which was a good move at the time considering the large number of films being made about the war - and also because Stanley had been a P.O.W., and somehow I expected understanding and preferential treatment. Foolish me! It all got a bit peculiar after Harry died. Harry was not unlike actor Gregory Ratoff in appearance, (Gregory was a Russian American, whose most famous role was Fabian in *All About Eve)*. He was very much in charge of things at the Regent Street office, which was fair enough as he was the big cheese! Unfortunately he had the bizarre habit of referring to me as "Sid". He invariably got my surname wrong too. For a long time he called me "King" – Sid King. Part of the preferential treatment? Oddly enough, I obtained a large amount of work under that nom de plume. When I went to the office to see him he'd say to me, "An' 'ow is you today Sid? Stanley out. Vot you wanting?"

All whilst speaking on the phone to a casting director:

"I got good h'actor for yer called Sid King. Very good gangster peckpocket parts. He was in "Blue Lamps."

Nevertheless it succeeded. He was how I imagined Samuel Goldwyn to be - Samuel Goldwyn, the 'G" in M.G.M., used to call Danny Kaye, "Eddie", possibly confusing him with Eddie Cantor, and was mythically known for the phrase "include me out" - only in Harry's case there were no Goldwynisms, only Dubenisms.

"Sid! You is perfect "boy with borrow.""

He meant "barrowboy". Basically he was kind and benevolent – a sort of volatile "Topol" from *Fiddler on the Roof*. Harry was happily married, with a daughter and two sons, and I believe the family originated from Russia, hence the fractured accent. When some deal of importance was in the offing, he was a great believer in the red-carpet treatment – lunch at the Caprice with champagne flowing. However, there was one thing in his make up to which I took exception: he would always be wary of accepting a reverse charge trunk call from me, and refuse it, if he didn't think it was worth it. I would be asked to drop him a postcard! I was once stuck on location and had a note to speak to him re a casting and had no money with me, as I was in costume. He still refused! He possessed an explosive temper which he vented on his secretary of the moment (they changed more quickly than the price of petrol) and Stanley came in for his share of the abuse. Eventually Stanley couldn't take it any longer and left to become a trainee manager with Marks & Spencer, but he later came back to the fold when the old man handed in his cards and joined the heavenly agents' Union, along with all the other agents and impresarios whose shows were closed for good. During the war years, Harry had been actively associated with the highly successful *Sweet and Low* revues starring Hermione Gingold and Henry Kendall at the Ambassadors Theatre. He also had a permanent interest in the Alexandra Theatre in Stoke Newington where he put on films and theatre and even the odd boxing match. Harold Warrender (a fine film actor, seen in "Ivanhoe" in 1952) and Kenneth Moore, were two of Harry's clients – both well known, but at that time Kenneth was getting into his stride as far as films were concerned. Both of them were in *Scott of the Antarctic* and Kenny (as Harry Dubens called him) was playing a smallish part, "Evans of the Broke", one of Captain Scott's team. Harry told me to make myself known to Kenny, "Very good h'actor who will be big star vone day an' you'll be in 'is pictures too!'"

So I introduced myself to Kenneth and we had a drink together; in fact during the next 10 years of my life I must have appeared in eleven or twelve films with Kenny. I was pleased to be his friend.

Having been "on probation" and a provisional member of the British Actors Equity Union, which you may remember I'd joined (well I'd been given a sort of "special case" status) during the war, I was permitted to become a full member. The 3rd February 1948 was the grand day I was officially allowed to ply my trade, for which I paid the sum of 5 shillings entrance fee (I hadn't paid it during the war), and then £2.12 shillings per annum (and a reduced sub of £1.12/- if my earnings were £5 a week). I had met the qualification requirements having been more than 40 weeks in professional employment! I was 4790, that was my number. The boys and I celebrated with a cream tea in the Chiswick High Road! We sang a song!

"Equiteeeeee! Show your narner to your father bang your smalls against the wall", to the tune of "Valencia", the big hit for Paul Whiteman. The manager came over and asked us to be less boisterous. I left my "Official Equity Card" lying on the dining table for Mother to take a look at, at her leisure. Naturally, she covered it up with a tea-towel.

Following on from *Scott of the Antarctic*, I was quickly on the move again, this time to Highbury Studios, to meet John Crichton and the lovely Andy Worker. Andy and John were responsible for Highbury Studios eventually becoming a sort of J. Arthur Rank tryout stable for small budget films, in which new writers and directors and actors would be given their chance. This opportunity arose because in 1949 the Labour government imposed a 75 per cent duty on imported films to give a boost to the British Film Industry and create more jobs. Domestically produced films that had to be shown by cinemas, were also increased to 45 per cent. J. Arthur Rank seized his chance and stepped up production. But of course there was a log-jam of American movies waiting to be shown, and they all had bigger budgets, longer periods to produce them, and proportionally better writers and facilities. And once they were let back in, the dam broke. Rank was soon in debt and boom time for the British film business was over. Highbury Studios were bought by A.T.V. who proceeded to record the soap *Emergency Ward 10* there and continued doing so for four years. I was in several episodes. But in January 1948 my first production for them (they thought I was Sid King for a bit) was entitled *Colonel Bogey* (playing another soldier) starring Jack Train, the very funny Colonel Chinstrap in *I.T.M.A. (It's That Man Again)* on B.B.C. Radio. The film was directed by Terence Fisher (with whom I was to do *Final Appointment, Hound of the Baskervilles* and *Island of Terror*); quickly followed by *To the Public Danger* as a policeman alerted to a supposed accident.

"Was there an accident? No sign of any broken glass. It might be worthwhile enquiring over there?" is the gist of what I said, analysing the scene with my torch, speaking to Barry Letts who had reported it. (Barry was of course to become a respected producer, especially of *Doctor Who*). And it turns out it wasn't a body at all, but a bike with a sack of potatoes on it! I got a credit at the end of the film but annoyingly my name was spelt "Kidd". (I suppose I should be grateful it wasn't "King"). This "morality tale", about the perils of drinking and driving, also directed by Terence Fisher, starred Dermot Walsh, (*Richard the Lionheart* on T.V.. We were to have big scenes together in *Hunted*. Very nice guy) and Susan Shaw, a beautiful young actress who was in *Train of Events, Pool of London, The Huggets* and eventually married her *Pool* co-star Bonar Colleano. Bonar tragically died young. I was to work with him on *Once a Jolly Swagman* and had been impressed by his energy and charisma. It was a huge loss to the business. He was a star of the future. She was deeply affected by his death.

I also crammed in a film for Fred Weiss called *Movie Go Round* for which I accepted £2! I can't remember why! I must have been mad! Perhaps my mother had been shaking her head at me again. It was a "conversation" between two film projectors in a cinema, one old, one new, and featured a lot of silent film clips. I played a character called Dick who repaired the projectors, alongside Donald Biset and Renee Goddard. My character dreamt that the projectors become human and they discussed the films they'd shown!

Meanwhile, back to cloak and dagger! Another buff envelope appeared in the post. I was to report to the War Office again. I did again. Again I was whisked down a labyrinth of corridors. But this was a different colonel. And a different room. 217? 271? 172? All much brisker. No tea and biscuit. Again the photographs.

"Yes I've seen him!" I responded eagerly.

"Where?"

"The Dorchester."

"When?"

"About a month ago."

"What was he up to?"

"Well I was having dinner at the Dorchester. He ran in and demanded my name".

"Yes. That tallies with what we know. The Norwegian woman you were with has vanished though."

They knew. They'd been "observing" me. Of course they had.

"Do you have any information on her?"

"Yes! She gave me a card and told me to pick up and deliver a package."

"You didn't."

"No."

"No. Do you have the address?"

"Ah. No. It was on a piece of paper. I left it behind."

Whoops this was embarrassing.

"….er…It was in Hackney if I remember rightly?.

"It doesn't matter. We know the address."

"She wasn't Norwegian you know. German. You made a good decision not to go to her room. Or go and pick anything up."

"Well I never intended to er…go to her..er…"

The possible lie melted away on my lips. I was abruptly ushered

My Mother Mary Kydd

JACK HYLTON presents

BACK HOME AGAIN

A Revue by ex-P.O.W.s from Stalag Luft III
and other Camps
Arranged and Produced by
VAL GUEST and PETER BUTTERWORTH
Dances arranged by Dorothy McAusland

1 "BACK HOME AGAIN"
The Full Company and The Pin-up Girl
Friends

2 4 HOME—I AWAY (Con West)
Compere, Talbot Rothwell ; Prisoner,
Peter Butterworth ; Wife, Hugh Elliott ;
George, Bill Rae ; Ted, Nat Hoffman ;
Charlie, Ken Morrison ; Mr. Lovejoy,
Stan Phillips

3 "WE'VE GOT RHYTHM"
Jimmy Prescott and Johnny Crowe

4 "ON MY RETURN"
Pete, Peter Butterworth ; Jonah, Frederick
Wood ; Lancelot, Arthur Butler ;
Tommy, Ken Morrison ; Arthur, Lionel
Baker ; Dick, Hugh Elliot ; Reggie, Stan
Phillips ; Johnnie, Sam Kidd ; and The
Girl Friends
(Script written and narrated by Talbot Rothwell, Music by
Bill Williams)

5 THE CONTEST

6 "A FEW WORDS"
(Peter Butterworth)
                    Peter Butterworth

7 DREAM BOOGIE
Terry Borrows, John Gaskin, Sam Kidd
Pianist : Stan Phillips

8 MANLEY & AUSTIN
                    "Gentle and Kind "

9 INTERVAL

10 "CALLING ALL BARS"
                    (Maschwitz and Stischer)
Bill Rae, Nat Hoffman, Stan Phillips and
The Girl Friends

11 "DR. FRADLER'S DILEMMA "
Dr. Fradler, Talbot Rothwell ; Mr. Bigley,
Hugh Elliot ; Whitewings, Sam Kidd ;
Phoebe Shaw, Barbara Young

12 "IT TAKES A TOUGH GUY TO BE A
LEADING LADY "
                    (David Porter, W. Wytson-Tadd)
The Dresser   Sam Kidd
The Ladies : Leslie Turnbull, John Gaskin,
Harold Burlton, John Mackwood, Arthur
Butler, Thomas Legowski

13 HELL FIRE BRIDGE
                    (Val Guest, Con West)
The Trippers : Talbot Rothwell,
                    Nat Hoffman
General Woodcock   Ken Morrison
Captain Belcher   Peter Butterworth
Sergeant Longhouse   Stan Phillips
Poughi   Hugh Elliot
Icilma   Barbara Young

14 ARTHUR BUTLER

15 HYDE PARK   The Full Company

16 LESLIE STRANGE
               The Famous Character Comedian

17 FINALE   The Full Company

Production Manager   —   ARTHUR LEWIS
Manager   —   PETER BUTTERWORTH
Stage Manager   —   BILL LEMON
Musical Director   —   DAVID POWLER
Wardrobe Supervision   —   MABEL AUSTELL
Press Representative   —   ROSA HEPPNER
                       (For JACK HYLTON LTD.)

Publicity stills & 'Back Home Again' programme

Snaps

Next Week's Play

MONDAY EVENING, FEBRUARY 25th

For Six Nights at 7.30 p.m.

MATINEES : WEDNESDAY, THURSDAY and
SATURDAY at 2.30 p.m.

"QUIET WEEK-END"

By ESTHER McCRACKEN

This fresh and delightful comedy is a sequel to " QUIET WEDDING " and might well have as a sub-title " The Further Adventures of the Royd Family." Its author now ranks as one of the most consistently successful of British dramatists. The secret of her appeal almost certainly lies in her ability to catch and faithfully reproduce the oddities and quiddities of English middle-class life. In other words, her humour and her sentiment develop naturally from the sort of situations which occur in the lives of the majority of her audience. "QUIET WEEK-END " at one time held the London Long Run Record at Wyndham's Theatre. The original company left that theatre to go on a long and outstandingly successful tour of the Mediterranean theatre of war, and then returned to London to continue its triumphant way. The play has not yet been generally released for performance by repertory companies and permission for us to present it now is a special privilege for which we wish to thank Messrs. Linnit & Dunfee.

"MEN IN SHADOW"

By MARY HAYLEY BELL

Moy	—	—	—	WALTER AMES
German Officer	—	—	PHILO HAUSER
First German Soldier (Willi)			SAM KIDD
Cherie	—	—	—	VIOLET GOULD
Kenny	—	—	—	VICTOR ADAMS
Polly	—	—	DOUGLAS MALCOLM
Commando Soldier		—	NEVILLE MAPP
Lew	—	—	—	PETER GRAY
Mordan	—	—	HECTOR MacGREGOR
Enshaw	—	—	GERALD ANDERSEN
Second German Soldier (Hans) :			KENNETH FRASER

The whole action of the play takes place in the loft of an old disused mill adjoining a farmhouse somewhere on the French coast

ACT I An afternoon in Spring, 1942

(INTERVAL)

ACT II The same. Twenty-four hours later

(INTERVAL)

ACT III Dawn. The following morning

The Play produced by KENNETH FRASER

Setting designed by Eric Rutherford, painted with the assistance of Christian Kappey and Ann Raley

China and Glass by The Token House, Windsor
Furniture by The Old Times Furnishing Co,
Cigarettes by Abdulla

The Windsor Repertory Theatre Orchestra
Under the Direction of VERNON CORRI
Leader and Solo Violinist

March : "Torch of Freedom" *Haydn Wood*

Overture : "Athalie" — *Mendelssohn*

Selection : "Perchance to Dream" *Ivor Novello*

Selection : "The Lisbon Story" *H. Parr-Davies*

Managing Director — — JOHN COUNSELL

EXECUTIVE STAFF :

Manager	—	—	ARNOLD PILBEAM
Assistant Producer	—	—	KENNETH FRASER
Secretary	—	—	DAPHNE COUNSELL
Stage Director	—	—	JENNIFER SOUNES
Stage Manager	—	—	PHYLLIS TRUMAN
Head Electrician	—	—	CYRIL DOUGLAS
Master Carpenter	—	—	ALFRED WEBB
Wardrobe Mistress	—	—	MABEL WILMER

MATINEE PERFORMANCE
AT 2-30 P.M.

NIGHT MUST FALL

by EMLYN WILLIAMS

MRS. BRANSON		Ann Jackson
OLIVIA GRAYNE		Pamela Roberts
HUBERT LAURIE		John Kydd
MRS. TERENCE		Olga May
DORA PARKOE		Cynthelline Brendon
INSPECTOR BELSIZE		Sidney Trevelyan
DAN		John Seebold

The Sitting Room of " Forest Corner," Mrs. Branson's bungalow in a forest in Essex.

ACT I.
A morning in October.

ACT II.
Scene 1—An afternoon, 12 days later.
Scene 2—Late afternoon, 5 days later.

ACT III.
Scene 1—Half hour later.
Scene 2—Half hour later.

Furniture kindly loaned by ... Antiques., Roman Bank, Skegness
Brass and Ornaments kindly loaned by Charles Frame, Lumley Road, Skegness
Cash Box ... ... Bewley & Sons, Roman Bank Skegness

THE PLAY DIRECTED BY JOHN SEEBOLD.   PRODUCTION BY DAVID FORBES-RUSSELL.

Manager	For	Bill Tate.
Stage Director	BUTLIN'S LTD.	W. Stiles.
Publicity Manager		C. S. Briggs.

MATINEE PERFORMANCE
AT 2-30 P.M.

WHILE PARENTS SLEEP

By ANTHONY KIMMINS

MRS. HAMMOND		Pamela Roberts.
" NANNY "		Ann Jackson.
COLONEL HAMMOND		Sidney Trevelyan.
NEVILLE HAMMOND		John Seebold.
LADY CATTERING		Olga May.
JERRY HAMMOND		John Kydd.
BUBBLES THOMPSON		Cynthelline Brendon.

Scene—The Drawing Room of the Hammond's House in Eccleston Square.

ACT I.
6.30 p.m.

ACT II.
1.30 p.m. and 2.30 a.m.

(During the course of this Act the curtain will be lowered for a few seconds to indicate the lapse of time.)

ACT III.
The next morning.

Brass Ware and Ornaments kindly loaned by Charles Frame, Lumley Road, Skegness.

THE PLAY DIRECTED BY JOHN SEEBOLD.   PRODUCTION BY DAVID FORBES-RUSSELL.

Manager	For	Bill Tate.
Stage Director	BUTLIN'S LTD.	W. Stiles.
Publicity Manager		C. S. Briggs.

THE Butlin Theatre SKEGNESS

THE "SHOW" THEATRE OF THE EAST COAST

PROGRAMME
of

JOHN WATT'S PRODUCTION

"THE STARS ARE OUT"

at 7.30 p.m.

PRICE 3d.

Programmes

The wonderful Cymbeline Brooks

'Hewers of Coal'

The Cast of 'Press On'

'Press On' poster

The 'Carrol Levis' sketch

With Pamela Cundell and Harry Secombe

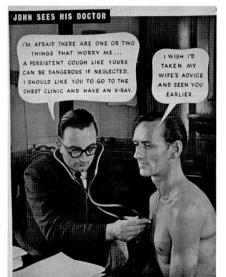
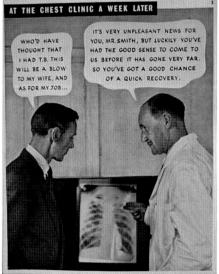

The government's 1946 Tuberculosis Awareness poster campaign

Publicity photo 1947

The Stage Cricket Club at Lord's

Pinkie Barnes

Night filming for 'Secret People'.
Valentina Cortese (on left) & Audrey Hepburn (on right)

Publicity photos

'Shout Aloud Salvation' & 'The Wonderful Visit'

Publicity stills

Wedding day. Best man Gordon Mullholland & Pink's sister Shirley Barnes

Sam Weller in 'Pickwick Papers'

At home in Melbury Road

out before what he said had sunk in.

Blimey!

I then embarked on a series of small parts which involved flitting from studio to studio which I have to say I rather liked. I'm happy to "flit" when there's work involved. Not flitting means no work! And I don't deal with that very well as I think you're beginning to understand.

Director John Irwin and producer Andy Worker, clearly taken with my performance in *Colonel Bogey*, got me in again at Highbury for *A Piece of Cake* starring the "Odd Ode" man himself Cyril Fletcher who had great success "odd-odeing" in B.B.C. T.V.'s *That's Life*. In fact, unbeknownst to most, he'd been doing his "Odd Odes" since 1937! This plot revolved around him creating an ode about a character named "Merlin Mound" who came to life, who would grant his wishes! But by stealing them! It was a comedy as you'd expect. Cyril was a lovely encouraging man who'd come up with a comedy idea that he lived off for the rest of his days. Good luck to him. I played a soldier!

Then I was onto another extravaganza entitled *Song for Tomorrow* at Highbury. Also directed by Terence Fisher. This time playing a Sergeant! It starred James Hayter, (fine actor with the lovely chocolatey voice). £20 for two days on that one.

Then *Trouble in the Air* a silly 51 minute Rank comedy for Highbury directed by Charles Saunders with Jimmy Edwards. I was the Police Driver. A few lines.

"Yes sir!" "Will do sir!" I was getting good at these "car driver" jobs.

Then *Fly Away Peter,* again for Charles Saunders. A comedy about kids leaving home featuring the marvellous Margaret Barton who should have become a huge star. I had the part of a man delivering a telegram and the line, "Here you are Miss! I hope it's good news!"

To which Margaret said, "Yes hope so!"

But the following day the First A.D. phoned to say that there'd been a problem with the exposure and the film hadn't come out properly and they didn't have the time (or money) to reshoot it with me, so had decided to give the part to a boy in the post room who merely delivered the telegram! So it's not me!

Then a small part in the sixty minute *Love in Waiting* about a restaurant ("Waiting" geddit?) starring David Tomlinson (Mr. Banks in *Mary Poppins*), with whom I was to have much fun in *Up the Creek*. It was about a group of waiters falling in love, with a few black marketeers thrown in, once again for Charles Saunders. Charles clearly liked me!

This was followed by *Hildegarde*, again for Rank (the title was changed to *Portrait from Life*) directed by the faithful Terence Fisher at the famous Lime Grove Studios in Shepherd's Bush, where I played another army driver - a soldier again of course. Mind you it was set in "Reconstruction" Germany and all the characters were either inmates of the featured Displaced Persons Camp or in the British Army. I was in one quick scene with a very handsome and friendly actor called Guy Rolfe who was brilliant in *The Spider and the Fly*. I had the simple lines:

"That's it sir. Camp 31." And followed this up with "O.K." when Guy said "I'll get out here."

All shot in a car in the studio. Three takes. Back projection. Mai Zetterling was in it. Again I'd have liked to have met her. But didn't. I got £12.

I was then in *Wedding Bells* (renamed as *Here Come the Huggets)* directed by Ken Annakin (hugely successful and at the beginning of his career. He ultimately directed *Battle of the Bulge*) and produced by Betty Box for Gainsborough Pictures. She was to produce all seven of the *Doctor* series - *House, In Trouble, At Large* etc.. Good old Jack Warner was in it, along with Kathleen Harrison (brilliant in *Scrooge*) and a little girl called Pet Clark, ultimately of course to be a hugely successful pop singer, shot at the old Islington Studios. I had a nice scene as Jimmy Hanley's soldier pal when he's back from his unit to get married. Another one that failed to make the final edit. Bloody hell.

EIGHT
The "Legendary" Michael Powell

Then out of the blue Harry got me an interview with Michael Powell. Yes! THE Michael Powell! I'd heard of him! What about that Mother? Ya boo sucks! Harry encouraged me by saying, "Sid! Look wot I agotta you! Michael Powell! Famous! Get this'un! It'll do you goods!"

Mr. Powell was shortly going to direct a film about scientific boffins, who were back room boys in the war, to be called *The Small Back Room*. It was about a crippled scientist who was the head of a government research station in wartime. While he's battling with his own personal problems, he also strives to unearth the secrets of a new kind of German "booby bomb". I was a little nervous about going to meet the "great man" in his office in Regent Street. I mean he was already a legendary director. I had heard stories relating to his furious temper and his odd attitude at times – especially when things weren't working out the way they should, but went with an open mind obviously. He along with Eric Pressburger had already made many fine films such as *Black Narcissus*, *The Life and Death of Colonel Blimp*, *The Red Shoes*, *A Matter of Life and Death* etc.. and was considered one of the finest film-makers of his generation. As I've said before, I'd already been subjected to belittling interviews where I'd failed to express myself and I went in hoping this wasn't going to be one of them where you get asked stupid lazy questions that reflect badly on the interviewer and always make you want to take the micky. It's the "What have you done?" "What are you doing?" and "Tell me all about yourself" sort of interview that leaves a bad taste. You long to reply "Had breakfast", "Talking to you." And "I love bathing in goat's milk." But surely that wouldn't happen with a "legend"?

The sun was streaming into the room straight on to me when I was ushered into Mr. Powell's presence. He was almost bald and had a small, fair, Hitler type moustache. He was seated with his back to the window so that I had to peer to see his face. After a few questions about the work I'd done and my war career, he suddenly said

"It's the part of a soldier – an old soldier who was active in the Great War. Do you think you could do that?"

"Well yes. Of course." I said. Falling over myself to please. (And secretly, within, asking myself why they weren't going to cast an older actor, who was the real age).

"Really play it, I mean."

(What else was I going to do with it? Ask it out?).

"I….."

"It would mean having your hair cut, army fashion. Would you mind that?"

"No. No. Of course not!" (I'd have had it all shaved off to get the part. Even my pubics if necessary.)

Mr. Powell suddenly said, "They tell me you're a bit of a comedian."

"Well….er…I …. (I was immediately all shy and covered in confusion) "I do know a few jokes……"

"Then make me laugh."

Oh bloody hell. The pressure. Would he like rude jokes? Jokes about Nuns? Nuns on scooters? Would he be offended if he was a Catholic? Would he be offended anyway? I went for it. I told him a near-the-knuckle anecdote involving pregnancy, a stork and a condom (yes, that one) which didn't amuse him at all (there was a heavy silence) and then, panicking, I tried to better it by recounting another one, this time about a baboon, a vicar and a call girl which again fell on stony ground. I foolishly tried a third. (I so wanted the job.) The two spinsters and the parrot. Nothing. I was annoyed now. I did Maurice Chevalier and added Flanagan and Allen. And Vic Oliver. Still nothing. So I shrilly did my Claude Dampier.

"It's meeeeeee!"

He just gazed at me. In fact not at me but slightly over my head. We just sat there. Finally he quickly ushered me out, shook my hand limply and said, "….yes well I'll think about it. Yes. I'll think about it and we'll let you know."

Ah the dreaded "we'll let you know." Which was tantamount to saying that I hadn't got it! I wandered home cursing him, myself, the profession I was in and even the next door neighbour's cat, "Pushkin" who had strayed cheerfully and foolishly into my path. On occasions like this you do a retake of it all, to try to work out how differently you could do the interview to make it better. I vowed to have better jokes and never to tell those again! And not get incensed. Claude Dampier? Oh why did I do him? And the baboon joke? Argh.

Harry phoned me the following day! I was going to apologise. He beat me to it.

"Sid! You goddit!"

"What?"

"Small Black Room!"

"What?"

"You forget already? What you meet Michael Powells for?"

"Sorry Harry, it was a disaster. I did my Claude Dampier and told a rude joke about a baboon. Sorry Harry".

"Sid. Sssh. You goddit!"

"You mean I goddit..er got it?"

"Sid. Why you think I ring you?"

"Ha ha ha ha!"

"Why that so funny?"

"Because I had a lousy interview Harry that's why!"

"You know what they say Sid. In this bizness, louzyness sometime not so bad."

"Ah. Yes. Of course. Thanks Harry."

He was saying you never can tell; which is true of course.

"I got you good rate!"

Well that was a surprise. Or perhaps someone else told worse jokes? I was called to Worton Hall, Isleworth (a friendly little studio) during the first week in May for my role as Private Crowhurst. I quickly got into my battledress, which was becoming second nature to me now, and was then taken by the third A.D. to the hairdresser for my Army cut. After he finished with the croppers, I was a candidate for the Kung Fu Academy or any obvious skinhead role. Thence to make-up, where they proceeded to whiten the remaining 48 hairs left standing.

"Mr. Powell said you were to look like an old soldier from the Great War." said the male make up artist.

"Yes. But is it necessary to take off my eyebrows?"

"Just trimming them that's all. We don't want any recriminations laid at our door, do we?"

He certainly made sure of that! I looked very peculiar. With a bizarre comedy white moustache. Was I playing comedy?

No one ever said! The first A.D. had barked.

"Get him done right away and take him to the governor to look him over. He may be in the first shot."

(I'd been called for 7.30 a.m.). So I was taken to the "Guvnor", Mr. Powell, and offered up for his appraisal. He nodded at me and said, "Okay he will do. But make sure no hair is sticking out from under his forage cap."

He must've been joking surely. The make up person had almost grovelled. He definitely touched an invisible forelock.

"Of course Sir. Mr. Powell Sir. Immediately Sir."

And then to me in the privacy of his room,

"He's a very meticulous man. Very meticulous. But a just one. Yes. Very just."

Blimey. This was all a bit peculiar! In case any hairs dared to peep out under my cap, he singed the remaining two or three offenders! I was ready. Eyebrow-less and hardly-haired perhaps. But ready! As it happened I wasn't used until very much later. Round about teatime in fact. Just for the record, I never removed my forage cap once throughout the whole shoot.

The stars of the film were David Farrar (he was the sleuth, Sexton Blake, in films and on radio and a huge hit in the Powell Pressburger *Black Narcissus*. He was to be in *Cage of Gold*. I'd been in a scene in *Frieda* with him.) Jack Hawkins, (one of the great British screen actors. Great at playing nasty and good characters, a brilliant skill. He was nasty in this. He was the star of *Cruel Sea* which I was in), Kathleen Byron, (a favourite of Michael Powell being in *Black Narcissus* and *A Matter of Life and Death*. It was rumoured that they were an item), Robert Morley, (a very amusing story teller - and upstager, according to Mary Merrall - who was in *African Queen* and was Oscar nominated in 1938 for playing Louis XVI in *Marie Antoinette*) and Cyril Cusack (the great Irish actor. Our paths crossed in telly and radio). I was established as the general man-of-all-work who was always present and greeted at the entrance of the scientific building. Things went along fairly smoothly without any hubbub, until the day that Robert Morley was called to the studio. Apparently, or so I was told, Mr. Morley was so expensive that they could only afford to use him for the one day. In other words, scenes had to be finished on the day that he was called, to keep in line with the budget. Of course, they could have gone "over budget" if necessary, but this was the sort of story that was put about so that the company wouldn't have to pay the other artistes any extra money. Presuming that his fee was something like, say, £250 for one day, they didn't want to fork out another £250 for part of another day. Robert was playing the government minister responsible for the scientists, and Jack Hawkins in this important scene, was brown-nosing the Minister as he had political aspirations. I had to come in, approach Jack and say, "A message sir."

Then I had to hand him the message, turn smartly left, and exit. Simple enough, it would seem, but it didn't work out that way. In order to help me and the camera, I was told by the cameraman to stop at a chosen spot, marked by a thin batten of wood on the floor which was out of sight of the camera, because it was essential for me not to "mask" (get in the way of, in the shot) Jack Hawkins and

Robert Morley. On the first take I came in and stopped short of the mark. On the second I overshot it. I could see the look of impatience on Michael Powell's face and I thought to myself, "Come on Sam. Get it right. Come on."

But on the third take, although I had marked out the number of steps, I foolishly looked down to find the batten, (why I did it I don't know) and Mr. Powell immediately shouted "CUT!" A still silence was allowed to hang for a few seconds. Then he blew up. He really let me have it. He said I was stupid. An idiot. An amateur. What did I think I was doing? Didn't I realise this was costing a hell of a lot of money? And in a loud aside, "That's all we need; some insignificant small part actor holding up production."

What a vile moment. How to react? I found myself standing to attention during his tirade and congratulated myself for being so "in-character." Then I thought of Basil Dearden and wondered how a Nazi salute would go down. A not so funny joke involving a vet and a giraffe entered my head as well and I had to prevent myself from telling it. Claude Dampier made an appearance. Should I do a quick impression? But no. I accepted the abuse and returned to my position for the scene to be re-shot. I asked God to guide me to the mark on the next take and sure enough I was spot-on. Phew! But just as I was congratulating myself, the cameraman said, "Sorry. Have to go again. No good for me."

He didn't explain why and Mr. Powell didn't question his decision. Going again and feeling about as tall as Tom Thumb and as stiff as a shop dummy and being very aware of the icy atmosphere around me, I made the next entrance with my fingers crossed and nearly dropped the message in so doing. But the scene was completed and after a short silence the cameraman sang out, "Okay for me."

I was tempted to do the same. But didn't. Luckily the Great Unsmiling Director whose brow was still dark from the previous "miss-takes" announced, "Right. Next set up."

Which was echoed by the First A.D. (and then of course the

Second. And the Third.) and there was general relief all round. But mostly on my part! Mr. Morley seemed to enjoy the situation – he always had a quip:

"Sam my dear chap, could you be in the next scene as well. I could do with an extra day".

Which was cruel but funny, and a large grin to go with it. But they finished his shots that day. After my embarrassment, Syd Streeter the First, winked at me as if to sympathise. This gave me some comfort; but later on I found out that he had an eye infection and was winking at everybody. And to cap it all, the whole "handing message" sequence was cut! In the actual film I merely stood about and said "hello" three times in long shot, looking oddly like Clive Dunn! But I think that that was the enhanced effect the director was after. It was all to do with the "film noir" and "expressionist" ideas of the time. I mean there was even a sequence where David Farrar was chased by a gigantic wine bottle!

Robert Morley didn't get a credit! He was referred to as "A Guest" in the cast list! I wonder what happened there? Something contractual no doubt! Or perhaps he fell out with Michael? Over money? Over taking three takes to hit his mark?

I was naturally very wary of the critical Mr. Powell, but it seemed to me that everybody was wary of everyone else on the set. When I eventually saw the film on television years later, I thought I looked very apprehensive. Even in long shot! My wife said, "No. You looked good! What I could see of you! You were mostly in the distance!"

Yes. Good but apprehensive. Even in long shot. You couldn't really make out it was me! But as I didn't get any money when the film was sold to a T.V. company, I wasn't all that keen on it anyway.

I was briefly called back for one day in case they were going to shoot another scene, (which they never did) and I saw a masterly and faithfully reproduced set-up in an Underground train (a brilliant set had been designed by John Hoesli) in which our hero, David Farrar, was obviously in great pain from his tin foot. I was not involved in this sequence but I watched it being shot. The train was seen moving along, when of course it's stationary, by means of back projection - a pre filmed sequence is shown on a screen in front of which the actors and the train are shot. The odd lurch which causes the actors to fall over or wobble on their feet is provided by the out of vision props men who jolt the "carriage" up and down. David was standing near the doors, and then the train stopped at the station, the doors opened, and our hero limped out with Kathleen Byron playing his girlfriend and their seats are taken by the throng. End of shot. The crowd workers (or extras, or supporting artistes) were all on board the train, sitting in the arranged positions. It was winter time and most of the men were wrapped up in their overcoats and duffle coats. There were lots of armed forces as you'd expect, it being a war film supposedly in 1943 - sailors and soldiers and R.A.F. The ladies too, were suitably clad in Macintoshes, tweeds and furs, or dressed as Wrens (Women's Royal Naval Service) and W.A.A.F.s (Women's Auxiliary Air Force) and A.T.S. (Auxiliary Territorial Service). Everything was ready to shoot. There was no chatter. They'd already been warned the action was imminent. When suddenly Michael called a halt. It appeared that there was some altercation going on with the person responsible for choosing the crowd players and I heard Michael shout… "I am not shooting this scene until we get proper, ordinary people in the train."

I was confused by this. The majority of the crowd workers had arrived by train on the Piccadilly line. I had spoken to quite a few of them, and they were all ordinary guys and dolls. No one was wearing a clown outfit. Or playing the spoons. Or tap dancing up the carriages. Eventually, after a calming down period when Michael disappeared for several minutes, some of the "extra" ordinary people were changed around and a few scarves and hats and coats were swapped, and he was suddenly happy, and the scene was shot. Michael may have been a genius but it was clearly built on irritatingly "waspish" foundations.

Paradoxically, working on the *Small Back Room,* Harry had got me the best daily rate - £15 per day - I had achieved up till then. I was on it for seven days so got £105! But I never got around to making Michael Powell laugh. Years later, when we were near neighbours living in Melbury Road, Kensington, he unexpectedly invited Pinkie and myself to tea in the garden of his house one afternoon. We'd encountered each other a few times in the street. He was quite charming, civilised, and human – even smiling several times. If I remember rightly, we had strawberries and cream and very strong tea, which I like. We talked about this and that – I was working at the time (on the T.V. series *Crane*) and he was in the throes of setting up a picture in which incidentally there was no part for me! He appeared to be a completely different man from the director I had encountered on *The Small Back Room*. He was full of old world charm, like Dr. Jekyll. Whilst working with him, I had encountered Mr. Hyde. Ah well. We're all entitled to our off days I suppose. Or in his instance, "off years".

Incidentally as a postscript to this story, my son Jonathan became friends with Michael's son Columba and was a frequent visitor to his flat. They played the odd war game scenario as kids tend to do and guess what? Columba played the Officers; and Jonathan was always the Private! He also told me that Columba had authentic prop machine guns from Pinewood; whereas Jonathan had his plastic Woolworth's F.N. Rifle. They all put on a short theatre production of *The Three Musketeers* which I went to see. It was really good. Except Columba as D'Artagnan, had complete 17th. century period costume. Massive 17th. century hat. Big plumed feather. Silk jodhpurs. Big heeled boots. Seville steel sword (sheathed). Jonathan (as Athos) had a cowboy hat with a pigeon feather stuck in it. And a little smock with a cross. And a plastic Woolworth's *Zorro* sword. And his plimsolls. He informed me that on one occasion, one of Michael's films, "Peeping Tom" was being shown in a back room. But he and his chums weren't allowed to see it. It was an X and they were too young! They tried to sneak in but were sent packing! I told him it didn't matter as it one of the few Michael Powell films that hadn't got very good reviews. Though now of course it's a classic!

Oh dear. I received another buff envelope from the War Office. I turned up again at the time stated and was again escorted down the lengthy corridors for what felt longer this time. Or had we gone round in a circle? The room numbers were either higher or lower. 913?319?139?… 275? Once again I can't tell you. I mean, I'm both not allowed and once again can't remember anyway. I was met by another officer with a thin moustache who offered me coffee. With Carnation Evaporated Milk. More photos were thrown on the table. Bizarrely they were of my house mate Johnny Gaskin.

"But this is my house mate Johnny Gaskin!" I blurted.

"Yes we know he lives with you. We want you to tell us if he ever meets this man….Yes?"

Several pictures of someone with very thin pinched features, clean shaven with blonde hair and a sort of haughty air in a sharp suit was slapped on the table in front of me.

"Can you remember this man for us?"

"Well yes….of course…I hope so!"

"Good. And don't tell Gaskin we've had this conversation."

This was a threat.

"No. Of course not!"

"Good".

I was thrown out at speed. I had met the man they'd shown me. It was Johnny's boyfriend Anthony. I had visions of having to report regularly on the both of them and becoming heavily involved in spying on my friend. I didn't tell them.

I went back to Ealing Studios in June for my next film, to play another (guess what?) soldier. Only this time it was a sapper. Another sapper (Harry Locke. We were to be in the same films a lot. Not very often in the same scene though! *Angels One Five, Carlton Browne, Reach for the Sky, Treasure Island, Barnacle Bill*, etc.) and I, were unearthing an unexploded bomb. When we eventually detonate the bomb, we expose a tunnel, in which there is a manuscript that says that some of Pimlico in London is actually part of the House of Burgundy and therefore not British at all and is exempt from post war rationing, and has to have border control! The film was called *Passport to Pimlico* and it was directed by Henry Cornelius, (later to do the famous *Genevieve* with Kenneth More). I had a nice scene with Harry. We're digging in the middle of a heatwave. We're bare chested. Harry is reading a paper. We two sappers are mentioned in the paper! We have a chat about the heat and the bomb which was called Pamela. Bill Shine - a friendly funny man, always playing posh army officers and aristocrats - then appears as Captain Willow, to tell us that we have to detonate it, as they've discovered another "last bomb" and our bomb is no longer as famous. Harry and I are not pleased. And that's it!

It was a sweet little scene. I enjoyed it. We shot the "hole" part in the studio in a rather well designed set. I had a nifty series of tattoos drawn on my chest by an enthusiastic make-up chap called Harry Frampton (well they were a bit basic and didn't take him very long, but nonetheless looked very authentic) one of which was the head of a long-haired comic book hero fellah with a mask on. Or was it a girl in dark glasses or a Red Indian chief? I never actually knew. There were lots of pointy symbols.

"It's Green Lantern" he said. I was none the wiser.

"Obviously I'll make you look sweaty as well, as you're digging. It's a good effect."

I was clearly his work of art. It was very well done!

He applied a lot of petroleum jelly for the sweat - Vaseline.

I was subsequently surprised by how many friends who saw the film either said

"Oooh show us your tattoos!" or looked down their nose at me.

"I didn't know you had tattoos."

As if I'd done something distasteful.

My Uncle Jack heard of it from somewhere and drawled at me in despair and disbelief, at the same time certain that this was another step on the slippery slope of the appalling career I had chosen.

"I've been told you have tattoos now. Who have you been mixing with who persuaded you to do that?" he said wincing and shaking his head.

I had to take my shirt off to show him it had been make-up.

The tattoos couldn't disguise how thin I was. I couldn't put those pounds back on, despite eating for England!

Passport to Pimlico turned out to be another winner for Ealing. And I did two days at £15 a day! One more success for the C.V..

I suppose emboldened by my "success", if you could call it that, I wrote a comedy poem and submitted it to the magazine "Film Industry" that I scoured regularly for cinema and casting information and gossip. The telling news of the day was that from April 18th. 1949 under the "Republic of Ireland Act", citizens of Eire would now be legally regarded as "aliens" in Britain. I sent the mag the following about what choices would the Irish actors make, to be British or Irish? Or could they be both? And they printed it! I called myself "Sham O'Kydd"!

"On Easter Day
Will Galway Bay
And the dreary mountains Mourne?
Will Keiron Moore
Be Anglo-pure
Or alien (Irish born)?

Will Cyril C-
And Brian D-
Abide the new decision?
Will Katheleen R-
(A "foreign" star)
Renounce - or show derision?

Will Arthur Lucan
Show that two can
Leave the Emerald Isle?
Discard the brogue
And start a vogue

"Mum Riley" -English style!
Ye sons of Erin
Shamrock wearin'
Rebel against the Order!
And with one voice
Make now your choice
To sink or swim with Korda!

So must we wait
Until that date-
Eire's emancipation
Yes - wait and see
How one can be
A "double" registration!"

I was pleased with that! All this was increasing my profile.

My reputation was growing and Harry Dubens got me an interview with director Jack Lee for *Once a Jolly Swagman* at Pinewood. He knew my work! Hooray! And I got the part and worked with Dirk Bogarde and Sid James! It was a movie about motorcycling and I played the captain of a Speedway team. I only had a couple of lines, but it was a nice dramatic scene and close up in a three shot.

Sid is Dirk's boss and tells him to take time off after he's just ridden in a race. I over-hear and enter the shot and offer him the chance of riding in my team.

ME: Come and ride for us Bill. How do yer feel about that ?
SID: He's contracted to me.
ME: I'm Captain of the Ilford lot. If you don't need him to ride for you...
SID: He rides for me!
And he's off! Two shot of me and Dirk looking at each other before Dirk rushes to confront him!

I got on extremely well with Dirk. I'd met him briefly on *The Blue Lamp*. Dirk enjoyed my sense of humour. And told me so. After we'd worked together on *They Who Dare* in 1953, he agreed to be Godfather to my son Jonathan. However he was filming when we had the Christening and after our flurry of films together, we lost touch. Jonathan met him once with me in a corridor in Pinewood. And never again. The world can be like that. He was a lovely actor and cleverly changed his career once he'd left Rank, where he was a light comedian in the *Doctor* films. *Libel*, *Victim*, *The Servant,* and *Accident* playing more complex, politicised characters, confirmed him as high-class. He was of course magnificent in *Death in Venice*. I should have kept in contact. But then so should he.

Next I was off to Highbury Studios with John Croydon and Andy Worker to interview for their next film, *Badgers Green,* a wonderful story about a dispute over a company who were attempting to build all over a small village, thus destroying the beauty of the area, and bulldozing the village cricket club in the process. The dispute is decided by a cricket match! I got the part, (I was Harry Parker) convincing them I could handle myself competently on the cricket field, but then I had been in the first XI at school so it wasn't too hard. Obviously, I thought this had been a prerequisite for being cast. To my bemusement though, I didn't have much to do in the cricket match, and more to do as a clerk in the committee meetings for the building company wanting to take over the town. The game was shot at the rather picturesque Odney C.C. in Cookham, next to a tributary of the Thames. It was on the film that I met Garry Marsh. I shall never forget warm-hearted and generous Garry. He was the star of the picture but he never behaved like some stars could. There was nothing aloof about Garry! He had been married several times, but when I met him, he was marking time on the women and concentrating on a different kind of game – cricket, which had obviously contributed to his casting in this instance. He needed to look competent at cricket to make the climax of the film work, and he was more than competent! I believe he actually thought more of cricket than the opposite sex. In fact he once said to me that if he could meet a lady umpire who enjoyed a drink, he'd ask her to marry him immediately, with the proviso that she wore only an umpire's white coat with a new ball in one pocket and a pair of bails in the other. And of course she must never give him out! She would also have to be prepared to discuss the laws of cricket well into the early hours when bad light stopped foreplay. Garry was a marvellous character and introduced me to the Stage Cricket Club for whom I was to play for the next twenty years and Captain for five. At that time, Garry ran the team practically single-handed and if he could arrange it, cricket would take precedence over work. He'd been known to book himself out of work for August and September and frequently turned up at tea time, when filming had gone on longer than expected. Although a bit on the tubby side he was a very good batsman and a more than useful off-spin bowler. As far as fielding was concerned, he was inclined to say "your ball" and leave it at that. It always amused me that for the more "competitive" matches, Garry would employ two ex-professionals to bolster the Stage's chances of not losing ignominiously and consequently forfeit the fixture! The match fee on those days reflected the better standard of our occasional team mates! And you had to buy them drinks! To be fair, they frequently deserved it, winning the game single handed, as was their wont! One of the cast of *Badger's Green* was Kynaston Reeves, (Mr. Quelch in the *Billy Bunter* T.V. series), an aristocratic looking actor with an air of authority about him, which no doubt accounted for his regular casting as a judge, a lawyer, or teacher. He would always arrive at the studio on a vintage bicycle. He did a whole scene in his cycle clips.

"Kynaston. You know you've got your cycle clips on?" I asked him. He replied,

"Indeed. My legs are not in shot."

I told Garry I'd played cricket at Dunstable Grammar. I had kept wicket and batted a bit and was a whippet when it came to fielding - so he invited me to go and see the Stage C.C. game the following

Sunday, which I gratefully accepted. There I met among others, Abraham Sofaer, a superb actor as well as a cricket fanatic. I was to play with him many times. He was a warm hearted man whose acting abilities were never really appreciated in this country. He eventually emigrated to Hollywood when he was about 65 and did marvellously well there, playing leading parts in biblical epics, like Joseph of Aramathia in *The Greatest Story Ever Told*, though I have also seen him as Chief White Buffalo in *Chisum* or Indians or Arabs in *Bhowani Junction* and *Taras Bulba*.

"Sofie", as he was known, was constantly telling anecdotes about well-known personalities and one of his favourites concerned the famous theatre actor, Robert Atkins, known in his later years for his Shakespearean productions in Regent's Park Open Air Theatre. He was the Vicar in Michael Powell's *Matter of Life and Death*. "Sofie" would boom out to all and sundry his imitation of Robert Atkin's fruity voice. It appeared that Robert, being in hospital for some minor complaint, was talking to another patient and began to quote from Shakespeare, as he tended to do. In this instance he felt a bit of *Hamlet* was appropriate as the odour in the room was not a good one:

"This goodly frame the earth, seems to me a sterile promontory.

This most excellent canopy…appeareth nothing to me but a foul and pestilent CONGREGATION OF VAPOURS."

He belted out the last few words as only he could. The head sister came dashing over to his bed.

"Please Mr. Atkins, please, no noise. The patient in the next bed (pointing to one on the other side of Robert) wouldn't appreciate it. He is very ill. In fact (she lowered her voice) he's dying!"

Atkins looked at her, but said nothing. When she had gone Atkins got up and went to the bed of the dying man which was surrounded by curtains. He pulled one of the curtains aside, and looked down at the grey faced, very ill patient. The man's mouth was open and he was breathing with difficulty. Atkins leaned towards him and said, "Hello old man, I hear you don't take too kindly to the Bard. Pity. It looks as if you'll be meeting him later this afternoon."

At this Stage Cricket Club match I also met the founder of the club, one Earle Grey (yes I thought the tea had been named after him, or he'd taken the name of the famous tea as his acting or "stage" name). He sounded very much like John Gielgud, with his immaculate pronunciation and elongated vowels, was match stick thin with a shock of thick white hair, cut very short but standing proud upon his head like a pipe cleaner, and had played cricket in the twenties for Sir Frank Benson's touring company. Benson was a keen cricketer who, when he was touring Hamlet, and playing cricket regularly in the morning and afternoons before a performance, had advertised in the Stage newspaper for a "Laertes. Must bowl off-spin."

Earle occasionally umpired, never ever giving anyone out - I'm not convinced he could actually see the batsman at the other end of the wicket - but mostly sat resplendent watching the game in a faded light blue and white Cambridge cricket blazer in a deck chair, or slowly wandered about the ground, "observing", as befitted his status. I always felt I should bow whenever I met him. Or at least scrape.

"Ah here comes Sir Two Sugars the founder" would be the affectionate cry as he approached, sedately. He was known for his whispered encouragement if you'd done well. Or even if you hadn't.

"Well played....Oh, well played young man" he would croak, elongating the vowels, never knowing your name and never lingering to expect an answer. Also there, was Tony Huntley Gordon, another affable cricketer, who was to be Stage Manager and Company Manager for *The Mousetrap* in the West End for 21 years. He was married to the silent film actress Muriel Martin Harvey, the ex-wife of Garry Marsh ("Just a bowling change" he used to say!) who I knew from Skeggy! Kenneth Milne Buckley, a B.B.C. producer who produced the soap series *Compact* was another member of the team. His mother, May Buckley, donated silver cups and bats for the best averages, in addition to handing out sweets to players and visitors alike. There was a rumour she was a silent film actress but when queried she suggested this was ridiculous. She was a wonderful supporter, often scored for us, and was sorely missed when she died. A match every year against the B.B.C. at Motspur Park, was named "The May Buckley Memorial." In due course Kenneth married the beautiful and beautifully spoken T.V. continuity announcer Sylvia Peters (she eventually presented *Come Dancing* amongst many other shows) and she would come to watch. Only when Kenneth was playing of course! The terrific actor Trevor Howard - who as I said I'd met in *They Made Me a Fugitive* - turned out from time to time. The great farceur Brian Rix - always losing his trousers in the wonderfully crafted *Dry Rot* and *Simple Spymen* amongst many huge hits - and writer/performer/producer Ray Cooney, who wrote *One for the Pot, What a Carve Up* and *Not Now Darling* etc. - put in guest appearances. But the eventual stalwarts during my years with the team, were the fast bowling star of I.T.V.'s *Top Secret* and *Ssshh You Know Who* Schweppes adverts, William Franklyn; Edward "Ted" Cast, beautiful left arm over bowler of immaculate cutters, who was a regular in the B.B.C. radio soap *Waggoner's Walk*; that excellent actor and big hitting batsman John Slater - Sgt. Stone in *Z Cars* for 7 years and Goldberg in Harold Pinter's infamous *Birthday Party* on stage. (Incidentally Harold Pinter himself was of course cricket mad and played for The Gaieities C.C. against the Stage on several occasions.) Hugh and Eric Goldie (Hugh was a producer/director and prolific run scorer and Eric was a singer for the B.B.C.); Russell Napier - Superintendent Duggan in *Scotland Yard* - and all rounder Philip Stone - he was eventually in *Thunderball* and *Where Eagles Dare* - who would use all his acting skills to plead with the umpire to give someone out and frequently succeeded when the batsman certainly wasn't.

"If you scare 'em, occasionally that finger raises itself of its own accord," he told me in his huge Yorkshire tones, which was of course similar to Ealing's Harry Kratz and his shouting. I'd have loved to have seen them bowling in tandem.

And I mustn't forget the charming and effervescent top West End musical performer Clive Stock - an opening bat who had a famous singing double act with Gwen Overton! Clive had been in the C.S.E.U. with Stanley Baxter and Kenneth Williams and was a master of publicity and was well known for advertising his act with Gwen in the top left hand corner of the Stage Newspaper!

The Stage Cricket Club's great day is always in September when they play at Lord's, M.C.C. headquarters, the shrine of cricket! In the fixture list, it is billed as Stage C.C. versus Cross Arrows, the latter usually being a collection of Lords ground-staff, some gentleman cricketers and one or two Middlesex players who are at a loose end. It used to take place on the hallowed turf of Lords itself, but now it is played on what is known as the Nursery - the practice ground, where the nets are. It is very rare for the Stage to beat the professional side. They do on one or two occasions, but usually the Cross Arrows team beat us out of sight or we scramble a so called "honourable draw". Garry habitually approached the match as if it were a military operation. At the Sunday game before the big day, all the chosen players were ordered to have clean and pressed kit: crisp shirts, creased flannels and whiter than white boots. The team would meet for one hour before the match to have coffee and discuss tactics, and then all progress to the ground in a hired char-a-banc. In fact this meeting was always a waste of time. There were no tactics. The opposing team always dictated them. The Stage always fielded first, expecting the Arrows to post a large score and then would endeavour to get as near as possible. On several occasions I was given the job of whitening all the pads, checking the new balls (both of them) finding the score book (it had a tendency to be left in the possession of whoever had been scoring at the previous game), and cleaning the wicket-keeper's box (it protected the meat and two veg and was attached to a dubious much stained white leather and fabric truss that was always tethered via belts and buckles and hooks and eyes around your waist. It looked like something you'd wield in a torture-chamber). In those days very few players had their own equipment so everything was piled up in a huge aromatic (let's be frank it had a very peculiar odour, a bit like slightly off Marmite) leather team bag that was impossible to carry, as it was chock full of so many extra bats and pads and balls in various states of decay; and also a treasure trove of peculiar detritus from the team's travels: many beer mats. "Guinness is Good for You", "Double Diamond works Wonders", "Make mine a Mackeson". Wrap around sausage batting gloves. A pair of very used enormous wicket keeping gauntlets with no pimples left on the rubber. Chammy leather inners - to wear inside wicket keeping gloves - with some fingers missing. A rusty tin box marked "First Aid" with nothing but a bandage and smelling salts in it. A few broken crisps - unflavoured. A restaurant menu for the Veeraswamy Indian off Regent Street. Various old team lists. Including a couple from the 30s with Boris Karloff on them. Also, a French pre-war rail timetable. And a couple of green sweat stained Stage caps size 6 and seven eighths. I decided not to tidy the bag in case there was a tradition to leave every item in situ. I got Garry to give me a lift! There was no way I was carrying that on the bus! I'd have done myself a mischief!

All the players, unless engaged in the theatre, were expected to stay after the match, which normally ended at 6 o'clock, to entertain our opponents at the celebrated Lord's Tavern. A collection was made to supply money for the large number of jugs of ale. If a player had done well, had scored 50 for example, he would be expected to buy his own jug, but would put up with the expense by enjoying the adulation when he went round pouring it, knowing his largesse would be reciprocated. Being good however could therefore be quite expensive! I rarely made fifty, though once bought a jug for getting five catches behind the stumps. And there was always the "skipper"'s jug which I was happy to purchase when captain. On one occasion in the early days, I was what is known as "12th. man". This was a polite way of saying that I had been appointed to be the skivvy and even if anyone did drop out, which of course sometimes happened, I still wouldn't automatically play. No, they used somebody else who they considered better than me, though officially I was still 12th. man and should have been substitute! If someone was late, the 12th. man would play until the latecomer took the field. I had my name on the printed scorecard, mind you, and that was an honour in itself I suppose. Another time when I was 12th. man I was watching the match from a comfortable seat in the stand and our opponents were 252 for four wickets. They were coming up for declaration time (meaning for all you non-cricketers out there, that they would declare their innings as finished and it would be our turn to bat). During a short break while the sight-screen was being moved - you move the large wooden white screen on wheels so that the batsman can see the ball coming out of the white background from the bowler's hand. The ball is more visible - one of the actors wandered over towards me and hissed something about "change". I looked in my pockets and said loudly. "Yes! I've got some! How much do you want?"

"Not "change". He spluttered. "Change!"

I obviously gave him a bewildered look. He shouted

"Change your clothes!" (I was in grey flannels and wearing a blazer) "You're supposed to be changed in case something happens and you have to field!"

At this stage of the game, the "something happening" was all of the players coming off for tea, and in any case I had "changed" earlier and had just "changed" back into my ordinary clothes. It was now a quarter to 4, declaration time, then there would be 20 minutes for tea, after which we would be batting immediately. According to the laws even if someone has broken an ankle, I wouldn't be allowed to bat.

"Oh yes!" I answered. "I shall do that immediately. How remiss of me and good of you to point it out."

The annoying man who'd requested I "change" was perturbed to see me at tea not having done so. The fool. We lost anyway and I vowed I'd never be 12th. man again. Happily the following year I was picked to play, and from then on was a regular. Incidentally Prince Phillip is 12th. man for the Lord's Taverners. I bet they don't ask him to whiten the pads and scrutinise the wicket-keeper's box and be a permanent stand-by!

Surprise surprise! After *Badger's Green* I was engaged by the B.B.C. for two radio jobs. Both were documentaries - once again using actors with a few scripted lines - and were written by Alan Burgess and Tom Waldron respectively. (Alan wrote Ingrid Bergmann's biography). It was no coincidence that they were staunch cricket lovers and always turned up to play for the midweek Stage matches whenever they could. I was cast because of my cricket! I'd written to producers at the B.B.C. on many occasions (Archie Campbell had used me obviously) erasing Charles Maxwell from my memory and fibbing that I'd broadcast to the forces in Germany, but this connection was a sweet success! Hooray for cricket! The very friendly David Jacobs and I (David was soon to present *Pick of the Pops* on the Light programme. He became a star after *Juke Box Jury*. We were to be at many Charity events together in the 60s) played several parts in Alan's *Goodbye to All This* programme and I narrated the other one whose name escapes me. As they were repeated and then sold overseas in what was called the "transcription service", the fee, although never enormous - 6 guineas in this instance - was another 6! Which is nice work if you can keep repeating it!

Some actors and actresses concentrate entirely on broadcasting. It suits their book and they are extremely good at it and are content to do that only, unless they are lucky enough to get some "Voice Over" work to augment their income. These are the voices you hear over the television commercials exhorting you to buy this or that. My good friend and colleague, Patrick Allen, has monopolised this side of the business for several years and has made oodles of money in the process. He has the perfect voice for selling the goods, be it tyres, chewing gum, shampoo, houses, etc., etc., and in his case I definitely mean etc., etc.! He even has his own recording studio in Soho! It's very well equipped, ultimately modern and extremely comfortable. He sprays his throat regularly – morning noon and night. And like Frank Sinatra, exercises and swims underwater to excess so he can say those long sentences without running out of breath.

"Today" he says. "Today I am off to record four 30 second

commercials. Let us spray!"

Well obviously he doesn't really, but he does take it very seriously. And rightly so! It is a great source of remuneration!

I got to know him rather well when we did the TV series, *Crane*. 39 episodes of it in fact. He's a good lad. What they call "canny" in the north-east. I am able to refer to him as "lad" because I'm older than he is. Older but not wiser.

There is also the B.B.C. Radio Repertory company known as "The Rep" which is a collection of elite (and sometimes aloof) actors who are contracted for one to two years to work only for broadcasting. I don't quite understand why you'd want to be "aloof" because you do radio, or anything in the Arts really, but there you are. There's nowt as queer as folk. Some actors get a sniff of stardom or even regular work, and they become "aloof". It's immensely tiring having someone you know well (or thought you did) look down their nose at you when you've spent days with them on a film and in the pub. They tend to get short shrift when the work dries up and they want to be your pal again. Naturally Radio Rep. actors are all very efficient, workmanlike and exclusive, enjoying a fairly lucrative living. One of my old sporting acquaintances, Douglas Blackwell, (*Z Cars*, *Ipcress File*, *I Was Monty's Double*) is one of the elite whose name is always appearing in the Radio Times cast lists. He is daft about cricket too. He's not "aloof". Quite a nifty bowler once upon a time. Now he's medium nippy!

After the broadcasts I was engaged to play an angry husband in a film called *It's Hard to Be Good* at Denham Studios. This was directed and written by Jeffrey Dell. I had a rather excellent comedy scene with the always warm Jimmy Hanley who was playing an army Captain in uniform.

We both got off a bus - the bus and the scenes were shot in the studio with outside filmed inserts - and I accused him of trying to pick up my wife, as he'd offered to carry her bag. Lots of "Oi what are you up to? That's my wife! I know what you're after" acting.

All in a rather fetching flat cap. Jimmy of course is taken aback as he was only offering to help. I say, "Come on then. I'll fight yer!" Or words to that effect.

I then gaze at the ribbons on his chest and am confused coz Jimmy's won the Victoria Cross! "'Alf a mo! If I'd noticed that V.C. before, I wouldn't have said what I did."

He then persuades me that the ribbon makes no difference and if I'm offended I should still be offended. I ponder a moment, stroking my chin, and then decide to punch him. And then wander off bandy legged into the distance with my "missus"! He was trying to be "good" you see. But as my actions emphasised, he was finding it "hard".

My punch (obviously I didn't punch him and he propels himself backwards) left him falling and ending up sitting in a dustbin! (which incidentally they had to shoot about six times to get the angle of his being stuck in the bin, right. They also changed the camera speed so that Jimmy could propel himself backwards at a leisurely pace and when played back it would look as if he'd been smashed into the bin. They padded the bin with blankets and cushions. Jimmy was either perched too high or went in too far). Whereupon - and here's another comedy moment - he's in the bin saluted by a couple of soldiers who happen to be passing by. (Shot much later after Jimmy was long gone. They didn't salute Jimmy obviously. They saluted the second A.D. standing out of shot, giving them the eye-line. Oh, the joys of the edit). And we cut back to Jimmy who salutes them stuck in the bin. Ho ho! I mean, as I say, I didn't actually punch him! I was standing opposite him in profile and I used my left hand to miss his face on the left hand side, and a "punch noise" was added on by a props guy hitting a board with a haddock. (Or possibly a cushion!) It looks as if I hit him! He then staggers back and "voila!" Binned! Ah the logic of assembling shots! This was a fine scene. It helped that Jimmy and I got on so well. He was great and encouraging as you'd expect. We had dinner! I got £15 again! P.S. When I saw it back in the cinema, I was intrigued to see that Jeffrey Dell used the two shot of Jimmy and I favouring me! All of it! So you see my face with the side of Jimmy's head! The camera angle featuring Jimmy which we'd shot, wasn't used! I took that as a big compliment. But in fact when you think about it Jimmy's character was setting me up for the gags so it was astute editing. Nice to be so favoured though!

In fast succession followed two episodes of *Mrs. Dale's Diary* for the B.B.C. Light programme. I was Wilkes, the car washer, who spoke "loike dat". A forelock tugger again, even in radio, where I can't be seen! But that's how I was viewed, so I just had to expect and accept it. Clearly there was something in my character that played deferential parts well. Perhaps the P.O.W. in me? The car-washing sequences, as usual, were done as special effects by the Studio Stage Manager, who had a whole series of brilliant radio spot S.F.X (sound effects) at her disposal, like small doors with door knockers on, so that she'd give the impression a door was being knocked on and opened or closed, all from her little F.X. trolley. In this instance she did a mass of sloshing and swishing and washing, with her shammy and a pail of water on the surface of a a metallic cupboard door, which she used to give the impression of a car's wing or bonnet being cleaned. Of course this was meticulously mic'd up! Quite a skill! Here's a tip: a box full of old magnetic tape, sounds just like a pile of old leaves if you swirl it all about! I got 5 guineas an episode!

I was to play Wilkes several times over the next two years, each time directed by Archie Campbell and Cleland Finn. I'd been recommended by cricketing chums Alan Burgess and Tom Waldron! I wonder if they all knew Charles Maxwell? (Sssh. Sam. Stop. No more Charles Maxwell. The reader will think you've got a complex.)

During this period, there was a big debate in the press (and was a hot topic amongst all film business employees), about star actors asking for too much money and preventing some films from making a profit. The film critic Milton Shulman consequently suggested in an article that acting roles should be offered to members of the public, obviously at very low fees, and thus save the film companies from going bust, due to the "excessive" demands from the greedy stars. My response to this was to send off another poem to "Film

Industry", referring especially to the fact that Milton hinted that after a few "goes", these "people on the street" would be as good as all the other actors! To have an eminent critic voice this view was possibly done deliberately by Milton to gain himself some publicity. But luckily there is a Union to prevent this scenario from ever happening. Having said this, this is something that the employers would secretly (and not so secretly when your daily rate descends to a ridiculous level) always seek: members of the public to do the work, so they can pay them very small amounts of money.

Here's my poem, which the charming editors of "Film Industry" rather enjoyed. And published! I called it "An Ode to Milton".

We hear it on the radio.
We read it in the press.
They all take pains to tell us,
"How we can solve the mess."
But the Brightest Brain of all
(Don't tell me you can't guess)
Is Shulman

Exhibitor - Distributor
And of course the T.U.C.
They're meeting almost daily
But talks have been N.G.
But away with all this parley-
Blind men never see -
Says Shulman!

A pruning of the budget,
Directors who direct!
It's all so very simple -
The least one can expect
"Is to turn out monthly features
And not have one reject."

Says Shulman.

He'll guarantee to find the stars
Upon the Central line.
A waitress or a postman
He'll get 'em all to sign.
What's the query. "can they act?"
Oh well, they will in time.
Says Shulman.

And if we take this choice advice
And weed out all the chaff
And cut down all expenses
By reduction of the staff,
He too should make a gesture
And reduce his pay by half.
What, Shulman?

No - I think the time has come
When we should tell him what to do.
He should stick to "Clever Cliches"
With the criticising few,
And let the men who *make* the pictures
Solve their problems too.
Not Shulman!

I met Milton a few times socially after this and he was always
very charming. Neither of us ever said a word about the poem or his
belief that any member of the public could walk on a set and act! I
think it was tongue in cheek.

I then found myself working for Cav again, in the opening titles
of a film where the camera concentrated on a group of convicts, of
which I was one, accompanied by a warder, who was Kenneth More.
I walked up the tortuous inside winding steps that connected all the

cells on all the floors of the prison, closely followed by Kenneth. The camera zoomed in on our feet – a low, quick, quick quick, low, foot shot, panning up the stairs and finally coming to rest on our hero, and star of the film, playing a convict, in prison for a crime he didn't commit, Richard Todd - soon to be the star of the iconic war film *The Dam Busters* and with whom I was to work in *Yangtze Incident*. The title of the film was, *For Them that Trespass*. Kenneth More told me that the film saved his life financially. He was completely out of money. Skint! Then Bob Lennard, the casting director, phoned him up one Saturday morning offering him the warder's job. No billing, but a quick fifty quid. He talks about it in his book *More or Less*. He took it, paid his rent having considered giving it all up and going back to the Navy, and never looked back! Kenneth's next film, a huge success for him, was the aptly named *The Chance of a Lifetime* (which I was in) and fate was to link us together once more, Mr. More! *Trespass* was shot at Welwyn Garden Studios.

I think it was the only time I ever worked there. I was on for two days for 15 guineas a day. And guess what? My scenes were cut! And the opening sequence was replaced with a single actor walking down the prison steps! We obviously still got paid! Though Kenneth did have a line spoken to Richard Todd with his back to camera:

"Don't let it get you down", in those fine modulated moreish tones of his!

But guess what again! That actor walking down the stairs in the prison on his own, was actually me! Cav had said

"Sam, let us do a shot of you slowly walking down the stairs and zen stop and look about you, half way up, and then walk down and zen straight up to zer camera."

So I did as requested.

"We may use for ze opening instead of ze ozzers." he said.

And they did! But as luck would have it, I'm utterly unrecognisable, covered by all the opening titles. And when I finally approach the camera, I'm in silhouette. (Obviously at the time I had no idea I'd be obscured by Times font!) When I saw the start of the film, I burst out laughing.

A pile of films came and went, now that I had the focal point of Harry: *Look Mum, Soldiers* a C.O.I. (Central Office of Information) film. I got £7.10/-, half my usual fee, as it was for the government. (I've never worked out why you weren't paid proper money. You were still acting. You weren't "half-acting.")

I was then in *Saints and Sinners*, directed and written by Leslie Arliss, where I was the rather uncomplicated "Man in Bar". I used my Irish accent for that one as it was set in an Irish village. Liam Redmond was in it. I wanted to ask him if he'd been arrested but didn't.

Then followed a few films I have in my diary but I'm sorry to say I can't remember much about them.

She Died Young. I did a day. I have a vague memory of turning up and hanging about and not being used and then being told they'd cut the scene and I was no longer required! Got £12 though. "Nuffink for munnie" said Harry.

A Drive in the Country for the Crown Film Unit, (£8.8/- a day, for two days. Another government film. Another smaller fee.)

Mr. Jolly's Journey. No idea. It says I did half a day. I got 3 guineas.

Floodtide playing a Scots barman. (Not quite "man in bar"). Gordon Jackson played the lead. He changes careers to become a ship designer rather than a farmer.

Private Angelo (scenes cut from that one). I remember I briefly met Peter Ustinov. He was friendly.

Mrs. Worth Goes to Westminster produced by Verity Films. It was a drama-documentary short, funded by the British Iron and Steel Federation. But in fact it was a sort of advertisement really. The plot involved someone (not me) visiting their M.P. at the House of Commons to ask about the state of...you guessed it...the Iron and Steel industry. Nigel Byass directed it. But my memory hasn't been jogged as to what I did in it. Sorry.

Feature Story directed by Michael McCarthy, starring the lovely Margo Johns who was to marry William Franklyn, was next. Once again my brain is a sieve. Other than Margo, who I was to see most Sundays whenever I played cricket with Bill.

Poet's Pub at Pinewood got me four days' work so that was £60. Though I was on call for four and only used for two. I was George the hotel porter in the "Downy Pelican". It was about a rowing-blue/poet played by Derek Bond who managed the pub/hotel. I remember a lovely actress called Barbara Murray was in it as a maid; who was actually a journalist! I don't mean Barbara Murray was a journalist. She was playing one. The marvellously unique Joyce Grenfell was in it too. But I didn't have a scene with her. I had a couple of words "Yes sir," at the beginning of the film, to the question, "Will you show Mr. and Mrs. Benbow their rooms?"

And took the bags upstairs for the new guests. And then brought them down again at the end of the film. Hardly in it. Though I did carry some more bags in a scene which was cut. And then, continuing the bag motif, had a scene in my next film carrying one, which was *Madness of the Heart*, playing a pilot carrying a large suitcase knocking into Margaret Lockwood, shot at the Kensington Airport depot in Kensington High Street, (which is where you checked in to get a coach to Heathrow in those days). Well I sort of backed into her to make it work, just before she walked off and had a funny turn. My line was the intricate, "Oh I'm sorry".

What was so ridiculous was the elaborate audition I had to do for this tiny part. Charles Bennett the director wasn't there and it was an assistant whose name I never caught (thank goodness or you'd know who to boo) who had me walking up and down carrying an imaginary bag and pretending to do "knocking into someone" acting.

"Could you be more aggressive?"

"Yes of course!"

I did it more aggressively. I was quite surly really.

"No that was too aggressive. A bit less aggressive. We don't want Margaret Lockwood injured. She's the star. "

"Yes of course she is. No of course not."

"Try just three steps. You don't need a run-up. And then hit her.

With your bag of course! Ha hahahaha. Not your fists!"

"No! Ha ha ha!"

Oh the wit. I three-stepped across briskly. But not too briskly.

"I'm not seeing the bag."

There wasn't one of course.

"Create a better bag for me."

So I mimed a better bag.

"A bigger bag please. It's too little for me."

I held up an invented trunk of enormous dimensions straining to put it on my shoulder.

"No that's too big. Make it like a sort of bag you can hold on your shoulder with a strap, but it might have a tennis racket or cricket bat in it."

"Alright!"

"Try again."

I wondered if he was deliberately seeing how far he could push me. I walked across again.

"Yes good bag. Now walk more deliberately. As if you've got a coach to catch!"

I created the long (ish) bag and walked in, in a determined but not too aggressive fashion.

"Yes that was great. Same again but now say the line "Oh excuse me.""

I did it, saying the line quite normally.

"The line needs to be more sympathetic. She's beautiful. She's Margaret Lockwood. You've smashed into a deeply attractive woman. You're aghast but worried and slightly in love with her at the same time. Try it."

I did.

"Now more love and shame. And slight irritation."

I did it again.

"And now be "devil-may-care!""

I was.

"Good. Thanks for coming in err…"

"Sam".

"Yes. Sam."

"We'll be in touch!"

What a pile of poo. You're always on the verge of saying

"For goodness sake you are such a twerp!"

(Or something like that.) I must have done it to his sadistic satisfaction as I got the part. When I shot it, Margaret and I just collided and I said sorry and that was that. Charles Bennett said, "Thank you. Well done!".

The First said "Moving on", I said, "Lovely working with you however briefly" to Margaret and she said, "Likewise!" as she was whisked off to make up.

I then did some post-syncing on *Now Barrabas was a Robber* for Victor Wark at Gate Studios playing a few cut-throats and prisoners. I had to vocally interpret being whipped, which is exhausting let me tell you!

"Sam I'm not getting you're being whipped" said Victor.

(This was becoming a theme after the "I'm not seeing the bag" scenario).

"Well I'm not Victor. I'm acting it."

"Well I could always hit you on the backside with this script."

"Ah. Possibly! Let me have another go before you do."

My next take was fine. I got 5 guineas! A young Richard Burton was in it! But I obviously didn't meet him as I was doing the dubbing. I got £6 for doing some voices at Gate Studios on *Lay that Ghost*. A bit of shrieking! I'm good at that! Mind you I think most actors are good at that. In the same way that most actors don't find it too difficult to play "mad" or "angry". It's not far below the surface!

And half a day's dubbing on *Silent Film* for £3. I did speak! I promise!

Plus some commentary on *Crystal Clear* at Merton for another five guineas. These little amounts always kept the wolf from the door.

I then had some terrible, bewildering news from Richard Stone, who I bumped into in town. Peter Waring, who had been so supportive towards me, had killed himself. I was completely taken aback by this. I never thought that such a gregarious, amusing, singular, friendly man could end his own life. He'd been fabulous to me. But of course we never truly know people, do we. For a start, he was not, I now learnt, who he had said he was. Far from being a Commander in the Royal Navy, who was invalided out due to his arm injury - he'd worked for E.N.S.A. as "Commander Peter Roderick-Mainwaring D.S.O., R.N." - his real name was Rodrigues, and he had in fact in his youth, stowed away on a cross channel ferry and burnt his arm on a pipe whilst doing so! This was his injury he'd supposedly got in the war. And he'd invented the Commander who never existed! He'd also been in prison for theft, had been to borstal for stealing jewellery and was a declared bankrupt. And according to the newspapers, he'd been using his celebrity with the B.B.C. after recording 6 episodes of the very successful *Heigh Ho!* to run up huge amounts of debt. I was mystified. I'd not experienced any of this behaviour on tour with him; I don't believe any of us had. Apparently he was also constantly getting engaged to be married to young daughters of very well-off parents, and would then break off the engagements having "borrowed" money from his would-be wives. And in fact already had an estranged wife and two children to whom he'd failed to keep up maintenance payments. He owed thousands of pounds. His fees for his comedy performances never covered the price of the hotels he was staying in, or the lavish parties he was throwing, or his constant hiring of private aeroplanes to take him to jobs all over the country. He was obviously completely living beyond his means. I suppose on reflection, having a manservant who he clearly couldn't afford, was an example of his profligacy. We just presumed he had a private income. The B.B.C., so I was told, had been fielding complaints about him from members of the public who had been his victims. His life was a minefield of criminality. As I say, not a single fraudulent event had we experienced on tour, though in fact I learnt he'd fitted the tour in in the period during which he'd been suspended by the B.B.C. for past financial wrongdoing, with which the public were filling up the Radio postbag and of course about which we knew nothing. But surely all of these lies and chicanery wouldn't have made him take his own life? But it must have been the shame and knowledge that no one would ever employ him again. He was a top comedian for whom one could only see a glittering future. And he'd thrown all that talent away. He hanged himself in his cell in Pentonville after he'd beed sentenced to nine months for fraud. It was all over the newspapers.

I was devastated. I couldn't believe it. He must have been at such a low ebb. I attempted to speak to his ex "man" Bill Montague, but had no idea where he was. He wasn't in the phone book, and the only number I had was the mews in Mayfair and he obviously didn't live there anymore. I despairingly tried it and was of course treated to, "Who? No one of that name here!"

I went round to the Forbes Russell Agency, but they'd heard of his "misdemeanours" and weren't very sympathetic. I phoned Harry. But he knew nothing about it and was shocked. I ran into a brick wall in fact. Some people almost gave the impression they thought he deserved it.

"Killed himself because of the duplicity."

"Couldn't have a career any longer after he'd been found out. He was a fraud and committed fraud. Good riddance".

I obviously didn't agree with these hardened attitudes. I mean obviously serve your time. But I could see how he must have felt. There were many I'd experienced first hand in prison camp who gave up when in the throes of despair. R.I.P. Peter. I was looking forward to working with you again. You were so kind to me. I wish I'd had the opportunity to talk you out of your decision.

I began to get jobs just by being with Harry. Obviously, for a lot of films, they still wanted to see you for an "interview" and occasionally you'd read the lines, but mostly if they'd worked with you before, they'd trust you to get it right and employ you if you were available. They'd send you the script. A cough and a sniff some of them perhaps, but work, nonetheless. Naturally each part required a costume fitting, which was either at a costumier like Berman's or at the studios themselves. Though frequently you'd just have to give your sizes to "wardrobe" over the phone and if you didn't fit the costume they'd pin you in. Many's the time I'm in a two shot and my shirt is two sizes too big and behind me, several safety pins are pulling the back of the shirt together. Occasionally wardrobe might tear the waist of a pair of trousers if it was too small and just have to deal with the cost! Some actors' waist sizes go up and down like escalators, so most wardrobe masters and mistresses have a larger pair put aside just in case, but sometimes on a low budget film, you just had to "make do". Sometimes they'd say, "Sam just wear your own suit".

These were the very low budget ones.

Trottie True starring Jean Kent - who was a very fiery energetic actress who'd recently been the lead in *The Good Time Girl* - was next in line. Set in 1890 and filmed innovatively in Technicolor, unlike so many of my early films which were in black and white, it was about a "Gaiety Girl", a music hall performer, who eventually marries a member of the aristocracy, but yearns for the balloonist she first went out with! Jean was perfect casting, as her parents were variety artists and like Trottie she'd been a child performer. I didn't actually meet her, or work with her, which was a shame as I thought she was great. (Though I fulfilled my ambition on *The Lost Hours*). It was a musical (though I didn't have a song), with several ditties of the period and shot at Denham Studios. I played the stage manager of the "Bedford" music hall (in fact we did it on location at the Camden Empire) , the scene of "Trottie's" first triumph, when Bill Owen - then known as Bill Rowbotham pronounced Rowbottom - mentors her first music hall appearance.

The director was a big bluff Irishman named Brian Desmond Hurst. He was, like me, from Belfast and had recently made the brilliant documentary about the Battle for Arnhem *Theirs is the Glory*.

He was to direct Alastair Sim in one of my favourite films ever, *Scrooge*. He was amusing, witty and rude, and could talk the skin off a rice pudding, creating a fun dynamic environment. He was always forgiven for having a spiky tongue on account of his Irish blarney. During the filming he kept referring to me and Bill as "the twins".

"Could the twins possibly do the scene a little bit more quickly as at the moment the acting is slightly on the slow side and that's not bad, but I have had two cups of tea, three sandwiches and a piss while you've been doing it."

They gave me a rather swish moustache, a centre parting, a lovely waistcoat and a small scene with a fifteen year old Dilys Laye (ultimately to be a terrific comedy performer. She was in possibly the best ever Carry-On, *Carry on Camping*) who was fabulous as the "Little Trottie", when Trottie was making her first ever music hall appearance.

"Run round the back and come on the other side" was my line to her.

She sang a little song and danced only to be heckled from the Gods.

"Look it's a baby!" said the heckler. "Where's your mother?"

"She's gonna get it in the neck!" I said to Bill (who was playing Joe the comedian who was in love with her).

But she heckled back "Next to you! About to hit you on the head!" and a Trottie star was born. I enjoyed working with Bill, however briefly. He was always cheery and friendly. We'd worked on *Once a Jolly Swagman* and were to be in *Rainbow Jacket* together. It's always good to do a scene with a friend.

After *Trottie True* I was involved in two more episodes of *Mrs. Dale's Diary*, again as Wilkes the car washer. At five guineas an episode with repeats, it was quite useful. I had some nice scenes with Mrs. Dale, Ellis Powell, whose car I cleaned.

"Oh dear Mrs Dale. Them pigeons 'as made a right mess of yer bonnet! I'll 'ave to apply all of me cleanin' skills! (CUE: Splish-splosh!)"

Despite all this work coming my way, my Mother, even after my speech on Christmas Day, was still at it, would shake her head and tut a lot when I came down for breakfast later than half past seven. She got quite cunning in her attempts to get me to reconsider my life. In this instance, her brother Jack, a landlord and ex-dresser in the theatre, who was disparaging about actors (he must have had a nasty experience in a wardrobe) had clearly been told to tell me tales of actors with no work, who had ultimately let down their families.

"It's not a profession for a responsible mature man you know", he said in his very superior, slightly camp "posh" Belfast accent. And continued,

"The actors I've known, became bitter and twisted. Or alcoholic. Or both. It's not too late to become an accountant. I have an opening for you."

Ye Gods. Accountancy. Well at least there was no connection with bedding. Meanwhile another Army picture, entitled *The Town Patrol* for Julian Wintle and directed by Michael McCarthy (with me playing my usual soldier, this time on a motor bike) for 8 guineas, came and went. It seemed as if I was never out of uniform for long; but at least I was getting well-paid for it!

I was employed as a stall holder looking to steal a "pitch' from the hero, American actor Douglass Montgomery, in a Blackpool Amusement Park. This was in *Forbidden* directed by George King. George was famous for the 1936 film *The Demon Barber of Fleet Street* and was a very thorough director, always marching about looking for shots, sizing things up, peering through a lens.

"Yes it would work if we shot it like that. Yes! Let's do it!"

Douglass had risen to fame in the U.S., having been in the huge success, *Little Women* in 1933. He'd made his home in England after fighting over here for the Canadian Air Force. His co-star was Hazel Court, who'd just been in *Bond Street*. I was Joe. I had a nice scene followed by a fight! The delectable Hazel - eventually a "Hammer Horror" starlet - was very friendly and approachable. Douglass was initially a bit distant and I thought uncomfortable, but to be fair to him, he seemed to think deeply about his character and was frequently looking at his script. Perhaps he hadn't learned the lines and was mugging them up? But he was friendly enough after our "fight"! All my scenes were shot at Riverside Studios in Hammersmith (just by the Bridge), although it was set in Blackpool, and there were some excellently lit clever sets, making it authentically look as if we were in the Amusement Park. Consequently, as it was set "up North", I had a gruff Northern accent, as did my co-antagonist Eric Whittle. Though Hazel's was a sort of mid well spoken cum cockney effort! I'm not sure anybody cared! It was Hazel Court after all, and she was gorgeous. In the scene which allowed Hazel and Douglass's characters to first meet, Eric and I were setting up a stall which was promised to Douglass - he had the chitty saying it was his - and we had strong words:

"You have to claim your pitch here" I say.
Hazel then sides with Douglass and intervenes with me and Eric and is then grabbed by Eric.
"Hey stop that!"
"And who's stopping him? says I.
"I am" he says.
Thwack. Douglass hits me!

Well, he doesn't actually hit me. We see him in close-up swing a punch and in the following shot on me, I leap backwards from the force (obviously he misses me) and smash back into the stall. In one of the takes I fell back slightly too off-kilter and demolished the awning! We shot this one several times and in both wide and close up, so they could cut between the two. I had to be careful not to smash my head leaping backwards and had to fall safely, but of course there was a mattress out of shot for me to fall onto, in the close ups. My character's reaction is to pile in. George shot that by just having me run out of frame, then he cuts to the wide of me and Douglass hitting each other. This big scrap between me and

Douglass, which annoyingly wasn't choreographed by a fight director
- I think they were saving money - when I saw the film, didn't show
my face at all! It's all on Douglass (well he was the star) and my back!
They'd shot several takes favouring me, but didn't use them! As there
was no fight director, we sketched out what to do between the two of
us. It was quite complex. I wrote it on the script:

"Two missing right cross punches, one each, where we both
duck.

A pulled punch from me into his side.

Followed by a non-contact kick from me then a clinch and a
right handed swing each.

Another clinch to the floor and then up on our feet.

And two more swings from me, left and right over his head as
he dips, and one from him, same again as I dip."

Complicated, but we worked it out. Though of course, I repeat,
there should have been a fight director. It shouldn't have been up to
us. However, after expressing satisfaction with what Douglass and I
had done, George King told the crowd of 30 supporting artistes who
had been observing the fight, that he now wanted a lifelike melee and
general stampede to take place involving everyone there! And he
added, "Keep fighting until I shout 'Cut'. Okay?"

He shouted "action" and all hell broke loose. Fairground stalls
were broken, beer glasses were smashed, specs were snatched off
faces and stamped on, false teeth were expelled never to be seen
again. I was the target for two or three pugnacious crowd workers
who guessed incorrectly that the camera was on certain actors, me
included - it was just a wide shot - so they made the most of their
obvious pugilistic abilities. I was bashed, pummelled, shoved, and my
hair pulled. I was punched on the nose, kicked in the goolies, and
finally my torn jacket was ripped off. No doubt Berman's, the
costumiers, got their compensation for it. I'm glad to say that I did! I
nursed secret bruises for days afterwards and when I came to do the

post synchronising for the scene (redoing my lines for the sound man who didn't get them the first time and emitting the odd "grunt" for the fighting) I complained bitterly to the casting director, Paul Sheridan, who had seen the rushes. He apologised and promised to make it up to me, being the gentleman that he undoubtedly was. (I'm not sure how you make it up to anyone as a casting director. You're either right for the part or you're not! Or possibly you get seen when you're not quite right? But he meant well.)

There are certain actors who enjoy a rough house such as the one I had endured. I think they like to prove how strong and virile they are. Some feel that their acting philosophy requires they do things "for real". One such was Richard Bradford, star of *Man in a Suitcase,* an episode of which I did in 1967. He was a terrific actor, and the well-scripted series was a huge success, but the whole thing was another example of fight scenes regularly not going to plan. Well they went to plan, but were much too real; in fact "Method Acting" gone mad. Richard as McGill, got so involved in his character that he frequently failed to "pull" punches and bore the bruises when actors reacted defiantly and questioned his approach. It lead to great "realism" but unbelievable antagonism. I was told that in an earlier episode, one of the other actors was so incensed, they hit him with a chair! Another of course expressed dismay and refused to act with him unless his "excesses" were curbed. He justified his actions angrily and accused them of not being proper actors.

"What is it with you Brits?" being his refrain.

"We're actors" came the response. "We act."

The only way to make a fight look completely authentic on the screen without harming the participants is to have it mapped out by an expert fight arranger: it saves time, money, bruises and bad feeling.

NINE
The Goggle Box

For a long time I had wanted to get into television which was very much the coming thing. Strangely enough, many actors and actresses shied away from it.

"It's not really anything to do with the theatre, is it dear?"
Or...
"It's like performing in an iron lung."
Or...
"Oh my God, it'll never catch on, surely?" they said.

However that didn't deter me from my desire to get onto the small screen. To be a part of the furniture in people's front rooms was surely something to aspire to? I told Harry Dubens of my wishes and his reply was... "Don't warry Sid, we warking on it. We warnt you get nice part, not just any old t'ing. Leave wit me."

"Leave it with my father" said Stanley. "We've got good contacts at the B.B.C."

Agents always say that of course. In fact they did have good contacts, but I was impatient. Fortunately I knew Angela Heathcote, a casting manager at the B.B.C. booking department - I'd met her at a party - and through her, I was introduced to Hilary Mitten, who was Ronnie Waldman's personal assistant. Ronnie was renowned originally for being presenter of *Monday Night at Eight* on the B.B.C. Radio Light Entertainment programme which ran all through the war and after it. His *Puzzle Corner* in which he'd stick a deliberate mistake that the audience would write in and "spot" was hugely popular. At the time he was a producer, but eventually became head of Light

Entertainment! I decided to go for broke. I phoned Hilary, told her I was an actor interested in doing some television and asked to take her out to dinner! She clearly admired my cheek… and accepted! Luckily I found she was on my wavelength, had a great sense of humour, and laughed at all my jokes. (Always a plus!) In addition, again luckily for me, she had seen me in a few films. Ronnie was currently producing a T.V. show called *Kaleidoscope* which was doing well. As the name suggests, the show was a mixture of different subjects. One item was called *Inspector Hornleigh Investigates* in which a police inspector was shown solving various crimes and a member of the public would be asked to spot the clues which led to the inspector apprehending the culprit. This would be followed by a T.V. version of *Puzzle Corner* concerning unusual origins, the return of the deliberate mistake, and the "get your wish" section where a viewer could wish for something - like "meeting top England footballer Stanley Matthews". The show would also be interspersed with musical items. Ronnie was clearly a power house! I remember Ronnie even having a board game out of the show! Hilary introduced me to Ronnie and the meeting went well and the following week I was cast to play a crook in two sketches. I was paid ten guineas for rehearsals and transmission. It was "Live" of course and although much more confined, the studio was not unlike a film set. When I became aware of the limitations, I acted as if I were on stage, except that I wasn't obliged to project my voice in the same way. Many performers become terrified at the thought of "drying" (forgetting one's words) and I've seen them shaking with nerves on many occasions. I must say I myself have suffered with nerves when something untoward has happened, but these days it's not so vital because most shows are pre-recorded on videotape. Anyway, there I was doing my first "telly" at Alexandra Palace and although my agent Harry Dubens didn't exactly approve - obviously I told him about my "short-circuiting" the situation - he didn't disapprove either. He'd got his ten per cent and appreciated I'd made a valuable contact. I don't think he even bothered to watch it! It was a tragedy when dear Hilary died of cancer a few years later; a great loss to all her friends of whom I was one. Angela Heathcote, whom I mentioned earlier was a loyal ally to me. She encouraged and advised me about various productions which were due for casting, one in particular being a play called *Take Back Your Freedom* which was to be produced by Michael Barry who was to direct *Stop Press Girl.* Coincidentally, Michael was a client of Harry Dubens, so everything was in my favour, except the remuneration which was in no way comparable to film money!

For two days on a film I earned as much as the weekly salary, including transmission fee, for television. I got £25/6/-.

The leading man in *Take Back Your Freedom* was Andrew Osborn, who also happened to be on Harry's list of clients! Andrew was always immaculately dressed and during the three weeks of rehearsal he never appeared in the same suit twice.

A little mannerism of his was to wear his jackets with the cuffs turned back! He drove a sporty looking Alvis car which suited his smart, moneyed, image. He was obviously doing well as an actor, or liked to give that impression. I liked Alvises! I'd briefly worked for Alvis before the war as a clerk in the accounts department. Before Whiteleys of course. Not a job for me, as I think you can imagine, despite my admiration of the cars. I was asked to leave. I flicked a rubber band at one of my colleagues. About forty times. Andrew was a debonair, polite and witty man and a fine actor. Though occasionally he could be very off hand, so it behoved one to be wary of him. It was a kind of competitive

"I'm doing a lot better than you. You can be my friend up to a point."

Which I'm afraid some actors embrace. He eventually tired of acting and became an executive producer for B.B.C. T.V. Drama. Unfortunately this became his undoing. He changed horribly. Well, he got worse. When he subsequently directed me in a crime series, he was adamant in getting what he believed was right and became a bully! He acted all the parts to show the cast how it should be done, giving everyone constant line readings. Now, this doesn't go down well with actors, who like to feel they have the intelligence to work out how to say their lines! Personally when this happens - and it happens a lot with some directors - I wait for the moment to pass, see if I agree, and if I don't, say the line their way for a bit, then on the recording, say it the way I was saying it before!

The plot of *Take Back Your Freedom* concerned a future dictatorship in England with Andrew Osborn as the "Fuehrer". Many distinguished actors such as Leonard Sachs (subsequently *The Good Old Days* chairman) and Charles Cullum (we were to be in *Barnacle Bill* together) were in the cast, and most of them, as well as myself, were dressed in khaki uniform somewhat reminiscent of the Nazi Labour Corps - a safari shirt with trousers to match. Having rehearsed for three weeks in a church hall in Kentish Town - I was playing Corporal Gosway - we duly arrived at Alexandra Palace, or Ally Pally as it was affectionately called, the day before the actual transmission, to have a run through of the play for the technicians. There were two large studios and also a "Green Room" which is a lounge for the artists, with a tea urn, a fridge for the milk, and lots of cups, obviously. Unfortunately the green room could only be reached via a long spiral staircase, thereby prohibiting any visit from those older actors with dodgy knees or breathing problems. Most of us were marooned in our dressing rooms anyway, being forbidden to leave the vicinity without permission, in case we wandered off when we were needed and thus missed our cue. It tended to happen that whenever you felt like a cuppa, they wanted you on set! The dressing rooms were all alike – six or seven people to a room with a huge bath in it. It was weirdly like a large sports changing room! Our plunge bath appeared recently to have been occupied by some tropical fish, judging by a strange green tidemark all around it! All the interior and exterior scenes were shot in the big studios. There were no location film sequences, so consequently there were lots of clever "outside" sets built. And everything was "live", meaning that it was transmitted to the viewers whilst being performed, because recording onto videotape had not at that time been invented (although obviously the boffins were working on it)!

The fact that it was a "live" transmission, as I've said, gave a lot of actors the T.V. jitters, and constant reference to it didn't improve matters. A voiced quarterly countdown of "We're going LIVE!" made some of the less fragile performers visibly jump! The only person who seemed unconcerned was Andrew Osborn. He was a steady as a rock and roared through the part with great aplomb and panache. In one scene I "doubled" for Andrew, pretending to be him, while he changed for another scene, and had to race along the corridor to the other studio with the camera peering over my shoulder (from the back Andrew and I looked alike. But only from the back. And of course I was wearing his jacket) but during the chase along the corridor from studio to studio I tripped and fell. Fortunately nothing was broken and it looked very real and dramatic and I picked myself up having luckily not revealed my face having fallen over still with my back to camera, and rushed into the set with Andrew taking over from me as himself, as if we were in a relay race.

In those days the shows were televised on Sundays and performed again (live) on Thursdays. Due to the gap the actors were often unsure of their lines, so in order to obviate this, a word rehearsal, or "line-run" as it was known, was usually called on the day before. Even then, some actors got flustered and "fluffed" on transmission, but true to tradition, they inevitably floundered on. Later on (much later on) a most valuable piece of equipment came into operation called a "Cut Key". This was a device which the stage manager used and was only brought into operation when signals of desperation appeared in the performer's eyes, and he or she was at the point of no return and obviously couldn't remember where they were (in the script obviously but occasionally, in reality!). The "Cut Key" was shaped like a bell push and on being pressed, it entirely eliminated the sound going out to the T.V. sets, so that the S.M., who would have been following the script line by line and word by word, would then prompt the helpless artiste. There was, of course, a slight pause in the sound received at the viewers' end, but nobody seemed to notice. They assumed, as I had until I found out, that there had been a break in the transmission for a few seconds – someone had stepped on a cable somewhere!

I particularly recall that in my early days of television, I was in a production where in one scene a man was being interviewed in an office. The interviewer asked a few questions which were hesitantly answered and it was obvious that the actor being questioned was a bit shaky (shaky? His lights were scarcely on at all!). Finally a blank, defeated look began to spread over the actor's face. The interrogator asked again, hoping to jog the actor's disappearing frantic mind. But to no avail. The helpless one looked about him for guidance and at that point the "Cut Key" was brought into operation. He was given the missing line. But relief did not appear on his face. He just stared, aghast, as if in a trance and said not a dicky bird. The folks at home, unaware of his predicament, were still seeing the picture of this dumb struck actor.

"Blimey! He's good!" they said. "Just look at that bewildered look on his face! And he's sweating like a dog! Wow!"

The interviewer, sensing all was almost lost, rephrased his question cleverly inserting the answer into it. All the interviewee needed to do was answer "Yes!"

"Let me put this another way. The name we're after is Jones isn't it?"

But it was no good. By now our hapless hero was looking around for the men in white coats to take him away, or alternatively show him the hole in the floor into which he could drop. Eventually the whole scene was faded out and the transmission Trade Card came into vision, with the announcer apologising for the breakdown….

"For reasons beyond our control……"

The play began again without the offending scene. Or the offending actor, poor chap. I heard he didn't do any more television for a very long time. And stayed gibbering in a darkened room. Who could blame him?

Apropos "live" television, we had one unrehearsed incident on

Take Back Your Freedom. I had completed my part in the play and had ventured back into the studio (making sure not to be in the way naturally) to watch how the rest of the production was going. In those days there was no such thing as a television monitor in your dressing room showing you what was going on on the studio floor. I very quietly crept in to see that very distinguished sweet actor Charles Cullum, lying on the floor having been shot dead by one of Andrew Osborn's henchmen. After a decent (or so he thought) interval he cautiously opened his eyes and thinking that everything was all clear he began to get up from his reclining position. The floor manager immediately hissed and waved at him. "No no no! Not yet! Not yet! You're still in shot!"

"Oh. Sorry" said the dead Charles to the floor manager and the viewers, lying down again rather hurriedly and bumping his head severely in the process.

"Dear Sam. Why do we do it?" he plaintively asked me in the bar afterwards, wearing a rather pristine bandage on his bonce.

"Why?"

"Well I do it for the money" said I.

"Yes, and so do I!" he replied, encouraged. "Drink up and we'll have another one!"

What a sweet man he was. By the way, Richard Wattis was also in it. Our paths crossed on many occasions. A very funny friendly man and fine actor. In both drama and comedy.

This was really my first television play and meeting Michael Barry was an extremely good contact for me, because I worked with him on numerous occasions after that. (He was later to become head of drama and eventually transfer to television in Eire.) He directed me at Pinewood for my small scene in *Stop Press Girl*, but after his departure for Ireland I lost contact with him. He was a charming and unassuming gentleman in the real sense of the word and did much for the drama section at the B.B.C., helping to raise the standard of television, much to the viewers' benefit.

I soon discovered that half of of the secret of becoming a

successful T.V. actor lay in the contacts or people one met.

I once knew an actor (no longer of this world, probably looking over my shoulder as I write to see if I mention him) who although he concentrated on T.V. work, was always aware of what was going on in every branch of the profession. He made it his business to be au fait with all the gossip. He cultivated producers, production managers, directors and secretaries. Cultivating people was a career in itself! Consequently he was very seldom out of work and often in the money. I won't say who it is, as I don't want to be insulting, but in fact he wasn't a very good performer, and to be fair, he himself didn't lay any claim to be "great shakes", but he had a good face, always tried to please, did as he was asked, and above all, socialised. I don't recall that he ever said in a production any more than, "Yessir, you can rely on me sir!"

Or…

"Over here mate!"

Or…

"It makes you think dunnit."

But he was very good at reactions. Indeed he excelled at them. Especially when they mentioned money.

"Oh really?" he'd say. "Not bad!"

Even when it was a "special low" fee!

I was approached by producer Ben Arbeid and director and writer Alan Cullimore to play an important part - well a huge one - Stacy, in *Vengeance is Mine*, a "second", a "B" feature film, to be shot at Carlton Hill Studios, St John's Wood. I'm not quite sure how I got such a large part, given my tendency to play small ones, but I jumped at the opportunity. Perhaps I was doing O.K? I was of course still self doubting. But that was my nature. It was a very small but efficient company – it had to be. They had to finish the film in under three weeks and everybody had to work very fast in order to keep to the inevitably tight schedule! Valentine ("The Man in Black") Dyall was the hero and I played his sidekick. He'd achieved the soubriquet "The Man in Black" by being the narrator of the B.B.C. Radio horror series *Appointment with Fear* and his dark sepulchral tones were his trademark. The feminine interest was in the capable hands of Ann Firth who'd been in *Scott of the Antarctic,* but we hadn't met. In the plot Val and I had just come out of prison and Val was determined to wreak his vengeance on the man who had wrongly put him there. I pleaded with him, Anne Firth pleaded with him, but it was all in vain: he was determined to liquidate his tormentor. With typical results. But there was a twist! Valentine's character supposedly had a terminal illness, and hired a hitman to kill him, Valentine, (what?) but then the idea was to frame the man who'd got him sent to prison, for the hit! (ah, I see) But then Valentine was told his illness wasn't terminal! (Oh no!) And the hit-man, Sammy Parsons, played by the very mole-like Richard Goolden, couldn't be found in order to have the contract cancelled, because he always disappeared underground (like a mole) before doing a hit! (Help!) Cue much mayhem and digging up of the underworld to find the hitman before he could fulfil his contract!

No doubt it will eventually turn up somewhere on television - probably not in the "Great Movies of our Time" slot - but definitely in the "ooh it's quite clever and well worth a look" section. What I remember vividly about this film is that I had a mountain of dialogue to deliver, which I managed to learn and spit out without accident or incident. Occasionally towards the end of the day, one would get "fluffy", especially if you happened to be doing a rather long speech, but according to Ben Arbeid, I was rather good! And all delivered in a well spoken accent! But Valentine Dyall had a photographic memory which impressed me enormously. He would arrive at the studio, always slightly late, always by taxi.

"What scenes are we doing?" he would ask me.

And then proceed to learn the dialogue while changing into his costume. He would repeat the lines to himself several times, keep running through the scene with me and would follow the same procedure for each subsequent scene. He learned his words instantly and I never knew him dry or fluff. Sometimes he would hesitate slightly until his brain gave him some alternative word to fill in, but it was never obvious that he had forgotten the original dialogue and what came out was often better! The budget for this type of picture in those days would be about £12,000 - £15,000. I did 12 days work on it and I was paid £12 pounds per day, less the usual deductions, and I certainly earned it! Ben Arbeid still talks about that film. I think he must have some money squirrelled away from the profits.

I had one interesting experience on the film: one day we were doing a scene in a pub (mocked up in the studio) and bottles of coloured water representing Whisky, Brandy, Gin etc. were used on the set - spirits were the most expensive so they were always fake - but the beer was real. The only snag was, as the beer was free, they were very careful to whom they handed it out – you'd think it was champagne we were drinking! Among the fellow beer drinkers was one whom I shall call Nigel. Nigel Richards in fact. Why be coy? Now he happened to be the original producer who had given me the sack when I was working at Skegness – for turning up late at Butlins – remember? Producing hadn't been kind to him. He was acting now. He had one line in the whole film. When he was pushed in the crowd by our hero Valentine who was anxious to get to the counter, he had to say, "Do you mind?"

I thought he did it moderately well and I went up to speak to him. I was pleased he seemed slightly embarrassed.

"Hello" I said. "Remember me?"

"Yes, of course" he said. And then hesitantly "…er.. you've changed your name to Sam?"

"Yes. Since I found work in the film world, I reverted to my first name, Sam. Your wife knew me as John."

"Yes. (Pause) "She's not with me now" he said, without any emotion.

"Oh really?" said I. "Where is she?" pretending to look for her in the crowd. Knowing full well what he meant.

"She left not long after you. And I haven't seen her since."

"I see." I replied.

The conversation came to a halt and then I said, "If you're still here at lunch, I'll buy you a drink."

He was. And I did. The moral is, even if you dislike your former employer, you should always offer him hospitality and have a large one yourself, preferably an expensive one! As I write, Valentine Dyall, the man with the wonderful deep voice, is billed in the T.V. Times as follows:

"12.25 Close. Valentine Dyall reads "Prayers for Impossible Days."

A far cry from *Vengeance is Mine*. Versatility is his name.

For me the year 1948 happily ended with more work. I did a Children's film for four days for £12 a day with Laurence Naismith called *Mr. Marionette* at the Gate Studios at Elstree directed by John Irwin with whom I was in *Badger's Green*. We were all slightly bemused when we turned up as it was shot on T.V. equipment - there were three cameras so the wides and close ups were all being taken care of in the one take - and then in an immensely innovative way for the time, this take was filmed off the screen of a telly. It was never released so possibly at this stage the technology didn't work. But of course later on "tele-cine" as it was called, became all the norm.

I then received 25 oncers for three weeks rehearsal of *Toad of Toad Hall* in a T.V. movie directed by Michael Barry on the telly, which went out on Christmas Day! £25, less of course the usual deductions. Andrew Osborn was in this one as well! He played "Ratty" and I was "Weasels, ferrets and stoats and the Welsh Rabbit!" (an airing of my Welsh accent boyo!).

I was to reprise my involvement in *Toad* in 1949, this time playing the "Chief Weasel" for Michael again, once more out on Christmas Day!.

Already lined up for me, starting January 5th., was the part of a black tie and tails steward employed in "The Liberal Club" in Mayfair (a set built at Pinewood) where I was to wait on, and converse with, Robert Newton, one of the great character actors of the era - Pistol in *Henry V*, and of course Long John Silver in *Treasure Island* (which I was to be in). This film was *Obsession* by Alec Coppell, a film about a psychiatrist called Clive Riordan, played by Robert, dealing with his wife's current lover by keeping him chained up in the cellar of a derelict building, until he felt the time was right to kill him (preferably when the police had lost the scent). It was directed by the soft-spoken Edward Dymtryk. Edward made his reputation with a film called *Crossfire* and I would've liked to have spent more time in his company. I was only on the film for 3 days (not used on two but £15 a day so £45) standing about as background in the club, and addressing Robert in two different scenes, which of course were shot on the same day, because we were using the same set.

"Excuse me doctor. You forgot to sign your bill," I said in the first one which was at the beginning of the film, and… "Excuse me sir. Will there be anything else sir?" I said in the second, which was at the end.

Naunton Wayne as the police superintendent, comes to arrest Robert, then wanders past me. So I got to work with Naunton Wayne as the superintendent. But didn't really. I didn't speak to Robert, other than to say hello, but neither did I speak to Edward Dymtryk (other than a few words at the interview I had with him for the job, and they were the usual platitudes). There wasn't much opportunity to speak to either on set. And anyway you knew your place really. You just did your job as professionally as you could and if you were given time to shake a few hands before you left to remove your costume and make up, you would. Normally it was the Second who wrapped you.

"Thanks Sam!" he'd say.

And that was it. In any case, Edward was a very shy softly spoken man, and he was off to the next set-up. But he got what he wanted from the cast with the minimum of fuss. I was told Edward was one of the fabled "Hollywood Ten" who had refused to cooperate with the chilling "Un-American Activities Committee" who were attempting to "root out" Communism in Hollywood. His refusal caused them to throw him in prison! I felt a certain sympathy for him as prison was clearly too much for him and he decided to tell all. Prison is a very intimidating environment. Naturally the whole Hollywood film community were aghast and bewildered by his about-turn and he was shunned. Unable to work there, as he was boycotted by the studios and considered persona-non-grata by fellow film makers, he'd been granted a permit to work over here. I saw the film months later. It was first class - Robert Newton and Sally Gray were terrific - in spite of the idiot in black tie and tails serving in the club who was the spitting image of me. With two lines in two scenes, there wasn't much I could get my teeth into.

Further films followed in rapid succession: *Stop Press Girl* (as I mentioned) starring Sally Ann Howes with whom I had my little scene. She was a girl with a strange super power. She could stop machinery! I played a clerk in the Railway booking office. It's one shot. From the rear of the office. I'm sideways on. She's facing camera.

"Ticket to London please," she says.

But I've got a newspaper propped up by the counter with her picture on it and I can't sell her a ticket as she'll stop the train with her super power. So I point at the paper with my pencil, and shake my head and gurgle! And that's it!

"Well done Sam!" said the director Michael Barry. "Do one where you take a little longer with recognising her would you? And one a little quicker?"

Three takes. James Robertson Justice, Gordon Jackson and Basil Radford and Naunton Wayne (again) were in it. But of course I didn't meet them on my half a day. Sigh.

Hard on its heels came *The Hasty Heart* for Associated British, which was shot at Elstree. Another soldier (for a change!) but this time with a difference. I played an Aussie jeep driver. Bob Lennard the casting director who had helped Ken More up the ladder to success, phoned to ask me if I could drive a jeep.

"Of course!" I replied. "I always drove one in the Army!'

(I hadn't, but I had driven a motorcycle, motorcycle and sidecar

- known as an M.C.C. - and also a lorry. But never a jeep).

"No seriously" he said (everything was taken very seriously by him). "You must be able to drive one properly and have had a great deal of experience with a jeep. You see, it has to be driven onto the set in the studio. It's bound to be very critical."

"It's easy Bob. Yes! Easy-Peasy. I'm a consummate jeep driver. Jeeps is my middle name," said this unmitigated liar. "I won't let you down."

Two weeks prior to my bits in the film, I searched around and found a jeep in a local garage in Chiswick. Ravenscourt Park actually. I gave a quid to the mechanic who owned the jeep and asked him to let me have a run in it, to accustom myself to the way it functioned. It was in fact, not difficult to drive, no different from any other car, so I drove it without any trouble. When I arrived at the studio I was again quizzed about my ability to drive a jeep by the Second A.D..

"Are you sure you can drive a jeep in the small confines of the studio?"

"Of course I can" I replied witheringly. "I was always driving vehicles in the Army. The only thing I haven't driven is a tank!"

He gave me a sceptical look.

"Listen," I said dismissively (tchah, these Assistant Directors!) "Last week I drove a jeep around Chiswick just to sharpen me up. So there!"

On the second day that I was called to the studio (they hadn't reached my scene on the first day) the first A.D. came to me and said

"Sorry about this Sam, but Vince, Mr. Sherman (the Director) has decided it won't be necessary to drive the jeep straight onto the set. It'll be too noisy and probably too smelly, in such a confined space. We'll push it on from behind and you can go through the motions as if you're driving, and we'll put the sound on afterwards."

"Oh I see" I said, disappointed. "I was looking forward to showing off my driving prowess."

"Well to compensate, he might do a couple of exterior longshots of the jeep going along in the country…" (then as an afterthought)

"but actually… you won't be needed for them. It'll be too far away to see if it's you or not so one of the drivers can do it. And as a matter of fact we might not be doing them at all."

I wouldn't let it go though.

"What about all the fuss saying I must be able to drive a jeep! It was essential for the part etc. etc.."

He pondered deeply, fingered his beard as if thinking deeply, and replied, "Well….That's showbiz!" Then he added cynically, "Don't worry. You'll get the same money!"

Cheeky devil! It was indeed shot from two or three angles and the jeep, when just on me and the vehicle, was slid into shot without seeing the pushers. I could only be seen in profile till the jeep came to a halt and I got out, looking all bandy-legged in my battledress, and rather cute Aussie bush hat!

Guess what. They didn't use this panning shot of me being pushed in, at all. They used another much wider shot we'd done, following Patricia Neal (the nurse) across to me, with me leaning on the bonnet! I'd arrived and been there for some time. No driving into the scene at all. And consequently no close ups.

"Sam let's shoot it with you discovered sitting on the bonnet." said Vince.

Here was my contribution:

PATRICIA: Are you Corporal McClauchlan's driver?
ME: That's me sister.
HER: He won't be ready for some time.
ME: I'll go get myself a cuppa!
Said in my Aussie accent!

But all kidding aside, I was pleased to be associated with such a fine film. Harry Dubens was pleased too!

"Anudder string to yer fiddle Sid! I've added "drives cheeps" to your C.V.!"

The stars of *The Hasty Heart* were Richard Todd and as I said,

Patricia Neal. Patricia is the kind of actress one always associates with award-winning performances and she was ideal as the sympathetic nurse with whom the dying Scottish soldier (Richard Todd) falls in love. Also in the cast was an unassuming American actor named Ronald Reagan, subsequently to play the real role of a rather competent politician - although at that time there was no hint of a political career - well, not that I knew of, the fellow who drove the silent jeep. Actually Ronald was a very good mixer - definitely one of the boys. I enjoyed his company and if he'd asked me, I'd have voted for him, despite being ineligible, due to the fact that I'm not actually domiciled in the U.S. and know very little about American politics.

Two radio shows winged their way over the airwaves for me. One was a play, *The Last of Mrs. Cheyney* produced by the very fine and encouraging Archie Campbell, who as I said had used me in *Mrs. Dale*. Archie was also considered eccentric - he had been known to turn up wearing two different shoes - and on this occasion demonstrated it by wearing two ties at the same time. We tried to work out if he'd meant it or had just forgotten. It seemed rude to ask. This had originally been a 1937 Hollywood film by Frederick Lonsdale, but in this instance was a Saturday Night theatre on the B.B.C. Home service. I played a servant. George. A footman. The always friendly Googie Withers as Mrs. Cheyney was my boss. Our paths crossed a lot! There was a singer and a pianist to contribute music between the scenes which was nice, and it went out live, which was as always a bit tense, but if you concentrated, was great fun, as you were never going to forget the lines as you were holding a script! Which of course you must never rustle as it would be picked up on the microphone! There was a specific technique to not rustling, which meant an almost balletic movement depositing pages of your script silently on the floor beside you. Many of the actors were experts.

"Up with the paper…and over…describing an arc…and slowly swoop down and deposit…and back up arching the back to the mic for the next line…and read…and read…and read…and then again…Up with the paper…and over…describing an arc…and slowly swoop down and deposit etc…and if you've finished, pick up your deposited script…as quietly as a mouse…and retreat from the mic onto one of the chairs to await your next cue which you've marked up ultra carefully in your script."

I had watched them diligently and copied them shamelessly. "Script rustle" was considered anathema. Though to be fair, some had their scripts in ring binders and silently turned pages, with all the aplomb of clandestine master spies moving papers about on a desk, to film them on tiny pen cameras whilst the security guard was doing his rounds feet away. (I've been watching too many James Bond films.)

On one occasion when we were going out live, Geoffery Sumner playing Willie Winton had a close call getting to the mic and afterwards confided to me he'd gone to the lavatory and turned the wrong way and got confused as to where the studio was.

"The red mist began to descend Sam and all my nightmares were coming home to roost as mutant chickens, when I recognised a fire extinguisher and made a correct turn."

He was very very red in the face and sweaty which everyone remarked upon, especially Louise Hampton as Mrs. Ebley, who shared a microphone with him and was visibly worried he was about to have a heart attack! I have to admit I'd be given a warning to play his part by the studio manager, the nearer we got to his cue.

The other radio was called *Country Magazine*, a discussion programme between horticultural experts and the public seeking answers to their gardening problems. A.G. Street was a genuine horticulturalist and I posed as an expert on gardening, (it was thought easier to get an actor to ask the questions) using my Beds. and Herts. accent which I had originally heard when I was at Dunstable Grammar School, where as I've said, Gary Cooper was a one-time boarder, although not in my time there, I hasten to add! His name is scratched on the wooden panelling of the common room wall and also on the lavatories' partition joining the swimming baths, though the latter signature is a fake because those particular bogs were not there when he was. But to return to *Country Magazine*. I had originally met the producer, Francis Dillon, in the "Stag" Club which was highly patronised by the B.B.C. radio personnel at Portland Place, W.1.. After the third or fourth pint, Francis asked me if I could do a country accent, so I gave him a mini audition there and then in the crowded saloon bar. He obviously liked what he could hear, above the noise of the boozing, because he subsequently employed me in several of his programmes which he himself scripted and produced. It's ironic but when I originally auditioned for Charles Maxwell he turned me down because he thought my voice was flat and monotonous. I wonder if he ever heard *Country Magazine*? Maybe he did, and thought he recognised that flat and monotonous voice – "Oi wunder?"

Starting on 18th. March 1949, I was contracted by John Redway, at that time casting director (later a leading agent) to work in a film called *The Chance of a Lifetime*, to be directed and produced by the actor, Bernard Miles (who was also in it). It was a tremendous task, acting, directing and being totally responsible for the financial setup. In addition, a very tight schedule had to be adhered to, as the factory location was in Stroud, Gloucestershire, with the whole film being shot in the working factory and its environs. But Bernard, with the cooperation of us all, kept to the schedule and we finished it on time. Though he tended to get a bit exasperated and irritated the more the film went on, trying to fit everything in. The cast and the film unit were spread out in various hotels and houses all over Stroud, because of the impossibility of one establishment taking them all.

Many well known actors and actresses were in the film: Kenneth More, Basil Radford, Bernard himself, Geoffrey Keen, Julian Mitchell, Peter Jones, Eric Pohlman, Frank Harvey, Hattie Jacques, Hilda Fennymore, Patrick Troughton, Uncle Tom Cobleigh, and all! The main scenes were all shot at the weaving factory just outside Stroud and because the actual workers were employed there every day, our filming activities had to be limited to long weekends, starting on Friday afternoons and shooting till Mondays at six in the morning. So consequently I was on it for six weekends from March till the end of May! At £30 a time I was quids-in!

Here's a brief outline of the film: the business (agricultural tool-making) was going through a difficult patch financially, and the workers suggested forcefully to the boss, Basil Radford, (once again I was working with him - what an actor!) that they could run it themselves – a sort of co-operative movement with workers' committees etc. - headed by Bernard and Kenneth More as the newly elected bosses. But the new setup also ran into difficulties - the big order of ploughs they'd just obtained was subjected to fluctuations in the currency market, and the "Zenobians" backed out of the deal which was worth £50 thousand. In the end the workers were helped out by Basil who re-routed all the stock via his contacts around the world, thus proving the workers still needed the boss, and they couldn't live without each other!

Apparently, unknown to us, the film Distributors hadn't taken too kindly to the "communist" theme when it was originally suggested, but Bernard, along with Filippo del Giudice (the owner of the "Two Cities" film company) had persisted and insisted, and the finance was secured. Eventually when the film was finished, another row blew up about showing it and it took a government order to enforce it. It didn't appeal to the general public though, who shunned it in their thousands! It was nominated for the 1951 BAFTA (British Academy of Film and Television Arts) for best British film, but I could see why it wasn't a success. It was actually more of a drama-documentary than a feature film, and to be quite frank, it was a bit dull. The inner workings of a factory making agricultural equipment possibly wasn't the greatest subject for a film-going public used to more exciting fayre that would take them out of themselves. And it did hint that a socialist team running the factory was quite feasible, which probably confused or alienated many Tory film-goers. Basil Radford was terrific in it. The scenes when he realises he is going to give his business up (even though he still got 6% of the profits as he owned the factory) are beautifully acted and packed with emotion. For my part, I was one of the "workers" and like in *Captive Heart* was everywhere, being prominent in crowd scenes, shouting out in panned close up, or getting splashed by lorries ("Oi! Watch it!") Or asking in the tool shop "What did you go there for?" after one of the workers has been summoned to see the boss, or cheering a late-comer clocking-in just on time, or cycling into the factory waving a newspaper and showing everyone an article ("the factory's in it"). And when a worker believes he's not being paid enough, everyone chips in by derisorally throwing in sixpence, and in rather nice big close up I shout "Gis us a halfpenny Fred!"

One day on the film, several of us were dismissed early from the location and we dashed back to the hotel/boarding house to have an early bath. There were only three bathrooms available and these were always occupied. I normally had to wait hours if I didn't get there early. I stripped quickly and wrapped a large towel around my frail body, forming a sarong with a slit to my waist where the towel met.

I charged into the bathroom and closed the door hurriedly behind me. But I found the bath was occupied. Hattie Jacques was in it, almost afloat, lying back luxuriating, supported by what looked like two baby dolphins with reddish purple cherries in their mouths.

"Oh sorry!" I blurted "Didn't know there was anybody here… Thought I was the first…Sorry."

Hattie, sliding down in the bath so that the water came up to the edge and the purple nosed dolphins disappeared, said roguishly, "C'mon in! The water's fine!"

She was kidding. I think. In my haste to retreat, my towel slipped down to knee level and I retired in confusion. About two months later John le Mesurier came over from Watford, where he was appearing at the Palace Theatre in a play, to pay his first love call to his fiancee Hattie. Later they made it official and lived in harness at Eardley Street, Earl's Court. Hattie was a great sport, a tremendous person and a delightful comedienne. She's terrific in *Chance of a*

Lifetime. In addition to her kindness and generosity, she was one of the leading organisers behind the British Leukaemia Society. I worked with her many times, especially in the *Eric Sykes Shows* - Eric got me in a lot - on B.B.C. T.V., and she never changed, being always kind and considerate. On festive occasions, for many years it was always a standing invitation to go to their parties – a sort of open house where you had to fight to get in!

I was on *Chance of a Lifetime* from March 18 to June 1 and had a lot of fun working with all the cast. One thing that stuck in my mind was Bernard Miles appearing on the set each morning and greeting the assembled actors and actresses with his favourite catchphrase, apropos starting the day.

"Accoutered as I was I plung-ed in!" (Shakespeare 'ennit) He sometimes made "plung-ed" sound like "plunged it".

Towards the end of the film I bought my first car, whilst on location, from the local butcher. It cost £75 (plus tax at £10/15/- and insurance £10. 2s. 6d) and apart from a puncture, I returned home in triumph – I mean, Austin. I left the car outside my mother's house with a hurricane lamp beside it as a parking light, to prevent it being towed away. (This was the protocol at that time with cars in 1949! There had to be a light beside it!) However it didn't deter some late night joyriding twit from nicking it. Fortunately, it was eventually found two days later by the ever watchful police, in Bayswater, intact except for a dry petrol tank and 50 stolen miles registered on the speedometer. The business being the business, I then had five weeks out of work and plenty of time to enjoy driving it around. But a day (£14) on *No Place For Jennifer* at A.B.C. where I met the lovely Janette Scott and re-met her excellent mother Thora Hird and some post syncing on the same film for £8 and a "Commentary" (equivalent to voicing a documentary) on *Grass Drying* for Nigel Byass again, kept me in funds. And then just when I'd given up and was contemplating bedding (oh where do I get these thoughts?) the dependable and hugely talented Val Guest got me in for a quick couple of days on *The Body Said No!* at Nettlefold as a technician in a T.V. studio with my bass voiced chum Valentine Dyall who was doing the T.V. announcements, as he frequently did in real life on radio. Ebullient American actress and singer Yolande Donlan - who was later to marry Val Guest (not Val Dyall!) was also in my scene, as was the charming and friendly Michael Rennie. Michael was playing himself, doing a broadcast. Yolande, playing a cabaret performer - something in fact she could do on her ear as she was a musical star - hears of a plot to kill Michael! Cue the unravelling of the plot!

Michael Rennie always interested me as an actor. I was in *Single Handed* with him three years later and he went out of his way to say hello then. What especially intrigued me was that he chose to be an American film actor when in fact he was from Idle in Yorkshire, had worked at repertory theatre in Yorkshire, and put the Yank voice on! He'd decided to become an actor having been a used car salesman and really worked at it! A hugely successful career in the U.S. and Britain was his reward. He will always be remembered for his alien in *The Day the Earth Stood Still* but he did a huge panoply of work in both film and television, especially the T.V. series of *The Third Man* where he played Harry Lime. Most of that successful long running series was shot at Shepperton and Elstree. I'd have liked to have been in that, but never was. I have to say, I take my hat off to him. A great example of pursuing his dream and achieving it. Mind you being dead handsome and athletic and 6 foot 2 probably helped!

TEN
Aharrr Jim Lad!

Maude Spector, a very distinguished casting director circumnavigated Harry Dubens and phoned me at home - mind you my phone number was in the actors' publicity book, "Spotlight" - asking me to go and see her at Denham Studios. She was keen to meet me! She wanted me to play a part in a big film!!! I met her. It went well. She said she'd been following my career closely!!!! Of course I told Harry I'd seen her. He was confused. But then I'd previously written to her. I wrote to everyone. You had to. Maude concentrated on casting for the big American companies – the Americans always called for Maude when they needed actors. It appeared that Byron Haskin, a very experienced and charming American director, was in London looking to cast a "motion picture". He had started out as a special effects genius, having been nominated for three Oscars as a technical guru, and was soon to make the acclaimed *War of the Worlds* which of course was a mass of brilliant Fx.. The telescope-legged aliens were a tour de force for the time. Anyway, Byron was looking for quite a number of British actors for *Treasure Island* (based on Robert Louis Stevenson's classic) which he was going to direct for Walt Disney Ltd.. As well as being authentic in the accent department, we were cheaper than U.S. actors. Harry was now involved.

"Sid they warnt see you at Dorchester Hotel for interview. It's to meet zer director and Maudie Spector. It's for *Treasured Island,* the film is call (ed)".

He did that agent thing of claiming he had made the contact when it was of course me. But I forgave him. As long as he got me a good deal! I duly went along. Maude was there of course, and a shuttle service of about 30 actors – no actresses. If we were all up for

254

pirates it made sense! When it comes to interviews, if things are going according to plan, one is usually seen within about half an hour of an appointment, which is fair enough. In my case I was on time and so were they, which was a rarity. But it was because Byron was so quick off the mark. Maude announced me to him giving him a short rundown of my history and credits. He shook my hand and told me to sit down, offering me a Camel cigarette which I accepted. He asked me what my latest movie had been, and I told him *The Chance of a Lifetime* and I briefly discussed my ubiquitous contribution, and then he cut to the chase. He wanted to know what part in his film Maude had me in mind for, and she said, "Well I thought Sam would be just right for Cady, the pirate who attempts to start the mutiny."

And he said, "Yeah. Why not?" (why not?!). "Thanks for coming. See you on set."

And that was how I became Cady in the immortal Disney classic, *Treasure Island*. In and out. About three minutes. Apparently he'd cast (or not cast) everyone like that! I wonder what he said to those he didn't like?

"We'll let you know?"

Possibly.

The great Robert Newton played the never to be forgotten "Long John Silver" and young Bobby Driscoll, who'd just been the recipient of a special "Juvenile Oscar" for *So Dear to My Heart*, was cabin-boy Jim Hawkins. As I said, or as Maude said, I was one of Long John Silver's gang - all cast realistically by Disney as British and Irish actors - and one of the first to hit the deck in the mutiny. My pirate garb included a long haired wig. I thought I looked rather fetching in a sort of "yonder varlet" way. Actually that's Robin Hood territory. I was more of a "salty sea dog".

Among the baddies engaged for the film were Geoffrey Keen - again. I was following him around - Ralph Truman - a wonderful voice. He was in epic films *Quo Vadis* and *El Cid* as you'd expect with a larynx like that - Harold Jamieson - a lovely chap later in the *Cruel Sea* - Patrick Troughton - an equally nice amusing man who of course

I already knew and we'd just been in *Chance*. The second *Doctor Who* after good old William Hartnell - Harry Locke - *Passport to Pimlico, Angels One Five, Reach for the Sky* - Stephen (what accent do you want?) Jack who became an esteemed dialect coach - William Devlin - he told me he'd played King Lear aged 22! - Gordon Mullholland - more about him below - and Scots John Laurie - of course subsequently a star of *Dad's Army* as "we're all doomed" Private Frazer. There were also several stuntmen who were additional members of Long John's outfit. Most of us formed friendships on the set, depending on scenes we were in together, and I found myself in a lot of shots with Gordon Mullholland and he was a very nice fella! (He was eventually a star of the soap *The Villagers*.) He lived in a small flat in the Cloisters in Sloane Avenue, Chelsea, and I, Harold Jamieson and Patrick Troughton would all go back together and finish the day at the bar there! Gordon hailed from Johannesburg and was very friendly with Sidney James and his first wife Meg who were also South African. He ultimately returned there and had great acting success. But before that, he was best man at my wedding! Gordon was great fun, was very good looking, and had a bevy of girlfriends. His favourite at that time was a beautiful slim creature called Hope Calvert, who was then Bruce Forsyth's sister in law. Gordon eventually married her! Hope was appearing at the famous Windmill Theatre as one of the celebrated "Nude Tableaux-Vivants" - Peter Waring's girlfriend had been one. Well, the one he had while we were on tour - and Gordon had some photos of her, post card size, wearing a little feather skirt and not much else! In fact they were real feathers on the photo! If you blew on them they would part to reveal.... a "We never closed" sign! (Which was of course the reputation the Windmill had in the war). All slightly bizarre, especially when Gordon would say with his tongue firmly planted in his cheek:

"Look at the brilliant photography on this one...... Blow!!"

I started work on *Treasure Island* on July 18th. and finished on Nov. 18th. Four months work at a stretch. I was not, I hasten to add, on call all that time. In fact, there were gaps which I was lucky enough to fill in with other jobs - always a nice thing to do - the main one being five days in the role of Charlie Fox in *Cure for Love* with the sensitive and charming Robert Donat as the star. He directed it and produced it, and wrote the screenplay, as well as being in it at Shepperton. He was great to work with and a wonderful listener and managed the acting/directing/producing/writing roles with ease. He was much less prickly than Bernard Miles had been on *Chance* doing all those jobs. The beautiful Renee Asherson played the love he had to be cured of.

I then did a day on *Seven Days to Noon* at Shepperton for Roy Boulting, as a soldier going house to house, searching for a scientist (Barry Jones) who's stolen a nuclear device, in order to blow up London, unless the government stops encouraging the arms race by stockpiling war-heads. Despite my fee now being £15, I was called for 6 days at £10 a day (it was always cheaper working for the Boulting Brothers) but wasn't used on five of them! Then we shot the scenes in an afternoon! This was to be the beginning of working for the Brothers a lot. They called me "Kyddie!" Roy told me he liked what I'd done in *Passport to Pimlico*. I had two good scenes first searching and then bunking off from the search to have a cigarette. And then one with the splendidly amusing Olive Sloane as the woman who'd been held hostage by the scientist in the evacuated area of London.

"What are you doin 'ere?" I asked her three times as well as a "Blimey!" when the cat knocked over a saucer.

The excellent Olive was really first rate in the part as the blousy ex-chorus girl and rightly earned the plaudits. We were to be in *The House in Marsh Road* and *Price of Silence*. The super efficient Shirley Barnes, my eventual sister-in-law, did the complicated continuity on it, which was a nice surprise. I also sneaked in (or squeaked in) a T.V. Movie called *The Squeaker,* written by Edgar Wallace. This starred two of my cricket chums! Sophie (Abraham Sofaer) and Russell Napier. And was produced by Kenneth Milne-Buckley. As you may remember, another cricket chum. And of course I didn't work with either of them. I was a reporter on a newspaper. It was all shot on film for the B.B.C. at Ally Pally.

Meanwhile back with the pirates, things were sporadic to say the least, owing to the calls being spread out between the actual boat and the studio. My mother, seeing me "lying around" at home from time to time hadn't grasped the essence of my being under contract and started again with her 'harrumphing'. I tried to explain I was being paid for the "lying around" but she never quite grasped it and once again gave me the fish eye. It was clear I needed to move out. I began to look at a few flats in the Chiswick and Stamford Brook area in my very low price range, but encountered the usual problems: "View of the park" was only achieved if you were six foot six or stood on a chair. "Roof terrace" was a gated French Window. And "Second bedroom" was arguably a cupboard. To be frank, I also had the ridiculous illogical fear of "sod's law" kicking in, and the moment I signed the contract on a flat, I'd suddenly break my leg or catch some incurable tropical disease or lose my voice and not work for six months and be unable to pay the rent. Consequently I merely avoided my mother for a bit. That made more sense. The reason I was on *Treasure Island* for so long, was that young Bobby Driscoll, playing Jim, was discovered not to have a licence to work as a minor in England. It seemed that no one had obtained permission from the London County Council for him to work in the film studio, or so we were given to understand. And apparently Disney and Bobby's family were fined and he was ordered out of the country! The film was of course in danger of falling apart as they had shot half the film with him, so Disney appealed and in the six week period allowed for preparing their case, Byron Haskin quickly and cannily rescheduled all of Bobby's scenes so he was doing them all at once, did a huge number of them in close up in the studio just prior to his being deported, and then shot around a stand in. So consequently the whole shooting schedule had to be torn up and rearranged, first around Bobby and then around the rest of us. It was a logistical nightmare. The scenes without Bobby with the stand-in, had to be very cleverly planned and shot, so we only ever saw the stand-in's back. We even had to re-shoot some of those scenes when Byron had looked at the rushes and the stand-in boy's face had crept in, especially in fight or chasing sequences. What a conundrum this had turned out to be for the production team! But it was excellently done, as if you watch the film, you can't tell at all. Bobby incidentally, was a super kid and not in the least precocious or big-headed as many film children can be. His mother and father were on the set as his chaperones and they too were very astute and friendly all through the problems the family were having. Bobby of course was to be the voice of Disney's iconic cartoon *Peter Pan* but according to what I heard, began to suffer from horrific acne and this was not what was required of a child star moving into adulthood. He made another couple of films including John Sturges' *The Scarlet Coat* with Michael Wilding and then appeared to vanish. I heard he was working as a petrol pump attendant in New York having allegedly been in prison for being caught in possession of heroin. A sad reversal of the usual process from working in a garage to stardom! Alan Ladd was originally a gas attendant and as far as I was concerned nearly always acted his roles like one. He was good as a monosyllabic cowboy like *Shane* but Americanised lines in the Biblical epics never worked for me. Stuff like "I guess we march on Rome, Caesar, that's for sure." Or "Marc- Antony ain't gonna like it, I know dat!" never quite had the ring of truth from any actor.

Robert Newton was one of the country's most successful actors at the time: he'd recently been Bill Sykes in David Lean's acclaimed *Oliver Twist* - and was infamous for his extremely hard drinking. However, he was apparently "nearly on the wagon" so he told us, but nonetheless drank Guinness and Champagne, "Black Velvet" at the end of every scene. He justified it by saying that this combination didn't count as "proper drinking" and was purely for medicinal reasons! But his consumption of alcohol didn't seem to impair his acting. He was very on the ball and conscientious, dealing with a very large star part and was noticeably very chummy with us all, even though he was under huge pressure. He used to arrive at the studio driving his Rolls Royce, looking very scruffy indeed, often in his dressing gown and slippers, having come straight from his flat. Several times he went home dressed as Long John in his huge sleeved red jacket and white stockings (even on one occasion with his sword apparently) and sometimes turned up the following morning in the same outfit. There was discussion amongst the cast and crew as to whether he'd slept in the costume, possibly in the car, he looked so much the worse for wear! But in fact it worked really well for the part and there was an astute hard working actor's mind on view. He was always "in character" when you think about it (or possibly just laziness!)! He never shaved, as the part never required it (the make-up department would trim his stubble) and he was stopped regularly by the police, who thought he'd stolen the Rolls. He seemed to revel in his notoriety.

"Well lads sorry to inconvenience you, but I've been stopped by the police again!" he would announce if he was late for his call, adding, "There is a problem though. Unfortunately they've confiscated my cutlass."

Cue much laughter! I mean the police stopping him made sense when you consider such a classy car was being driven, possibly slightly erratically, by a pirate! Or a man in his pyjamas! And there was also the likelihood the coppers all wanted to meet one of the most popular actors of the time, so were keen to stop him, even though they knew who it was and where he was going. He certainly gave a brilliant portrayal of a villain - a likeable one - which became one of the seminal Disney films of the period and spawned another pirate film for Robert as *Blackbeard* and then a Long John film, and a T.V. series shot in Australia - *Long John Silver* - which was cult viewing for children. Unfortunately the drinking took its toll and Robert was taken from us soon after this T.V. series, far too young, with cirrhosis of the liver in 1956. He was 51. A great loss to the profession. He was certainly a character. Even today people are still impersonating him: "Aharrr Jim Lad!".

A source of huge embarrassment for him, was the fact that he kept getting cramp in his left leg, doubled up uncomfortably behind him and secured with tape and straps to give the impression it was missing from the knee down. He'd started off with a peg-leg, with his knee inserted into a sort of cup and that used a bizarre combination of even more straps as well as those doubling his leg up, but that was soon dispensed with. It was so painful that Robert displayed his displeasure by throwing the wooden leg over the ship the first time he wore it. However even with just a strapped-up leg and a crutch, he suffered. Just standing still was so uncomfortable (he obviously wasn't hugely fit, what with all his drinking) that even that required great courage and tenacity, and then he had to act at the same time! But moving - that required another set of skills entirely! Co-ordinating his crutch and stepping on his unstrapped leg, was frequently too much for him , as we often found out.

His parrot, called Captain Flint in the film, wasn't helping the situation either. He fell off Robert's shoulder on numerous occasions, squawking, unused to the shoulder being at a tilt and the up and down motion of Long John lurching along on his crutch. The bird and his handler, consequently spent so much time on the film, I believe they made more money than the actors. The number of retakes necessitated by "the bloody bird" as Robert called it, could have financed several crews!

"Sorry lads. The bloody bird's orf again" Robert would say through gritted teeth as it flew away squawking, ruining the take. "I'm thinking of having parrot soup tonight!"

This, coupled with Robert's milk curdling cries of anguish when he was getting cramp, were enduring memories. A scene would be going well when suddenly he'd yelp repeatedly in dismay and then fall to the floor writhing in agony.

"My leg! My bloody bastard leg! Aaaaaargh!" he'd cry.

In addition there was always a liberal scattering of sunflower seeds, the bird's feed, actually supplied in abundance by the film company, littering the set, and of course free nibbles from the actors who'd surreptitiously given it snacks, so consequently it was always looking around the floor - or at the pirates - for some tasty morsels! On several occasions Robert's crutch gave way, having slid on something edible. The Parrot had a double (stuffed of course, which was a relief) who was always on standby should the original prove to be too difficult! Memories of the *Scott of the Antarctic* cat! If only they'd had a stand-in then. At least the Parrot didn't fly off and hide amidst the arcs!

One particular sequence was unbelievably stressful for Robert. Long John and his mutineers had taken over the ship and were plotting what to do next. It was a longish scene. Long John had suggested that George Merry (played by Ralph Truman, another stalwart British actor of the era. He too had been in Olivier's *Henry V*) be "clapped in irons" for disobeying orders for starting the mutiny too soon, which had led to my death. He'd wrongly encouraged me to attack Redruth, who was a sailor working for Squire Trelawney. Israel Hands (the versatile Geoffery Keen) persuades Long John not to lock him up, as George is too useful to be imprisoned. The pirates all agree and call Long John "Captain" for the first time. Long John is flattered and then orders everyone to fight. Robert, hissing expertly, got the rehearsal right perfectly. But as we know, the longer the leg was doubled up, the more uncomfortable it became. Consequently, these lines, towards the end of the scene, spoken to Israel and Haggott (played by Harry Locke), became problematical. You could see the sweat pouring down his face as the scene reached the end and he'd been lurching all over the set:

"Guard the ship. If there's difficulties, you fires the cannon. An' when you're on lookout, don't drink the rum…Understan' Aggott?"

To which everyone laughs and aharrs and aye ayes! And off they rush to fight Trelawney and his men in the stockade on the island.

"Final checks" was announced by the First A.D.. Everything had been scrutinised: the cyclorama, the lights, the camera. Make-up had looked at everyone, to see whether all wigs were on straight, (Geoffery Keen's had a tendency to shift to the left) and continuity were similarly verifying with wardrobe that everyone was wearing everything properly; in fact everything was in place for the take. Robert had his doubled up leg undoubled and then doubled up again, his sweat was mopped off his brow, and the preening green Parrot, Captain Flint, not there for rehearsal, was put on his shoulder in all its feathery glory. The usual "Quite pleases" were bellowed out by the First and Second A.D.s, and Byron Haskin looked about him and gave the go for the take to take place.

"Action" he said quietly. Robert began beadily. The scene crackled. He got to, "Guard the ship….. If there's difficulties, fire the 'Aggott……..'Aggott?…What's that?… It's "cannon"!…. Sorry!"

"O.K." said Mark Evans, the First, "Settle down. We're going right away."

After a brief break when everything was checked once again, so it wasn't really that brief, and it didn't really go right away, everyone was ready to carry on.

"Action" said Byron once again.

Sweating profusely Robert sailed beautifully through the scene. But he hit the rocks again.

"Guard the ship. If there's difficulties, fire the 'addock. … 'Addock?…..Aaargh!. …..Sorry everyone."

"All right. All right!" said Mark Evans. "We've had our fun."

(What fun? It was purgatory for Robert. No one was laughing!)

"Settle down. We're going right away."

"Quiet please! Going right away" echoed the Second.

A make up lady came on and fiddled with someone's wig (probably Ralph Truman's which was a hairy affair and needed much combing). A sparks decided an arc wasn't behaving or had moved and shouted a lot as a ladder was hoisted. The cameraman wasn't happy with something. The gate was checked for any hairs or fluff in the lens. So after an even longer break, they were ready for a third take. Robert by now had a strange demented look in his eye. Perfect for Long John but somewhat disturbing for him and the rest of us. The tension on set was electric. Everyone was willing Robert to get it right.

"Action" said the patient Byron, still in control.

Robert was now sweating cobs and tottering slightly on account of the pain and discomfort in his leg. He was leaning at a slightly bizarre angle to accommodate it. Captain Flint was giving him a strange parrotical look. But obviously Robert soldiered and pirated on. Everything went well. He approached the slippery lines ultra gingerly:

"Guard the ship….. If there's difficulties, …. fire the cannon. (everyone sighed inwardly. He'd got that stumbling point right) An ' when you're on lookout….. don't drink the rum…Understan ' Parrot?…PARROT? (He glared at captain Flint as if it was his fault). PARROT? IT'S 'AGGOTT!' FUCKIT! FUCKIT! FUCKIT!………..Sorry!"

The "Sorry!" was tiny and slightly ashamed of his sweary outburst.

He collapsed under the strain of it all and lay on the floor muttering. Byron said "Cut" and we broke for tea. Robert unstrapped himself and sought a seat and another seat so he could raise his usually strapped leg and rest it, and immediately after tea (or was it coffee laced with scotch?) without Captain Flint this time - he was clearly too much of a distraction - he got the take in one! And Byron shot a mass of leering close ups - in which Robert had dispensed with the strapping - that he could edit into the previous takes. From this moment on, if Byron could shoot Robert from the waist up, he'd try, so Robert didn't have to have his leg doubled up. He just acted it! It's fun watching the film and noticing where Robert is either standing in front of a table, or in close up, with the crutch under his arm but clearly not leaning on it. It means he's just standing on his own two feet doing the scene.

All the sea-going scenes in the film, that is, those on the ship the "Huispaniola", were shot in the studio in an environment where the dialogue could be properly recorded. Many outdoor action sequences, where the dialogue could have been "muddy" because of the many exterior noises, were shot by the second film unit on a sea-going replica just off Plymouth. The back "lot" at Denham was used to depict the island where the treasure was buried. The ship itself, built entirely to scale, was on rockers or rollers to simulate the motion of the waves, in the studio. The seemingly blue cyclorama (which took hours to light with arcs) represented the horizon. When the ship was at rest, anchored, in the harbour, it was found that the rollers were too violent, so a gentle up and down motion of the camera was sufficient to convey riding at anchor. This was achieved by the camera operator, the inimitable Skeets Kelly. Another ex P.O.W. incidentally! He did all the aerial photography on *Battle of Britain* and had a fine career behind the lens. (And the actors as well had to sway slightly to complement the camera when given the direction. "And sway!" would shout the First A.D! This could occasionally lead to re-takes when one of the actors was swaying the wrong way to everyone else).

I had a good death scene! Shot in the head! My character Cady was killed by a young John Gregson as Redruth, in a fight next to the ship's wheel. Well I say "fight". I leapt on him, armed with a knife, grabbed him round the neck, he shrugged me off, we struggled and then he shot me! And that was the end of me. Blood already set on my face and I leap backwards in a separate Big Close Up with hands to my head. The first pirate to be killed! As well as that I'd been in lots of group shots on the ship as you'd expect being one of the pirates, and in the Inn sequence at the beginning. And in a little scene about starting the mutiny. And had another line about rum. This is what I expected to do at this stage of my career in big films. The odd line and a lot of set dressing, if I was lucky. Like *They Made Me a Fugitive* but without the tongue twisters. Like *Chance of a Lifetime*.

I enjoyed working on this Disney epic very much indeed. This was another big film for my C.V..

Nothing was in the pipe-line. Except the good old staple,

dubbing. I'm never going to sniff at that. I did some post-syncing on *They Were Not Divided* at £9 for Terence Young playing a…soldier… and some narration on a piece called *Crystal Clear* for 7 guineas for Ronnie Riley at Merton Park, a documentary about diamonds.

Then, early in 1950, January 16th. to be precise, I was asked to play the part of a "heckler" in a film for the Conservative Party. So putting my Socialist leanings behind me, I have to say I'm not a particularly political animal. My mother had voted Tory all her life, but I was never a "dyed in the wool" anything. I had however voted Labour at the 1945 election. I'd been attracted by the idea of a National Health Service and had been bewildered by the amount of unemployment in the 30s under the Tories. In those distant and "not so bad as we thought they were" days, Party Political Broadcasts were done in the form of ten to fifteen minute films and shown in the cinema. They were a bit of a yawn then, as now, and became either an opportunity for a visit to the lavatory, or a topic of vocal derision. Mostly the latter with hoots and catcalls and raspberries. Nevertheless I enjoyed my three days of heckling, which were shot almost entirely in a Tory party H.Q. at Harringay just opposite the greyhound stadium. They gave me scripted heckles but I was given free rein to improvise a few. "Rubbish" and "you twit" were some of the less political I came up with. Though a few of the lines were very topical e.g.

"If you win the election, are you going to abolish the welfare state?"

I got carried away by asking what the M.P. thought about nationalisation. But was actually encouraged by the director to be as active as possible.

"Very good Sam. It's keeping him on his mettle,"

I was paid the titchy rate of a fiver a day. Even for making some of the lines up! From this of course, the usual deductions were made! Luckily no contributions to the party were asked for or given. The party agent gave the actors a glass of Cyprus sherry and handed around some petit fours that looked and tasted as if they'd seen better days! Harry Dubens saw the film at a private screening and said he'd put me up for every "Hickler" part that came his way from then on.

"You were terrivic Sid! Do the Communist party next! *Chance of the Lifetimes* prepared you for that."

Harry hadn't been a fan of the film's message.

I did some post-syncing on *The Intruder*, cast by John Redway and then my first feature film of the year was *Cage of Gold,* directed by faithful Basil Dearden. David Farrar I knew of old from our *Small Back Room* days. We had a non-committal, "How have you been doing?" type of conversation with an "Oh you two know each other then!" from Basil, and that was that!

David wasn't easy to talk to, despite being a terrific actor. He'd been wonderful in *Small Back Room*. But as a communicator, he had a habit of lapsing into long silences. It was much easier to converse with Jean Simmons who was not only pretty, but very friendly, into the bargain. I renewed acquaintance with Douglas Slocombe, the lighting cameraman who had lit *The Captive Heart*. He and Otto Heller - another top lighting cameraman - were very popular at Ealing Studios and I was to work with them many times in the future. Alan Donald was the boyfriend in the scene. We did it in very few takes. It's the "old husband who is thought to be dead in the war, reappears after his wife has remarried and demands money" story. I played, not a soldier (hurrah!) but a waiter in the "Palette" club. It was a lovely scene with me delivering champagne to Jean Simmons and Alan Donald (Jean had recently been Oscar nominated for her Ophelia in *Hamlet* and Alan was to be brilliant in *Bridge on the River Kwai*) sent by the cunning David Farrar who wants to take her away from her fiancé. And Alan sending it back! We did a whole load of set-ups with close ups and then shots back to David alone at his table, but in the end they decided just to use the set-up all on the Jean Simmons - Alan Donald table, with David Farrar in the background and me coming backwards and forwards from his table to theirs. The focus puller certainly earned his corn! We rehearsed this set-up about half a dozen times.

"Champagne from the man at the back sir" etc..

It worked beautifully. I was proud of that! This was another terrific film to be associated with.

After my waitering job with Ealing, I did a day on a film at Elstree called *The Miniver Story* (for £20!), a sequel to the successful *Mrs. Miniver,* once again starring Greer Garson (marvellous in *Random Harvest*) and Walter Pidgeon, neither of whom I remember meeting despite my being in a scene with them. I was…wait for it…no not a soldier. A removal man.

I was then forced to wait some considerable time for my next employment. Harry could provide no solace. "It's kwite as a field cat Sid" he said.

I was out of work for 41 days. Not huge for an actor I know. But enough to drive my mother round the bend. I hid from her even more than usual. I'd shelved my thoughts of finding somewhere else to live because I'd been busy filming. Now I rekindled my idea of moving. But the doubts re-surfaced. What if this period of unemployment were to last? What if I got involved in a brawl and my features were re-arranged (mind you that might get me more work. Basil Radford had a scar and that seemed to enhance his looks) and I never worked again? I hastily repaired to Power Road Chiswick where they handled the unemployment side of things. I hadn't been there for a bit. I was in good company! Jack Howarth, eventually Albert Tatlock in Coronation Street, used to meet me there. He eventually had a cottage in Wales, a suite at the Midland Hotel, a flat in London and an enormous number of repeat fees. "Good on yer Jack", as they say in the Oz parts of Earl's Court. As for me, I transferred to another office of unemployables at Hammersmith, Brook Green, W.6. They failed to get me anything; but Mother came up with something. Of course she did! She knew someone in Kingston. In Bentalls. Her department store tentacles were insidious. For three weeks I helped run a recording kiosk where people shouted stuff into a mic. like

"Hello Mum! Bet this will surprise you! This is Alf wishing you a happy birthday!"

And I handed them the little silver "record" to take away which could be played on their "gramophone". My mother was very pleased. A foot in the door for her scheming. But the proviso was that if acting work came up I would leave as soon as possible, which she didn't like at all.

Fortunately, it did. I did two days on a B.B.C. Radio drama for Francis Dillon with Cyril Cusack. I was an Irish soldier! It was called *Padraic General*. I earned 8 guineas. Then close on its heels was *Teatime Story* at Merton Park for Imperial Chemical Industries (I.C.I.) playing almost a soldier (security) followed by more B.B.C. Radio at Ally Pally called *With a Blunt Instrument* which was annoyingly three days for only 6 quid!

ELEVEN
Raoul Walsh and Doo-Nan

The inimitable Harry, agent for a chosen few, told me to hold myself in readiness for an interview, "For very beeg Film called *Capitan 'Oratio 'Ornblower* which iz to be film beeg at Denham Studios, Sid. Maude Spector spoke to me zee otter day and want to know if you speak American? I told her, like me, you speak all accent. O.K?"

I of course agreed. Always say "yes", that was my motto. My Yank accent wasn't bad actually.

The American stars were Gregory Peck as Horatio Hornblower R.N. and Virginia Mayo as the Duchess. I, together with Patric Doonan - who was an actor on the up also with Harry's agency - were to go along to Claridge's (top U.S. directors always stayed in swanky hotels) to meet the director, the well known Raoul Walsh. He turned out to be a very tall Irish-American. He'd literally been in at the birth of the movies, having made many famous and memorable films in Hollywood. He'd worked with all the great stars: Chaplin, Barrymore, Theda Bara, Gloria Swanson, Marlene Dietrich, Clark Gable, Errol Flynn etc. etc.. Walsh wore a permanent patch over his right eye, since it was damaged in a motor accident. He spoke in a vigorous and abrupt manner, as if reluctant to speak at all. I had been ushered into the room by Maude and motioned to sit down with a gesture from Raoul.

I tried not to look at the eye patch but found myself strangely drawn to it.

"Done any sea pitchers before?" he said very quickly and seeming to be looking past me.

"Oh yes I've just completed *Treasure Island*. I was one of the pirates!" I said enthusiastically and possibly fawning a little. He

270

looked me up and down and rolled his eyes as if to say "big deal."

"Yeah but have you spoken lines in pitchers" he spat out at speed, sneeringly as if the reply would obviously be, "No. Never".

Instead I snapped back. "Of course Mr. Walsh. I'm an actor." (Gulp)

He looked at me again with seeming disbelief. "Yeah?" He said, looking me up and down once more. "Yeah but can you talk with a transatlantic accent?" he sneered again, determined to catch me out.

"Well yes." I put on my best American "How-ja wan me to taak sur?" voice.

Unimpressed, his one eye panned past me and landed on a script which he picked up and thumbed through. He pointed to a page and said, "Read that - Trans-atlantic-wise."

It was a short speech relating to a ship called "The Witch of Endor" which was supposed to have sunk in the Mediterranean and the part I was reading for was "third lookout". I read it with the restless rolling foamy Mid Atlantic in mind and not too badly I thought. He made no comment on the accent but said, "O.K. We'll let you know Mr Doo-nan."

"Kydd! K-y-d-d." I corrected. "Not Doo-nan." I murmured transatlantically.

"How's that?"

"Not Doo-nan. Kydd. K-y-d-d. My name is Kydd."

"Oh yeah?"

He gave me the look of death. As regards interviews that was down there with the worst.

I realised it was a mistake having gone there with Patrick Doonan, but it was too late. As it turned out, the fault was minimised by our both being summoned to Denham Studios and being told that we were to wear sailor's uniforms of Nelson's era with black boaters, plus have pig tails put on us by make-up. The crew were going to be chosen from this motley lot. And there were indeed a lot of us! We were then lined up and photographed individually. Sideways, backways and frontways. And then the whole crew assembled as if for a school photograph. Raoul himself then came and inspected his matelots by tracking past us, looking us up and down. He stopped at me and said, "You're Doo-nan, aintcha?"

I replied Trans-atlantic-wise, "N-o. I'm Kydd. K-y-d-d. My name is Kydd."

He looked at me suspiciously as if I was playing some trick on him. "Where's Doo-nan then?"

I pointed him out and Raoul moved over to him. And that was that! I heard nothing. Harry then phoned and told me Patric was a crew member but I wasn't But I had been given the part of the "Third Lookout", the one I'd read for, who stays on dry land. The sailor who never went to sea! I was not to be a member of the crew. Maybe my Transatlantic accent hadn't gone far enough out to the U.S., or maybe I looked too much like Patric Doo-nan. Perhaps Raoul's eyesight made it difficult for him to judge faces? Anyway, on the plus side, I had a part, and after a bit I was called to Denham studios.

On the first day I was called at 7 a.m. and by 8 a.m. I was dressed and made up, patiently waiting, but was never summoned to the set. At the end of the day, the Second came and told me that the call for the next day was exactly the same: 7 a.m.. The same routine occurred the following day, with me waiting patiently in my dressing room. At the end of the day the Second appeared again but this time informed me that, "Things are a bit hectic on the set, but in all probability you'll be used tomorrow."

I wasn't worried. At this stage of my career, I enjoyed going to the studio not to be used. Like the gas meter, my rate was "ticking-up" all the time. Regardless!

On the third day, just as I was thinking that another free day was about to be chalked up and I'd been in my sailor's outfit reading the paper, they came for me in a hurry. The First A.D. himself explained to me breathlessly, "We have to be off this particular set tonight…and we only have half an hour to shoot the scene. Is that O.K.?"

I don't know why he was asking me if it was O.K. I was hardly going to say, "No it's not. How dare you? I'm off!"

This was the way films were/are shot. You spend all day painstakingly on a couple of scenes and then cram in another one before the overtime kicks in. So I said, "Yes of course!" And added "What about my companion in the lookout post, the other actor according to the script? I haven't met him."

I hadn't. And hadn't recognised anyone in the canteen in a sailor's outfit like mine.

"No don't worry. There isn't one at the moment," said the assistant. "Mr. Walsh is choosing one of the extras to play the part."

As I registered immense surprise, he added quickly, "He's only got a couple of lines, hasn't he?"

"Yes" I said. "He says "It's the Witch of Endor" and the slightly more complicated "Well the Dutchman came in ahead of him and ran up a flag saying it was him".

This was going to be interesting. Raoul was going to get an extra to play a part with no idea of the scene, with a brief time to shoot it, and he had lines he'd never seen before, let alone learnt.

I arrived on the set to find that it was indeed hectic. Everyone was busting a blood vessel to get off this set in the allotted time. My part of it comprised peering out of the inside of a "look out post" situated above the mouth or inlet of a harbour. This "post" was obviously cleverly constructed in the studio. Naturally we shot it without a rehearsal. You always do when it's going to be disastrous. It's almost as if the filmic Gods line up and shout out, "For it to be truly dreadful, and leap grotesquely into overtime, make sure to shoot it without preparation."

The supporting artiste and I hastily shook hands. He was Tom. He'd barely had a chance to look at the scene and of course told me he'd never spoken dialogue before. I somehow knew that was going to be the case. I suspected mayhem, and indeed got it. What were they thinking of? Here's a synopsis:

When the scene opens, I'm in the background writing in the logbook and a figure in the foreground - my assistant, Tom - is looking out of the window through the telescope. He then lowers it, looks through it again, and then in his best transatlantic accent (he didn't have one, despite this being so important at the audition, and in fact was Australian) says, "It's the Witch of Endor, Cobber!" (Well he didn't say "cobber" but I felt he should have with his pronounced accent.)

"The Witch of Endor? Hornblower?" queries the Third Lookout (me), even though there are only two lookouts, coming forward to him and taking the telescope from him to look himself, also saying

"It cain't be! She was sunk in the Meditarraney some time ago!" (In my best Transatlantic West Country sailor-speak accent).

I then put the ridiculously long almost comedy telescope to my right eye and take a long look.

"How kin that be? If you're tellin' the truth then I must be drunk, and there's a corpse sailing a sunken ship"

And that's when the be-hatted-sailor-never-said-a-line-in-a-film-before-and-has-had-no-rehearsal Tom says his complicated

"Well the Dutchman came in ahead of him and ran up a flag saying it was him."

(Well not complicated if he'd had the chance to learn it.)

I then put the telescope to my eye again, say,

"Heavens! It IS the Witch! I'd recognise her in a storm! I'll telegraph 'em!"

And then I go to signal, by cranking a lever connected to the signalling paddles. End of scene. There is then, amidst stirring end-of-film music, a separate shot of the paddles, perched upon our hut, doing their signalling and allowing the ship into harbour.

So we stood on set in our positions. The First briefly explained the action to us, told us our moves and shouted "going for a take."

Of course we were. Time was not on our side. Tom froze.

"What's the ship called?" Tom asked frantically.

I told him. ""The Witch of Endor" Look. Hide your script behind something. If you're stuck grab a quick look at it if you can!"

"I haven't got a script," said unprepared and rabbit stuck in headlights Tom.

"Here. Have mine." I said. "Look. Quickly. Let's run the lines."

We got about halfway through when "ACTION" bellowed Raoul, surprising us all, as no one was ready. The scene was rubbish. Tom was fine with the words, if a little tentative, but when it was my turn to look through the telescope, I was thrown by the fact that it had been blacked out. I don't know why I did this, but when I couldn't see anything out of my right eye I moved the telescope to my left eye and obviously couldn't see out of that eye either, so examined the telescope.

"CUT! CUT' Fer Chrissakes CUT!" shouted Raoul "Wassa matter wid dat guy there? Whass he doin'?"

("That guy?" He obviously didn't recognise me in my sailor's outfit.)

"Somebody's blacked out the telescope" I said. Holding it up for all to see.

"Open the other eye to look. We'll never see it from here." said Raoul.

"But you don't look through a telescope with both eyes open" I said plaintively. "It looks kinda ridiculous!" I said emphasising the transatlantic qualities of the 'kinda'.

"Well Mr. Doo-nan" He remembered me! "Just try it for me…..WOULDYA?"

I scuttled back to my first mark, behind the writing desk. Raoul made you scuttle.

"O.K. ACTION" rasped Raoul, as if his epiglottis was scalded. It made Tom audibly gasp in fear. Tom peered out of the window, lifted the telescope up and after a super long pause - had he forgotten or was it for dramatic effect? - he said, "It's the er…the er….What's the name of the ship again?"

He looked pleadingly at Raoul and then at me. He obviously hadn't taken my advice and put the lines down anywhere.

"Cut it. Cut it. CUT!" yelled Mr. Walsh and then with an

exaggerated icy calm he said, "It's the Witch of Endorre. The Witch.... of..... Endorre.......... THE WITCH OF F*CKING ENDORRE!..... GOT IT?............."

Then quickly as if we had ten seconds to fit it in before we all turned into lizards, "O.K. LET'S GO. FIRST PLACES. TURN OVER. ACTION!"

The inkwell on my desk shivered at the volume.

"It's the Witch of Endor!" said Tom in a whisper. I replied with the lines you already know and by the time he got to, "Well the Dutchman came in ahead of him etc.," his nasally "strine" voice was getting stronger and more confident, now that he'd remembered the name of the ship. In fact he was pretty good. Good for him! I ludicrously put the telescope between my eyes in the middle of my forehead, and closed them, said my lines and retired to my desk in the background and proceeded to answer the "Witch of Endor's" signals by rapidly cranking the lever that operated the exterior paddles. (I mean the device wasn't practical. There weren't any paddles I was connected to. This would be an exterior shot. But I had to act as if I was operating something, even though it wasn't actually there.) In my over-enthusiasm the pillar to which the crank was attached overbalanced and fell into the set with a large crash! (If you look carefully at the final edit, I'm holding the pillar up with my left hand.) There was a short silence and then Raoul's voice was heard screaming:

"SEE WHAT YOU DONE DOO-NAN! SEE WHAT YOU DONE!"

It took half an hour to repair the prop – as I've said, the handle wasn't a practical handle and was attached to a wooden batten that had somehow got stuck in the hole it was being cranked in - and fit it back up again. We got the shot eventually, after two and a half hours overtime and a ludicrous number of takes, in which Tom forgot the ship's name again and his other line (mostly his other line) Raoul shouted at me to look through the telescope another way ("STICK IT ON YOUR RIGHT EYE DOO-NAN OR I'LL STICK IT

SOMEWHERE FOR YOU!) and the lever jammed and the camera jammed and Raoul jammed, and ranted and raved and referred to me constantly as "Doo-nan" ruining his "pitcher". I thought of the money the overtime was earning me and wondered if he referred to Patric Doonan as "Kydd".

I've read Raoul's autobiography, *Each Man in his Time*. ("Each Man In His Overtime" I called it.) My wife, Pinkie, bought it for me as a birthday present.

"Cheer you up! Bring back happy memories!" she said. It's a good read. Jimmy Cagney wrote the foreword and said

"Raoul Walsh's autobiography has it all, with laughter prevailing throughout."

Surprisingly, I'm not in it. Perhaps I encountered his evil unfunny twin who stood in for him occasionally. Or the real one had been abducted by aliens and replaced with a look alike.

The real Patric Doonan, who said Raoul didn't actually call him anything, told me of an incident that occurred on the film between Stanley Baker and himself. Stanley was playing the First Mate and Patric, as we knew, was a crew member. In the scene Patric had to complain to Stanley about the Captain, who was Horatio Hornblower (Gregory Peck) not having a plan.

"…he doesn't know where we're going….we're lost I tell you….lost!"

The camera was tracking from right to left along the deck and Stanley and Patric were walking past the camera, slowly. Raoul, who didn't, as always, waste much time rehearsing, suddenly without warning, decided to shoot. He must have thought this somehow improved performance. Oh how wrong he was.

"O.K." he said. "Let's go!" Then "Hey you two!"

(pointing to the two sailors directly behind Patric)

" You repeat those lines, "we're lost. We're lost I tell you". Ad-lib till the camera is past you, O.K?"

The two sailors who were of course crowd workers, nodded in the affirmative. They couldn't believe their luck. They had lines and would be paid extra, for they were now "actors". Their Christmasses had all come at once. Perhaps they could get agents on the back of their small parts? Start a film career? Go on to greater starring roles? Who knows? On "ACTION", the camera tracked and as Stanley and Pat walked past it, Patric said his lines:

"Hornblower shouldn't be in charge of this ship. He doesn't know where we're going. We're lost. We're lost I tell you".

The camera tracked past them, to reveal our two "extras" who expertly improvised:

"Ere. Rodney."

"What?"

"Yer know what?"

"What?"

"We are completely lost."

"I know".

"LOSSST"

"Yes,"

"LOSST I TELL YOU!"

"You are not wrong."

"The captain's a fool!"

"He's more than that. He's insane!"

"Ooh you are so right!"

"Bonkers!".

"Ooh yes."

"Completely loopy."

"Oooh oooh yes. Loopy."

"I don't know about you but I'm not happy."

"Me neither."

"Ooh no. No no no no no no no."

"Noooooooo. Happy we are not!"

There was a pregnant pause. The supporting artistes beamed at their own fluency and skill. All eyes turned to Raoul.

"CUT!" he apoplectically screamed. "CUT! CUT! CUT! CUT!

CUT! CUT! CUT! CUT! CUT! CUT!"

Then pointing in their direction,

"GET THOSE DAISIES OUTTA HERE!"

Incidentally when I saw the "pitcher", I was dubbed! With a gruff George Woodbridge-like English voice about 20 years older than mine. (I think it may have been him!) Tom wasn't dubbed and was still Australian. Not a Transatlantic vowel or consonant to be heard anywhere in the vicinity. It was as if Raoul was wielding his power from the other side of the world!

"Ha ha! I got yer Doo-nan!"

In the final edit, Tom's first line "It's the Witch of Endor" was cut. Though to be fair, it was a nice two shot and the scene looked O.K.. Despite my voice. In truth it's a fantastic film (and a really terrific "pitcher"). Gregory Peck, James Robertson Justice and Robert Beatty are excellent.

Following my hectic stint with Captain Eyepatch, I sailed into calmer waters with B.B.C. Radio, doing two Documentaries under the banner of *Now It Can be Told, Canoe Raiders* - which concerned the Cockleshell Heroes that I was to be in a film about - and happily (about cheating at cricket) *Not Out*. I got £6/6/- for each one.

Once again, although of course a lot of the programme was about real people talking, there was the odd scripted insert that I was used for, which was great fun and very handy.

Dear Harry Secombe asked me to go along to see him in a B.B.C. Home Service production of the series *Music Hall* which starred Ben Warris and Jimmy Jewel, stars of radio's *Up the Pole* - and cannily suggested I meet Bill Worsley the producer to see if he could give me any work in the future. As it happened I didn't ever work with him. He was a nice guy though! Harry's "turn" was peppered with song as usual. He gave me his script! Which of course he'd written!

BEN WARRIS: And now ladies and gentlemen, it gives me great

anxiety to present you the resident comedian of "Welsh Rarebit", that amiable maniac, Harry Secombe!

HARRY: Well - hello there - what did you call me Ben?

BEN: A Maniac?

HARRY: (SINGS) A maniac bird in a Gilded Cage -

BEN: Oh no! Who taught you to sing?

HARRY: My sister - George Secombe.

BEN: But Harry - George isn't a girl's name -

HARRY: I know -

BEN: Then why call your sister George?

HARRY: Well when she knew I was her brother she took it like a man.

BEN: Harry - you're completely incomprehensible. (EXIT)

HARRY: Well hello there! (GIGGLE) and thank you Ben Warris for your kind words. However this is no time for compliments, but time instead for one of Secombe's Bedtime Stories for Children - bless 'em all - (SINGS) The long 'uns, the short 'uns, the - Oh I beg your pardon - I got carried away - I'm not usually carried away till after the broadcast - by two big men in uniform - (LAUGH CUT SHORT) To resume tonight I wish to tell all the tots - big tots - small tots - (SING) Tots as heavy as lead - aaah - there I go again - I just don't care - that's all - The story of Dick Cattington and his Wit - er Dick Wattington and his kit - Kittington and his wat

- (SCREAMS) The story of Little Red Riding Good - Once there was a jockey called Fred, and when he rode a winner, people used to say - "Isn't Fred riding good?" - so when he had a daughter with black hair, she was called <u>Red</u> Riding Good. Aren't some people obstinate? When Red was still a girl of some thirteen runners - and about thirty six winners, Fred retired and bought a fish shop - a nice plaice with a sole agency for selling skate on thin ice, delivered C.O. D. (LAUGH) Etc. etc.!

Harry as always, went down a storm.

Then, in fast succession, small parts were the order of the day and I lapped them up. Harry Dubens was happy I was so busy - I did a brisk one for Val Guest and Danny Angel in a Douglas Fairbanks film *Mr. Drake's Duck*, a movie about a duck laying uranium eggs, as a news editor. I was on the phone at a desk in a newspaper office. Just one set up. One mid shot. Asking the war office what was happening at a farm in Sussex where tanks had been sent that had been designated as a prohibited area (because of the uranium eggs)! Brisk shouty journalist acting! This was a new venture. Perhaps it would open up a new area of work for me? Loud newspaper men! It didn't. I did play one in *Love in Pawn* though. In and out in that one. Incidentally the cameraman was one Harry Gillam who played for the Stage C.C.!

Then I was employed by John Baxter in *The Second Mate* (doing a smuggling villain routine on board a Thames-going barge and some warehouse acting.). We had some exciting chase sequences both on the barge on the river and on the replica in the studio. Gordon Harker was playing a double game working for the crooks, but informing the police! More in and out.

Then by Ralph Thomas in *The Clouded Yellow* at Pinewood, playing a wireless operator. Scenes with good old Kenny More. The police are scouring the Lake District for Trevor Howard and Jean Simmons. They believe Jean has murdered someone. I'm in direct contact with the helicopter which is flying over the area.

"They've been seen near Copley's Wood."
And then:
"The helicopter says there's no one in Copley's Wood."
Then:
"Couple seen at Sour Milk Gill."

All shot in the studio. Trevor Howard is great in it as an ex spy who resembles a 1951 James Bond 007. Of course I had no scenes with him. In and out again.

Then came *The Magnet*, with me as a postman opposite a very young James Fox, who I remember was then called "William". This was another Ealing film, with all the top guns - written by T.E.B. (Tibby) Clarke and directed by Charles Frend. We shot in New Brighton, Merseyside. I did my Northern! I should have done my Liverpudlian which I could do as well. Three days, not used for two, so not quite in and out.

Next I was in a sweet little *Passport-like* film, starring the always working convivial Basil Radford, *The Galloping Major* for director Henry Cornelius. The horse that the community of "Lamb's Green" had bought and was supposed to have been on its way to Aintree for the Grand National, had been mistakenly painted white and driven away to be in a medieval jousting scene in a film in Chester and everyone was searching for it. (Ooh these plots!) I was a newspaper seller who shouted, with his back to camera, (well a part of me was in profile)

"Standard-Star-News! Horse still missing" as the van with the horse in it drove past.

A one take, two second wonder. Well we went again a couple of times as the timing of the horse-van coming out of the studio gates could have been better (not quite sure why a paper seller was outside a studio, but never mind. Not much foot fall there!). To rub salt into a very brief wound, I was dubbed. A deep throated voice nothing like me! I experienced what I'd been doing myself to some actors for several years. Like with *Hornblower*, I slunk away from the cinema. But you just have to accept it don't you. At least I hadn't been cut out! In and out again, again.

Then a quick car mechanic in a tale of blackmail murder and deceit for a Roy Baker and Monty Berman produced film, directed by John Gilling called *No Trace* starring Hugh Sinclair (he'd played *The Saint* a lot) at Alliance in both Southall and Twickenham once more scrutinised continuity wise by Shirley Barnes. This sentence was as long as my part.

And finally, again as a soldier, (First Soldier said the cast list) on a film called *Man Detained* also called *The Dark Man,* shot mainly on location at Littlestone in Kent. Not in and out here. I had much more to do in this one than the previous four. The atmospheric film was produced and directed by the old firm of Julian Wintle and Jeffrey Dell. Most of my scenes were spent searching along the pebbly Littlestone beach with William Hartnell, who played the Sergeant Major. Though I had a cameo firing a Bren Gun! All that training came in handy! The little stones may have been easy on the eye, but not on the constitution or the feet, and to add to our discomfort it was extremely hot weather!

We were looking for the chief villain, Maxwell Reid (who at that time was married to Joan Collins, but not for long!). Bill Hartnell, bless him, was inclined to treat us all as if we were still in the army, and was always checking our mode of dress to see if we'd omitted anything! He was a stickler for being correct, but could never catch me out, as I had a great deal of experience behind me and a number of mental bruises to prove it. He meant well though. It was just that when he donned a battle dress - and even out of it - he imagined he was back in Service! Quite a number of the actors objected, but I didn't mind - it rather amused me in fact! When he played the Sergeant Major in Granada's T.V. comedy *The Army Game*, he behaved in exactly the same way - always correct and insisting everyone else be so. Army medals, badges, stripes, boots, belt, cap and stick, haircut, always perfect. Geoffery Sumner played the Commanding Officer, and even when they went to the pub for a drink, Bill would call him "Sir". There's realism for you! A good guy

Bill, a terrific actor and of course the first Dr. Who. I can honestly say, he was one of the best actors I ever worked with. Maxwell Reid, who wasn't very communicative, and especially not with Bill who was very critical of his unshiny shoes, ("The shoes need a bit of a buff Maxwell, don't you think? And while you're at it, I would suggest you have a trim. I'm standing on your hair!") eventually emigrated to Hollywood and paradoxically gave up the film business. He gave up Joan Collins too. Or maybe she gave him up. He strangely enough, always spoke in a "kinda" American accent anyway, but occasionally the cockney showed through! Unlike Michael Rennie of course, whose American accent was so good, his Yorkshire never surfaced! Years later I met a well known actor who would sometimes play cricket for the Stage C.C. when we were very short of players. He was American. Or at least everyone thought he was, including myself. He was always talking about baseball and American football, and what a great country the U.S.A. was. And how bigger everything was in America than "little 'ole England". Then came an occasion when I was match manager, and responsible for getting the team together, and we were a few players short. I rang his number in desperation, but there was no reply. After a few abortive attempts with the phone just ringing, I looked to see if he was in the phone book and I had the number right, and saw his name with an alternative number. I rang it. The address was in the East End. Whitechapel in fact. And the person who answered the phone in a broad cockney cum Jewish accent turned out to be his mother! She somewhat spilt the beans and told me he was born within the sound of Bow bells but pretended to be an American, as that was the only way he could get work! He had never been to the U.S.A. in his life! He came clean at the game, but I have to admit I slightly resented being so easily fooled! After that match he never played cricket for us again. Possibly it was bad for business if too many cricketing actors knew his cover was blown. But when you think about it, if he was getting work, which he was, good for him! It's a bad reflection on the business though if he felt he couldn't just be "an actor". I suppose he thought maintaining the fiction offstage meant he would never be doubted.

I had a day on Roy Baker's vehicle for Margaret Lockwood, *Highly Dangerous* at Pinewood, taking a poorly Victor Maddern's place as a "Customs Man" with good old Patrick Doonan (Victor had the flu apparently) - Victor and I were to overlap in many many films and tellies: *Malta Story, I'm Alright Jack, Mess Mates* etc. - but my first involvement in his career was replacing him! I had a bit with Dane Clark the American star of the piece (the number of films at the time where the lead was American!) asking if he had anything to declare. When I saw the film I wasn't in it! Another one I'd been cut out of! Always a problem when you're only in one scene.

Then Roy (Hurrah!) got me in again to dub another crime film, *Blackout,* starring Maxwell Reid (again). Roy had been churning 'em out for Tempcan Productions and Monty Berman would shoot it (and Monty would produce it with him), and in this instance director John Gilling had written the screenplay. They were a scintillating team. It was dubbed at Alliance Twickenham where they'd shot the interiors. I played two very different parts. One was an ex army hall porter and the other was a police inspector. The porter was a bit wheezy so perhaps you could see why he was being dubbed. The policeman looked the part. Unfortunately, he didn't sound much like a policeman - not that all policemen sound the same - but he was lacking in authority and was slightly wooden. And whispery. And let's be frank, dull. In fact he made so little mouth movement, anything I did looked as if it couldn't possibly be coming out of his mouth. But after several passes we came to a sort of clenched teeth 'light and shade' compromise. As the hall porter I had to say to Maxwell Reid, who was looking for one of the murderous gang: "Number 70 fifth floor. I think he's out sir!"

And to another gang member:

"Sorry sir. There was a gentleman who wanted your flat number. I told him you'd left." I was nicely crusty and "cockney trying to be posh" for that one. A bit like Irene Handl.

The copper had to say: "Alright Dale. Throw the gun down. We've arrested your friends. We've got you surrounded."

And after poor old Dale had fled and quite rightly fallen off the balcony (coz he was the baddie), I said to the other copper: "I'll take this lot to the ambulance. You stay behind and clear things up. And you sir had better go to hospital (Maxwell Reid had been shot in the arm but was so manly he still had time to walk the heroine out of the crime scene.) All of this in my slightly stilted "evenin' all" policeman's voice. £12 for the day. I thank yew.

Because work was looking sparse - if I wasn't working constantly, it was always sparse! - I decided to brush up my tap dancing. Before the war, having been fired with optimism by having seen Fred Astaire and all the other tappers, I had avidly and patiently learned two routines that I trotted out at all the Talent Contests I entered, painstakingly taught to me by a former Tiller Girl whose brother was in the local choir. She charged me half a crown an hour and all the lessons took place in the kitchen which was covered with linoleum and therefore highly suitable. I was an eager pupil and in no time at all - well three months later - I was doing a duo with her as part of the cabaret at the Church Ball in Porchester Hall. We sang one chorus of "Let's Fall in Love", did some cross talk, sang two choruses of "Nasty Man" and then performed the tap dance. It was to become immensely useful in Prison Camp and in subsequent auditions. After that, every Tuesday and Thursday, I attended the Buddy Bradley School of Dancing - at five bob a time - which was to be found almost opposite the Windmill Theatre in Soho. It had been advertised as "Musical Comedy Dancing and Tap" in "The Stage" Newspaper and I applied myself assiduously to learning one of Mr. Bradley's intricate routines. Sometimes in a lull in rehearsal for a play, I have gone into the routine and some actresses have looked on admiringly, but most of the actors have said, "Swank. Showing off."

So I am loath to reveal my er "capabilities". Only if I'm pressed and coerced! Years later I performed a dance routine with Max Wall and Julia McKenzie in a pantomime, *Jack and the Beanstalk,* at the Bromley Theatre. But Max - one of the great comics of my era and someone I was proud to call a friend - was so marvellous and brilliant, I felt and looked like a self-conscious impostor.

I was in a neat flow of work. Not great parts but more regular than ever before. Harry was happy. Mother wasn't scowling. Jack wasn't shaking his head and tutting. I'd saved a bit for any rainy days. I did a day on *Hell is Sold Out* a film about someone impersonating a supposedly dead author who comes back alive from the war to confront the impersonator, played by the versatile Herbert Lom, at Nettlefold. This was directed by the perennially young Michael Anderson, who of course directed *The Dam Busters.* My bit as a waiter in a nightclub never made it to the final edit. Another one!

Then another Francis Dillon *Country Magazine* B.B.C. Radio. And another *Now It Can be Told* B.B.C. Home Service Radio for Tom Waldron. This one was called *The Visiting General* and was about a U.S. General attempting to prevent an invasion of North Africa diplomatically. Guess what? I played a soldier!

I then did some post syncing and acted in a couple of scenes for a new young director called Don Chaffey. He eventually did the classic *Jason and the Argonauts.* The film was a children's film with a child sleuth and lots of falling into puddles, as adults always tend to do in films like this. This was *Case of the Missing Scene* set in Norfolk on the Broads, for Rank's Children's Entertainment Films, known as "Gaumont-British Instructional", a sort of precursor to the Children's Film Foundation. It was a rather lovely little movie about a camera crew and poachers both seeking a bird, a "bittern", for different reasons: the camera crew to film it, the poachers to kill it and stuff it and sell it, and the camera crew inadvertently filming the poachers and consequently getting them arrested. I dubbed three parts that featured technicians at the film studio (in the film) that was making the film about the bittern:

One character handed over the cans of film:

"There you are Tony. Just sign for 'em!"

Slightly London that one.

I then played a driver, saying:

"I had to go to the station and pick up the film from Norfolk!"

An older projected voice, not difficult to dub, as the actor playing him was turning away, so you can fit the line in when his back is towards you.

And then I was a technician in Denham Laboratories in the cutting room looking at the film they'd shot on the broads. This character was quite well spoken. I made him a bit deeper:

"What's this scene? Two men in the reeds with a gun? Perhaps they're working up a poaching sequence?"

I acted in the film as well. I was a station guard, picking up the cans of film off the London train which replaced the ones that had been stolen by the crooks, so the cameraman had enough film to shoot the bittern eggs hatching. (It was very educational as you can imagine. Not only about birds but about camera equipment as well!) The boy picking the film up is very eager and in the scene I have to quell his enthusiasm:

"You'll have to come along to the goods office first son."

And

"Just a minute! I've got to enter it into the book!" as he grabs the film.

Needless to say I didn't get a credit for the guard, which was always disappointing. But enjoyable work with a director eventually to become a huge success. Perhaps he'd use me again? He did!

I was soon to be another crook. I was Bert in Michael McCarthy's *Assassin for Hire* with the excellent Sydney Tafler as the assassin. He's a nice chap. And a Chelsea fan. And likes a bet on the horses like me. This was at Merton Park Studios for Julian Wintle, who used the studios so frequently I began to think he must've had a financial interest in them. So what? At least he did make films, albeit mainly second features and as far as I was concerned, although the money was inevitably low in comparison with first feature rates, the experience was well worth it. Usually I had much more to do in these small budget pictures, which I enjoyed. One always hoped that eventually the small producer this year, would turn into the big producer next year and of course in Julian Wintle's case this happened. Two or three years later he was installed in an office at Pinewood Studios for his first big feature, *Passage Home*. Not of course that there is any guarantee that you'll be cast in the major production, but the chances are better if you've already worked for the producer. And in fact I was in it! In a nice part!

I did a day at Southall for Kenneth Hume on *Cheer the Brave* for half my usual rate, ("Sid it's half!" "I'll do it Harry."), as a boy of barrow, and then three separate days of post syncing on *Pool of London* playing a variety of sailors on board the "Dunbar" which was the boat at the centre of the drama (myself and Victor Maddern had actually been in it but were cut out!) and then some more dubbing on *Man in the White Suit* for Ealing. I suppose some actors would have been cowed by the lack of visibility when I was dubbing or being edited out. But I was still working. I mentioned it to Harry. He wasn't sympathetic.

"Youse gettin the work Sid. If they makin decision ter cut you out it's not yer fault. Doan take it to heart. They still gettin yer back for oddar picture."

That was certainly true.

TWELVE
Corpsing

It's a unique thing to be cast as a corpse. I have had that distinction. It was in a picture called *Another Man's Poison*. It was made at Walton Film Studios, Surrey, starring the unforgettable Bette Davis - Academy award winner twice for *Dangerous* and *Jezebel,* and nominated 10 times. Yes that Bette! - and the multi talented actor-playwright-author Emlyn Williams. He of *The Corn is Green*. Andy Worker, who was production manager on it, who I've mentioned before, telephoned me. The following conversation ensued:

ANDY: How would you like to play Bette Davis's husband in a film called *Another Man's Poison*?

ME: (Overjoyed) Oh yes! Oh yes please! That's marvellous! I'd love to! When do I start?

ANDY: It's not as thrilling as it sounds. You don't get an opportunity to er ...embrace her.

ME: Ah. So… we obviously don't get on very well do we?

ANDY: Indeed, You get on terribly. Really really badly.

ME: Oh. Are we divorced then?

ANDY: Well no. You're dead.

ME: What?

ANDY: You've been done in. And she did it. And it's not as thrilling as it sounds (He'd said that before).

ME: So I'm her dead husband?

ANDY: Yes.

ME: (I began to see where this was going) Are there any scenes where I'm alive then?

ANDY: No.

ME: Ah. Not even in flash back?

ANDY: No.

ME: Ah.

ANDY: It's easy. As the "stiff", all you have to do is lie on the floor for a week - or in a chair - we haven't worked out what's happening yet - and we'll look after you. But you do get to act with her. Sort of. And Emlyn Williams is in it!

I said to myself, unconvincingly, that the experience would do me good. I'd make new contacts etc.. I'd get to know Emlyn Williams!

I didn't.

He wasn't in any of my scenes. I'd get to know Gary Merrill, Bette's co-star and real life husband! They'd met in *All About Eve*!

I didn't.

He wasn't interested in chatting to me. I'd get to know the great Bette herself, as I was in several scenes with her, bolt upright in the chair with my hand in the air! Carried by her outside!

I didn't.

I was ignored completely. The director, Irving Rapper, who had directed Bette in Emlyn Williams' *The Corn is Green* (ah the connection: Emlyn wrote *The Corn is Green)* never actually spoke to me. Irving always asked the 2nd. A.D. to deal with me as if I wasn't actually there. Despite both of them being a few feet away.

"Can you tell the corpse to put his hand up as if it's a sort of "grizzly claw?" he said.

"O.K" said the 2nd .. "Sam. Can you put your hand up as if it's a sort of "grizzly claw?"

They were both standing over me.

I did so.

"Tell the corpse to put it higher."

I did.

"Sam. Can you put it higher?" the 2nd. A.D. would ask.

"I have." Said I.

"It's not looking like a claw. It needs to look more like a claw. Can we get a wooden claw? The man playing the corpse can just hold it there," said Irving.

"Sam. Can you make it look like a claw?" asked the 2nd.

"Or you're getting a wooden one. Yes! Yes! I heard!"

I was exasperated. And then slightly ashamed, as I'd answered back. Bloody hell. I was trying my best. In the end, make-up were asked to make my hand look "dead" whatever that means. They blackened it a bit. I'm not sure that helped. Bette and Gary had the task of carrying me outside and dropping me in the nearby lake. We didn't see this happening obviously. There was to be a shot of the lake and on set they lugged me outside and then spoke about having put me there. So there was no "body-in-the-lake acting". There was a "being-picked-up-and-dropped-outside" sequence that was quite demanding though. Not for me obviously as I was being carried. But Irving wanted a shot of my feet being dragged and Gary and Bette naturally weren't present for that. It was a muscly "sparks" dragging me. And in fact, Irving didn't like my shoes, so we had to get a well polished pair of black shoes from wardrobe and they didn't have any my size, so in the end someone in the office with the right shoes stood in for me, wearing my trousers and socks, and was "dragged" with a close-up of his feet. So that foot-corpse bit in the film isn't me. Then in the plot I had to be taken through the French windows and dumped outside because Emlyn Williams turned up and Gary and Bette had to hide me. That wasn't too convivial, as when we did a rehearsal, Gary just dropped me.

"The corpse is too heavy" he said. "Can we shoot higher and pretend we're carrying it?" he asked.

Bette agreed.

"Yes that would be a great idea. It weighs a ton."

Notice I'm referred to as "it". And "weighs a ton"? I was about 9 stone 6. I mean let's be frank, they really weren't happy having to carry me out. Bette gave up. Gary got brusque. Bette asked for someone lighter. Gary asked for a dummy. And I mean I was hardly a bag of cement! Bette did speak to me once though.

"Hello Mr. Corpse," she said. "Could you move? You're on my foot."

Gary then finally acknowledged me.

"For f*ck's sake! Could the body not snore? He's supposed to be dead".

I admit it. I'd dozed off. Andy had taken me to lunch trying to make up for the way I was being treated, and I'd eaten rather well. And possibly had too much to drink.

Harry Dubens phoned. He said there was a play for me at the Watergate Theatre.

"Sid. Theatre. The money is louse - £5 a week"

"What?"

"But it good contactz! And the writer is up and going! I know you haven't Theatred but when you get it, do it if you can fit it."

Of course I had "theatred". But not with him as my agent.

"Watergate" was of course nothing at all to do with its American namesake. About 15 years too early for a start! But in fact "controversial" productions were known to be put on at this "fringe" establishment. There'd been a flash of nudity and some shouty swearing in a recent previous production that had caused a stir so I was told.

It was situated in London not far from the Players Theatre in Charing Cross. The play was *Nothing up my Sleeve* written by Ronald Duncan who had achieved fame with his verse drama at the Mercury Theatre, *This Way to the Tomb*. I was told to meet someone just out of college called Kenneth Tynan, who as well as being the producer also directed and cast it. I met him at a house just off the Kings Road in Chelsea. He was very young, tall, slim, stuttered when he spoke and chain smoked. He weirdly held the cigarette between the two end fingers. He was surprisingly nervous and seemed rather ill at ease, but I think it was the first show he'd ever produced. And directed! I mentioned to him that I wasn't completely sure about the dates as I thought that a B.B.C. T.V. commitment might conflict with two nights of his play. He told me not to worry about that as arrangements could be made to cover for me. I read for him. He was clearly keen to have me which was nice! Harry phoned.

"Sid, he like you! You god it."

It could hardly be called a memorable piece. I think it was a "work in progress" as they say, as it reappeared at the Royal Court as *St. 'Orace* in the 60s. Gwen Nelson and Alfred Burke were in it. They were friendly. Also in it was the inimitable Harry Fowler - known for his cheeky chirpy cockneys. Harry was a "character". He treated the whole thing as a joke and behaved outrageously. To be frank, Kenneth Tynan couldn't cope with him and being a youngster, obviously wasn't looking for confrontation, as nothing was said. I mean it was a ludicrous performance. Freddie Schiller, my lovely erstwhile German acquaintance from *The Captive Heart* was also in it, but seemed a little disconcerted and bewildered by Harry's zany behaviour which turned the show into a sort of *Hellzapoppin*. In this 1941 film the actors break the "fourth wall" and speak directly to the audience. It was considered very avant grade at the time. I never saw it, just heard about how "outrageous" it was after the war. Harry did just that. He had a running dialogue with them. It wasn't in the script; this was definitely not supposed to take place. And Freddie frequently came off stage shaking his head. In the pub afterwards he said

"Zat man has destroyed this play completely."

I must admit that to my shame I joined in at times. He did get the audience laughing. Always when they shouldn't have been. Harry would stutter his lines a lot, mimicking Kenneth Tynan mercilessly, and pick on people in the audience with whom he'd discuss what they had for dinner! The production staff perhaps seeing the play wasn't working and anything to brighten the show up, were schtum. After a three weeks profitless run - we got below average notices and small audiences (Harry Dubens, hoping to surprise me, forgot I had two days when I wasn't doing it, and came to see it on the night my understudy was on) - the show finished and the theatre closed down for good. It was due for demolition anyway, but I think our show hastened it's demise! On reflection, with Ronald Duncan's reputation, Harry Fowler didn't do us any favours. Kenneth didn't appear again after a couple of nights, so maybe he'd washed his hands of it! And us! To this day I regret mucking about in it. But several people associated with *Nothing up my Sleeve* went on to make a successful career in showbiz. Harry Fowler became even more well-known - he was an effervescent Sam Weller in the film of *Pickwick Papers*, and of course was in the T.V. series, "The Army Game". Alfred Burke starred in the successful television series *Public Eye*, as the hugely popular rain-coated detective Frank Marker. And Kenneth Tynan, apart from becoming an eminent writer/critic, especially for the New York Times, was a brilliant literary manager of the National Theatre, rewrote and put on the outrageous *Oh Calcutta!* in the West End, and most infamously of all, was the first man to say "F*ck" during a live T.V. transmission!

The Courts of Justice for B.B.C. T.V. followed my flirtation with fringe Theatre and Mr. Tynan. He wrote thanking me for my contribution, which was very decent of him. Few people bother! In the first episode of the B.B.C. series, which concerned juvenile delinquency, I played a carpenter whose son was one of the juveniles being brought before the court. I pleaded in court for my wayward offspring, but without success, mainly because it was his second offence; in fact I got a wigging from the magistrate for not keeping a proper eye on my boy. Ian Atkins, son of the famous actor Robert Atkins (who I've mentioned before!), directed the show, and begged me and several other members of the cast to do their best, as our work up until then had clearly not impressed him! He was rather a dour task-master who didn't smile much. I preferred his wife, Freda Bamford, who was also in it, a marvellous character actress with a brilliant expressive face whose potential has never been fully realised. Though she did pop up all over the place in tellies much to my great pleasure. She, oddly enough, smiled a lot! What a lovely funny woman. We rehearsed for three weeks at a church hall near Russell

Square, suitably marked out in tape to represent the Magistrates' Court and shot the show on film over two cheerless days at mocked up Courts in the studio. Ian didn't appear to like any of us. What a strange experience this was.

After the *Courts* I seemed to monopolise the B.B.C. airwaves. For instance, I was in Edgar Wallace's *The Ringer*, playing a policeman, P.C. Field. Victor Maddern was in it playing a crook! This was followed by *And Now It Can be Told: Frogmen*. A story about the brave men who worked fearlessly under the water for the war effort, and then Rex Tucker's *The Man in Armour*, for *Children's Hour* playing (unusually!) a pickpocket called "Fingers". I then supplied Alan Burgess, B.B.C. sound producer and author, with information about the tough and chaotic fighting in Calais during the War (May 1940 to be exact - I was captured there) for a programme called *St. George's Day*. That brought me 10 Guineas.

I slipped in a quick day on *Mr. Denning Drives North* starring John Mills as a plane technician, but had my scene cut. (Argh!) Then an odd film, *Penny Points to Paradise* came up. Actually, "chaotic" would be a better description. So much of it seemed to be done in one take. Even if we'd mucked up! Naturally some of these never made it to the final edit, so the plot became slightly bewildering. Some did and were all a bit, how can I say, "tentative". I had one scene on the beach which they had great difficulty setting up - there was confusion as to who had been called, and someone was missing, so just gave up! It never made it back into the schedule.

The film starred Harry Secombe - dear Harry got me in - Spike Milligan, Peter Sellers - the fabulous soon-to-be *Goons* - the ebullient Alfred Marks - later a big star in his own T.V. show *Alfred Marks Time* - Bill Kerr - great with Hancock - the multi-talented comedienne Paddy O'Neill, later Alfred's wife - and Freddie Frinton, doing his famous drunk routine for no apparent reason other than he was amusing doing it. It certainly wasn't anything to do with the plot. It was directed by Anthony Young. Well, Anthony shouted "Action" and Spike did the directing! Alan Cullimore tried to produce it, and raise the money. Most of the film was shot at Brighton, in the streets and in the studio. I played three parts (it was that kind of movie): a cross eyed railway porter at the beginning of the film, who kept veering to the edge of the railway platform with the bags, a la Ben Turpin; a cross eyed Taxi driver with an exploding car who drove half on the pavement, which was very disconcerting for the Brighton populace, especially as the police hadn't been informed by the film company that I would be doing so. And finally a cross eyed news vendor who always handed the newspaper to the next customer. There was a theme here you may have noticed! But like the beach scene the news vendor never made it to the final edit. Moyra Secombe, Harry's lovely wife, came down and had a short holiday. She was in the picture too, watching the shot-putting dream sequence with me, in which I played myself, standing next to Peter Sellers observing the trajectory of the shot-putt! So in fact I did have three parts in the film after all!

Harry was playing a football pools winner, Harry Flakers, who'd won £100,000, and everyone was trying to remove him from his money. The film didn't really work. It was a mixture of slapstick, bits of the cast doing their turns (Harry mimed a surgeon doing surgery in the same vein as his 1946 shaving routine) peculiar editing, (where they'd clearly not got another shot to cut to) Spike and Harry in plot sequences where I think Spike was making it up, and incomprehensible story moments. The crooks finding the suitcase full of the pools winnings in the fireplace and putting it back so they could replace it with fake money later, was just peculiar. Why didn't they just steal it? Similarly just as if to confirm the-kick-bollock-and-scramble nature of the film, my driver character reappeared on several different occasions in the film in the comedy car, frequently with the hood of his duffel coat up. This was because that on those occasions, they shot it with someone else driving! In fact there are several shots where the edit leaps from me wearing just a cap, to some other bloke with the hood of his duffel-coat up, and then back to me again in the cap. I have no idea why. Other than I presume I wasn't about when they shot the inserts? In which case, why not? I was there for all the filming! I enjoyed myself though! But mostly in the hotel afterwards! Spike, Peter, Harry (as delightful as ever), Paddy and Bill were great company. I know they weren't happy with it at the time, especially Peter, who, ever the perfectionist, was disappointed with the character of the Major he was playing, but he struck me as fine in it. But as an overall advertisement for the soon-to-be-*Goon* comedy team, it needed work!

Another *Courts of Justice* happened - *Trial by Assize* - again for Ian Atkins, who this time greeted me with a wintry smile, which was a step in the right direction, though the production was still too chilly for me! They gave me a rather fetching moustache to try and differentiate me from my previous character!

And to complete my popularity with the B.B.C., I got a feature part in a play entitled *Shout Aloud Salvation*, about the birth pangs of the Salvation Army, directed by my fan Michael Barry, the heroine being the beautiful and brilliantly talented "newcomer" Virginia McKenna - soon to be a star in *A Town Like Alice* and *Carve Her Name with Pride*. Jessica Evans played opposite me as a woman of ill repute, while I was the rat-like leader of a "pro-war" pack. My large "lively" performance (so the papers said) entailed addressing the rabble and stirring them up. Unhappily, having to shout so much at rehearsal, I completely lost my voice. I could only croak my lines. In despair, I pursued any remedy no matter how ridiculous, to regain it. Everyone made suggestions with the best of intentions. The ubiquitous "don't speak" wasn't helpful. Salt water had no effect other than to make me think of the sea. My Aunt suggested I chew a piece of ginger root and then eat a marshmallow. I couldn't find any root, but ate a lot of marshmallows which of course are tasty but had no effect at all and I think rendered me flatulent. A fellow actor swore that if I tried to sing in falsetto, my voice would return in no time. I had a go, emitting a series of squeaks and getting a lot of funny looks from the cast as you would expect. But that didn't work either. All I could do was whisper and that was it. Then a saviour appeared, in the shape of someone in the cast, the venerable, great, Lewis Casson, who was a "Sir", a very distinguished actor and director and recently head of British Actors' Equity and the husband of Sybil Thorndike. He had lost his voice with the best of them. He advised me to purchase a bottle of "Sanderson's Throat Specific" and to be very diligent about the doses I took, and to take it sparingly, but to have a larger dose before the show.

"It's powerful stuff you know Sammy. Be very careful" he told me, looking secretively under his eyes as if he'd confided which end of the rainbow the leprechaun had buried the gold or that my vital organs might drop off if I took too much. So, as a last resort I tried the Sandersonian elixir. It magically worked! It may have tasted like a mixture of castor oil and snake juice, with a vinegary under-taste and a hint of mouse, but there I was back to normal! And then, immediately the show was over, I became a croaker again, and remained so for another two days. Miraculous! Hats off to Mr. Sanderson! And Sir Casson of course! I have carried a bottle with me to every show just in case, ever since! Ignore people when they tell you it can shrink your follicles!

So…Like all actors, I was keen to keep working. And I did! Next I was in a B.B.C.T.V. of *Just William* for *Children's Hour* for Joy Harington about William and Ginger trying to catch a jewel thief. Guess what I played? No not a soldier. The jewel thief!

The wonderful Ealing Studios once again required my services, starting on Tuesday 15th. May, this time as a Detective Sergeant in plain clothes. I was a good guy for once, with Joe Linnane, an amiable Irishman, also in *Penny Points to Paradise*, as my superior. I gave 'em my Irish accent. The film, *Secret People* was directed by Thorold Dickinson - he'd made the well known football film, *The Arsenal Stadium Mystery* and shot Audrey Hepburn's screen test for her hit film *Roman Holiday*. I'd had a quick interview with him.

"Your excellent reputation goes before you" he told me, which was nice.

It was a political thriller involving refugees and terrorism. It apparently wasn't hugely impressive, according to the reviews, which was rare for Ealing, and I have never seen the finished product. All I can say is that I spent a week on night work in Richmond Park in the charming company of the stars:

Serge Reggiani, the French/Italian actor later to become a celebrated "chanson" singer in France. We shared war stories. He had been a French resistance fighter and been in the thick of it. He got quite good he said, at blowing up trains!

Valentina Cortese, who had become a huge success in Britain with her role in *The Glass Mountain* and gained a best supporting actress Oscar nomination for Francois Truffaut's *Day for Night* in 1973.

And a very pretty elfin creature called Audrey Hepburn!

This was Audrey's first big film part - she'd had a few small ones in *Young Wive's Tale* and *The Lavender Hill Mob* - and she was playing a ballerina which was of course why she'd been cast, having studied ballet with the famous "Ballet Rambert" in Notting Hill. She told me she'd been having elocution lessons, as English wasn't her first language, although her father was English. But she was actually Dutch and the Flemish vowels occasionally came through. You wouldn't have thought so, as her accent was perfect, but she said it was all down to the beautifully spoken and much imitated actor Felix Aylmer who'd been coaching her for both film and stage! No wonder her diction was perfect! She was a total delight and despite my brief association with her, I was as pleased as punch when she won an Oscar for *Roman Holiday* in 1953. She made it very clear to everyone she was spoken for. She was seeing James Hanson and was very happy (he was later Baron Hanson of the Imperial Tobacco group). We talked about the war. She'd had an awful time of it in Arnhem in Holland; and like me had been almost starving. She and her family had been forced to eat tulip bulbs. We had a lot in common! Alas I never saw her again as our paths diverged completely, but she was utterly charming, and I think this shone through in her performances. It may have been brass monkey weather, but the night was illuminated by the presence of the two ladies and the Italian matinee idol, warming themselves around the red hot brazier as the early dawn streaked the sky. They had a caravan of course, one each, but they seemed to prefer the company of the riff-raff who were pressed close to the fire roasting their freezing feet! And of course their chestnuts!

Because we worked through the nights from 7 p.m. to 5 a.m., the actors were entitled to time and a half, i.e. one's daily rate and a half again. As my rate was £15., I collected half that amount again, namely £7/10 shillings, making £22/10s in all, which when added to my one day in the studio at £15 worked out at £120, less Harry's 10% and National Insurance and Income Tax of course. And as a bonus, the company of two wonderful women.

THIRTEEN
Stooging with Joanie

On 24th. May, John Baxter rang to ask me if I was interested in "stooging" with some actresses who were being screen-tested for the important part of an "ingenue" - the naive , innocent role - in his new film, *Judgement Deferred*. (this was the first "Group Three" film by the way). As I said before, with regards to *Nicholas Nickleby,* this "stooging" meant being the other actor behind the camera in their screen tests. I think the term has died out and you now just "read-in". But then you were "the stooge" which wasn't a bad thing, though a "stooge" is now someone who's been set up for a crime. Ah the evolution of the English language! I agreed to do it, influenced by his half-promising me a part in the film, and the fact he would pay my expenses. Expenses? I would've done it for nothing. It was a pleasure to do it. I was clearly trusted! I told Harry.

"I'll get a fee if you liking Sid!" he said.

I said no. Expenses were fine! I got 3 guineas!

I arrived at Southall studios at the civilised hour of 1.30 p.m.. You're usually at the Studios at the crack of dawn! Most of the five girls concerned were very nervous and anxious. Two of them wore very tight-fitting dresses, to show off their er charms and beauties, (it was that kind of part) hoping that it would impress the director. The "stooging" part of the tests, as far as I was concerned, consisted of my never appearing in shot but reading from the script as if it were a radio play. I stood either to the left or right of the camera, slightly behind it, so that the girl would almost have to address the camera in close-up, although she was answering me. The five aspiring Starlets had been sent a copy of the dialogue about a week earlier and of course were expected to know it and play it as if they had already got the part! Each screen test lasted approximately four minutes and would be viewed by the director (but not by the artistes) the following day, after it had been processed.

John Baxter went out of his way to put the girls - all up for the role of Lil Carter - at their ease, gently explaining what he wanted. It was a big emotional almost flirty, scene from the film. Nearly all screen tests are scenes from the film you're up for. He rehearsed slowly, always asking each girl if she was alright and to stop if she felt unhappy. They were all good actresses, but the one who stood out was called Joan Collins. She was very pretty and gave the impression she was interested in you. Well, not with me, the "stooge" who was assisting her with the test, but she was certainly interested in John the director. Her demure look and the discreet fluttering of her eyelashes had him eating out of her hand! During the break for tea John peered at me over his horn rims and said, "Well Sam. Made your choice yet?"

I told him, sotto voce, as not too far away, Joan was sipping a beaker of char. She was surrounded by the A.D., the focus puller, and the Lighting Cameraman, like bees round a honeypot, all trying to outshine each other. I said that she was easily the best, not only for her outstanding qualities, but also for her bags of confidence. She certainly had a "je ne sais quoi" - in fact, more than that. A "je sais exactly what it is", and the techies were clearly after it!

"Hmmm. It would be interesting to see how it works for her on the film," I said from my great height, realising I'd slightly exaggerated my status!

He nodded sagely (he was good at that) and replied, "Yes I think you may be right." And added "Now the next thing is to find a part for you!"

"Good idea!" I said. " I'll do a test for you if you like. Shall I drag up?"

"Well you never know! Perhaps in the continental version! How are you with no clothes on?"

"Well I'll have a go at anything me!" I replied.

And of course I would have! Anyway as it turned out, Miss Collins got the part, and never looked back! There was only a very small part for me in the film - Ambulance Man! And cricketing chum Abraham Sofaer was in it. And John and I didn't get a mention in her autobiography! I did however sit behind her father at Stamford Bridge in the middle of the East Stand block E, row M, seat 21, watching dear old Chelsea's indifferent progress (other than a flukey season in 1954-55 when they won the league) and we would occasionally converse at half time. I would ask after her and he'd say, "Joanie's doing alright in Hollywood! She's got something good coming up!"

And then once the match had restarted we'd get down to our usual grumbling and join together in cries of despair like:

"Ref! The eye test didn't work then?"

"My gran in leaded long johns runs faster than him!"

And

"I've brought my boots! I'm going on in the second half!"

On 25th. May I hied down to Kenley Aerodrome where George More O'Farrell was on location directing a film called at the time, *Hawks in the Sun*, later to become *Angels One Five*. You may have seen it on T.V.? It gets regular repeats. It's become quite "iconic" about the Battle of Britain. Jack Hawkins and John Gregson were the leading principals, but every well known (and quite a few not so well known) character actor was in it somewhere! Michael Denison, who makes an appearance in my previous book *For You the War is Over* as the haughty Officer who tells me to forget my idea of leaving the army as we're off to fight the Russians, was in it. I avoided him. Not that he would have remembered me. He was far too important for that.

This was George's first major feature, so he was naturally keen to make it a success! I was cast as the Chief Mess Steward and my contribution was originally simple: as well as handing drinks and eats around, saying "very good sir, here you are sir etc." in the pilots' watering hole, the Mess, (these interiors were shot in the studio) I had to walk out on to the tarmac in the wake of an emergency take-off - known as "Bandits One Five" - and shielding my eyes from the sun, salute the fighters as they zoomed off to do battle with the German Luftwaffe. We did the shot on the tarmac several times.

"Sam I think you obscured your face a bit with that salute".

"Oops sorry George. I'll cheat it a bit."

"Yes Sam that would be great".

("Cheating" is when you don't quite do the action as it was really happening, you "cheat" to accommodate the shot; for example, you have a different eye-line to the one that would be "real", but from the P.O.V. - point of view - of the camera it's fine. In this instance you'd salute slightly behind to the right of your head so your face is visible).

"Sam can we try one where you follow the flight of the planes with your eyes? We've got one where you're just looking and that one may be O.K., but let's try this one just so we've got one?"

"Sure." (You are in fact pretending you can see the planes, as there aren't any.)

"Sam this time can you cheat the look just to the left of camera. Don't look at where the planes would be. Just look at that cloud would you?" - and then George finally approved.

He took great pains to get everything absolutely right and as it became apparent that the Mess was an obvious focal point for the film, I was called to Elstree to be background (or even foreground) more than was on the call sheet. I hadn't expected that!

But, guess what. My role as "Bandits One Five saluter on the tarmac" was cut. But at least I knew it was. I didn't have to wait till I saw the film in the cinema. I found out during the filming. The First phoned and said they'd had a script change and decided they wanted to create a more poignant moment, wanting me to do a toast, instead of a salute, and in the mess rather than on the airfield.

"Sam, the pilot, Squadron Leader Ponsford (played by would you believe it, Mr. tell-you-how-to-say-it Andrew Osborn) leaves a glass of sherry on the mantlepiece clock, for when he's back after the mission; but he doesn't come back, and you take it off the clock and toast him and drink it. It's kind of "life goes on but you're proud". Yes?"

"Oh O.K. Yes. Of course!"

"We're going to do that tomorrow. Your call is 7.30 a.m.." he said.

So the following day, which originally had been a day off for me, they shot the new scene of Andrew leaving his sherry behind - I was in that too, handing out drinks - and immediately afterwards, the sequence of me wandering in and tidying up, spotting the sherry, taking it off the clock, toasting him (and all other pilots) and drinking it down. George gave me the opportunity to do several thoughtful takes, some quick, some slow, and said, "I think they were all very good Sam. My favourite was the first one. But we've got a lot of choice. Well done. I'm very happy. Very moving. Thank you."

It's a small moment, but I believe I did it justice. The sherry was black tea by the way.

In the middle of shooting, there was a lightning strike by the electricians for more pay. This lasted for three days, resulting in loss of money for the actors - we weren't paid during a strike, this was written in our contracts - and the breaking of contracts for some who had expected to be available for other work by a certain date, who consequently had to be replaced and their scenes re-shot with new actors. In addition, my Austin Seven car battery was stolen during the night by some heavy fingered thief who must have been an ardent battery collector! I can remember it as if it were yesterday. Some things are peculiarly etched into the memory and this was one of them. I came out of the house at Chiswick, got in the car to go to the Studios, but on pressing the starter, there was complete silence. After several more minutes fruitless pressing, and then swinging the starting handle till I was blue in the face, I lifted up the bonnet and saw there was a gaping hole with dangling wires where the battery should have been. I phoned the police. They clearly didn't have battery theft as a priority and didn't even send someone to have a look!

"Could you drive over and show us sir?" the desk sergeant suggested.

"I can't officer. THE BATTERY'S BEEN STOLEN."

Until I had time to acquire another battery, I had to get up two hours earlier and travel to the studio by Tube train, train and bus. After buying a new battery I had locks put on the bonnet fasteners and a thick leather strap to go all the way round it. Would you believe it somebody at the Studio pinched the strap!

I was employed for twelve days on *Angels One Five* - this was good, as the original guarantee was for four! It was one of the first films that led to me being recognised by the public.

"Ere you're that bloke who does the toastin' in that film with the planes incha!" was a regular statement. Or something like that. Sometimes it was, "Don't I know you?

"Well I'm an actor, " I would reply. "Perhaps you've seen me at the cinema?"

"What. Are you an usher?"

It was about this time June/July, that I cemented my off/on relationship with Lavender "Pinkie" Barnes, my favourite number one Table Tennis Player and Advertising Copywriter. (She was one of the first female copywriters. It was she who had invented the line for Veet underarm hair remover "Veet. It's always Summer under your arms" as well as gems for "Jansen Swim Wear" and many others). We'd actually split up and then got back together. Initially we'd just been too busy. She'd been away - she was champion of the Netherlands several years running - I'd been away. I'd not been in her good books when I'd got large numbers of the *Treasure Island* crew to watch her play table tennis and there'd been a lot of drunken cheering, and we had a fractious phone call, but I'd meant well. But then I realised I was missing her a lot, so asked her out again. She coolly pondered, gave a quizzical look… (well I suppose it was quizzical. I'd phoned her)… paused for what seemed like a lifetime…("are you still there?" I'd asked)… and said… "Yes I'd love to!"

Phew!…

She frequently practiced her sport at St. Bride's Club in Fleet Street and I had the gall, cheek and temerity to challenge her. Regularly. Of course she pulverised me out of sight every time I attempted to wrest her worthy crown from her - I mean she was an England International and World Doubles finalist! - but when it came to the in-fighting of the love stakes, she could never win and had at last met her match. In the ping of pong, what usually happened was that she'd obliterate me in the first game - she had a terrific forehand and a devious chopped defence - and then after giving me a ten points start and still winning, she'd take pity on me and allow me a few points by playing left handed. Thereafter, when she played left handed with a blindfold and gave me a start, she was putty in my hands! We became engaged one night in a Fleet Street hostelry after she'd put up token resistance - in fact she proposed to me! - and finally I gave in! And so it came about that I was affianced and betrothed all at the same time. My mother was delighted, saying what had I been waiting for and I should have done it ages ago and that she was too good for me and I'd have to pull my socks up! And now that I was settling down perhaps I could get a proper job with a pension! And the rest of the ex P.O.W. fraternity residing off and on at Fairfax Road - Cliff Winterbottom, Frank Coburn and Johnny Gaskin - agreed with my mother! The cheek of it! (Well the "me-not-being-good-enough-for-her" bit. They were happy with me being an actor). But they did take me out for a tip-top meal to celebrate: Fish and chips in the Chiswick High Road! I had the cod! No vinegar. Lots of ketchup! And lashings of 7Up! Yum yum!

But before the nuptials I managed to slip in a quick appearance in *High Treason* for Roy Boulting as a fuming political agitator printing "peace rally" leaflets at a printer's. It was a very quick scene, only one shot of me and the policeman in a wide shot, with my assistant and another policeman in the background, panning across from the printing press. Roy made it clear that that was the way he was going to shoot it, and that was that. One rehearsal, all done in one shot. All over in two takes. Gilbert Taylor the cameraman, asked to do another one as he thought he could do better, but the first take had worked as well.

"Thank you gentlemen moving on."

The scenario was this. The police arrived while I was printing the "peace" leaflets. They asked me about a man they were pursuing. Did I know where he was? I said, "If I did know I'm not likely to tell am I?"

The policeman replied, "We thought he'd have been back."

My irritated response was, "Well he hasn't been. He was kicked out of the country by you lot. You know that."

"Well in that case, I'll leave you to get on with the revolution eh?'

And then I got a nice medium close up. The camera panned in on me and I said, "Bloody Nazi," angrily.

Incidentally, I was using my real voice. No cockney or Irish here.

"Well done Kyddie" said Roy. I dubbed some of it as well, some of the London dockers who were loading the soon to be blown up cargo. I dubbed *I Spy Strangers* for Roy as a bonus. It starred Liam Redmond and Patric Doonan by the way! They'd played rather a large part in my career so far. Liam, as you know I nearly got arrested. Patric was my alter ego.

I didn't have a scene with them though, as you will have gathered.

Almost immediately, I had to go on location for a Beaconsfield Group 3 film called *Brandy for the Parson.* Being a Group 3 meant it was £7 10/- a day! Half my daily rate!

("You sure you vant do it Sid?

"Is there anything else?"

"No."

"I'll do it.")

Starring Kenneth More (Yes, he took me out to supper, dear Kenny), it was to be directed by John Estridge and produced by

309

Alfred Shaughnessy (later the writer and script editor of *Upstairs Downstairs*). I had a nice scene with the stars, James Donald (with whom of course I'd been in *Cage of Gold*) Kenneth, and Jean Lodge. The constantly amusing Charles Hawtrey was in the scene as well. It was shot in Dorchester. I was playing a workman who loads barrels of brandy (that have been smuggled from France and left on the roadside - ooh the plot!) onto his van, thinking they're tar, when the smugglers see him doing it and stop him! I did a rather broad Dorzet accent!

ME: Ah. Zo it's not tar then? No it don smell like tar! Mind you it don smell like fish either....Ere, you know what I think......?"
KENNY: You know I think we'll give you a couple of quid to forget all about it."
ME: Oh. That's be nice!".

There was a steam roller in the shot. I didn't have to drive it. But I could have done if asked. (It's not that tricky really. Point and steer and brake.) I added "steam roller man" to "jeepboy" and "cat handler" on my C.V.. I made £59/10/-. I was called for four days and we shot it in one! Pinkie came for a long weekend to test out my location facilities and was pleasantly surprised! We climbed up the giant "Man of Cerne Abbas" carved out of the hillside and took snaps of each other sitting on him! Pinkie had never seen anything like it!

On my return to London, Harry got me an introduction to dubbing maestro Major William De Lane Lea ("lots work be 'ad zere Sid"), who was a veritable ball of fire, at his studio in Moore Street in Soho. (I say studio, but of course at this stage it was like someone's bijou flat.) Sadly he is no longer with us having called time on his career by shooting himself! He had been a French Intelligence attaché during the war and had come up with the idea of dubbing French films. He expanded his business from French to foreign films which he adapted for showing in this country, and that meant a lot of dubbing, and after being interviewed by him very quickly, "I know your work Sam!" (I love it when they say that. Saves so much time. It's when they say "I've never heard of you" that it becomes difficult) I was given a voice test to see if I would be able to deal with his unique and unusual system of post-syncing, which was unlike what I've explained to you before. He bought Yugoslavian films, Swedish films, Indian films, German and French films, and for all I know, Tibetan films, although I never post-synced (or "sunk") any of the latter. (Well I don't think so. Occasionally you were in and out if it was a small scene!). Then the Major employed translators to translate the dialogue into English, to match the voices. This was a skill in itself. The translations were then transferred to a running band of film which was projected onto a screen under the scenes to which they applied. To be more explicit, a scene or loop from the film was projected onto the screen to coincide with another band of film beneath it on which the English dialogue was written out like a "cue" card. Each piece of dialogue tallied with the character speaking on screen and the translation was such that when re-recorded the character's lip movements almost matched the English words. The actor's job was to read the English words written on the band underneath (which were being recorded while he did so) and not to get confused by watching the actors performing in the film. The knack was to get the right pace and retain the essence of the character. Some actors were hopeless at it. I was fortunately pretty good. Well the Major thought so! And I had had plenty of experience! When the loop had been satisfactorily recorded, it was the Major's custom to play it back for all to hear. The effect on the listeners was uncanny. The lip-matching was so good that you'd swear the characters in the film were speaking English! Most critics seem to hate dubbed film and prefer sub-titles. I don't mind them and at least they supply a certain amount of work for actors which is always a good thing. My first job with him was a Brigadier in *Les Miserables*. Over the years I was to put my voice on many of the De Lane Lea films. Quite a number of foreign children's films I voiced, were shown on B.B.C. T.V.. Working with the Major was a pleasant and not too arduous task and at times, when a large crowd of actors were fighting to get to the microphone in a place no larger than the average bathroom, japes and giggling were the order of the day, only to be brought to a halt by the laconic North Country tones of the Major.

"All right lads. Settle down now. Settle down. You're destroying the ambience."

This was his favourite word relating to the recordings, "ambience". He was always demanding "More ambience please gentlemen!" Which I think ultimately meant "please concentrate and stop mucking about!"

I should mention by the way, that for the use of my voice and my time on the recordings, (and acting skills!) I was now paid seven guineas (seven pounds and seven shillings) in all for the day, which was par for the course for a dub.

Another Group Three, *The Brave Don't Cry* filmed at Southall Studios, despite being about a mining accident in Scotland (well the exteriors were obviously shot at a mine) for Philip Leacock, had me as a railway porter dispatching homing pigeons.

"I'll see they catch the 11.30" I said in my Scots accent whilst writing out the dockets (Yes! I was doing acting and writing at the same time!) and commenting on the sweet actress Wendy Noel's father and brother on their shift.

"Nice to have a roof over their heads," I said as it was raining torrentially. Which caused the mining incident! Plot plot plot, you see! I remember we had to do the scene several times because the soundman wasn't happy with the volume of the cooing pigeons! The "pigeon handler" was asked to quieten them down, but failed miserably. I mean how do you quieten a pigeon?

She gave them some more seed to munch, but that only seemed to encourage them further. So she tried taking a few out.

"It looks like there's nothing in the basket" said Philip.

So they were put back in again. When I saw it in the cinema - as

I've said I was very keen to see everything I was in, if I could, as I was sure there was room for improvement - I still thought the pigeons were far too loud! And from the three shot you could only make out a single beak anyway! Blimey! Upstaged by pigeons! And all for fifteen pounds.

I did three days on *Saturday Island,* cast by Paul Sheridan. You may remember he "owed me one" after *Forbidden.* I don't think this was the "owe.". He was a nice chap who combined both casting with acting, which was no mean feat. I didn't know any one else who managed it. Paul's advantage, which I suppose gave him a head start on other actors, was that he'd been born in Paris, and spoke fluent French and tended to play Frenchmen in England. And Englishmen in France. I wonder if he ever cast himself? Stuart Heisler directed it. He was a directing and editing legend, having worked with Mack Sennett for the "Keystone Cops", did the successful *The Star* with my "friend" Bette Davis, and ultimately directed T.V. shows *The Lone Ranger, 77 Sunset Strip* and *Rawhide,* all worldwide successes. As usual I didn't get much of a chance to chat with him. But he was charming and efficient. I played a soldier, yes, but an American one! A wounded marine, in the hospital ship which hits a mine and there are only two survivors. And I wasn't one of them. I saw this film at the cinema with Pinkie. It starred Tab Hunter and Linda Darnell, both of whom are marooned on a desert island after escaping from the sinking ship. Pinkie couldn't work out why they didn't become lovers in the film, as neither of them was wearing many clothes, and both were rather attractive. I have to say I agreed. The American title was *Island of Desire* which was distinctly more appropriate. The location stuff was shot in Cuba which would have been lovely had I been in any of the location shots, but annoyingly I only managed to work in Nettlefold in Walton, in a set that resembled the interior of the boat. I was next to the very amusing Peter Butterworth - who I knew of course if you remember from the Jack Hylton Revue *Back Home Again* - who told me that despite having, like me, been a P.O.W., he never got any prisoner parts as they said he didn't look like one! I suppose it helped in my case looking emaciated and slightly desperate!

A quick B.B.C. Radio followed for Alan Burgess called *The Undefeated* and then I was back with the *Goons* again on a B.B.C. T.V. movie - it therefore wasn't live - called *Goonreel,* taking the micky out of "Newsreels" in a series of sketches linked together by announcer Andrew Timothy, directed by the hugely successful comedy producer Michael Mills, who ultimately produced *All Gas and Gaiters, Wooster* and the *Stanley Baxter* series. Harry Secombe had been very loyal to me, having recommended me as he did with *Penny Points to Paradise* and I clearly hadn't disappointed, as here I was back again! The whole famous radio crew were in this one (and I think it was the first time the Goons had been on T.V.): Michael Bentine, Peter Sellers, Spike and Harry, along with a sweet young funny beanpole of an actor called Leslie Crowther, destined for great things, and a slightly spiky competitive comic actor called Graham Stark. The beautiful Euncie Gayson - later James Bond's girlfriend in *Dr. No* - played most of the women in the sketches, which she did with great aplomb, though she tended to be more set decoration in some of the skits. Though I remember the choreographer Clementina Stuart - yes there was dancing! And singing! My tap dancing skills were required! - being roped in to do her acting bit. And naturally if there weren't enough men to go around, the women would put on a moustache. There were some very funny moments indeed, amidst some complete madness. And some scenes I just couldn't grasp, as they seemed to me to be nothing but silly noises and Spike shouting incomprehensibly. These were dumped. Peter Sellers' characters were already top-notch, though he tended to take it much more seriously than the others, but could improvise brilliantly. It was a question of working out when to speak and whether you could improvise with him. I played a few soldiers as well as some crooks and an M.P.! I was on the cast list as "various", as one tends to be in this kind of show, and indeed I was in a lot of the sketches as it was forty five minutes. It was much better organised than my previous involvement with the team. For a start, the Michael Bentine, Jimmy Grafton, Spike script was finished before we started it! Having said that, we all chipped in with ideas and I was told I'd be listed as a "contributor". So some sketches "evolved" even while we were shooting them! They're a talented bunch!

FOURTEEN
Not a "Herbert" at all

I did a couple of Classics for the B.B.C. Radio Drama department, *Daniel Defoe* as a sailor and *Sherlock Holmes* as a policeman. In the latter, the marvellously named Laidman Browne played Sherlock to Ivan Samson's Watson. It was scenes from the books narrated by Wynford Vaughan-Thomas. Laidman had read "The Speckled Band" on *Book at Bedtime* which I believe was the first book ever to be read on the programme. I was tempted to abbreviate his name when addressing him but wasn't sure what to call him.

I was then called to Shepperton Studios by Pat Smith, (Herbert Wilcox's casting director) to meet Mr. Wilcox for the part of Harry Bunn the bookie in their new production *Derby Day*. I had of course played a bookie in the final scenes of *The Blue Lamp* at White City Stadium. Mr. Wilcox apparently said he wanted me for the part which was nice. I phoned Harry to tell him.

"What's goin' Sid? Why does no one call me anymore? Are you gonna to e'range money yerself? I still get 10%."

He did have a point of course. I think I'd sent Pat Smith an introductory letter with my phone number on it. I was good at writing to people, something I have kept going all my career.

I had never met Mr. (call me Herbert) Wilcox before and was agreeably surprised by his courteous and thoughtful manner dealing with actors and actresses. He treated them like human beings, not automatons, as some directors are wont to do. His wife, the celebrated actress Anna Neagle, later a Dame, to whom I was introduced, had been voted "most popular" in the U.K. in 1949 and was a huge star, and was the epitome of kindness and charm. And hugely talented of course! They were a smashing couple, and he obviously adored her. And she was dotty about him! But there was much disquiet about their relationship. The problem they had, was that in an age of not showing your feelings in public, they were overtly affectionate to each other. And there were many willing to criticise this, as they were both middle aged and not "in the bloom of youth". Personally I think a lot of it was jealousy.

A quick note about Herbert Wilcox: He was the great British producer of his time. He'd had huge recent hits with *I Live in Grosvenor Square, Piccadilly Incident, The Courtneys of Curzon Street* and *Maytime in Mayfair.* So this was, to say the least, a feather in my cap. So all systems being go, Pat asked me if I could attend the studio the day before my shooting days, to be put through my paces by two or three genuine bookies who would give me the run down on the correct "procedure", such as calling out the odds, marking up the odds, and learning the basic elements of the "tic-tac" system. I agreed of course, and after a heavy "bookies" lunch on the day, finishing with liqueurs, brandy, and cigars all round, and feeling slightly all of a glow, I was initiated into the mysteries and glamour (?) of yer average bookmaker's working day on the rails! (Some of which I'd picked up on *The Blue Lamp*). Not that I was going to be that heavily involved in the film, but the whole purpose of the exercise was for me to look as if I knew what I was doing in the sequence. The bookies - Wilf, Joe and Gary - were all keen to make a good impression and after the free lunch and drinks - they clearly weren't being paid for their expertise, this was their payment - were inclined to overwhelm me with advice, so much so, that if I wasn't careful, I would be paying too much attention to the detailed actions rather than the dialogue. However I learnt enough to look as if I knew what I was doing and it all worked out to everyone's satisfaction. "Five to four" which was touching your left wrist with your right hand was an easy one, as was the "double carpet" of "thirty three to one", which was arms crossed with your hand across your chest. And of course the well known "lug 'ole" "six to four" odds where one hand touches the opposite ear - hence "ear or lug 'ole". I also learnt a few terms to shout out.

"Evens" was "Major Stevens". "A hundred to thirty" was "Scruffy and Dirty". My favourite was the Romany backslang of "four to one", "rouf", (which is "four" backwards). As it happened, and is frequently the case, I didn't need to use any of this nicely (hic) discovered tic-tac information (which was just as well as most of it had disappeared into an alcoholic haze) as the following day I had two proper tic-tac men next to me on the bookie's "shelf" where I was standing next to my board of odds, who were doing all the tic-tacing! I merely shouted the odds out very loudly (it was a very shouty part. I made sure I'd brought the Sanderson's with me) and marked them up on the blackboard with a piece of chalk, which was something I'd remembered how to do. Then I took the punter's money, my assistant Pat wrote the bet in his book, I gave them their change and handed them the slip with their number on it. My role was ultimately to collude with the police, who asked me if I'd seen the murderer, Tommy Dillon, (played by John MacCallum). I had! I'd taken his bet! And Alfie Bass had seen him giving me the money! Hebert Wilcox shot all these scenes with wide tracking shots to emphasise the teeming crowds at the race track. Though I did get a nice close up when "alerting" the policeman.

"Anyone laid a £15 quid bet on Starry Night?" said the copper approaching me, played by the cheery Hugh Moxey. (Obviously not cheery in the scene, as he was trying to catch a criminal, but a friendly chap when we'd finished a take.)

"Starry Night? said I.

My assistant looked the bet up. Yes! And 03 was the ticket number.

"I remember he looked as if he'd been sleepin' rough! Needed a shave" I said.

Hugh then asked me to point him out to him if he'd won, while he lurked nearby. He did win! He duly came to collect his winnings.

"Ticket 03! Starry Night! £150!" said John, accompanied by Googie Withers.

"Ticket 03" I repeated loudly, (this was my close up) nodding to

Hugh the policeman, who ran up with several other policeman and nicked him.

Incidentally it was shot on the lot at the back of the studio and not at Epsom at all, although they'd obviously filmed a great deal of "real" footage at the race course that they could intercut it with. The lot I was in, was crammed with well rehearsed extras as milling spectators, and was a huge set with masses of booths and a fair ground. (By the way, in this instance the extras got a separate cue from the rest of us. There'd be two lots of action; the first for the extras to "mill" and the second for the artistes to do their action. That way you wouldn't have anyone looking as if they'd been standing still and only just started moving in the main shot, which created nightmares for the editor.

After the sequence was finished, Mr. Wilcox - I couldn't bring myself to call him Herbert yet - asked me to go and see him in his office before I left the studio. I was intrigued. What could this be about? Had he spotted something in me? (you're always hoping this is the case) …. And guess what…He had! In fact it seemed that he was more than pleased with my performance and told me over a scotch and water from his well stocked sideboard, that he might have a nice part for me in his next production! And true to his word, he did! The bookie character in *Derby Day* is only small in the scheme of things, although most important plot wise, and only took three days to shoot. But the part he was referring to, that of Detective Inspector Murch in *Trent's Last Case* was much larger and more significant. More part equals more visibility. (and more money as your daily rate goes up). It didn't come to fruition till March of the following year mind you, but it did happen. Sometimes of course you get earmarked for jobs by a director or producer and nothing happens - the script changes and your character is no longer in it. The director sees someone else he thinks might fit the character better than you. Or sometimes the money is lousy and your agent argues that to accept the fee offered would do your career no good at all, so you learn to have a thick skin. But this one actually took place. And thereby hangs a tale, albeit a little one. I went to Berman's, the Theatrical Costumiers, to get myself fitted out in a Detective Inspector's uniform as requested, which was a suit of course, but a specific kind of dark "policeman's" suit. Very natty I looked too. When I arrived at 7.30 a.m. for my first day's call at Shepperton Studios, I was asked by the A.D. if I would go and see Mr. Wilcox in his office. I was ushered in and Herbert (he was Herbert now) immediately asked me if I'd had any breakfast. No matter, he had ordered eggs, bacon, toast and a pot of tea for me and whilst I was talking to him it was brought in by a waitress from the studio restaurant. Whilst I chewed, he chatted about the part - we decided I should use my Irish accent. I read a bit for him - and asked if I would mind putting the Inspector's uniform on for him, after I had breakfasted. I duly donned the uniform for his perusal, but he took an immediate dislike to it. Then he said, "Did you come in a suit? No of course you didn't. You wore a sports jacket and flannels didn't you?" I nodded.

"Would you mind (I waited, not knowing what was coming).... would you mind going back home and bringing a choice of say, three suits, to see if there's something I might like better? Use my Rolls, the chauffeur will drive you. Where do you live?"

"Not far from the Chiswick High Road" I replied.

"You don't have to hurry" he said. "Michael (Wilding) isn't expected until this afternoon, so we've plenty of time."

So I went back to Bedford Park in Herbert's Rolls Royce, chauffeured all the way, and collecting three suits from my bulging wardrobe (I only had three suits) - all three suits hand-made by those high-class tailors, Messrs. E.J. Barker of Turnham Green (now alas retired) - I returned in triumph to Shepperton. (Incidentally, whilst I remember, I was up for "Best Dressed actor" in 1959 because of E.J.'s great style and tailoring!)

Back at the studio, I dutifully modelled the three suits, one after the other, twirling and twisting for Mr. Wilcox's approbation or otherwise. He eventually settled for my dark sober grey flannel one. However, once we got on the set filming the big scene in the large office of the recently dead tycoon - I was investigating the death and was writing my notes when Trent was ushered in to question me - Herbert asked me to remove my jacket. And that is how it was finally played - in my shirt sleeves!

Michael Wilding, who was playing Trent, and with whom I had my long scene, was a bit hesitant over his lines. In fact I had a shrewd suspicion that like Valentine Dyall, he hadn't looked at them until he'd arrived at the studio. Moving from place to place he went through his script, marking the scene in his head as he went and eventually after several rehearsals when we came near to shooting, he substituted words of his own which seemed to fit, or at least satisfy Herbert. You had to concentrate to work out what your cue was, as he'd changed the lines around quite a bit. Herbert was obviously good chums with Michael, (who had a long term contract with Herbert after the success of *Piccadilly Incident* in 1946) putting his arm around him in an endearing fashion when he was speaking to him. Often they would share some little joke together and burst out laughing. Sometimes Michael's fooling around stopped the shot, but Herbert was more concerned with Michael's performance than the shot being held up. Wilding, of course, was a charming man – light hearted, amusing and very "hail fellow, well met". In fact, off the screen he was rather like the type of relaxed characters he played with such success on it. Later he succumbed to the lure of Hollywood and achieved another sort of fame by marrying the beautiful Elizabeth Taylor. One or two others followed in his footsteps and did equally well for themselves in the "I too married Liz Taylor" serial.

Trent's Last Case eventually turned up on T.V.. I always thought I looked too young for the role of Detective Inspector Murch. And I didn't like the shirt sleeves! It was a terrific part though. Almost three and a half minutes with me talking most of the time. I was proud of that one. Herbert used a two shot for the whole thing - there was only one edit in it when John McCallum briefly comes in to talk about his gun - with Michael looming over me sitting on the desk I was working at, and then walking round me as he returned to sitting on the corner. Herbert tracked in slowly as I gave Michael more information about why I thought it was suicide, leading to a kind of mid close up. I had the great line "the thing that puzzled me, was finding his false teeth beside his bed" which seemed to confirm my conclusion that he must have been in a terrible state when he "killed himself".

"He'd been in such a queer state of mind lately."

Of course Trent investigates and suspects it's murder. But ours was a "set-up", a long informative plot scene, with me talking all the time filling in Trent, with masses of info, about the bullet, the gun and how he died. It was very informal though, which I believe was the effect Herbert was attempting to achieve. For a change, when I saw it, other than the sleeves and my looking very young, I enjoyed it. And hoped it would get me a mass of work. Oh I forgot. Orson Welles was in the film, playing the murdered tycoon Sigsbee Manderson in flashback. I didn't meet him. I'd like to have done.

I did two more pictures with Herbert Wilcox: *Yangtze Incident* and *Lilacs in the Spring*. And he was always the same. Courteous, unruffled, reasonable, and very much in love with Anna. It was a great loss to the profession when he died.

Quick as a flash I dubbed *Behind Close Shutters* at De Lane Lea for £11/7/- , did a day on *Curtain Up* as an ambulance driver for Ralph Smart (£18), and several days on a comedy called *Hot Ice* directed by Kenneth Hume, with Michael Balfour and Barbara Murray, about a group of people being invited to a country house to be robbed! This was another driver part. I was Adams. (£40)

I next did three days on *The Hour of 13* at M.G.M. studios at £20 a day, playing a reporter for director Harold French. Harold had been an actor and it showed. I'm a great fan of actors directing as I've said. They understand it. They're not just shooting the scene. They're working out the relationships. They're looking at "the book of words". This was set in Victorian London so I had a costume call at Berman's Theatrical Costumiers to wear the authentic clothing.

"Ooh Sam you're back again! What are you this time?"

They knew me there! That was nice! I ended up with a brown bowler and a rather snazzy check suit. This was an interesting film for me, in that I was called back to do a mass of "re-takes". In fact everything I'd been in was re-shot! I was told there'd been a problem with the film and all the day's work had been exposed and consequently erased. But I do remember the lines changing and wondered if there'd been a plot change. These murder mysteries - this was about a maniac killing lots of policemen - do occasionally throw up the odd anomaly which is only spotted as the film is being made:

"Oh dear he's supposed to be dead according to the plot. Why is he in this scene?"

Or even a dreadful continuity error that can't be rectified at all:

"He's not wearing the suit he wore in the scene where he's running up the High Street and it's a continuation!"

I never got to the bottom of it. All I know is I had to reshoot all my scenes and I got four more days out of it.

I managed to fit in *A Tomb with a View,* a B.B.C. T.V. movie at Ally Pally, as a policeman, for Lance Sieveking, who was originally a big radio producer and had heard my efforts on the airwaves, so he told me, and was very impressed.

I had a double dose of comedy involvement. Firstly I worked with the young Tommy Cooper in a B.B.C.T.V. show called *It's Magic.* This was an education, despite him not being the experienced comic he was to become. I had to bite my tongue to stop myself from laughing. And Tommy doesn't always do on transmission what he does at final rehearsal, which could lead to everyone with him seeing something go completely differently to what he'd supposedly rehearsed. That's why he sometimes looks more astonished than usual during the show! And this was live! This of course is what made it all work, the uncertainty; and his infectious laughing at his own jokes. He's almost improvising; and reacting brilliantly to everything and anything. Nowadays of course all Light Entertainment and Drama on T.V. is recorded, so mistakes are eliminated. Although with Tommy of course the mistakes are 95% of his act! Along with his gags! Here are some of my favourites:

"I went to buy some camouflage trousers today but couldn't find any anywhere."

"I dreamt I was eating flannel cake! And when I woke up the blanket was gone!"

A man takes his Alsatian to the vet. "Hello there. My dog is cross-eyed, is there anything you can do for him?"
"Hmm," said the vet, "let me have a look at him."
So he picks the dog up and examines his eyes. Finally, he says, "I'm going to have to put him down."
"What? Because he's cross-eyed?"
"No, because he's really heavy"

"A man walked into the doctor's. The doctor said "I haven't seen you in a long time". The man replied, "I know I've been ill."

Cue masses of throaty laughter from Tommy!

And of course we had the madness! So there he was in his fez. I'm playing a crook trying to steal his wallet. I'm not supposed to get the wallet out of his pocket. This was the sketch. And a mass of doves and flowers and other tricks are supposedly set off by our struggling! But the wallet came out first time! So there's no struggle and no reason for all the tricks to be set off!
"Put it back in and have another go" says Tommy.
So I do. Even though I'm doubled up with laughter.
"That's it! Is it in? Yes. Try and take it out now."
And all the tricks then work. I pull out the coloured hankies and a bunch of flowers. A dove flies off. Cards spew out of his jacket. A policeman then walks by and I'm arrested for stealing his tricks!

Then I was a poker player in a poker sketch. He played the wrong cards!

"Ah can I do that again?" he asked looking at camera. Then he knocked a glass over. Cue cackles! Then he dropped all the cards. But then picked 'em up…and got four aces! Quite brilliant! You could tell this was a unique comedy talent!

And then, my second helping of excellence. What an interesting period of my career this year was turning out to be:

I worked with the marvellous Terry-Thomas at Lime Grove who had sprung to fame in the hugely successful *Piccadilly Hayride* which starred one of my all time favourites, the wonderful Sid Field. I must talk a bit about Sid. Every character of Sid's would have his famous "stage trip" at one moment in the act which would deflate his character immediately, every time. (When he was about six, I managed to get my son Jonathan to perfect this. We would "trip" and do "double takes" in the kitchen religiously.) Sid's golf sketch when he plays someone learning the game, is a combination of slapstick and mime and complete idiocy. "Keep your eye on the ball" says his straight man the ever reliable Jerry Desmonde, who was of course straight man for Norman Wisdom too, and Sid lies down with his eye up against it.

"Let's go" says Jerry.

"When you say "let's go. You don't mean "let's go". You mean stay here" says Sid. He takes everything literally. There's an enormous amount of hilarious over the top idiocy in some of his reactions, which have clearly influenced other comics.

Back to Terry-Thomas: Terry (or Tom as people called him) was known for being a brilliant zany musician cum comic, who could play a variety of instruments and do a multitude of accents, as well as his trademark gapped teeth grinning, ultra upper class character. His piano playing Russian opera singer featured people like Serge Napkins and Tania Pantsov and his guitar playing Austrian yodeller was fabulously silly. His "piece de resistance" was a very funny and skilled sketch called *Technical Hitch* which he'd been doing for years on the cabaret circuit and had honed to perfection. It was about a radio disk jockey, who'd broken all his records whilst on the air and consequently had to impersonate the artists instead of playing the disks. Naturally the impersonations were mad. He had a huge range and went from basso profondo to shrill falsetto; and all his impressions including Paul Robeson and Maurice Chevalier, the tenor Richard Tauber , a bizarre Yma Sumac (which made me laugh so much. She was the high pitched Peruvian) and then his piece de resistance, the Luton Girls Choir, (brilliant idiocy) were very clever and over-the-top as you'd expect.

The series I was in with him was called *How Do You View?* for B.B.C. T.V.. Part of the novelty and humour (and appeal) of the series was seeing "Tom" wander through Lime Grove Studios' control rooms and offices until he'd "stumble upon" a sketch, as it were, in which he'd take part. In one sketch, I was William Shakespeare, a Bard, struggling, without inspiration, which was provided by Terry, who comes up with the plot of *Hamlet!* Most of the shows were produced by Bill Ward, who later became one of the hierarchy at A.T.V.. Bill was a great help to Terry, falling about with infectious laughter at rehearsals. Terry, although seemingly confident, needed encouragement to survive and Bill's approval helped him along. Unfortunately it's the same old story with comedy; unless you have belief in the material, the gales of laughter at the first rehearsals begin to die down after constant repetition, when the jokes have become familiar. Then the comedian begins to have doubts about the gags and after a lengthy discussion sometimes the sketch is cut entirely. What replaces it is not always as amusing, often because it's rushed and re-written in a near panic. And unless the producer retains a strong hand, the whole show can lose its original humour. Terry, ever the perfectionist, was convinced he wasn't being funny, when of course he was! I tried to convince him the sketches we were in were good ones and worked, but they slowly got chipped away. It was very frustrating. Most of the shows were rather like a revue with blackout sketches, "cod" interviews and a longer sketch involving

Peter Butterworth (who was mostly the chauffeur "Lockitt"), Michael Balfour and often myself. Terry was very aware of the pitfalls and watched over the show like a worried mother hen; but the odour of bad eggs can linger! It was a difficult slightly bitter environment to inhabit unfortunately. But on the positive side, catchphrases which Terry-Thomas was using at the time, became famous, like "good show", "you're a shower, an absolute shower!", and "you complete stinker!", which reappeared in *I'm Alright Jack* and *Private's Progress*. Basically he was always the same outraged, terribly English, funny guy – just in different apparel. However he was always looking for a better "funny". It was a fine thing, but dangerous at the same time, when what you've got already works!

He of course ultimately put his sketch years behind him, and became a major star in such films as *School for Scoundrels,* and eventually in the U.S. in films like *It's a Mad, Mad, Mad, Mad, World.* Good luck to him. He deserved it. Despite his self doubt, he was a very funny man.

I did some "stooging" for a fiver, for a film called *The Cruel Sea*, a film about the Navy versus German Submarines. Charles Frend, who I'd worked with on *Scott* and *The Magnet,* asked if I'd read in for the screen-tests of two characters, Tallow and Bennett. The best Tallow, the Petty Officer, was Bruce Seton who was streets ahead of the rest. I'd worked with Bruce in *Scott* and consequently Charles knew him anyway. His screen-test was a very relaxed, confident affair and he sailed through it. In the "stooging" we did the scene where Jim Watts the Chief Engineer (played in the film by good old Liam Redmond) says he's going to marry Tallow's sister. As Tallow had initially been talking about provisions - about loading "560 sausages" on board - there were some fine mood swings in the scene. "Oh that's so good Jim. She'll be as pleased as punch!" was his joyful reaction to Jim's proposition. I have to say Bruce was fabulous in the film. A beautifully observed and sympathetic performance. He subsequently became a Baron! Whenever I met him, I'd curtsey!

There were a couple of actors who hadn't learnt the lines and didn't impress! One was quite well known! I shan't name him though. There were extenuating circumstances, as his wife had just had a baby prematurely. He apologised profusely but couldn't really pull it off, which was understandable.

Donald Sinden and Glyn Houston were both up for the part of Bennett, the power crazy First Lieutenant. They were both excellent actors and charming courteous men and I thought either could have played the part of the decidedly nasty character. I had to be on my metal to read-in amidst such intense aggression. We did the scene where Stratton and Lochart are abused by Bennett when they both come on board the ship. I played both Stratton and Lockhart! And then we did the one where Bennett comes in drunk and rants at the Officers before puking up and running out. I played all the officers! In the end, Donald was chosen for Bennett; and Stanley Baker after further "stooging" (not from me, I was doing *The Steel Key*) was chosen for Lockhart; but on Jack Hawkins' recommendation, Stanley swapped roles with Donald, (which made sense as Stanley Baker played "nasty" brilliantly) and Glyn played another character called Phillips! Charles promised me a part! As always I thanked him, but didn't believe it would happen. But it did! And I would die a watery death!

I got a run of radio and dubbing: *The Small Voices* playing a soldier called Sparrow for the Overseas Service; and one and a half days playing a major character Gennaro on a 1949 Italian film called *Wolf of Sila* at De Lane Lea for the Major. Gennaro was a nasty piece of work! And then I was engaged to play a couple of very silly parts in B.B.C.T.V's *Children's Hour*, in *Billy Bunter of Greyfriars,* about the guzzling schoolboy himself, played by Gerald Campion. In the episode *Bunter's Bicycle,* I "gave" my Postman. (Not a big part. Amusing comedy letter delivering with my letters being handed back to me - "No you keep that!"- and Bunter searching for cake in all the packages I had and then the contents of my sack are poured all over me) and a much bigger part, in *The Report,* that of Nosey Jenkins, who you can imagine poked his nose in and suffered the consequences.

An immersion in custard was my reward! Ex-actress Joy Harington for whom I'd done *Just William* both directed and produced. Later she did the same with *Jesus of Nazareth*. It was supposedly a big leap from Children's T.V. comedy to Biblical drama but she was very talented and won the 1956 T.V. Guild Prize for it.

I renewed my acquaintance with Kynaston Reeves who was the poor put-upon schoolteacher Mr. Quelch. He still wore his bicycle clips when you couldn't see his legs, but only in rehearsal!

I continued to mix television and films as the mainstays of my career, concentrating on film. By now there were one or two stage feelers for me, but after deliberation with Harry we decided not to pursue them. His advice was, "We see wot ze play is. In meantime, stick with flims Sid. More money. And maybe fitz in television!"

Of course the occasional odd broadcast and dubbing added to my income. But on reflection, perhaps I should have done more theatre to "legitimise" my career. Theatre was apparently where the "craft" was. And the snobbery! My reputation as an actor would have been enhanced. But the money was nowhere near as good. It was a difficult decision to make. And the films were there and I was getting them.

In January 1952, I found myself in one called *The Lost Hours,* a 67 minute "film noir" - for Bob Baker and Monty Berman, shot at Denham - in which I played a mechanic called Fred. It was directed by David MacDonald, a lovely Scot whose recent film *Christopher Columbus* had been something of a disaster for Rank, so I was told. I hadn't seen it, but he was now on 'B' pictures like this one, so his reputation at the time was apparently nose diving, which didn't seem to be reflected in this film, which ticked all the required boxes for me. He was very encouraging and easy to work with, and there was a nice atmosphere on set. I'd met him for a chat and a brief read, and Harry was told the part was mine.

"Well done Sid. Anozzer notch to ze bow-tie. And a car mechanic man! I add to the resume."

This had a decent cast. The gorgeous Jean Kent was the heroine

- I missed her in *Trottie True* but worked with her here. She was a terrific vivacious actress and despite her being in stuff everywhere and anywhere since, I've only worked with her once more, in a B.B.C. T.V. show called *Pantomania*, which is a shame as I'm a big fan! She gave me a signed pic! To Sammy! John Bentley was the villain. (Oops if you haven't seen it, I've given it away) We were to be opposite each other in *Final Appointment.* He was very much a leading man, and soon snaffled by Hollywood, but didn't enjoy it there he told me, and came back to Britain to latterly star in *African Patrol* which was very popular on T.V.. I enjoyed his company very much and was to meet him socially on many occasions over the ensuing years. Dear Garry Marsh was in it playing the Inspector who solves the case. I was soon to be his assistant on *Voice of Merrill* but in this instance we didn't meet. Though I had a phone conversation with him, but shot on different days! You can do that with film!

I had several nice sequences in this (under the car and serving in the office - one with American Mark Stevens who'd been the star of *Between Midnight and Dawn*) including a big plot scene in the garage where the drama intensifies as my character is ignorant of the fact that Jean is with the murderer! The audience know! She's left alone in the garage office for a minute as I exit with the killer and she phones Scotland Yard to try to get them to send out the patrol cars; but is interrupted before she can tell them to rescue her as the killer comes back into the room with me! She even hides a note under a towel telling me to call the police which I fail to see after she's left, as I'm distracted by the phone ringing - it's the police asking why did I phone them? And I of course say "Not me guv, I haven't phoned you?" (oh no!) which of course I haven't. This was when I was about to pick the towel up! Which I didn't! But eventually - of course much later on (ooh the plot) - I pick up the towel to dry my hands, see the note, dial 999 and am put through to Garry.

"I've got a message here. It's from a Miss Parker. It says it's urgent. I'll read it to yer", I say.

And I do and Garry sends out the cars!

Having phone calls when the other person isn't actually there on the line speaking - which is nearly all the time in fact - is dealt with by actors in different ways. Some just say their own lines and pause a bit, adopting a "listening face", knowing that there will be an edit around them. I think this is dangerous as it can make the call seem flat or not sound as if it's giving anyone at the other end any time to speak! I normally write out what I believe is being said to me and have it approximately in my head so it makes it flow and seem real and hope I'll transmit that to the viewer. In this instance, although he wasn't present and we shot it on different days, I knew what was being said to me, as Garry's lines were in the script and I'd learnt them. Incidentally, while I'm on the subject of "phone-acting", it's always a good idea when ringing someone, to choose a number that won't take too long to dial. You obviously need to use 7 numbers as in WES 9150 or it's not authentic. And don't use 111 1111 as it's clear you're not dialling a proper number. But "Can you dial a bit quicker and choose some numbers nearer the top of the dial please Sam?" is a direction I've had to deal with. When you're with an actor or actress phoning and he or she laboriously dials a long number, they'll frequently be told by the Second (or even continuity) to get a move-on. Not that the phone will be in close-up! It's just a bit boring! So I choose numbers like 232 1211. Try and avoid 7s 8s 9s and 0s. Having said that when you have to dial 999 you dial 999! If you don't, there'll be some Herbert who will write to you via your agent telling you, "when you dialled 999 the other day in that film I was watching and you dialled emergency services, I listened to the dial noise and you dialled 776. Why? You destroyed the verisimilitude of the piece. I thought an actor of your reputation and experience would be more careful… etc. etc. etc." Yawn.

Here's a funny thing. When I came out of the lavatory looking for the towel - the one Jean had used to hide the note beneath - I decided to add some colour to my part by whistling. And I whistled a tune called "Confucius Say" that had been made popular before the war by Guy Lombardo. I don't know why I chose that to whistle.

These things just pop into your head don't they? But I used it again in the film *They Who Dare* which I did the following year. But more of that later.

I met Douglas Allen, a mild mannered B.B.C. T.V. producer who seemed to take kindly to me. He asked me to do the part of The Tramp in *The Wonderful Visit*, a sort of theological play in which Barry Jones was the leading actor. Barry was great at playing wise old men and aristocrats. He played one in the big Hollywood film *Brigadoon*. And of course had been the philosophical scientist in *Seven Days to Noon*. The angel who made the "wonderful visit" to Earth was played by the unknown, but highly professional and friendly Kenneth Williams - complete with halo. What a comic institution he became, starring in all the *Carry Ons* and delivering wonderfully funny cabaret and sketch shows with all his diverse characters. I had previously met him briefly on *Trent's Last Case* where he had acted the small part of a gardener's assistant who found the body at the beginning of the film, and he had regaled me with his life story - true and possibly embroidered! And of course very amusing! He was (and is) a very humorous loveable fellow. Underneath the banter and outraged behaviour is a well-read erudite humanitarian. *The Wonderful Visit* was televised - live - from Alexandra Palace on Sunday February 3rd. and again on Thursday February 7th. and was well received. I got a review stating "a performance of note on T.V. in the last week was Sam Kydd's as a tramp in "The Wonderful Visit" providing a lively and thoroughly realistic character study, to demonstrate his versatility."

Ha! I could add "lively tramps" to my C.V.!

After the second transmission, whilst having a drink together, Duggie Allen informed me that there was a fair chance of his producing *The Pickwick Papers* by Charles Dickens later in the year.

"Oh yes Duggie" said I. "That would be good!"

(Well what can you say. To criticise would be foolish! If I'd said "Ha what do you want to do that for?" it might have been the end of a blossoming relationship. But of course I liked the book and the idea anyway and I felt he was telling me for a reason. I was correct.)

"How do you feel about playing Sam Weller?"

How did I feel? How did I.......? I couldn't believe it! I agreed enthusiastically and hastily bought another round of drinks in my elated confusion! He naturally cooled my euphoria - they always do - by adding that it wasn't absolutely certain, but there was a chance of it coming to fruition.

"You can have first refusal of Sam Weller, if of course you're free."

Bloody hell I'd make myself free. I'd not take any long term work if necessary! I was very very pleased, but the snag about this kind of situation is that if the actor has no dates, no <u>solid</u> dates to work on, he is completely at the mercy of Fate. It can happen that he starts working on something else and can't be released from it or the dates on various jobs clash. As it happened it was the year of the Aquarian and everything worked out all right for me!

FIFTEEN
Honeymoon interruptus

Pinkie and I had finally set the date for the nuptials: June 6th, Invasion Day. D Day. She had advised her employees, Masius and Ferguson, that she was getting married on that day and was given a fortnight off to languish in the luxury of the honeymoon, which was to be spent at a hotel in Devon. In actual fact it was situated on a small island located in Bigbury Bay and except when the tide was out, one had to use a Heath Robinson type of car-cum-boat-cum-ferry which took us and the other so-called honeymooners, across the stretch of water – the Bay of Delight and De-lovely!

I had planned to finish on a film at the Alliance Studios in Southall (*The Steel Key*, where I'd played the nice part of a rather villainous chauffeur. I had several good crooked scenes, and a credit! Which was rare! As I've said, film companies frequently weren't good at providing the whole cast list in the end titles!) by the 30th. May, so as to give us ample time to savour the delights of the luscious moon of honey. And I did. I'd had a rather devious looking pencil thin moustache in the film and I suggested to Pinkie that perhaps I should keep it for the wedding. She suggested if the glued-on bit of hair stayed on my face, then she should have one too. Funnily enough we were married facial hair-less.

In the film I was in a lot of the action. Lots of shifty looks and shifty tasks to do, dressed as a chauffeur. In fact my billing was "chauffeur", but I was only seen driving a car in my chauffeur's uniform, once! This kind of skulduggery was rare for me! I had to hit a policeman over the head and kidnap a girl from a hotel room with a gun and flee down a fire escape from the star, Terence Morgan - who was eventually Sir Francis Drake in the T.V. series - and who duffed me up in the film and abandoned me in a country lane without any trousers!

I had lots of lines like:

"A car just drove up with three men. One's Inspector Forsythe of the Yard. We know each other well."

And the most scary:

"Hello Miss Wilson."

(Gets out gun).

"GET YOUR COAT ON. COME ON! COME ON!

"What do you want with me?" says Joan Rice as the heroine.

"You'll find out." I reply, escorting her down the hotel corridor.

And then I'm off following people, being shifty and lurking again.

Anyway, back to the honeymoon. As I said, I finished on 30th.. But fate, in the shape of Andy Worker, talked me into taking part in another film which almost overlapped, called *The Voice of Merrill* produced by Tempean Films, the company belonging to Monty Berman and Bob Baker.

"There's only one snag" said Andy. "We'll need you for a couple of days during your fortnight away, then you can return to your love-nest!"

I naturally passed it by my wife to be, who sympathetically realised how the land lay and agreed that I should fit it in, as you never knew where it might lead! How lovely! But then she was a bright knowledgeable and knowing thing, who knew that you never knew with acting!

And so it came to pass that on the morning of June 6, 1952, I and my best man Gordon Mulholland, without the postcards of his girlfriend, arrived at the Kensington Registrar's office at the time stated, 11 a.m. for 11.30 a.m. along with Pink's sister Shirley Barnes, and by 12 noon, it was all signed and sealed and was just another entry in the registry records.

We returned to Fairfax Road for the cutting of the cake, the telegrams, speeches and the drinks.....and the drinks....and yet again the drinks. At this juncture of my narrative, I should state that before we were married, Pinkie had been diligently searching for a home for us both, in Central London, which wouldn't be too far from her place of employment or the film studios, etc.. Then a few months before we were due to tie the knot, she heard of a house in Melbury Road Kensington, which was in the process of being converted into flats. During her lunch period she dashed along from Berkeley Square, where she worked, to see it. She was so delighted with the re-build, the road and the environment, not far away from the Gothic "Tower House", the pre-Raphaelite painter Holman Hunt's Studio, and the acres of Holland Park, that she staked her claim immediately to the smallest flat, before the conversion was completed. Our future home for some years to come, consisted of an enormous parquet floored sitting room-cum-dining room, one huge bedroom and one small one, kitchen and bathroom. We had it decorated according to our requirements, furnished by Liberty's, Barker's and Derry and Tom's, plus knick-knacks from Harrod's and Hampton's and finally curtains and cushions courtesy of an upholsterer I knew at Shepperton studios. Anyway, while the wedding celebrations were still going on, we slipped off to Kensington where we spent the first flat in the new night - or something like that!

After what seemed like a very short time, we were up with the lark and set off early for Bigbury Bay in my (well it was "ours" now) 1938 Austin Ruby saloon. She - the car - was loaded with our four suitcases and two holdalls, plus two adults (us of course) and made very heavy weather of the hills. A particularly steep one, necessitated going up in reverse like the Oozlam Bird (known for its backwards movement and disappearing up its own fundament). Fortunately there wasn't much traffic about to impede the eccentric ascent. The radiator let off a lot of steam on two occasions, and so did I. And at some stage Pinkie got out to push while I steered. (What a woman!) But in the end we managed it. Slightly weary and travel worn, we arrived late at the Bigbury Bay Hotel, having left the car on the mainland and humped our cases onto the ferry. Tired but happy, we dined on lobster Thermidor and champagne and retired to the honeymoon suite to explore and meditate! I was due to spend the two days of filming for *Merrill* on the following weekend, so I'd have a week of the "nuptials" before going back to London and then I'd return to Pinkie on the Monday.

In the morning however I received a message from Andy Worker (who else?) of Riverside Studios, Hammersmith, who said that, "Owing to a change in schedule, your presence is required tomorrow. Apologies. Know it's unbelievably inconvenient. I'll make it up to you etc., etc.."

Up till then it was the best honeymoon I'd ever had!

I returned to London to film in the open air, all through the night, which was quite a contrast to the night before. I was joined by Teddy Underdown and Valerie Hobson outside the portals of the B.B.C. at Portland Place while we enacted the scene in which our villainess Valerie rushes out into the traffic to tell her lover Teddy not to tell the police he has killed her husband as in fact he died of natural causes and not poisoning, and is smashed into by an oncoming car. (Yes it's another complicated plot. Good film though!) I was necessarily present, but had no lines in the scene where she expires in the middle of the road. After a long and cold, stopping and starting, night - in fact very little was shot - I returned to spend the day in bed at the flat - alone!

My filming in *Merrill*, which was a very clever "who-dunnit!", in fact took eight days. Four more than I'd been booked for. And four more out of my honeymoon. The schedule moved all over the place. I did three days in a row Tuesday to Thursday, wasn't called for the Friday but then was, wasn't called for the weekend so tentatively returned for two days to Pinkie, and went back again for the Monday and Tuesday. And then did another two days. And I've forgotten the one I did before I went on honeymoon! Nine days! And then I did some post syncing! I played an Irishman again, a police officer assisting my friend Garry Marsh in his murder investigation - he was Inspector Thornton, I was Sergeant Baker - with lines like:

"He's at the Flamingo restaurant. Shall I get him?"

And in response to Garry Marsh's, "The highway of success is filled by men being pushed along by women" saying, "I could do with a shove myself!"

Garry and I were a sort of double act, which worked very well to create another rhythm to the piece, one of amusement amidst the drama. It helped that I got on so well with him. I suppose you could see why I was cast, having a foot in both camps, doing drama and comedy as I did.

It's a terrific film with Valerie Hobson and James Robertson-Justice superb. Garry was excellent as usual - always a hugely credible copper - and as I say, a joy to partner. James was very convivial, and very bright. It was no surprise to me he'd tried to be a Member of Parliament. I got a credit in the opening titles (well I was in it a lot) and if you notice, in one scene, where Garry tells Valerie, as Alycya, that there will be an autopsy on her husband's body, I'm only seen in long shot, by a tree. It's because after I did this shot, which they did first, Andy Worker and John Gilling the director, decided it would be too cruel to keep me from my love-environment and deliberately put me as far away as possible from Gary so I wouldn't be in any other garden shots, of which there were several, so I could leave early. Well that was nice of them!

And then I was back with the newly wedded bedded Mrs. K.. In my absence, apart from fretting for me - we'd had several phone calls where I had bemoaned my fate - she'd not done much. Oh I forgot. She'd had a near brush with death, as one frequently does on honeymoon. She had been swimming in the sea when she had become caught in the undertow, and carried a long way out. Fortunately she had managed to cling onto a buoy, until she was rescued by a passing trawlerman! She told me all about it as she lay in my arms and again got carried away, ending up clinging to her boy (boom boom). The rest of the honeymoon was spent walking along beautiful country lanes, bathing, enjoying the food and lying in bed. Counting the cracks in the ceiling of course.

On our way back to London the car behaved admirably and we returned in record time, making a bee-line for our new flat in Kensington, anxious to get settled in. For the next 14 years it was to be a marvellous abode, ably managed by Pinkie who from that day to this has retained her sense of humour, which is something of a record being married to an Irish Aquarian actor, and an ex-P.O.W. to boot! Eventually, in 1967, we extracted our roots and moved to Barnes in South West London.

One Saturday in late summer, a Pedigree Cat Show took place at nearby Olympia - I think it was called "The Cat Show" which made sense as the dog show was called "The Dog Show" - and having a weakness for furry felines, we decided to pay a visit. It was a wondrous sight. Cats of every known and unknown type were present: Persian Reds, Abyssinian Greens, Manx a Million, Siberian Whites, Scottish Hoots-Mons, Welsh Cariads, Irish Shamrocks, you name it, they had it. After traipsing around the whole show, it was getting near closing time when we passed a cage holding a solitary small Siamese kitten. He was a "Blue Point" (grey with blueish ears in fact) and looked quite wistful and forlorn; yet in spite of that there was something special about him. When Pinkie spoke some soothing words to him, he answered in hugely empathetic tones, naturally with a Siamese accent.

"I am Siamese if you please" he may have said, like the cats in the *Lady and the Tramp* cartoon (played by one of my favourite singers, Peggy Lee). We were both enthralled and he was ours for a fiver. The money changed hands, watched by the sleek kitten. After having been given his posh pedigree - "Poncojo Azure Kim" was his Sire, and "Banchon Blue Misty" was his Dam, bred less exotically by a Mr. Macpherson of Balcombe - we carried him home triumphantly in a cardboard box, deciding to name him "Birra" after the popular Siamese Prince, Birra Bongse the Grand Prix Racing Driver. And like him, Birra had an impressive turn of speed! He complained unceasingly about the unprincely mode of transport in the cardboard box, when a chariot filled with diamonds would have suited him better, but at least he was talking to us. Within a few weeks he appeared to understand English, but did not deign to speak it. He was sharp and very noisy and could Siamese-talk the hind leg off a Cheshire Cat with no trouble at all. He was completely unafraid of dogs - in fact it was quite the reverse. They weren't prepared for his attitude and many a dog cowered like a cat in his presence. He took our flat over and dominated it entirely and when he was fully grown we had a cat-flap made for him in the kitchen wall, which gave him access to the garden to go marauding whenever he felt like it - which was often. We grew so fond of that intelligent furry fellow that when Pinkie and I were both working, she sometimes dashed home from Berkeley Square during her lunch break, to see if Birra was O.K. Directly he heard her key in the lock, he would come running down the hall complaining about her absence, interspersed with brushing himself against her legs and making a noise like a Siamese generator!

Away from Birra, I was working on a film called *Appointment in London* which despite its name, was on location at an airfield in Peterborough. The Director, a very gentle and courteous man indeed, was Philip Leacock. He of course had used me before in *The Brave Don't Cry* and had clearly spotted something in me he liked! He subsequently moved onto Hollywood and became involved in big T.V. series like *Bar-bar-bar-bar-bar-bar...Hawaii Five O!* The producers were Aubrey Baring and Maxwell Setton. *Appointment* was a terrific dramatic film about Royal Air Force Bombing raids involving Lancasters, during the war. The final bombing sortie is brilliantly edited and assembled. You're almost with them on the raid! The "appointment" is the medal ceremony that the pilots eventually attend at Buckingham Palace, hence the title. It starred Dirk Bogarde as Wing Commander Tim Mason, and I played "Erk" Ackroyd, who is Bryan Forbes' - Pilot Officer Greeno - mechanic. I have three nice early scenes with Bryan on the tarmac and when I'm working on the plane, but I had a really lovely moving and sympathetic one in a hangar with Dirk. Greeno has just left on a raid and I'm polishing and playing his mouth organ which he'd accidentally left behind. Dirk hasn't been on the bombing raid but has seen Greeno off, and initially when Dirk hears the mouth organ he fears he's hearing a ghost, but sees me and questions me. It's a long emotional scene veering from comedy to pathos. I'm giving it my northern, as Erk is from Sheffield. Dirk laughs when I tell him I've got two children and another one "on the way". And how my "missus" is scared I'll be killed in the bombing. But my line "I keep telling 'er it's not like I'm flyin'" sends Dirk morose as he's been on 20 plus raids and there have been hundreds of deaths. Dirk suggests I don't polish the mouth organ too much as it'll taste nasty. My line "It's tasting quite fruity already sir," got a big laugh when I saw the film in the cinema. Of course Greeno doesn't make it back.

This was possibly my best scene ever in a film up to that point. *Trent's Last Case* had been good all over. And so had *Vengeance is Mine*. But this felt **so** good. It veered between comedy and pathos once again. I could clearly do that well. When I'd done it, I thought of the "pond" scene in *The Captive Heart*. It had the same impact on me. My career might have been different if that had stayed in and not been cut. But no regrets. I was doing O.K.. Dirk had been fabulous to work with. When the scene was over he paid me the compliment of saying, "Well done Sam, that worked really well".

There was great simpatico between us and I was sorry when he eventually left England to live in France; but the change of scene evidently inspired him to become a best selling author. He was a fabulous actor already of course. As I've said before, I never visited him there which was a shame. Incidentally you're always on a hiding to nothing when you're playing a mouth organ, as they tend to over-dub the mouth organ tune afterwards in post production. Even if you happen to be a virtuoso harmonica player, the chances of them using what you're playing on set, are slim. So you have no idea what tune you're actually (eventually) miming to. Luckily the mouth organ's shape means you can always "palm" it and cover your mouth and the mouth organ. Mind you, if you've got small hands, it's not as easy to disguise! If you look at Bryan Forbes playing it in the film he's suffering from the "curse of the harmonica". Whatever he's playing (well he couldn't play it anyway) it's obvious it isn't what we're hearing!

The beautifully mannered Aubrey Baring produced the picture for Mayflower Films and it was from this movie that I was chosen for another with the same company called *They Who Dare* which was scheduled to start in January 1953. Dear Dirk suggested me for the film! During a lull in the proceedings at a dubbing session for *Appointment* - I was voicing a ground staffer who was describing the bombs (who had his back to camera so was easy to dub) in a cockney accent... "We've done the incendiaries and are loading the rest: 25 one hundreds and each plane has a cookie." - Dirk said to Aubrey, "What about Sam then for *They Who Dare?*"

And Aubrey, as charming as always, said (I was there by the way, listening.)

"Dear old Sam! Of course! Why not? I'll bear him in mind and we'll discuss it nearer the date."

He obviously didn't commit, but Dirk nodded and winked at me and I suspected it was on!

I did a quick day on a film called *Love in Pawn* starring popular husband and wife team Bernard Braden and Barbara Kelly (famous in the sixties for I.T.V.'s consumer programme "On the Braden Beat") at Alliance in Southall for Charles Saunders, for whom I'd done *Trouble in the Air* and *Fly Away Peter*. I got a tenner! I did the shot completely on my own and didn't meet anyone. That kind of pressure can be big, but it's part and parcel of doing the job. You really need to be on top of the lines. I was a reporter, similar to *Mrs. Drake's Duck,* offering Barbara Kelly - Bernard's wife who had "pawned" him for a fiver - money for the rights to sell his story to the newspaper. It was a nice mid-close-up whilst on the phone:

"Mrs. Fox! The paper is willing to pay you £100 for the story of your married life, under the title, *The Cost of Loving*!".

One take. Delivered quickly and earnestly. Followed by another for luck. But I was happy with the work, as I fitted it in rather nicely during a day off, while I was doing a telly for the B.B.C. called *My Wife Jacqueline* which starred Leslie Phillips ("Helllohhh!") and was produced by Dicky Leeman who went on to produce some episodes of *What's My Line* (which I'd have liked to have been on, but never was! Though Dennis Main Wilson the producer did enquire about my availability in 1958, but alas I wasn't free).

Then I was lucky to be heavily involved at Merton Park for Julian Wintle in a film called *One is Guilty* or *Death Goes to School*. (They changed the title). Directed by Stephen Clarkson, this starred Gordon Jackson as a detective who endeavours to track down the murderer of a school teacher, when anyone in the school could have done it. It wasn't me, as I was playing Sergeant Harvey, his occasionally comedic assistant - our double interviewing act worked well. He's good fun is Gordon. In one scene in the school's sports' changing area we both got the giggles as did the crew and the director, when we were searching in the contents of pupils' shoe bags and a props person had set the biggest bra anyone had ever seen.

I took ages getting it out of the bag and then of course, once I'd got it out, amidst the laughter, I tried it on! Weirdly it never made the final cut! I was a gratifying 12 days on this, surrounded by Barbara Murray - Pam Wilder in *The Plane Makers* and terrifically vivacious - and that fine actress Beatrice Varley - I was in a *Charlie Drake Show* with her - amongst others. Bizarrely enough, even though I was Gordon's sidekick, I don't get a credit in the film!?

Good old cross eyed casting director Ronnie Curtis, cast me in a David Villiers training film, for the *Vacuum Oil Company*. I was a crook stealing secrets! And I fitted a film in at M.G.M. called *Time Bomb* for Ted Tetzlaff playing a ticket inspector on the train where the bomb is defused. Victor Maddern was in it playing the saboteur. We didn't have a scene together. Though we did have a drink!

I embarked on a few sketches for B.B.C. T.V. in *The Eric Barker Half Hour* playing a soldier, a crook and a policeman. They'd been watching my films! I had some funny moments arresting the effervescent Nicholas Parsons with whom I was to later do *Here and*

Now. The multi-talented Eric - he'd written this and played many different characters - who was later in many of the *Carry-Ons*, was great at being inept bureaucrats or befuddled policeman and strangely we never coincided in a single film together! Eric was a fascinating character who in actual fact had "peaked too early" in my opinion. These sketch shows - on the back of his excellence of radio series like *Merry Go Round* - were beautifully crafted and he did three series of them. But once the series ended he never quite obtained the level of stardom that he deserved. Sure his ability as someone playing "figures in authority" still meant he worked steadily, but to me he was a star who didn't manage to maintain his momentum, which was grossly unfair. But then when has this business been "fair"?

Next off, I scooted to Ealing for a huge film where I was lined up with the other 99% of Britain's character actors - including Glynn Houston, Meredith Edwards, Megs Jenkins, June Thorburn, Barry Letts, Harold Goodwin etc. etc., all doing their nuts for the impressive *Cruel Sea* starring the brilliant Jack Hawkins. There's a story attached to Jack's bravura performance, concerning his famous scene after he's had to depth charge British sailors in the water in order to destroy the U Boat, in which he gets blind drunk and confides in Lockhart about the appalling dilemma he faced and how deeply his choice has affected him. He reshot this iconic scene over and over on different days; some close ups and performances were bigger, some smaller, as the director, Charles Frend, having seen the rushes, thought his original performance, in which he broke down in tears, had been too large! In the end they went back to Jack's instinctive first take! It's frequently thus. The first take has a freshness and reality that can sometimes never be duplicated. His was a marvellous piece of acting. He was superb in the film.

I gave my "steward" performance as Carslake (I waited on the officers in their dining room. "Aye aye sir!") - well Charles Frend had promised me something in the film after my "stooging" - and I eventually succumbed to the massive waves that producer Leslie

Norman conjured up. We had to act with a huge wall of water being thrown at us! We did it so many times that I formed the impression that Leslie was indulging in some sort of secret vice called "how to wash the actors away!" I not only felt like a drowned rat – I looked like one! I swallowed so much H20 that I gave it up for years and even now I only take a minute amount with my Scotch! Despite all the permutations Charles Frend shot that I was in, I'm only visible climbing up a ladder and struggling to get past someone going in the other direction to retrieve his life-jacket. All the sinking sequences were shot in the Ealing Tank - the huge tank area dedicated to sea shots - and the water was supplied from overhead tip up trolleys or wagons, and to swell the volume of water, these were augmented with fully turned on fire hoses, the spray and force channelled by aeroplane propellers. The "below decks awash" shots were beautifully reproduced, but when five or six actors are scrambling up a single ladder and the wall of water crashes down on them, somebody is bound to get hurt. And they did! I was a mass of bruises, cuts and scratches, all in the cause of realism. Leslie Norman (father of Barry Norman the presenter of "Film… whatever the year was") said it was looking fabulous, but the director Charles Frend kept saying, "I think we'll go again". He was finally happy on the 25th. take! I was sure all that constant water pouring on me had grown me a couple of gills!

Incidentally as well as my role in vision as Carslake, I dubbed three characters in the film: the toothless old bloke who'd injured his arm on whom Donald Sinden puts a bandage, who says "Perfect for swimmin' d'yer think?"; the light northern Lord's Prayer voice-over when all the sailors are struggling for their lives when the Compass Rose has been torpedoed; and a rating at the end of the film helping a German from the blown-up sub get on board the ship "I gotcha mate! I gotcha!". Enjoyable work as three different sailors! Four if you count Carslake!

I managed to play a train fireman in *The Titfield Thunderbolt* (for Ealing again. They were so good to me) but wasn't credited. Michael

Crichton got me in for a couple of days. It was about the local railway line being closed down and the villagers' attempts to get it reopened. It was another Ealing success. And as usual I was pleased to be involved, even in a small way.

SIXTEEN
Maltas Two

There then followed a very pleasant overseas location with Roy Boulting in a film called *Single-Handed,* based on C.S. Forester's *Brown on Resolution. Single-Handed* was a 20th. Century Fox film and starred American actor, Jeffrey Hunter, who was the epitome of modesty and charm. (He later had huge success in John Ford's *The Searchers*, and was subsequently Jesus in *King of Kings*. And Captain Pike in the *Star Trek* pilot, *The Cage*.) Added to which he was extremely able at his job, a willing helper and one of the boys! We got on very well! I got his phone number! We promised to see each other again! We haven't so far!

The film was produced by Frank McCarthy, another likeable American who'd been the secretary of the General Staff of the U.S. War Department in the War, a quite Gigantic Cheese in fact! We had a few nice chats about our war experiences, which were slightly different to say the least! He was a Brigadier General who won a Distinguished Service Medal and the Legion of Merit! I was a private in a prison camp lugging bags of sugar and planting telegraph poles! (He was later the producer of *Patton* which won the Best Picture Oscar in 1970.) We were all booked in at the Phoenicia hotel in Valletta, Malta, which was known as the "George Cross" island, having been awarded the medal, because of its staunch resistance in the war. The "all" included Victor Maddern, John Horsley, Robin Bailey and myself. Later we were joined by a little known, nervous actor named John Schlesinger, later an esteemed director - the Oscar winning *Midnight Cowboy* was one of his - playing the part of a German guard on board the German ship, the "Essen", that was being pursued. The prestigious "Times of Malta" reported the arrival on the island of the *Single-Handed* film unit, stating that the film starred Jeffrey Hunter, Michael Rennie and Wendy Hiller. It went on to say that, "Jeffrey Hunter will be filming a lot of the scenes on the island of Gozo. Wendy Hiller would not be coming to Malta because her parts will be filmed in London!" (Oooh! Stop messin' about, as Kenneth Williams would say).

Then it added… "Staying at the Phoenicia Hotel are actors Samuel Kydd and Robina Bailey".

I looked in vain for Victoria Maddern and Joanna Horsley – directed no doubt by Rona Boulting, and felt the urge to change my name to Samantha Kydd.

Victor and I were the "other ranks" in the film. We had some nice scenes with Jeffrey Hunter who was signalman Brown.

"What I can't work out Brownie is why you ever came into signals? And not gunnery? You'd be a bit good at that wouldn't you?"

Said in my best Belfast. "Brownie" is of course a fabulous marksman, which he employs brilliantly "single-handed" in the second half of the film. But we were then all blown up as our ship the "Amesbury" was destroyed by the Essen.

Jeffrey was one of only two survivors, and then "single handedly" again escaped from the ship and shot at the German sailors while they were making repairs in a lagoon, thus delaying the ship, so the H.M.S. Stratford could then find it and sink it. John Horsely and Robin Bailey were cast as officers. When we finally got around to filming on board a warship, Robin and John were approached by a well-meaning Navy officer who, after asking

"Are you chaps connected with the snaps?" (snaps being the "film" I presume) invited them to the officers' wardroom, ignoring Victor and myself because we were dressed as "other rankers". He ludicrously had so little idea about the fact we were actors, that even the supporting artistes dressed as officers gained entry, and we "rankers" actors were denied access! However we soon got our share of the alcohol on board, being over-plied with offers of the hard stuff (not to mention their rum issue) by the kind and thoughtful <u>real</u> Navy "other ranks". Oh well!

We spent the first four weeks doing very little, mostly lying around in the sun, sampling the vines and virtues, while the rest of the unit worked like beavers - hauling ropes, cameras and themselves up and down the slippery rocks of Gozo Island. Our unexpected holiday arose because the ship on which we were due to shoot, began to leak, which necessitated her going into dock for modifications, and until she was ready - and you couldn't hurry the dockyard workers - we were literally, beached. Not that we complained. We drove about Malta in our hired cars as if we owned it! We made daily trips to the fabulous bay not far from Sliema, where we swam, sunbathed and picnicked! In the evenings we visited the bars and clubs which abounded at that time in the (in)famous "Gut", patronised by thirsty sailors and servicemen, as the Mediterranean fleet was based there. One evening we all had to be sartorially turned out and on our best behaviour. We were due for pre-dinner drinks with Earl and Lady Mountbatten at their charming establishment just off the Main Street in Valletta. We were all slightly trepidatious initially over how this would go down, as he was of course the ex Viceroy of India! Should we bow? Curtsy? Genuflect? Throw flowers? Robin Bailey seemed to know all the answers.

"Never call him "my Earl" he said. "Lord is the proper form of address. And she's "my Lady"."

But we were wary that he didn't really know what he was talking about or was "muckin abaht!" Fortunately there were others there to introduce us. And anyway there was a certain informality about the formality and we had nothing to worry about. At the plush reception - there was champagne! Cheap champagne but champagne nevertheless - we found them both very approachable and amusing. They were most interested in the film and keen to see some of the shooting. We had an enjoyable couple of hours and when we all lined up to say farewell - it's expected, the "lining-up"- they told us not to hesitate if we needed their help at any time. We racked our brains to work out how they could be of use! Perhaps they could make an appearance like Alfred Hitchcock? And flit across the screen? No. They'd be too easily recognised. I did suggest this though and Mr. Mountbatten (sorry, Lord Mountbatten) was highly amused and said he'd be keen if the makeup department could provide him with a bushy beard!

Halfway through our stay in Malta another film unit appeared from Pinewood with Anthony Steel, Jack Hawkins, Muriel Pavlov, and Alec Guinness as the stars. They were there to make *The Malta Story*. It was directed by the affable blarney merchant himself Brian Desmond Hurst, who of course knew me from *Trottie True,* and the Unit planned to be there for five weeks, including two weeks after we left from *Single Handed*. Lady Luck was being kind to me because Victor Maddern and myself were taken aside and asked to play the parts of First and Second Soldiers in this Pinewood production, and after consultations with Roy Boulting and Frank McCarthy, it was agreed that we could work for the Rank Unit, provided we only stayed one week, that is one week after the *Single Handed* Unit had left. We had to be back for Roy and Frank to film interiors! In addition they would be obliged to pay our hotel expenses and our air fare home, to be recouped by 20th. Century Fox. As almost thirty of the *Malta Story* personnel including their stars and feature players were already booked in at the Phoenicia Hotel, plus most of our Unit (in addition to holiday-makers) the place was fairly bursting at the seams! We were asked if we minded sharing rooms until things became easier, but annoyingly they drew the line when I asked for the Continuity Girl as my room-mate!

I never quite understood why we were in both films. Had the *Malta Story* forgotten to cast the two parts in England? That was what Victor Maddern was told. But Brian Desmond Hurst said they'd only just written the two characters in and it was easier (and cheaper) to use us. But this still didn't make sense. Why have two actors in one war film set in Malta, in another war film set in Malta, being produced at the same time? Wasn't that a bit artistically lazy? And why did *Single Handed* agree? Still I wasn't going to complain. I got a phone call from Harry late one evening and apparently he'd phoned a few times and missed me.

"Sid!" He said. "Zere you are! You are one lucky one! Two films in tha same place! Two monies! First the ship break down and zhen zey lose two actors!

"What, they died?"

"What?"

"The two actors. Was there an accident?"

"No they clash wiz ozzer vork!" (Ah, Harry had another reason for our being cast) I prezume you are happy be in it?"

"Does Archie Leach prefer to be called Cary Grant?" I replied.

"Who is Archie Leach?" replied Harry clearly bewildered.

"Cary is Archie!"

"In zer film?"

"No no. I mean.....Is the Pope a Catholic?"

"I 'ope so! 'E's not Jewish."

I felt I should just say yes.

"Yes Harry! I am very happy to do it."

"But wot about Pinkie? She O.K.?"

He'd made a good point of course. Another week of being away. But Pinkie as always "got it"; this was my career, and was immensely understanding. And we had been regularly exchanging letters.

"Can you phone her Harry?"

"About wot?"

"To tell her about the extra week."

"Yes. 'Course!"

"Just in case I fail to get through. What with the hours being different and me working. And a letter might go astray. Or something. And she might worry."

"Good idea, Sid!"

He did. Pinkie didn't correct him when he referred to me as Sid. She found it rather endearing! He also informed me that Douglas Allen, true to his word, had cast me as Sam Weller in *Pickwick Papers* which started after I'd done the film interiors when I was back.

Everything dovetailed beautifully. I gave my imaginary rabbit's foot a kiss and rubbed my invisible magic lamp and turned my money over in my pocket. Things were looking good!

My stint on *The Malta Story* involved doing shots on an airfield, as sappers filling in the holes created by air raids, before, during and after the bombing and I have to admit to being scared. The charges let off were immensely realistic. It reminded me of being straffed and bombed by a Stuka in Calais when I was delivering messages and I had to throw myself into a ditch, before I was captured in 1940. I know it's all safe as it's a film, I know I'm thinking "I have to run from here to there and I know exactly where the explosion is, it's behind me."

But occasionally mistakes are made, so it's a jolly good idea to pay attention when the Assistant Director explains the action. One of the supporting artistes didn't listen and got burnt by straying too far out of shot.

From an acting point of view, I was another Irishman. Victor though gave us his "northern".

"If it takes thirty tons to fill one hole and we've filled 25, how many tons is that?"

"Far too many" says Victor.

"The rumour is that there are fifty Spitfires coming," I reply.

"There have been that many coming since I've been here and all that's come is 600 Germans," says Victor.

And then the bombing starts again and we flee behind the sand bags. Then we realise that the tractor, "Millie", has been left out!

"There's "Millie! Out in the middle of the bombing!" I say.

"Millie! Oh no!" shout all the other actors crouched in the shell holes. And a brave soldier leaps up and drives the tractor away from danger amidst the explosions. I had some very nice close ups. Incidentally Victor and I had to do several big two shots reacting to the bomb falling near us, seeing and hearing it and ducking down. In fact we did about six takes. This was of course the First pointing at us to give us a cue to duck, once we'd worked out our eye line. The bomb falling and exploding was in another shot, and consequently had to be edited together to get our reaction.

The "Gut", so called by English sailors because of its reputation as the seediest part of Malta, was at the end of Strait Street and seemed to be populated by ladies (and men) of the night, of all shapes and sizes. They swarmed everywhere in the slightly mad, licentious atmosphere. Apparently they were good at taking money upfront and disappearing in an instant into the nightclubs. Victor and I and several crew members were constantly propositioned if we dared to stray into the area, on our search for restaurants, and one ample lady pursued us the length of Strait Street not taking no for an answer. She kept calling us "sailors".

"Hey sailors. You like a good time?...Sailors! Hey!"

After a particularly loud "Hey sailors!" (we were obviously not dressed as sailors) I foolishly replied indignantly,

"We're not sailors actually. We're actors!"

"Actors? You don look like actors."

Charming.

"Can you introduce me Alan Ladd? I love him! I give you free session?"

She clearly wasn't a film fan.

On one occasion some of us decided to visit one of the clubs, and the tables were very crowded and noisy. The Cabaret was being performed by one of the proprietors in drag. In a pre-war dress and armed with a huge fan made of ostrich feathers, he was giving a fair rendition of the classic "All of Me" in a high falsetto.

"Take all of me....take my...."

We never heard what the thing was going to be that was to be taken, because there was a sudden commotion at one of the tables jammed with sailors. Two of them started squaring up to each other like fighting cocks.

"Oi!" said one to the singer , with one eye on the stage, "Take all of me, Gel."

"Nar!" said the other. "Take all of me. Not 'im. Choose me."

"It's me 'e wants" said the other.

And they continued scrapping. In a deep baritone voice greatly contrasting with the high falsetto, the "Gel" said

"Do you mind buttoning up your bleeding mouth? I'm trying to do me number 'ere!"

There was a momentary pause and then another sailor with a cockney accent shouted:

"Ah bollocks you old poof!"

Some adjacent voices yelled

"And bollocks to you mate. He may be a poof but he's my poof. Just you leave my mate alone!"

The fighting started immediately and that was the cue for our exit. There were crashing bodies and falling tables and hurled glasses and plates and food resounding in our ears, as we hurried back to the Phoenicia, then pursued by our newly found number one fan.

"I like to meet John Wayne too! Remember I give you free session!"

Next morning quite a few of the crew aboard H.M.S. Cleopatra, the ship we were filming on, sported black eyes and grazed cheeks. They clapped when Victor and I sang the first verse of " Why not take all of me!" In perfect harmony of course.

Altogether I was six weeks in Malta. Five weeks "relaxing" for 20th. Century Fox whilst they fixed the boat, including four days filming with Jeffrey Hunter, and ten days for Rank's "Malta Story". On my return from Malta to London my contract reverted to 20th. Century Fox and I was required to hold myself in readiness for two days filming, or more if necessary, on *Single Handed* which was already settled in at Shepperton Studios. However I wasn't "used" as they say, until Saturday, December 6th. and then only to do some post-syncing of the scenes we shot in Malta. It was a very foggy day in London town and in Shepperton too. I think it was the last of the pea-soupers, those appalling yellow tinged fogs that were clearly very bad for those with weak chests, caused by coal fires I believe! I didn't fare too well in them what with my T.B.. When we came out of the recording studio, John Horsley and myself were shrouded in this eerie mist. We retreated into the entrance, only to bump into Roy Boulting and one of the technicians.

"Oh the fog's not a problem!" said Roy. "Hop in the Rolls and I'll give you a lift back to town!"

I knew he had sharp piercing eyes, but fog penetrators I wasn't too sure about. Notwithstanding, we all piled in and settled down in comfort. Half an hour later we had progressed only 80 yards outside the studio gates. Roy's eyes continued to burn as fiercely as his fog-lamps, but it was to no avail. In desperation he shouted like a good striking Union man, "All right! Everybody out!"

Roy, of course, stayed in the car to drive it, while John Horsley and myself shared the piddling torch that Roy provided. Naturally he directed the proceedings, and provided the commentary in that terribly clean cut, cold aristocratic voice of his.

"I say Kyddie, keep your eyes open. You nearly guided me into a f*cking lamppost. I haven't finished the picture yet, you know!"

By the time we got to Hammersmith, fog flares were out in full force (these were paraffin fuelled flames set up at key points in roads to act as guides and warnings) and we found ourselves directing other cars to the correct side of the road in the friendliest fashion. It always is friendly in fog, until you get hit! Eventually - I'd lost count of how long it took us walking from Shepperton (well John and I took it in turns to ride in the Rolls and find a way through the fog with Roy's torch) - we arrived at the King's Road in Chelsea, where Roy lived, and were invited in for a generous nip of fog-removing-from-throat-and-lungs Scotch.

At this time, out of curiosity, I totted up the number of films I had appeared in from 1945. Including *Single Handed*, the grand total was 119. And I may have inadvertently excluded a few. So 1945 to 1952 worked out at an average of 16 films a year. Penelope Keith says that any success she may have achieved is to be put down to, "Graft, talent, and a large slice of luck."

I second that. The luck is essential though. If I hadn't seen that advert in the paper that evening I would never have applied for *Captive Heart* and would possibly now be selling wardrobes in John Lewis. And I'd never have met Pinkie.

I realised that if I could keep up that average of 16 a year for the next seven years I could legitimately say that I was making a success out of acting, despite the smallness of some of the parts. As it happened though, this number became impossible to adhere to, on account of the doldrums into which the British Film Industry drifted, finally to become almost completely becalmed. For example, whereas at one time, covering all the Studios, sixty pictures were being made in one year, suddenly Studios began to close, and the output dwindled to a trickle; and sixteen productions seemed a lot! Among the Studios closed were Islington, Isleworth, Gaumont British (Lime Grove), Riverside, Walton on Thames, St. John's Wood, Southall, and countless smaller ones. What happens to all the technicians when their place of work disappears? The editors, cutters, electricians, soundmen, cameramen, assistant directors, etc. etc.? I know a few survive, but in comparison with actors, who are used to being out of work anyway, what do they do? Over 3/4 of the industry must've been lost. I know of one chap in charge of production who eventually managed an ironmonger's, with great success. And another, with a family, who started a café, which failed.

SEVENTEEN
What the Dickens?

On Tuesday, December 9, three days after the fog "adventure", I started rehearsing with Duggie Allen who, as good as his word, had asked me to play Sam Weller in *Pickwick Papers* for B.B.C. T.V.. It gave me a great fillip being involved in such a prestigious production and playing such a key part. However, one day Duggie and Wyndham Goldie (the latter had adapted the series from the book and also had a part in it) took me aside and began questioning what I was doing. Wyndham Goldie was worried about my interpretation of the character and hinted that I wasn't quite getting it to his satisfaction. In fact he gave me the impression that I wasn't anywhere near what he wanted. Duggie nodded but didn't say much and after another run-through he said that I was much better…

"What do you think, Wyndham?"….

Wyndham half-heartedly nodded and said

"Yes….Not bad."

While of course he looked as if he meant

"No that's not what I want at all".

Naturally, he had me worried. But this was only the first episode and I wasn't really noticeable till later on in the show when I first met Mr. Pickwick. There was a brief discussion about the make up. Not including me.

"So you're saying Wyndham that Sam should have his nose elongated to make it look like the drawing in the book?" asked Duggie loudly. It took place only a few feet from me and I heard it all.

"Oh yes definitely. It must be! He must look as much like the illustration by Phiz as possible!" said Wyndham.

"Well. I'm not convinced!" said Duggie.

"No no no! He has to!"

"Well I'm not so sure!"

"Well I am!"

I didn't get to have an opinion. In the end they compromised. The nose was built up very slightly, but it became a nuisance, because it kept falling off under the heat from the lights and my sweaty endeavours. Somehow Wyndham blamed me.

"Sam. Your nose needs to be kept under control" he said.

"I'm doing the best I can Wyndham, but it's very slippery!"

What a weird conversation. I was wary of Wyndham Goldie. He wasn't exactly a ball of fire – a cold, vinegary man, a little on the haughty side, perfect casting for his role of Mr. Perker - and he was never satisfied with the way I played it. We rehearsed at a hall in Gower Street, not far from the Royal Academy of Dramatic Art and as Sam Weller would've said, "Quite a bit of h'actin' goes on in that there 'all, I can tell you!"

Wyndham always wandered up to Duggie during my scenes and whispered into his ear. Duggie would then give me a line reading or a note. It was very disconcerting. As it turned out, despite my nose and Wyndham looking down <u>his</u> at me, in the end, I was the one who got all the good notices!

I was in five of the six episodes, all shot at Alexandra Palace, and after my first one had safely gone out - live of course - I began to enjoy myself. George Howe played Mr. Pickwick, and Peter Copley was Mr. Dingle. Geoffrey Sumner was also in the cast and the ladies included the excellent Petra Davies, Betty Marsden - multi talented of course in *Round the Horne* — and the lovely character actress Fanny Carby. Peter Bull played my father - he was great in *African Queen* and *Dr. Strangelove* - whose immortal line on top of the coach as we careered along, was, "Give 'em a touch ov yer 'orn, Sammy!"

Whereupon I put the hunting horn to my lips and blew a long ear-shattering blast! I didn't do badly considering I'm not a trumpeter and haven't got the proper "embouchure"! Actually it wasn't as easy as it sounds, for the rocking and rolling of the coach (they only shot the top of the coach and had the scene going past on "moving scenery" like sideways roller blinds) was being done frenetically by the over-enthusiastic props men and Peter was lashing at the imaginary horses with his whip at the same time! Just in case he dropped his whip over the side (which he did!) he had a spare one placed on top of the coach. In addition, both he and I nearly fell off the top – once during the camera rehearsal, and again during the transmission where the "shakers" got carried away and the bucking and bumping became even more manic.

Oh, we earned our money alright! I hugely enjoyed all the scenes with Peter. He was on my wavelength. He had the odd moment of panic, line-wise, but we'd made a pact to help each other out if anything went wrong so we were well "on the ball" with ways out, like "What do you think ofs" and "we could mentions" to put us back on track. On one occasion he was on the verge of going out through the wrong door, but a hasty grab and redirection solved his error. Peter Copley, who played Mr. Dingle was absolutely spot-on - a fine reliable sympathetic actor who featured in many tellies, especially *The Troubleshooters* - and George Howe excelled as Mr. Pickwick. We all got on marvellously as a cast. It was a delight to be in. Wyndham still found fault with everything I did and was still suggesting things to Duggie, but as the series went on, Duggie didn't pass the notes on and eventually Wyndham gave up.

A couple of times during his rehearsals as Mr. Perker, I wandered in and observed and whispered in Duggie's ear just to be fair. Mostly things like, "Would you like a cup of tea Duggie?" And "They've got very good cake!"

At the end of it all, the critic Maurice Wiggin wrote me a personal note stating his desire to further the Kydd cause, saying he had loved my performance, and adding rather poetically, "…any help I can give you in my small and choleric way will always be freely given. It is my cross and necessitation as a critic, that loyalty once given, is given for aye…"

Blimey. How about that! Maurice has been true to his word and has remained a supportive friend ever since. To be embraced by a wordsmith like him has been a truly emotional experience.

And then a distinguished critic, Miss C. A. Lejeune of the Observer had this to say:

"Pickwick Papers which has just ended, left me with the continued respect for the producer Mr. Douglas Allen and a belief that in Sam Kydd who played Sam Weller, England has found a new, sharp, sensitive and lively actor."

I bought six copies and posted one to Wyndham, marking the "crit" with a pencilled red ring.

I wrote to C. A. Lejeune at the Observer, thanking her. I got back:

"How very nice of you to write! You know, although nobody will believe it, critics like to be told they've given pleasure, just as much as actors. ...I'm told by people who have worked with you in the studio, that you're just as nice and intelligent as you appear to be."

Aw. Sweet! How kind was that?

I also got another lovely review:

"Sam's "Weller" is delightfully handled on television, and the lad reveals a supreme ability to submerge his personality and produce the character, one quite different from anything he has given us before but delightful and believable with a performance that is full of vitality. Watch him in 1953!"

I'm sorry to say I don't know who gave me this one. But thanks in retrospect and my apologies!

I also had a rather nice exchange with T.V. and radio critic, Ian Low. He put in his regular column, "The fourth episode of "Pickwick Papers" contained the best of the portraits I have seen - Peter Bull's Tony Weller. Indeed the Wellers, father and son, may save this not-too-happy experiment."

I wrote to him!

"How would you feel if all your news

Was signed by "Our Reporter".
Or, plagiarising Wednesday's views,
By "Ian Low and Daughter"?
But this, kind sir, is what you did.
To Tony Weller's son - SAM KYDD!"

I only wish you 'arf a werry 'appy '53
The other 'arf I'll send you when you choose to mention me!

Next week he wrote:

"A hurt little verse points out that in last week's notes, though I praised both Wellers I named only Peter Bull. Let me make amends to Sam Kydd for such unmannerliness".

I enjoyed playing Sam Weller immensely. He will always remain one of my favourite heroes, not only as a character to portray, but also as someone to emulate. And in addition I made a lot of new friends including Peter Bull and Fanny Carby, both of whom I'm very fond.

I worked with diminutive comedian and ball of energy Arthur Askey in a small part in *The Love Match* for the B.B.C. - hugely enjoyable as he was a consummate professional and warm inventive performer with whom I was to perform a lot in the 60s in his *Arthur's Treasured Volumes* series; then did a quick dub for Jack Lee for *Turn the Key Softly*, voicing a passer-by who has just seen Kathleen Harrison (brilliant in this film by the way as an old lady just out of prison) run over while crossing the road to get her lost dog.

"Yeah, must have been killed outright"

And managed to fit in a day on *The Saint's Return* which starred Louis Hayward (who I was to work rewardingly with later). And did a week playing the part of a character called Johnson in a live episode of a B.B.C. serial by A.P Dearsley, (whose film *Fly Away Peter* I'd been in and not been in) starring the lovely actress Joy Shelton, called *My Wife Jacqueline: The Agonies of Courtship*. And then did a quick scene on a film directed by Val Guest called *The Runaway Bus* playing a security guard opposite the very up and coming and friendly comic Frankie Howerd who was a "relief driver", taking stranded passengers away from a fog-bound London Airport to another airport to get to Dublin and had got lost trying to find his bus and had entered our office through the window. (Plots can sound so complex when you try to explain them!)

When I watched it, I was a bit fed-up, because despite Val having shot all my reactions to Frankie's story-telling, none of them were used. The scene was edited all on Frankie, and you could only see the back of my head! Mind you, he was being amusing, and was the star, so it was fair enough. Then, suddenly, in the middle of it, I had a rather nice close-up! Frankie said, "It's me granny, poor old thing".

I replied "Is she dead?" I think my line was supposed to be funny, or at least set-up Frankie's reply, which was, "No, she's home on leave."

I agree with you. I don't think it works either. But as I say, my line was in close-up!

Harry phoned. Would I be interested in being in a film called *They Who Dare?* Starring Dirk Bogarde? For Mayflower Films? Aubrey Baring? This was the film that dear Dirk Bogarde had suggested me for, to Aubrey. I of course said I was.

"Good. I wait for zem to arrange interview."

Harry phoned back a few hours later.

"Sid! You goddit! Zey fone to tell me you goddit! No interviews require'. Decen' part. Zhey send script!"

"Well done Harry!"

"I do nuzzing! It's you! Ze say you impress in *Appointyments in London*. It film in Cyprus! We wait for money discuss an' orf you goes!"

"Hooray!"

"Hoorays indeed! Hep hep!"

Prior to leaving for Cyprus, I was invited onto a radio show on the B.B.C. Home Service called *I Know What I Like,* which was a sort of precursor to *Desert Island Island Discs.* Three quarters of an hour of your favourite tunes and a discussion about your career! I was a bit taken aback to be asked. I mean I was hardly a star attraction, but I was billed as, "One of the star British actors now filming in Cyprus".

How about that? I mean I wasn't actually in Cyprus when they recorded it. It hadn't gone out live. I was soon to be in Cyprus. It was recorded on magnetic tape and went out in April when I was filming. But I suppose it was also a sort of publicity machine for the film I was about to do. But hang on a sec! Me! Billed as "this week's guest star!" Cor! I chose a mass of dance songs that we'd listened to in prison camp. And some Oscar Rabin stuff I'd liked since before the war. And early Sinatra. I was a big fan of his. And Bing. And the Andrews sisters. And some Vic Lewis. Peggy Lee I loved. ("Why Don't You Do Right?") And I chatted about the huge number of films I'd done, Sam Weller in *Pickwick* and my frequent Light programme appearances, and occasional moments on *Mrs. Dale*, and of course my wartime experiences, shows I'd done in captivity, the cat in *Scott, Treasure Island*, etc.etc. and it flew by! I got quite emotional discussing those who never made it back from captivity. Danny Faulds was one. I'll never forget you Danny. I was rather pleased about being invited onto that. Pinkie was overjoyed. My mother was very impressed, but didn't go overboard with her praise.

"I think you might have chosen some church organ music" she suggested. Uncle Jack missed it.

In March 1953, I took off by chartered plane for Cyprus to film *They Who Dare.* The title was taken from the motto of the S.A.S. which was "He who dares, wins." The director secured for the filming, by Mayflower Productions, was a real coup. It was the very famous Lewis Milestone who had achieved lasting acclaim in the film world's hall of fame by being director of *All Quiet on the Western Front.* I briefly met him in Mayfair prior to leaving for the location, and he warmly told me I was earmarked for the role of Marine Boyd. Dirk was the star of our film supported by Akim Tamiroff, Denholm Elliot, Gerard Oury, William Russell, David Peel, Alec Mango, Peter Burton, Michael Mellinger and myself. Akim, Gerard and Alec were playing Greeks and the rest of us (apart from Michael Mellinger who played a gypsy who knew the terrain) were to be British.

This was a great opportunity for me. I had a decent part. Quirky as well. With a legendary director. If the film was successful, my career might take off. It was a very exciting moment. This was a big big chance. Harry was excited as I was. He hadn't known it was Lewis Milestone.

"Sid! Lewis Milestone from *All Quiet!* Sid! *All Quiet!*"

"Yes Harry! I know!"

"This could be big, Sid!"

"I know Harry! I know!"

"This iz it. You play cards right you could be big star! Doan muck it Sid!........"

"No Harry."

"Lewis Milestone, Sid! LEWIS MILESTONE!"

The pressure was on.

TO BE CONTINUED

IN

VOLUME TWO

OF

SAM KYDD'S UNPUBLISHED MEMOIRS

"NEVER MIND THE ACTING, JUST SAY THE WORDS."

1953-1960